FOUNDATIONS OF COST CONTROL

Daniel Traster, CCC, CCE, CCP

PEARSON

Boston   Columbus   Indianapolis   New York   San Francisco   Upper Saddle River
Amsterdam   Cape Town   Dubai   London   Madrid   Milan   Munich   Paris   Montreal   Toronto
Delhi   Mexico City   São Paulo   Sydney   Hong Kong   Seoul   Singapore   Taipei   Tokyo

Editorial Director: Vernon Anthony
Senior Acquisitions Editor: William Lawrensen
Editorial Assistant: Lara Dimmick
Director of Marketing: David Gesell
Curriculum Marketing Manager: Thomas Hayward
Senior Marketing Coordinator: Alicia Wozniak
Marketing Assistant: Les Roberts
Associate Managing Editor: Alex Wolf
Project Manager Editorial: Alexis Biasell
Production Editor: Alexis Biasell
Production Manager: Laura Messerly

Art Director: Jayne Conte
Cover Designer: Mary Siener
Cover Art: Erika Cespedes
Media Director: Tim Peyton
Lead Media Project Manager: Karen Bretz
Full-Service Project Management: Kailash Jadli/
   Aptara®, Inc.
Composition: Aptara®, Inc.
Printer/Binder: LSC Communications
Cover Printer: LSC Communications

Credits and acknowledgments for materials borrowed from other sources and reproduced, with permission, in this textbook appear on the appropriate page within the text.

Many of the designations by manufacturers and seller to distinguish their products are claimed as trademarks. Where those designations appear in this book, and the publisher was aware of a trademark claim, the designations have been printed in initial caps or all caps.

Library of Congress Cataloging-in-Publication Data
Traster, Daniel S.
   Foundations of cost control / Daniel Traster.
      p. cm.
   Includes bibliographical references and index.
   ISBN-10: 0-13-215655-5
   ISBN-13: 978-0-13-215655-4
   1. Education—United States—Finance.   2. Education—United States—Cost control.   I. Title.
   LB2825.T73 2013
   371.2'06—dc23   2011037950

ISBN 10:   0-13-215655-5
ISBN 13: 978-0-13-215655-4

257 2024

For my parents, whose love is immeasurable

Brief Contents

Contents

Preface

On July 7, 2009, I received the results of a survey of cost control instructors conducted by Pearson Education earlier that year. The results mirrored my own teaching experience that the biggest obstacle to student success in the typical cost control course is math. Simply put, many cost control texts put forth little effort in helping students understand the math behind cost control.

Math is an essential component of cost control, but it is hardly the goal of any serious study of the subject. Cost control is about maintaining quality and quantity standards for a business while maximizing that enterprise's profitability. Math aids a manager in making smart business decisions; it is a support, not a substitute, for a good manager. However, culinary students who get bogged down by a textbook's poor delivery of math instruction never get beyond the basics of mathematical computation to experience the excitement of generating profits through informed decision making. Teaching how to compute basic mathematical equations becomes the overwhelming (and unintended) focus of chef-instructors using these ineffective books. I believe that culinary students and chef-instructors deserve better.

Foundations of Cost Control begins with key culinary math basics that, when mastered, make all other cost control equations much easier to comprehend and learn. By taking the time to learn these math skills first, students will find the text's subsequent equations much easier to use and compute accurately. Math is a critical component to cost control, but it is far from the only element of cost control worth studying. As students master the math more easily, they free up mental energy to focus on learning the more important conceptual elements of cost control. They also begin to welcome the role math plays in cost control as an information provider that guides decisions rather than as an exercise unto itself.

This book does not attempt to be a comprehensive tome addressed to MBA students and thirty-year industry veterans. There are already plenty of those on the market. Instead, it focuses on the foundations of cost control that every culinary student must master to work his or her way up from cook to chef to general manager. In fact, this natural progression in the career path is the framework for the organization of the book.

The book opens with a brief overview of the many areas in the flow of food in which proper control supports profit generation. Then, as described earlier, the text provides a chapter on math basics to make the rest of the text easier to digest. After the chapter on math basics, the book moves to the cost control information needed by line cooks—specifically, recipe and unit conversion. The book then progresses to those cost control tools and concepts employed regularly by chefs and purchasing managers— yields, recipe costing, sales price determination, special concerns related to beverages, and control of the purchasing, receiving, storing, and issuing processes. The next few chapters deal with those cost control concepts utilized regularly by general managers (and in many operations, by chefs as well)—employee organization, labor management, forecasting, and revenue management. The book concludes with the material most often controlled by owners or very senior managers—income statements, budgeting, and expenses beyond food, beverage, and labor. The organization of the content reflects the typical order in which culinary professionals acquire and apply cost control knowledge over the course of their careers. That each chapter builds on the previous ones makes new content that much easier to understand.

Having been a chef-instructor, I recognize the delicate balance between needing students to understand cost control conceptually and training them to use computers, which speed math computations but provide little assistance in concept mastery. I also firmly believe that cost control concepts are best learned in a class with a textbook and teacher, while computer skills are best learned on a computer. (Is a student more likely to master Excel by reading about it in a textbook or by actually using an Excel worksheet?) Therefore, this text focuses on the math and management concepts behind cost control. An online educational companion to this text is currently in development. This online support will help students to learn and practice on some of the computer software available to today's culinary professionals. Having the textbook as the primary classroom tool ensures that a deeper understanding of cost control is delivered in class, while the online companion to the text gives students familiarity and competence in the laborsaving software common in today's industry. Through this two-pronged approach, neither foundational understanding nor computer competence is sacrificed.

In addition to the book's content, certain chapter elements to *Foundations of Cost Control* enhance the student's educational experience and the classroom dynamic. Intrachapter examples explain the mathematical equations provided in the text, so students can see how those equations are applied. End-of-chapter summaries recap each chapter's essential elements while end-of-chapter comprehension questions confirm that students have grasped the material delivered in the chapter. The discussion questions at the end of each chapter ask students to go beyond traditional equation application and fact regurgitation. The discussion questions do not necessarily have a single correct answer but rather invite students to share their insight and opinions on complex cost control challenges. These types of questions aid an instructor who wishes to challenge students to a deeper understanding of cost control.

Readers will notice that the text alternates by chapter between male and female pronouns. While men and women both have much to contribute to and to learn from the culinary industry, the English language makes gender-neutral communication difficult and clumsy. Rather than using "he/she" or similar constructs, I have opted to use male pronouns in odd chapters and female ones in even chapters. The use of one set of pronouns in a given subject area is not meant to insinuate anything about the relationship of one sex to that particular material. Rather, the alternation is an attempt to convey the relevance of the book's entirety to both sexes equally.

Finally, I have made every attempt in the length and organization of the chapters to make the book flexible enough to accommodate quarter and semester system schools as well as to serve the needs of teachers with mathematically adept and numerically challenged students. The first chapter is a short introduction to cost control that is easily covered in a class day abridged by a syllabus review and student introductions. The second chapter on basic math can be skipped entirely for students who are strong in math without losing any knowledge specific to cost control. Alternatively, the second chapter may be covered with the entire class present or as part of a supplementary session specifically for those students who need the math review. The final chapter, "A Discussion of Other Expenses," is short enough to be covered in class on the same day as a final exam review. It could alternately be eliminated from the course entirely without detriment to a student's understanding of the remaining text's content. In short, *Foundations of Cost Control* is designed to support each instructor's disparate needs, not to place artificial constraints on a class.

To access supplementary materials online, instructors need to request an instructor access code. Go to www.pearsonhighered.com/irc, where you can register for an instructor access code. Within 48 hours after registering, you will receive a confirming e-mail, including an instructor access code. Once you have received your code, go to the site and log on for full instructions on downloading the materials you wish to use.

No book is perfect for all audiences, but I hope that this approach to cost control will help culinary students comprehend better the mathematics and the broader concepts behind cost control. Rather than inciting fear in students, *Foundations of Cost Control* is designed to inspire students to learn cost control as an essential skill for any future chef or foodservice manager. No restaurant, no matter how talented its chef, survives if it cannot generate profits. Conversely, any culinary professional who masters cost control becomes a valuable asset, desirable to any foodservice business. This text works to ensure that culinary students do not just "go through" a cost control course but rather learn all the material that such a course ought to offer.

—Daniel Traster

Acknowledgments

All my hopes and dreams to provide a better educational tool for cost control students and teachers would still be languishing on my computer rather than in the hands of eager readers were it not for the efforts of an extraordinary team of people. To my editor Bill Lawrensen, developmental editor Alexis Biasell, and editorial assistant Lara Dimmick, I owe the greatest debt of gratitude for guiding me through this multiyear project. My thanks go out as well to Nicole Beveridge-West, St. John's University; Jonathan Deutsch, Kingsborough Community College; Kirsten Tripodi, Fairleigh Dickinson University; Kenneth Bourgoin, Valencia Community College; Larry Canepa, the Art Institute of Phoenix; Andy Chlebana, Joliet Junior College; Chris Crosthwaite, Lane Community College; David Derr, the Art Institutes International–Kansas City; Mathew Kline, the Art Institute of Phoenix; Tianshu Zheng, Iowa State University; Mark Zink, the International Culinary School at the Art Institute of Charlotte, Dan Beard, Orange Coast College; Valentina Columbo, Le Cordon Bleu College of Culinary Arts; Richard Harnden, Oxnard College; Joe McCully, Lane Community College; and Daniel Taylor, The International Culinary Schools at the Art Institute of Raleigh Durham, who took seriously their role as peer reviewers, so I might further polish and refine my text. I am grateful to Gregory Steis and Louise Casamento for teaching me about MICROS and the technological wonders that POS systems can perform, and to Jim Laube and Myra Weinberg for their help in ensuring that my readers would get a taste of the National Restaurant Association's standard format for income statements. Nate Auchter deserves recognition for his help in navigating the occasional disconnect between cost control theory and industry reality. For introducing me years ago to educational tools like the Magic Box, Paul Hutchinson merits high praise. I would be remiss if I did not acknowledge the many teachers who over the years advanced my skill in math. To my parents, who encouraged me to value and to embrace math, thank you for all of your years of love and support. And finally, to my wife and daughter, who, despite having no background in foodservice, patiently endured my many monologues about the inner workings of restaurants, thank you; this book is only made possible through your endless support of my work.

About the Author

Author of *Welcome to Culinary School: A Culinary Student Survival Guide*, Daniel Traster CCC, CCE, CCP has over twenty-five years of experience in the culinary industry, including eight years in culinary arts education, mostly at the program management level. He worked as the dean of Culinary Arts and Hospitality Management at Stratford University in Falls Church, VA, and as the academic director for Culinary Arts at The Art Institute of Washington. Additionally, Traster served two years as the chair of the Cooking Schools and Teachers section of the International Association of Culinary Professionals after already serving two years as the section's vice-chair. Currently the culinary director for the Metropolitan Cooking and Entertaining Show and a freelance writer, Traster cherishes his experiences in the culinary field. Before teaching, Chef Traster cooked in various types of foodservice operations including "Bagels and …" in New Jersey; the Four Seasons Hotel in Philadelphia; Provence Restaurant in Washington, DC; Occasions Caterers in Washington, DC; and a university president's residence as a private chef. Over the past decade, he has served on the boards of the Restaurant Association of Metropolitan Washington and its Education Foundation, the Nation's Capital Chefs Association (a chapter of the American Culinary Federation), the Epicurean Club of Washington, the National Capital chapter of The American Institute of Wine & Food, and the advisory boards for DC Central Kitchen, the Center of Applied Technology North, Stratford University, and Lincoln College of Technology. A strong believer in lifelong education, he holds a B.A. in English and Theater from Yale University, an A.O.S. in Culinary Arts from the Culinary Institute of America, and an M.S. in Adult Learning and Human Resource Development from Virginia Tech. Daniel Traster lives with his wife, Katie, and his daughter, Abigail, in Washington, DC.

As any textbook can be improved through the collective input of culinary school students, teachers, and industry professionals around the country, Daniel Traster welcomes feedback, comments, and suggestions for future editions. He can be reached via email at WelcometoCulinarySchool@gmail.com.

Introduction to Cost Control

Cost control and its corresponding math components sometimes bear a reputation for eliciting boredom among students. The reputation is undeserved. Cost control is a challenge more similar to an adventure game than to a math class. While math is involved, it is there to inform one's decision making rather than to stand as a final goal unto itself. There is treasure to be won in the form of profits, and there are enemies—loss and inefficiency, for example—to be vanquished. Like any game, cost control has winners and losers, too. A successful manager can generate enough profit to expand a business, fund employee raises, and/or merit a promotion. With enough training, every future manager can become such a winner. However, unlike a computer or board game, cost control comes with real-world consequences. Poor decisions can result in dissatisfied customers, unrealized profit, or overworked employees. Can this make real-world cost control intimidating? Perhaps. Boring? Never.

While cost control may seem like a math class, it is best to think of it as a companion to a management course. Every foodservice operation (every business, for that matter) has inefficiencies that develop naturally over time. Food has value that chefs increase when they prepare and present it, with the addition of customer service and ambience. Likewise, food loses its value if it spoils or ends up in the trash can. Employees contribute to a restaurant's bottom line by working productively to add value to the operation's food and service, but unethical employees can undermine the same company's existence by stealing from the business. A foodservice manager who markets to increase revenue can fund employee raises and greater investor profits, but one who manages sales poorly may not even cover current expenses. Food, employees, and dollars are but a few of the many resources that managers control to support a company's financial viability. Whether those resources become assets or liabilities to the company depends on managerial decisions.

The purpose of studying cost control separately from a broader management course is to learn the mathematical tools and financial theories that inform a manager's decisions. However, it is important to stress that these tools and theories only provide information. The responsibility of identifying appropriate solutions and strategies for business challenges lies solely with the managers and owners (and employees, in more progressive companies), who must take into account all nonfinancial variables as well. That said, trying to make a managerial decision without financial information and an understanding of cost control is equivalent to guessing and does not serve the manager or the company well. By learning and utilizing cost control tools and theories to guide decision making, a manager not only better serves the interests of his company but also makes himself more valuable to potential employers as a capable, competent manager.

Objectives

By the end of this chapter, you will be able to:

- Describe the role of math and financial information in making management decisions
- Identify revenue and expenses as the resources that managers control to generate profit
- List the primary types of loss that occur in a foodservice operation
- Describe the flow of food in a foodservice operation and pinpoint where cost control points are most critical
- Describe the importance of learning cost control theory and mathematical calculations in an industry that often relies on computer systems to collect data and perform calculations

1.1   THE PURPOSE OF MATH

Some of the people reading this book (perhaps you) may believe that the primary purpose of math is to scare or to intimidate culinary school students. Nothing could be farther from the truth. In the foodservice world, math is a tool, no different from a chef's knife or a computer, to help culinary workers perform their jobs better. Without math, chefs could not convert recipes, calculate food orders, or determine menu prices. There once was a time in your life when you could not use a chef's knife; imagine trying to cook without it now! Math is no different. You may not know any cost control formulas yet—you may not even be very comfortable with math in general—but there will come a time when you will view cost control math as just another useful tool in your arsenal. And, you won't be able to imagine working without it.

Like all tools, math cannot function without a craftsman. In the hands of a talented chef, a knife can produce a fabulous meal; in not-so-skilled hands, knives are dangerous and potentially destructive. Math requires an individual who knows how to use it, how to interpret its results, even when not to use it for making management choices. Inaccurate calculations, which can occur simply by entering the wrong data into a computer, can result in disastrous business decisions. Imagine a chef who invests thousands of dollars to market and promote a new signature dish only to find out that due to a calculation error, the dish actually loses rather than makes money. Such an error could shut a restaurant down.

So what should you do to become a master craftsman with math? First, you must learn certain formulas and know how to use them. Second, and more importantly, you need to understand what those formulas represent. For example, a computer can calculate food cost percentage, but if you do not know what food cost percentage is, why to calculate it, and what to do with that information, the computer will not be helpful at all. Similarly, understanding a formula's goal may help you to catch basic math errors. For example, if you have a recipe that uses 1 quart (qt) of apples and you are asked to reduce the yield for that recipe, you would easily recognize a calculation error that asks for 1 gallon (gal) of apples—an increase rather than a decrease in the recipe quantity.

Finally, the most important concept to learn about math and cost control is when to use it and when not to use it to make management decisions. Penny-wise and pound-foolish people fail to see the impact a decision has on the big picture because they are so focused on saving an additional penny. For example, math might tell a manager that his steakhouse can save ten cents per portion by ordering wet-aged, precut steaks instead of dry-aging large primal cuts and portioning them in-house. But if customers choose that steakhouse over others primarily because they can see the meat dry-aging through glass windows, the manager would be foolish to switch to an option that eliminates his marketing edge. Math can provide lots of valuable information, but that information is typically only one factor among the many variables that come into play when making a management decision.

1.2   REVENUE, EXPENSES, AND PROFIT

Most businesses have a mission, vision, and values. Rarely is making money the sole mission of a company, but no company can survive without covering at least its expenses. In fact, generating a fair profit is typically a key element of any business's vision. Managers are the ones most responsible for achieving an organization's profit goals.

Profit is a function of two primary variables: revenue and expenses. When a company brings in more money than it spends, the surplus money is termed "profit." If expenses outpace revenue, then the business experiences a "loss." Mathematically, the concept is expressed as follows:

$$\text{Profit (or Loss)} = \text{Revenue} - \text{Expenses}$$

Example 1.1: If a business brings in $100,000 in revenue and has $95,000 in expenses, how much profit or loss will it generate?

$$\text{Revenue} - \text{Expenses} = \text{Profit (or Loss)}$$
$$\$100,000 - \$95,000 = \$5,000 \text{ Profit}$$

Example 1.2: If a business brings in $100,000 in revenue and has $105,000 in expenses, how much profit or loss will it generate?

$$\text{Revenue} - \text{Expenses} = \text{Profit (or Loss)}$$
$$\$100,000 - \$105,000 = -\$5,000 \text{ or } (\$5,000) \text{ Loss}$$

When Revenue minus Expenses is a positive number, the business makes a profit. When it is a negative number, it incurs a loss, often expressed on financial statements in parentheses "(loss)" to show that it is a negative number. (Red ink and minus signs are alternate ways to designate a negative number.) Sometimes the equation is expressed as "Profit = Sales − Costs," but the concept is still the same. Profit is all of the money coming in minus all of the money going out.

1.2.1 Types of Revenue and Expenses

Cataloguing types of revenue is straightforward. Revenue, for the most part, is the money coming in from sales of products and services. For a typical restaurant, sales are of two types: food sales and beverage sales. Additional revenue may come in from fees charged to customers for special services, such as room rentals or separate charges for service staff (especially for catered events). Some companies also make money selling T-shirts or other logo items. In many operations, further revenue may come from a return on investments, such as interest paid for money in the bank account, but for most foodservice businesses, this is a very small proportion of the overall revenue. (For the purposes of simplicity and applicability to the majority of foodservice businesses, this book will focus exclusively on revenue sources from food and beverage sales.)

The categories of expenses are far more varied in most foodservice operations, but they fall under some common broad headings, as follows:

- *Food Costs* These are the costs paid for the ingredients used to generate food sales.
- *Beverage Costs* These are the costs paid for the ingredients used to generate beverage sales. (*Note*: Some managers only include alcoholic drinks in beverage costs, while others include both alcoholic and nonalcoholic drinks. The choice depends on the manager and the type of operation.)
- *Labor Costs* These are the costs associated with having employees. Labor costs include wages (payments to hourly workers), salaries (payments to workers as an annual salary), and employee benefits.
- *Direct Operating Costs* These costs relate to the supplies that go directly to customer service activities, such as flatware, china, linens, uniforms, and flowers.
- *Marketing, Advertising, and Promotion* These costs stem from activities designed to generate sales for the foodservice operation. Examples include paid advertising, printing and distribution of coupons, food "comped" to a potential or current customer, or staff paid to present at a food show.
- *Music and Entertainment* Just like it sounds, these are the costs paid for music and entertainment. Depending on the type of foodservice operation, these could be very small or very large expenses.
- *Utilities* These costs include payment for gas, electric, water, and sewer expenses.

- *Repair and Maintenance*   These are the costs for repairing and maintaining expensive pieces of equipment with long life spans as well as for maintaining the larger facility and grounds. (Inexpensive equipment is typically replaced rather than repaired.)
- *Equipment Purchases*   These costs apply not only to inexpensive kitchen utensils, but also to equipment designed to last for multiple years, such as chairs, ovens, or computers. In many cases, these costs are thought of in terms of the equipment's cost per year over its life expectancy, also known as "depreciation."
- *Administrative and General Costs*   These are the costs that come from the supplies and infrastructure one would find in a typical office, from paper and pens to internet and phone connections.
- *Occupation Costs*   These costs include rent, property and related taxes, property insurance, and any other costs required to occupy the business's physical space.
- *Interest*   This is the expense that comes from paying interest on loans owed to investors or banks.

Managers must control for all sources of revenue and expenses, though for certain expenses, all a manager can realistically do is account for them in planning. Because profit relies solely on two factors—revenue and expenses—by properly managing revenue and expenses, a manager can help a company reach its profit goals.

1.3   TYPES OF LOSS

The concept of "control" from a cost control perspective effectively means eliminating unnecessary expenses while maintaining essential ones at the proper levels; in terms of revenue, it means driving business to hit forecasted levels. For some types of expenses, the cost is not eliminated so much as it is made more efficient. For example, a chef cannot sell food without spending some money on ingredients and labor, even if both of those costs can be reduced slightly through efficiencies. However, there are a few "costs" that managers try to excise completely from their departments because they provide no return to the business. These costs are commonly referred to as "loss," and they typically fall into one of the following three categories:

Theft.   While theft has no place in any business, rarely does a year go by in a foodservice operation without an employee or customer attempting to steal from the business. Theft can be as dramatic as a burglary by armed robbers or as subtle as an employee sneaking saffron off the storeroom shelf and into his pocket. An employee may not even realize that his action is considered theft, such as grazing from a cook's mise en place instead of eating the staff meal. Theft may include money or property (food, equipment, etc.), but the result is the same either way. The business loses something of value that takes away from its potential profit.

Waste (via production).   Loss through waste is typically the result of poor training and by extension, poor management. Waste through production usually comes in three forms. The first type occurs when an employee trims too much of an ingredient. For example, a cook might peel 4 ounce (oz) from every pound of carrots instead of the chef's specified 2 oz of peelings. Such waste may not seem significant for a single pound of carrots, but over hundreds of pounds of carrots, the waste really adds up. The second type of production waste results from an employee ruining a dish through a cooking or cutting error. This form of waste can occur if a cook burns a pot of rice, drops a steak on the floor, cuts a prime rib too small for sale to a customer, or otherwise makes food unusable. The third type of production waste is poor portion control. When a restaurant plans for a 10-oz portion of pasta and one cook typically serves customers a 12-oz portion, it is a form of waste. A customer may not reject a larger-than-necessary portion, but he will not be dissatisfied with the standard portion either. In fact, if he returns to find that the portion sizes are normally smaller, he may be disinclined to return. Thus, a too-large portion size is not only a wasted cost, but it can undermine future sales. These forms of production waste will never be eliminated from professional kitchens completely, but with proper training and management, the incidence of such waste can be greatly reduced.

Spoilage. Sometimes considered another form of waste, spoilage is less the result of poor training and more commonly the result of poor planning by management. Spoilage occurs when food goes bad before it has a chance to be prepared and sold to a customer. With proper forecasting, purchasing, and receiving procedures, a restaurant can ensure that it only receives quality ingredients that can be used up before they spoil. As with waste via production, spoilage is difficult to remove entirely from a foodservice operation, but with proper management, spoilage can be kept to a minimum.

All three forms of loss—theft, production waste, and spoilage—work directly against a manager's attempt to generate a profit. One of the primary responsibilities of a manager, from a cost control perspective, is to keep loss from gaining a foothold in a business's daily operation.

1.3.1 Control through the Flow of Food

Just like a HACCP (hazard analysis critical control points) manager monitors food sanitation at several critical control points, a cost control manager controls most of the business's expenses at certain points in the flow of food to make those expenses as efficient as possible. While subsequent chapters of this book go into great detail on these control points, this section offers a brief overview of the many areas a manager can and should control.

Purchasing. The journey food takes through a foodservice operation begins with the purchasing process. Purchasing is the point at which a purchasing agent, chef, or other employee determines how much to order, when to order it, and which purveyors to patronize. Done properly, good quality food is purchased at a competitive price in enough quantity so that the ingredients neither run short nor spoil. Uncontrolled, the purchasing process can wreak havoc on a business's costs. Without effective inventory and purchasing systems, the purchaser may not know how much to purchase. Over-purchasing may lead to product spoilage, which is money down the drain. Ordering too little or too late could render the kitchen unable to produce food for sale. Last-minute purchases through a retail supermarket to make up for inaccurate ordering can be expensive enough to make a dish unprofitable. If food needed for a special event is delivered too far in advance, the business will again experience spoilage before the food is needed. Finally, the process of selecting a purveyor and a specific set of products is critical to avoid cost overruns. The purchaser determines, often through a bidding process, which purveyor provides the right product at the best price. However, while price is important, it is not the sole factor to consider when choosing a purveyor. Food delivered on an unreliable schedule may arrive too late to be of any use. Food at a lower price per unit may not actually be the best deal if the kitchen cannot use the entire product. In short, the purchasing process is the first opportunity for a manager to control costs in the flow of food.

Receiving and Storage. Once food has been ordered from a purveyor, it needs to be checked and stored upon its arrival to a foodservice business. Receiving is the process through which an employee confirms that the food received matches both the invoice and the order placed. Unethical purveyors have ample opportunity to take advantage of a business that does not receive food properly. The invoice may list a higher weight or quantity for food than what is delivered. The prices quoted during the purchasing process may be higher on the invoice. The food delivered may be of poor quality and thus unusable or likely to spoil before it is used. Potential food safety hazards, such as perishable products in the temperature danger zone, should be caught during receiving, and employees should quickly and properly store wholesome foods to avoid initiating sanitation problems themselves. Proper receiving and storage help prevent theft from unethical purveyors and spoilage from poorly inspected or improperly handled food.

Issuing.   The storeroom is another cost control opportunity for management. Controls in issuing help to ensure that food is tracked, so undetected theft becomes more difficult. Stock rotation helps minimize loss from spoilage. With proper issuing procedures in place, all of the food purchased for the business ends up in the kitchen for its intended use rather than in a trash can or in an employee's home.

Recipe Production.   A well-controlled kitchen uses standardized recipes to help control costs and minimize waste. Some loss, however, is natural to the cooking process and must be accounted for rather than eliminated to control it properly. For example, large cuts of meat, fish, poultry, and produce have trim, even when properly fabricated. Most food loses weight during the cooking process as well. When trim and cooking loss are calculated properly, recipes can be costed correctly and accurate sales prices can be determined.

Presentation and Portion Control.   Even when a recipe is properly followed in the kitchen, if it is portioned inaccurately, expenses will increase. Since menu prices are calculated on the basis of an expected portion size, an employee who serves too large a portion may turn a profitable dish into a losing one. Too small a portion may result in customers returning food; food that ends up in the trash represents a loss no matter what the reason. Presentation and portion control must be managed for a restaurant to remain profitable. Keep in mind, too, that presentation and portion control, like all of these other steps in the flow of food, relate equally to beverage as they do to food. While there are special concerns for beverages elsewhere during the flow of food, one of the greatest opportunities for loss with beverages comes from a lack of portion control.

Sales Control.   While one might assume that sales control simply means collecting money properly from a customer, sales control goes well beyond the delivery of a guest check. Managers must properly calculate sales prices to make sure that a dish brings in enough revenue to cover its ingredients, labor, overhead, and profit. Effective marketing helps to drive sales to increase revenue for the business. Insufficient sales and poorly priced items will drive a restaurant out of business as easily as will a slew of dine-and-dash customers. The flow of food ends at the point of sale and consumption, but two more areas impact expenses so greatly in any foodservice business that they merit mention.

Employee Scheduling.   While labor is technically not part of the flow of food, employees are mentioned here to acknowledge the potential for significant cost savings through efficient scheduling (or for loss through poor scheduling). Hourly employees are paid for each fraction of an hour that they are at work, even if they are not truly productive. When two employees are getting paid to do the work that one employee could easily handle, that is wasted money that could go toward increased profits. While cutting an employee's hours to make more money for a faceless company may seem cruel, a manager's allegiance must be first to the financial health of the business. A company that does not operate at a profit will soon go out of business, and then everyone, including the manager, is out of work.

Forecasting. Though the flow of food ends once it is consumed by the customer at the point of sale, each sale provides historical information that helps a manager to continually improve his performance controlling inefficiencies in the flow of food. The business's historical data on customer buying patterns helps a chef predict which dishes will sell better and thus which need more (or less) mise en place prepared. This predicting or forecasting helps a purchaser order ingredients properly to avoid overpurchasing and spoilage. Forecasting also helps a manager to schedule the right number of employees to handle customer needs without paying workers to kill time. Through forecasting, managers begin anew the process of controlling the flow of food. The flow of food may be thought of as a cycle, but all of the elements in the process operate continuously and simultaneously. Learning to set up systems and procedures to manage all of these processes (and others) at the same time is the purpose of studying cost control.

1.4 HUMANS VERSUS COMPUTERS

Unlike restaurants of yesteryear, today's foodservice operations typically use computers, especially through point-of-sales systems, to collect data on customers, sales, expenses, revenue, and other information unimaginable even a few decades ago. The information can be processed in real time (i.e., immediately) and broken down by almost any variable (e.g., sales by month, day, day of the week, shift, or even hour). Computer systems can help a manager calculate recipe costs, sales prices, food cost percentages, theoretical inventory values, and even expected profit for a given period. Computers are wonderful components of a well-managed business. They are sometimes considered a chef's most valuable tool. But computers do have their limitations.

The greatest restriction a computer has is its inability to do anything other than what it is programmed to do. For example, if a user sets up a formula in an Excel worksheet to calculate food cost percentage, and that formula is entered improperly, the program will reliably calculate food cost percentage exactly as instructed—incorrectly! While some computer programs have preset formulas, a manager needs to understand the purpose of each formula and what information each calculation provides if it is to be of any use at all. A program that gives numbers for labor cost percentage and food cost percentage is valueless if a manager does not know what those percentages mean and what to do with that information.

The other main limitation of a computer is that it can only work with the information entered into the program. Even if the formulas are correct, a program with inaccurate data input will provide inaccurate data output—garbage in, garbage out. If a chef needs to calculate the cost of a recipe and the computer asks for the ingredient quantity and unit price, it may not calculate the correct answer if the chef lists the ingredient quantity in ounces and the unit price in dollars per pound. As with entering the formulas, the computer is only as smart as the user. Current and future managers who do not understand cost control and the math involved, will not find a computer of much value. The computer can do the monotonous work of performing calculations, but the managers must set the computer up for achieving success.

Finally, as mentioned earlier in the chapter, the results provided by a computer, no matter how complex and accurate, are simply data. The numbers can tell managers almost anything they want to know except what to do with that information. This is perhaps the most important reason to understand cost control and the purpose of each calculation. For example, a computer can determine that over a three-month period, a restaurant's food cost percentage increased a full percentage point, its labor percentage increased three percentage points, its sales increased 2% over the time period, and its profit dropped by $30,000. While this information may indicate a problem in the business, it does not tell a manager how to fix it.

Often, problematic results on a computer spreadsheet are merely red flags that alert a manager to conduct an investigation into the cause of the problem to determine an appropriate solution. For example, the solution to the earlier scenario is not obvious from the given facts alone. The food cost could be the result of increased loss through spoilage or theft, or it could be the result of increased purveyor prices. Different causes require different approaches. Spoilage and theft might be corrected through better controls in the purchasing and issuing processes, while increased purveyor prices are accounted for through adjusted recipes or sales prices. Similarly, the labor cost could be the result of poor management and scheduling, or it could be a logical, temporary increase that resulted from employees retiring and cross-training their replacements before getting off the payroll (which may require no managerial intervention at all). The increase in sales should be a positive thing, but perhaps it should have been greater based on the levels of expense increases. In short, an investigation and a talented manager can determine the proper solution for the drop in profit; a computer spreadsheet cannot. Computer data only highlights where the problems may lie, so the manager knows where to begin researching. That is the reason why math and computers play the roles that they do and why only human beings—knowledgeable, well-trained human beings—can effectively perform the role of cost control manager.

SUMMARY

One of a manager's key responsibilities is to generate profit, which is a function of revenue and expenses. Revenue can come from several sources, but the main ones in foodservice are food sales and beverage sales. Expenses are the costs of doing business, and they come from a range of areas, including food and beverage ingredients, labor, direct operating costs, marketing, advertising, promotion, music and entertainment expenses, utilities, repair and maintenance, equipment purchases, administrative costs, occupation costs, and interest. Loss, while a common "cost" in foodservice, is not a necessary expense and should be reduced as much as possible. Loss comes from three main sources—theft, waste, and spoilage—and can occur anywhere in the flow of food. Math plays an important role in helping a person manage a foodservice operation, but it is only one factor to be considered when making management decisions. While computers can perform many calculations for a human being, they are no substitute for a well-trained manager, who can interpret mathematical calculations and consider them along with other variables to make decisions that maintain a business's profitability and long-term success.

COMPREHENSION QUESTIONS

1. What two variables determine a business's profit?
2. If a restaurant has $178,000 in expenses and $190,000 in revenue, does it make a profit or operate at a loss? How much profit or loss does it have?
3. List three categories of common foodservice expenses. State what costs are typically included in each of those categories.
4. List the three types of loss common in foodservice. Which type is often the result of poor training?

Which is typically the result of poor forecasting and planning by managers?
5. List two areas that are not part of the flow of food that impact expenses significantly.
6. Why must a future manager learn cost control and its corresponding math when a computer can perform mathematical calculations much faster?

DISCUSSION QUESTIONS

1. Where have you ever seen a foodservice business generating revenue from something other than food and beverage sales?

2. Have you ever seen or heard of a theft at a foodservice business? What happened? How did the business respond afterward?

3. Have you ever been to a restaurant that did not utilize computers (as far as you know)? Do you think the restaurant would have been better off with computers or would it not have made a difference?

4. Imagine a large restaurant that loses twenty pens a day because customers take them after signing their checks. The lost pens cost the business $20 per day because they are specially made with the restaurant's logo on them. Is this cost a loss or an expense? Because the manager did not originally expect the pens to be taken, the business spreadsheets calculate a profit that is $600 per month less than expected based almost exclusively on the lost pens. How should a manager deal with this situation, if at all?

2
Basic Math

Objectives

By the end of this chapter, you will be able to:

- Round numbers to the appropriate decimal for both practicality and accuracy
- Convert fractions and mixed numbers to decimals and decimals to fractions
- Reduce fractions
- Multiply and divide fractions
- Convert decimals to percentages and percentages to decimals
- Calculate part, whole, or percentage given two of the three

*[**Author's Note:** My experience in culinary education has shown that students in culinary schools arrive with a wide variety of math capabilities. Some excel in math, while others have always struggled. Cost control is not solely about math, but in classes where students get bogged down in the execution of math computations, the class never progresses beyond the math component to a more complete understanding of cost control. For this reason, I have included this chapter on basic math to bring all students up to the same minimum competency level for cost control math. My hope is that by taking the time to gain some math foundations now, the entire class will be able to progress through the math in future chapters more easily, thereby allowing more class time for the discussion of nonmath cost control principles.]*

The math involved in cost control is elementary considering the difficulty of math used in other fields. Cost control does not employ calculus or even algebra, but it does rely heavily on fractions, decimals, and percentages. Hopefully, that doesn't make you cringe. You use this kind of math in your life all the time. You probably just don't think of it as math. Consider the following example.

Without using a calculator or even a piece of paper, try to calculate 25×9 as quickly as you can. If after five seconds, you still don't have the answer, try this question: How much money do you have if you have nine quarters? You probably came up with $2.25 almost instantly, and that includes putting a decimal point in the right place! Well, $25 \times 9 = 225$. Why is the money example so much easier to calculate? Simply put, most people have more experience doing "money" math than they have doing other types of math. With enough practice, you will soon do all of the calculations required in cost control just as quickly and easily, though probably not in your head.

While some culinary students may already be experts in fractions, decimals, and percentages, not all are. If you are one of these experts, this chapter will be a simple refresher for you. If not, this chapter will provide you the mathematical foundation upon which cost control calculations are built. Make the effort now to gain comfort and mastery of the material here quickly before moving forward in the book. While the math in the rest of the book is quite simple to perform, it is impossible to do so without an understanding of fractions, decimals, and percentages.

2.1   ROUNDING

Converting fractions to decimals sometimes results in numbers that run on far too long to be useful, so before progressing to fractions and decimals, a discussion on rounding is in order. Rounding numbers to shorten the string of digits after a decimal point is a compromise between accuracy and practicality. Though 2.37512 oz is more precise a measurement than the same number rounded to 2.4 oz, both have their place in cost control. Imagine that you are working with a recipe that (because it was reduced from a large commercial-quantity recipe) requires 2.37512 oz salt. You normally round the quantity to 2.4 oz because your digital scale only measures to one-tenth of an ounce. In effect, you have no way of measuring the impractically accurate 2.37512 oz. But today, your chef asks you to multiply the recipe by 1,200 because you are catering an enormous event. If you use 2.37512 in your conversion, you'll see that you need 2,850.144 oz salt; this equates to 178.134 #. If, however, you start with 2.4 oz salt in your calculations, you'll come up with 2,880 oz or 180 # salt. The difference between the two calculations is 1.866 # salt. While such a quantity difference might not be noticeable for some ingredients in a recipe of this magnitude, this much extra salt might push the final dish from flavorful to unpleasantly salty. If we change the ingredient in this theoretical recipe from salt to something pricier, such as ground cardamom, an extra 1.8 # would drive up the cost of the recipe significantly. For a large quantity conversion as this, the more accurate 2.37512 oz should be utilized in the calculations. In short, numbers with multiple digits after the decimal point are best maintained as precise as practically possible until they are applied to the real world.

2.1.1 How to Round

The process of rounding a decimal is quite simple.

Step 1:   Determine the desired accuracy of the number. In other words, to what "place" should the final number be written? Do you want two digits after the decimal point? Three digits? No digits?

Step 2:   Look to the number immediately to the right of the "desired" final place. (For example, if you want to end up with two digits after the decimal point, you look at the third digit after the decimal point.) If that digit is less than 5, you are rounding down. If that digit is 5 or more, you are rounding up.

Step 3:   If you are rounding down, then simply remove all of the digits to the right of your final desired place. If you are rounding up, then you must increase by one the number in the final desired place after dropping the digits to its right.

Rounding is explained more simply in numbers in the following examples.

Example 2.1: Round 4.87315 to the nearest hundredth (or two places past the decimal point).

───The "7" occupies the final desired place, two places past the decimal point.

4.87315

───The "3" is immediately to the right of the desired final place.

Since 3 is less than 5, round down. Drop all of the numbers more than two places past the decimal point.

The answer is 4.87.

Example 2.2: Round 4.87315 to the nearest tenth (or one place past the decimal point).

⌐——The "8" occupies the final desired place, one place past the decimal point.
4.87315
⌐——The "7" is immediately to the right of the desired final place.

Since 7 is greater than 5, round up. Drop all of the numbers more than one place past the decimal point, and increase the 8 to a 9.

The answer is 4.9.

If the number rounding up is a 9, you will need to "carry the 1" just as you would with basic addition. Thus, if you are rounding 3.897 to the nearest hundredth (two places to the right of the decimal), the answer becomes 3.90 or 3.9. The 0.89 is rounded up to 0.90 just as if you were adding a one to the column with the nine.

Notice in both examples that any digits more than one space to the right of the desired final place are irrelevant. So 4.87, 4.8731, and 4.87315 all round to 4.9 when rounding to the nearest tenth. Do not confuse the length of a series of digits after a decimal point with its size. You can always add a series of zeros after the last digit to the right of the decimal point without changing the number's value. So 3.8 is larger than 3.758. If this isn't obvious, add those zeros to compare 3.800 with 3.758. That may help to evaluate number sizes if you aren't already comfortable with decimals.

One final note on terminology: the position one digit to the right of the decimal point is called the tenth's place; two digits to the right is called the hundredth's place, and three digits to the right is called the thousandth's place. When a question asks to round to the nearest hundredth, the final answer will have two digits to the right of the decimal point, to the nearest thousandth will have three digits to the right, and so on.

2.1.2 When to Round and by How Much

Since rounding compromises accuracy, it should not be done at every step of a multi-step problem. When performing a series of steps on a calculator or computer, there is no need to stop and round the answer at each step of the process. Simply leave the full number in the calculator or computer until you have completed your series of calculations. Even a computer that is programmed to display only a certain number of digits on a spreadsheet will use the unrounded numbers in its calculations to preserve accuracy. If you must record your work on paper as you go, a good rule of thumb is to write four digits to the right of the decimal on every step. At this degree of detail, the final answers, once rounded to a practical measurement, should be identical or nearly identical to those performed with numbers rounded only at the final step.

How much rounding should be done to make a measurement practical? In truth, it depends on the accuracy of one's measuring devices. For example, a digital scale designed for kitchen use can typically weigh items to a tenth of an ounce, but a balance beam scale can only weigh in quarter-ounce units. Thus, if you use a balance beam scale, you would round numbers to the nearest quarter ounce, not the nearest tenth of an ounce. For example, 3.31 oz would be reduced to 3.25 for measurement on a balance beam scale while it would be reduced to 3.3 for measurement on a digital scale.

Not all calculations result in weight or volume measures. Sometimes, the calculations result in dollars or in percentages. Dollars cannot be divided any further than penny units, so money is always rounded to the nearest penny or to two places past the decimal point. Percentages can be infinitely detailed, but for the purposes of this book, we will always round percentages to one-tenth of 1% (or 0.1%). As the chapter discusses later, this equates to recording numbers three places to the right of the decimal point before those numbers are converted to a percentage format.

Finally, many chefs advise their trainees always to round money up, no matter what the rules of rounding would advise. While there is some logic to this approach (mainly, that rounding up keeps the business from losing a portion of a penny on the sale of certain items), the "always-round-up" rule is unnecessary when one remembers that math gives guidance and information to management, not fixed answers. As evidence, consider the last time you read a restaurant menu. Did the prices look more like this ($12.23, $8.71, $14.09) or did they look like this ($12.50, $8.95, $14.00)? The first set of numbers would be a common result for a chef to see after conducting calculations on suggested sales prices, but she would almost always adjust them up or down to "nicer-looking" numbers (the second set) on the basis of the menu and customer psychology. Whether or not her spreadsheet rounds money up or down to the nearest penny will be irrelevant to the final menu price, and when her costs are rounded properly, they are slightly more accurate than when they are always rounded up.

2.2 FRACTIONS

Fractions are commonplace in the professional kitchen. Simply put, a fraction is a way of numerically expressing a portion of a full unit. One third of a cup (c) of flour is the quantity you would get if you divided one cup of flour into three equal portions and measured one of those portions. Conversely, if you measure out three $\frac{1}{3}$ c of flour, you will have one full cup.

Fractions can come in the form of mixed numbers, whole numbers, or pure fractions. With the aid of a calculator or computer, fractions can be converted to decimals or percentages. They are useful ways of expressing a ratio (and ratios are common ways of expressing recipes in the culinary field). They come in handy when a cook needs to scale recipes up or down, to convert units for ease of measuring, or to adjust portion sizes for a dish. In short, fractions are indispensible to the efficient operation of a professional kitchen.

2.2.1 Fractions, Whole Numbers, and Mixed Numbers

Before working with fractions, one must first understand fraction shorthand. A fraction is commonly written as one number over another. In these cases, the top number is called the "numerator" and the bottom number is called the "denominator" (see Figure 2.1).

Writing a numerator over a denominator is equivalent to writing the numerator *divided by* the denominator. So $\frac{1}{4}$ is the same as $1 \div 4$. (If you tend to think of fractions as the denominator "divided into" the numerator, $\frac{1}{4}$ as four into one, for example, switch your thinking immediately. There is no "into" button on a calculator, only a "divided by" button. "Into" makes it impossible to use a computer or calculator when doing math!)

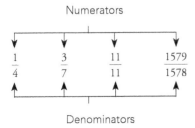

Figure 2.1
Numerators and Denominators

When the numerator is smaller than the denominator, the fraction has a value less than 1. When the numerator is greater than the denominator, the fraction has a value greater than 1. Most importantly, when the numerator and denominator are the same, the fraction is equal to 1. In Figure 2.1, the fraction $\frac{3}{7}$ is less than 1, $\frac{1579}{1578}$ is greater than 1, and $\frac{11}{11}$ is equal to 1.

Whole Numbers.   Although whole numbers (1, 2, 3, 4, 5, etc.) are commonly written without a denominator, they can be expressed as a fraction simply by putting the whole number in the numerator and a "1" in the denominator. Thus, 3 is the same as $\frac{3}{1}$. 18 is the same as $\frac{18}{1}$, and so on. This concept may seem unnecessary, but it helps greatly when multiplying and dividing fractions as well as when converting units of measure.

Mixed Numbers.   A mixed number is one that combines a whole number and a fraction in the same expression. For example, $2\frac{1}{4}$ (spoken "two and a quarter") is a mixed number. It is the same as saying "$2 + \frac{1}{4}$" or "two whole units and one quarter unit." Mixed numbers are difficult to manipulate in their current form, so they are often converted to a single fraction.

To convert a mixed number to a single fraction, multiply the whole number times the fraction's denominator. Then add the result to the fraction's numerator. Finally, place the total over the fraction's denominator.

Example 2.3: Convert $2\frac{1}{4}$ to a single fraction.

Numerator

$2\frac{1}{4}$

Denominator

Whole number

Step 1: Multiply the whole number (2) by the fraction's denominator (4). $2 \times 4 = 8$.
Step 2: Add the result (8) to the fraction's numerator (1). $8 + 1 = 9$.
Step 3: Place the total (9) over the fraction's denominator (4). $\frac{9}{4}$.

The answer is $\frac{9}{4}$.

Example 2.4: Convert $7\frac{3}{8}$ to a single fraction.

Step 1: $7 \times 8 = 56$
Step 2: $56 + 3 = 59$
Step 3: $\frac{59}{8}$

The answer is $\frac{59}{8}$.

Reversing the process, going from a fraction to a mixed number, is much easier. Divide the numerator by the denominator. You will have a whole number and a remainder. The whole number is the whole number component of the mixed number. The remainder is the numerator of the fraction. The denominator remains the same.

Example 2.5: Convert $\frac{7}{3}$ into a mixed number.

Step 1: Divide the numerator (7) by the denominator (3). $7 \div 3 = 2$ with a remainder of 1.

Step 2: The whole number result (2) is written next to the remainder (1) over the original denominator (3). $2\frac{1}{3}$.

The answer is $2\frac{1}{3}$.

The process is slightly more complex when using a calculator. The calculator does not list a "remainder." It only lists a decimal. So, when using a calculator, divide the numerator by the denominator. The number to the left of the decimal is the whole number part of the mixed number. Subtract that whole number in the calculator, so you are left with only the decimal. Multiply the decimal by the original denominator to get the numerator for the mixed number. Write the mixed number as the whole number followed by the new numerator over the original denominator.

Example 2.6: Convert $\frac{53}{16}$ into a mixed number using a calculator.

Step 1: Divide the numerator (53) by the denominator (16). $53 \div 16 = 3.3125$.

Step 2: Subtract the number to the left of the decimal (3). $3.3125 - 3 = 0.3125$.

Step 3: Multiply the decimal (0.3125) by the denominator (16). $0.3125 \times 16 = 5$.

Step 4: Write the whole number (3) followed by the numerator (5) over the denominator (16). $3\frac{5}{16}$.

The answer is $3\frac{5}{16}$.

While this process might seem too complicated to be worth the trouble, switching back and forth between mixed numbers and single fractions is quite common. The single fraction format is essential for conducting calculations when converting recipe units. The mixed number form is the only practical way to measure ingredients. For instance, in Example 2.5, it would be a waste of time to count out seven $\frac{1}{3}$ c of flour when a baker could measure out 2 c and $\frac{1}{3}$ c of flour much faster. Conversely, if you needed to multiply the recipe times 11 to get a higher yield, it is easier to work with $\frac{7}{3}$ c (or 2.333 c) as the starting unit than it is to multiply $2\frac{1}{3}$ c. With time and practice, these computations become second nature for a chef.

2.2.2 Multiplying and Dividing by Fractions

Able to convert whole and mixed numbers to fractions, one can multiply and divide one fraction by another fraction. To multiply two fractions, multiply the two numerators to get a new numerator, and multiply the two denominators to get a new denominator.

Example 2.7: Multiply $\frac{2}{5} \times \frac{3}{4}$.

$$\frac{2}{5} \quad \times \quad \frac{3}{4} \quad = \quad \frac{2 \times 3}{5 \times 4} \quad = \quad \frac{6}{20}$$

Dividing fractions is just as easy. To divide one fraction by a second fraction, invert the second fraction upside down and multiply the two.

Example 2.8: Calculate $\frac{2}{5} \div \frac{3}{4}$.

(Note that the second fraction is upside down)

$$\frac{2}{5} \quad \times \quad \frac{4}{3} \quad = \quad \frac{2 \times 4}{5 \times 3} \quad = \quad \frac{8}{15}$$

Multiplying and Dividing by One.   Recall from earlier in the chapter that a number with the same numerator and denominator equals 1. For example, $\frac{14}{14} = 1$. Since any number multiplied or divided by 1 is the original number, we can make fractions look different without actually changing their values.

Example 2.9: Reduce $\frac{12}{16}$ to a more user-friendly measure.

(Note dividing by 1, in this case $\frac{4}{4}$, doesn't change the original fraction's value)

$$\frac{12}{16} \quad \div \quad \frac{4}{4} \quad = \quad \frac{12 \div 4}{16 \div 4} \quad = \quad \frac{3}{4}$$

A similar process could occur by multiplying both numerator and denominator by the same number. You would change the fraction's appearance without actually changing its value, but in the professional kitchen, the reduction of fractions is more useful than their increase. Though common in pure math, in the kitchen, reducing fractions is generally limited in the kitchen to making measuring easier. As evidence, look at a set of measuring cups. Which is more practical to measure, $\frac{12}{16}$ or $\frac{3}{4}$?

2.2.3 Converting Fractions to Decimals

While fractions are more useful for cooks, cost control managers tend to find decimals and percentages preferable to numerical forms. Calculators work with decimals, not fractions. Dollars and percentages are written as decimals. Fractions are important for measurements and unit conversions, but decimals are essential for most other kitchen calculations. Fortunately, converting from fractions to decimals is easy with a calculator or a computer.

To convert a fraction to a decimal, divide the numerator by the denominator, and let the calculator or computer do the rest.

Example 2.10: Convert $\frac{3}{8}$ to a decimal.

Enter $3 \div 8$ into a calculator. The result is 0.375.

While it would be difficult to measure 0.375, this number is far easier to use for other cost control operations than the fraction $\frac{3}{8}$ is.

Going from decimals back to fractions is slightly more complicated. Any decimal can be converted to a fraction, but making that fraction practical for measuring requires a little memorization and sometimes a bit of rounding.

To convert a decimal to a fraction, one can always place the decimal, without the decimal point, over a denominator that represents the number of "places" the decimal goes to the right of the decimal point. For example, if the decimal goes to the hundredth's place, then the denominator is 100. If it goes to the thousandth's place, then the denominator is 1000. Basically, the number of zeros after the 1 in the denominator is equivalent to the number of places the decimal goes to the right of the decimal point.

Example 2.11: Convert 0.078 to a fraction.

> *Step 1:* Place the decimal without the decimal point (078 or 78) in the numerator.
>
> *Step 2:* Since this decimal goes three places to the right of the decimal point, put a one and three zeros (1,000) in the denominator.

The answer is $\frac{78}{1000}$.

Example 2.11 deals more with abstract math (which is always exact) than it does with applied kitchen math, which requires accommodations for the measuring tools used in a kitchen. While $\frac{78}{1000}$ can be reduced to $\frac{39}{500}$, that fraction is still not useful for measuring. So next, we must discuss the decimals that convert easily to "useful" fractions (in culinary terms) to see if 0.078 is relatively close to one of them.

Most American kitchens operate in fractions of $\frac{1}{16}$, $\frac{1}{8}$, $\frac{1}{4}$, $\frac{1}{3}$, and $\frac{1}{2}$. Since there are 16 oz in a pound (and 16 Tbsp in a cup), $\frac{1}{16}$ or 0.0625 is a "useful" fraction of a pound (or of a cup). Measuring cups are commonly available in $\frac{1}{8}$-, $\frac{1}{4}$-, $\frac{1}{3}$-, and $\frac{1}{2}$-c measures, so decimals that convert to these units are easy to measure. To make the math a little easier, the best thing to do is to memorize a few common fraction–decimal equivalents (see Table 2.1). Then, when you see these decimals on a calculator or computer, you will know their fraction equivalents without having to do any further calculations. Any decimal that does not appear in Table 2.1 can also be rounded to the nearest $\frac{1}{16}$ or $\frac{1}{8}$ measure by multiplying it by 16 or 8, respectively. In other words, if you multiply a decimal by 16, the result (if it is a whole number) is the numerator for a fraction in which 16 is the denominator. If you multiply a decimal by 8, the result is the numerator for a fraction in which 8 is the denominator.

Example 2.12: What is the nearest "useful" measure for 0.4375 #?

> $0.4375 \times 16 = 7$ (7 is the numerator of a fraction in which 16 is the denominator.)
>
> The answer is $\frac{7}{16}$. (Because there are 16 oz in a pound, $\frac{7}{16}$ # = 7 oz)

Sometimes, the math does not work out quite so neatly. In these cases, the cook must round to the closest useful measure.

Example 2.13: What is the nearest "useful" measure for 0.721 c?

> $0.721 \times 8 = 5.768$ ⟵——— Not a whole number

TABLE 2.1
"USEFUL" FRACTION–DECIMAL EQUIVALENTS

$$\frac{1}{16} = 0.0625$$

$$\frac{1}{8} = 0.125$$

$$\frac{1}{4} = 0.25$$

$$\frac{1}{3} = 0.333$$

$$\frac{1}{2} = 0.5$$

$$\frac{2}{3} = 0.666$$

$$\frac{3}{4} = 0.75$$

Since 5.768 is not a whole number numerator for a fraction in which 8 is the denominator, we need to round 5.768 to the nearest whole number. In this case, we round 5.768 up to 6 to yield the fraction $\frac{6}{8}$. When both the numerator and denominator are divided by 2, we get the equivalent fraction $\frac{3}{4}$. Measuring $\frac{3}{4}$ c is easy. Of course, in some cases, like this one, the answer may seem obvious without any math at all. We know from Table 2.1 that $\frac{3}{4} = 0.75$. Since 0.721 is quite close to 0.75, it is safe to round 0.721 c to $\frac{3}{4}$ c.

Let's return to Example 2.11, in which converting 0.078 to $\frac{78}{1000}$ doesn't give us a useful number. You will notice from Table 2.1 that 0.078 is close to 0.0625. Thus, 0.078 is approximately $\frac{1}{16}$. This unit can be measured much more easily than $\frac{78}{1000}$ using common kitchen equipment. ($\frac{1}{16}$ # is an ounce, and $\frac{1}{16}$ c is a tablespoon.) Thus, $\frac{78}{1000}$ may be the most accurate answer to Example 2.11, but $\frac{1}{16}$ is the most practical answer for kitchen use.

While converting from decimals back to fractions (at least to useful fractions) is a little more complicated than going from fractions to decimals, both can be done fairly quickly with a basic understanding of common fraction–decimal equivalents and the rounding process. Because the process of going from decimals to fractions may involve rounding, to maintain as much accuracy as possible it is best not to convert back to fractions until absolutely necessary for measurement purposes. Thus, in calculations with multiple steps, stick with decimals until the final step is complete. Only then should you convert a decimal to a fraction, and even then do so only if the final answer is a measurement of volume or weight commonly divided into $\frac{1}{8}$ or $\frac{1}{16}$ units (not dollars, percentages, or even ounces that will be weighed on a digital scale).

2.3   PERCENTAGES

Before working with percentages, you should understand what a percentage is and what it means. "Percentage" is simply a way of expressing a fraction in which the denominator is 100. For example, most people use the term "50%" to refer to half of something. Fifty is half of hundred, so 50% mathematically is equivalent to $\frac{1}{2}$. However, you can determine 50% of any number, not just of 100: 50% of 10 is 5; 50% of 18 is 9; and 50% of 122 is 61. In all cases, 50% is always half of the base number, the same proportional relationship that 50 has to 100. Thus, percentages are merely shorthand for decimals and fractions.

2.3.1 Converting Numbers to Percentages

While converting fractions to decimals sometimes requires a calculator, calculators are not necessary at all to convert decimals to percentages. To change a decimal to a percentage, simply move the decimal point two places to the right and add the percent sign (%).

Example 2.14: Convert 0.47 to a percentage.

0.47

Move the decimal point two places to the right. Then add the percent sign.

The answer is 47%.

Example 2.15: Convert 0.078 to a percentage.

0.078 after moving the decimal two places to the right becomes 7.8%.

Percentages return to their decimal form by removing the percent sign and moving the decimal point two spaces to the left. If the percentage is a whole number, then the decimal point is assumed at the end of the last digit.

Example 2.16: Convert 12% to a decimal.

12

Assume the decimal comes just to the right of the 12, that is, 12.0. Moved two spaces to the left, the answer is 0.12.

2.3.2 Working with Percentages

Future chapters focus on using percentages in numerous ways. This chapter introduces just three concepts: how to determine a percentage given a portion of a whole quantity, how to determine a percentage of a quantity given a specific percentage, and how to determine a whole quantity given a portion and percentage.

While the three formulas needed are stated separately later in the chapter, they can be combined into a single graphic formula as follows:

To use this graphic formula, simply cover up the variable you wish to find and do what the remaining formula tells you to do. Recognize, however, that the percentage will always be written in its decimal form (without the percent sign).

For example, the formula to determine a percentage is:

$$\text{Percentage (as a decimal)} = \frac{\text{Part}}{\text{Whole}}$$

Example 2.17: 12 is what percentage of 16.

$$\text{Percentage} = \frac{12 \ (\text{part})}{16 \ (\text{whole})} = 0.75 \ (\text{or in percentage form, 75\%})$$

In word problems, the number near the word "is" or "are" is the "part," and the number near the word "of" is the "whole." This trick becomes handy because the part is not always less than the whole. For instance, a business could ask what percentage of sales their expenses are. If expenses (part) are $110,000 and sales (whole) are $100,000, the expenses are 110% of sales. This represents a business that is losing money, but business practices can be corrected once the problems are accurately identified. Assuming that the part is sales rather than expenses, simply because the sales number is smaller, would be a major error. It would suggest a profitable business on a spreadsheet when the business is actually operating at a loss. No manager can manage effectively with bad information.

The second concept to learn is how to calculate a percentage of a quantity given a specific percentage. To do so, multiply the whole quantity times the percentage in its decimal form. Expressed mathematically, this is:

$$\text{Part} = \text{Whole} \times \text{Percentage (expressed in its decimal form)}$$

Example 2.18: What is 31% of 800?

$$\text{Part} = 800 \times 0.31 = 248$$

This is 31% in its decimal form.

One of the most common mistakes in working with percentages is forgetting to convert the percentage to a decimal for calculation purposes. For example, 31% equates to 0.31, not 31. Some computer programs, and even a few calculators, adjust the decimal for you when you hit the percentage sign, but unless you know how to make your technology do that, adjust the decimal yourself. Moving a decimal point two places to the left or right is easy enough to do in your head, and it can keep you from making a very common but very basic math error.

Finally, the third concept is to solve for the whole quantity given a part and a percentage. From the graphic formula, this is expressed as:

$$\text{Whole} = \frac{\text{Part}}{\text{Percentage}}$$

Example 2.19: 42 is 30% of what number?

$$\text{Whole} = \frac{42 \text{ (part)}}{0.30 \text{ (percentage as decimal)}} = 140$$

These formulas, involving whole, part, and percentage, arise in various forms throughout cost control. Sometimes food cost is the part, sales the whole, and food cost percentage the percentage. Sometimes, edible portion is the part, as purchased quantity is the whole, and yield percentage is the percentage. The names may change, but the graphic formula and the math calculations remain the same.

SUMMARY

Rounding numbers up or down is a simple process that reduces precision but allows for practical measuring in a professional kitchen. It should be done only in the final step of a multistep process to ensure that the result is as accurate as possible. Fractions mathematically express a portion of a whole unit. They can be expressed as single fractions or as mixed numbers. Mixed numbers are easier for measuring while single fractions are easier for computations. Single fractions can be multiplied or divided as well as reduced to more user-friendly terms. Converting a fraction to a decimal is as easy as dividing the numerator by the denominator with a calculator or computer. Going from decimals to fractions is just as easy, but not always practical. In those cases where a decimal does

not readily revert back to a fraction that is a multiple of $\frac{1}{16}$, $\frac{1}{8}$, $\frac{1}{4}$, $\frac{1}{3}$, or $\frac{1}{2}$, it is often best to round to the nearest "useful" fraction on the basis of the available measuring devices. Percentages are similar to fractions and decimals in that they represent a portion of a whole. Converting a decimal to a percentage is as easy as moving the decimal point two spaces to the right. Going from a percentage to a decimal reverses the process by moving the decimal point two spaces to the left. When performing calculations, it is best to use a number in its decimal form rather than in its percentage form (unless you know how to program your computer or calculator to read a percentage accurately). Fractions, decimals, and percentages may seem complicated, but in time every chef gains comfort with them.

COMPREHENSION QUESTIONS

1. Round 12.083 to the nearest tenth.
2. Round 1.98 to the nearest tenth.
3. Round 0.8693 to the nearest thousandth.
4. Round 9.013 to the nearest hundredth.
5. Round 2.36 to the nearest whole number.
6. Convert $2\frac{3}{4}$ to a single fraction.
7. Convert $1\frac{1}{3}$ to a single fraction.
8. Convert $3\frac{3}{16}$ to a single fraction.
9. Convert $\frac{11}{8}$ to a mixed number.
10. Convert $\frac{15}{2}$ to a mixed number.
11. Convert $\frac{19}{3}$ to a mixed number.
12. Convert $\frac{121}{8}$ to a mixed number.
13. Calculate $\frac{4}{3} \times \frac{3}{2}$. Reduce to lowest terms.
14. Calculate $\frac{3}{16} \times \frac{8}{10}$. Reduce to lowest terms.
15. Calculate $\frac{9}{4} \div \frac{3}{5}$. Reduce to lowest terms.
16. Calculate $\frac{10}{3} \div \frac{7}{8}$. Reduce to lowest terms.
17. Convert $\frac{3}{8}$ to a decimal.
18. Convert $\frac{7}{16}$ to a decimal.
19. Convert $\frac{5}{3}$ to a decimal.
20. Convert 0.125 to a fraction.
21. Convert 0.875 to a fraction.
22. Convert 0.6667 to a fraction.
23. Convert 0.75 to a fraction.
24. Convert 5.3333 to a mixed number.
25. Convert 8.0625 to a mixed number.
26. Convert 0.1333 to the nearest "useful" fraction for measuring cups.
27. Convert 0.289 to the nearest "useful" fraction for measuring cups.
28. Write 0.684 as a percentage.
29. Write 1.05 as a percentage.
30. Write $\frac{1}{8}$ as a percentage.
31. Write 54% as a decimal.
32. Write 4.3% as a decimal.
33. 18 is what percentage of 24?
34. 35 is what percentage of 50?
35. What is 33% of 64?
36. What is 12% of 153?
37. 90 is 25% of what number?
38. 12 is 34% of what number?

DISCUSSION QUESTIONS

1. What are the typical measuring devices in a kitchen that could be considered fractions of a larger unit? What are their typical fractions?
2. Why would a company list a long, nonuseful decimal in its master recipe instead of converting it to something useful? What potential problems could occur as a result of this practice?
3. What ingredients could have a potentially significant impact on the outcome of a recipe if their quantity is rounded too greatly?
4. If fractions, decimals, and percentages all express the same thing (a ratio between a portion and a whole quantity), why are all three employed in different situations?
5. What math do you use in your daily life that employs fractions, decimals, or percentages?

3
Unit and Recipe Conversions

Objectives

By the end of this chapter, you will be able to:

- Convert measurement units by weight and volume
- Convert recipes to generate new yields

One of the most important skills for a line cook or pastry cook to possess is the ability to convert between units of measure. Novices to the industry may assume that cooks always follow the same recipes in the same quantities every time they make a given recipe. Nothing could be farther from the truth. Some days are busier than are others, so cooks have to adjust the quantities they prepare, sometimes on a daily basis. Imagine how difficult it would be to control costs if cooks could only prepare a given recipe to yield twenty portions. What would they do if there were only ten reservations on a particularly slow day? One of the biggest tools to prevent spoilage and waste is to prepare only the amount of food needed for a given day, event, or meal period. To do so requires chefs and cooks to convert recipes to a desired yield.

Converting a recipe to yield a different number of servings is quite easy. The most challenging part of the process is converting between units of measure. Most nonprofessionals can double a recipe with ease. Going from 1 teaspoon (tsp) to 2 tsp simply requires a cook to measure the ingredient twice in 1-tsp increments. However, imagine that a recipe needs to change from serving four to serving four hundred. It isn't practical for a cook to measure out 1 tsp 100 times. Not only does it increase the likelihood of error, but it also causes a waste of money to have an employee measure something one hundred times when he could simply measure 2 c and 4 tsp (the equivalent of 100 tsp). Equally challenging is reducing the yield of a recipe. If a recipe calls for a gallon of milk and a cook needs to halve the recipe, it is easy to find a $\frac{1}{2}$-gal measure. But let's say, the recipe needs to be reduced by one-sixth. Good luck finding a $\frac{1}{6}$-gal measure in a kitchen. Measuring $2\frac{2}{3}$ c ($\frac{1}{6}$ gal) is infinitely easier.

Once a cook learns how to convert units of measure, converting recipes is a snap. It requires a small amount of memorization, but the rest of the process is simple multiplication and division.

3.1   CONVERTING UNITS OF MEASURE

Before converting units of measure, one must first learn some ground rules regarding weight and volume. "Weight" measures how heavy something is, while "volume" measures how big something is or how much space it occupies. The two can be interchanged, often imprecisely, with the use of a chart that lists the weight and volume equivalent of a specific ingredient. The reason the result is imprecise has to do with the form that an ingredient takes. For example, 10 oz whole peanuts take up a certain amount of space, but if those peanuts are chopped, they will take up a different amount of space. Even then, the space they occupy will vary depending on how finely they are chopped. White flour, which seems to be uniformly ground, will hold different amounts of air between the particles depending on whether it is sifted or tightly packed into a volume measure. Four ounces of flour might fill less than 1 c or more than 1 c depending on how it is treated before measuring.

In most cases, cooks should not convert from volume to weight or weight to volume on a daily basis. (It might be valuable to do it once using a chart to convert a home-cook recipe to a professional kitchen standardized recipe, but even then, the recipe should be tested to confirm its accuracy.) If a recipe asks for an ingredient in a unit of volume, it should be converted to a unit of volume. If a recipe asks for a weight, it should be converted to another unit of weight.

Fortunately, there is one convenient exception to this rule. Water converts easily between volume and weight measures. Eight ounces of water equals 1 c of water. (The mnemonic "a pint's a pound the world around" applies specifically to water.) Since some ingredients, such as eggs, are made up almost entirely of water, they, too, can convert between weight and volume easily. However, don't confuse "water" with "liquid." Honey, for example, weighs far more per cup than 8 oz.

The 8 oz to 1 c ratio for water creates two shortcuts that come in handy in a professional kitchen. First, the ability to measure water and mostly water ingredients by either volume or weight is an obvious benefit to a cook who prefers one form of measuring to another. Second, and more importantly, the volume–weight equivalency for water allows a cook to convert back and forth between weight and volume on paper for any ingredient as long as he converts the final answer back to the original measurement type in the last step (i.e., volume stays volume and weight stays weight). In other words, if it is easier for you to convert all volume measures to ounces when converting recipes, you can do so as long as you convert back to volume in the final step.

There are many units for weight and volume, but the ones most common in a professional kitchen are listed in Table 3.1.

TABLE 3.1
UNITS OF MEASURE BY WEIGHT AND VOLUME WITH ABBREVIATIONS

Common Units of *Volume* in Kitchens	Common Units of *Weight* in Kitchens
Teaspoon (tsp or t)	Ounce (oz)
Tablespoon (Tbsp or T)	Pound (lb or #)
Cup (c)	Gram (g) (metric)
Pint (pt)	Kilogram (kg) (metric)
Quart (qt)	
Gallon (gal or G)	
Milliliters (mL) (metric)	
Liter (L) (metric)	

TABLE 3.2
COMPARATIVE SIZES BETWEEN COMMON UNITS OF MEASURE

3 tsp = 1 Tbsp 16 Tbsp = 1 c 2 c = 1 pt 2 pt = 1 qt 4 qt = 1 gal 5 mL = 1 tsp 1,000 mL = 1 L	16 oz = 1 # 28.3 g = 1 oz 1,000 g = 1 kg 2.2 # = 1 kg
For Water: 1 c = 8 oz 1 L = 33.8 oz	

3.1.1 Measurements to Memorize

Before you can begin converting between units, you must learn the comparative sizes between the units. For example, unless you know that a pint is twice the size of a cup, you cannot convert between cups and pints. The comparative sizes of the units are listed in Table 3.2. There is no way to learn this information other than to memorize it, but once you have it memorized, you can convert from any one of these units to any other among them.

Although all of these equations become second-nature with practice, culinary students sometimes have trouble memorizing all of them. A simple mnemonic device that may help you to memorize the relationships between some units of volume measure and ounces is called the Magic Box (see Figure 3.1).

The Magic Box is formed by memorizing the order of units: cups ➤ pints ➤ quarts ➤ half-gallons ➤ gallons and by remembering the ratio 1:8 or 1 c equals 8 oz. The rest of the columns are formed simply by doubling the previous column. The pints column becomes 2:16; the quarts column becomes 4:32, and so on. Once you have drawn the Magic Box, you can simply look across the chart to see how many cups or ounces are in each unit of measure. Just remember that the ounces work only for water and similar ingredients.

3.1.2 The Conversion Process

Having memorized the comparative sizes between the various units of measure, you are now ready to convert from one unit to another. To convert between units, simply multiply or divide by the ratio between the two unit sizes. For example, the ratio of cups to ounces (for water) is 1:8 (1 c of water equals 8 oz). The ratio of cups to tablespoons is 1:16 (1 c equals 16 Tbsp). The ratios come from the memorized formulas. The only challenge is determining whether to multiply or to divide by the ratio. There are several approaches to figuring out whether to multiply or to divide, but you only need to learn

Unit of Measure	Cups	Pints	Quarts	Half-Gallons	Gallons
No. of Cups	1	2	4	8	16
No. of Ounces	8	16	32	64	128

Figure 3.1
The Magic Box

one—the one that works best for you. As you read through the following three techniques, choose the one that makes the most sense to you.

If you are already familiar with the relative sizes of the various forms of measure, then this technique may be for you. It works particularly well with visual learners who can visualize the relative sizes of the units of measure. The simple logic to it is this: As you go from a bigger to a smaller unit, you multiply; as you go from a smaller to a bigger unit, you divide. The result is that as the units get bigger, the number of them needed gets smaller. In shorthand, this might read Unit(↑):Number(↓) and Unit(↓):Number(↑). Example 3.1 illustrates how this method works.

Example 3.1: How many pounds equal 24 oz?

Here, we need to go from ounces (which we know) to pounds (which we need to find out).

An ounce is smaller than a pound, so we are going from a smaller to a bigger unit. As the unit increases in size, the "number" decreases. [Unit(↑):Number(↓)]
To get a smaller number, you divide.
Our ratio is 16 oz = 1 #, so we divide by 16.

$$24 \text{ oz} \div 16 = 1.5$$
$$24 \text{ oz} = 1.5 \text{ \#}$$

Example 3.2: Three quarts is how many cups?

A cup is smaller than a quart, so we are going from a bigger to a smaller unit. [Unit(↓):Number(↑)] or as the unit decreases, the number increases.
To increase the number, you multiply.
1 qt = 4 c (per the Magic Box), so we multiply by 4.

$$3 \text{ qt} \times 4 = 12$$
$$3 \text{ qt} = 12 \text{ c}$$

Sometimes, you may need an intermediate step if you don't know the ratio between the two units directly.

Example 3.3: How many grams of water are there in 3 pt?

A gram is smaller than a pint. Our units are decreasing, so the number increases. We don't know the ratio between pints and grams, but we do know the following:

$$1 \text{ g} = 28.3 \text{ oz}$$
$$1 \text{ pt} = 16 \text{ oz}$$

So we can go from pints to ounces and then from ounces to grams. The units get smaller in both steps, so we multiply both times.

$$3 \text{ pt} \times 16 = 48 \text{ oz}$$
$$48 \text{ oz} \times 28.3 = 1,358.4 \text{ g}$$
$$3 \text{ pt} = 1,358.4 \text{ g}$$

If you are not yet familiar with the relative sizes of the units of measure, this modified approach, which relies on the same logic, may work better for you. It is a good crutch until you become more comfortable with measurements over time.

To use this technique, you must memorize the following sequence in order:

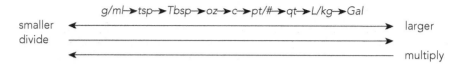

The slashes occur because, for water, $1 g = 1 mL$, $1 pt = 1 \#$, and $1 L = 1 kg$. Otherwise, the size of the units goes from smallest to largest as you move from left to right along the line. Thus, a teaspoon is smaller than a cup, and a kilogram is larger than a pound. This simply puts in words the relative sizes of the units of measure.

Now, to convert from one unit to another using the ratios, just look at the unit sequence line. As you move from left to right, you divide; as you move from right to left, you multiply.

Example 3.4: How many quarts are there in 2 c?

Going from cups (which we know) to quarts (which we want to find out), we go from left to right.

Left to right means we divide.

$1 qt = 4 c$ (per the Magic Box), so we divide by 4.

$$2 c \div 4 = \tfrac{1}{2} qt$$

Example 3.5: How many teaspoons are there in 7 Tbsp?

Going from tablespoons to teaspoons, we move right to left on the unit sequence line.

Right to left means we multiply.

1 Tbsp = 3 tsp, so we multiply by 3.

$$7 \, Tbsp \times 3 = 21$$

$$7 \, Tbsp = 21 \, tsp$$

As with the previous method, you may need to insert an intermediate step if you do not know the ratio between the two units directly.

Example 3.6: How many pints are there in 2 L?

We can go from liters to ounces and then from ounce to pints.

$$1 L = 33.8 \, oz$$

$$1 pt = 16 \, oz$$

Going from liters to ounces, we move right to left, so we multiply.

$$2 L \times 33.8 = 67.6 \, oz$$

Going from ounces to pints, we move left to right, so we divide.

$67.6 \, oz \div 16 = 4.225 \, pt$ (which could be rounded to $4\tfrac{1}{4}$ pt for practical measuring).

METHOD 3: DIMENSIONAL ANALYSIS

Those students more comfortable with fractions, and math in general, may prefer the dimensional analysis technique. Dimensional analysis simply writes the ratios you have memorized as fractions in which the top and bottom units continue to cancel each other out in subsequent steps. To convert from one unit to the next, write the starting quantity and unit on the left. Then multiply by a fraction, on the basis of one of the ratios you have memorized, in which the denominator is the same unit as your starting unit and the numerator is your target unit (or an intermediate step toward your target unit).

Example 3.7: How many quarts are there in $2\frac{1}{2}$ gal?

$$2.5 \text{ gal} \times \frac{4 \text{ qt}}{1 \text{ gal}} = 10 \text{ qt}$$

The fraction is based on 1 gal = 4 qt; you are essentially multiplying by 1 because the numerator and denominator are equal.

In dimensional analysis, the units cancel each other out. Since "gallons" in the example is in the numerator on the left and in the denominator in the fraction, it is removed entirely from the equation. Only "quarts," which is now in the numerator, remains.

Dimensional analysis may seem confusing at first, but it helps keep track of units. If a unit is not canceled out, it remains in the answer *in its location in the equation* (either in the numerator or in the denominator). Thus, unless you are looking for a number per unit (e.g., dollars per ounce), your target unit should always end up in the numerator.

Example 3.8: How many quarts equal 1,200 mL?

We know the following from Table 3.2:

$$1 \text{ L} = 1,000 \text{ mL}$$

$$1 \text{ L} = 33.8 \text{ oz}$$

$$1 \text{ qt} = 32 \text{ oz}$$

Now, we just set up the equation, starting with 1,200 mL, so the units cancel each other out and leave us with quarts, our target unit.

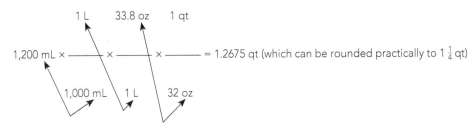

Each fraction is oriented to cancel out the previous unit. Only "quarts" is left.

In dimensional analysis, the fractions come directly from the memorized equations, and they are oriented so each fraction cancels out the unit from the previous fraction. To enter the equation into a calculator, simply enter the starting number, then multiply by any number in the numerator and divide by any number in the denominator. Thus, Example 3.8 is entered into a calculator as:

$$1,200 \div 1,000 \times 33.8 \div 32 = 1.2675$$

Whether you use the Unit Size–Operation Technique, the Left/Right-Operation Technique, or Dimensional Analysis, you can convert easily between units using the comparative size equations you have memorized. Chefs convert recipes often. Sometimes they learn a recipe from another country, and they need to convert metric units to the American or British units of their kitchen tools. More often though, chefs convert recipe units when they increase or decrease the yield of a recipe to accommodate a different number of customers.

3.2 ADJUSTING RECIPE YIELDS

When a chef needs to adjust a recipe to increase or decrease the yield, the process is always the same, assuming the portion size does not change. It requires only two bits of information: the old recipe yield and the new or desired recipe yield. With these two pieces of information, a chef can calculate a conversion factor. This conversion factor is then multiplied by each ingredient in a recipe to create new quantities for each ingredient. These quantities will generate the new, desired yield.

3.2.1 Calculating Conversion Factors

The formula to calculate a conversion factor is as follows:

$$\frac{\text{New Yield (N)}}{\text{Old Yield (O)}} = \text{Conversion Factor (CF)}$$

This formula assumes that the portion size does not change.

Example 3.9: What conversion factor should a chef use if he wants to convert a recipe yielding 6 portions to one yielding 15 portions?

$$\frac{\text{New}}{\text{Old}} = \frac{15}{6} = 2.5$$

The conversion factor (CF) = 2.5

If the portion size of the recipe changes, then the formula to determine the conversion factor requires that you find the total yield (in weight or volume) for each recipe. To do this, multiply the number of portions times the weight or volume of each portion to get the total yield for both new and old recipes. Be sure that both recipes use the same units (i.e., both are in ounces or both are in cups, etc.); otherwise, you will need to convert them to the same units.

$$\frac{\text{New Yield (total portions} \times \text{portion size)}}{\text{Old Yield (total portions} \times \text{portion size)}} = \text{Conversion Factor (CF)}$$

Example 3.10: What conversion factor should a chef use to convert a recipe yielding twelve 4-oz rolls to a recipe yielding eighty 3-oz rolls?

New Yield = total portions × portion size = 80 portions × 3 oz = 240 oz total

Old Yield = total portions × portion size = 12 portions × 4 oz = 48 oz total

$$\frac{\text{New}}{\text{Old}} = \frac{240 \text{ oz}}{48 \text{ oz}} = 5$$

Conversion factor (CF) = 5

3.2.2 Adjusting Ingredient Quantities Using a Conversion Factor

Once you have calculated a conversion factor for a recipe, you simply need to multiply each ingredient by the conversion factor to get the new quantity for each ingredient.

New Ingredient Quantity = Old Ingredient Quantity × Conversion Factor

The catch is that often the units must be converted to something practical for real-world measurement. For example, if the conversion factor is 64 and one ingredient is $\frac{1}{4}$ c milk, it would be best to convert the new quantity of milk ($\frac{1}{4}$ c × 64 = 16 c) to something more practical to measure, say 1 gal.

Example 3.11: Convert the recipe below to yield 18 portions.

Chicken Parmesan	Yield = 24 portions
Chicken breast, boneless, skinless, 6 oz each	24 each
Tomato sauce	36 oz
Mozzarella block, sliced $\frac{1}{8}$" thick	24 slices
Parmesan, grated fine	$1\frac{1}{2}$ c

Step 1: Calculate conversion factor.

$$\frac{\text{New}}{\text{Old}} = \frac{18}{24} = 0.75$$

Step 2: Multiply conversion factor times each ingredient quantity. Units remain the same.

Ingredient	Old Quantity	CF	New Quantity (Old × CF)
Chicken	24 each	0.75	18 each
Tomato sauce	36 oz	0.75	27 oz
Mozzarella	24 slices	0.75	18 each
Parmesan	$1\frac{1}{2}$ c	0.75	1.125 c or $1\frac{1}{8}$ c

In this particular example, the new quantities are best left in their original units. Example 3.12 illustrates an instance in which the units should change.

Example 3.12: Convert the recipe below to yield 150 six-ounce servings of soup.

Vegan Vegetable–Barley Soup	Yield = 12 portions; Portion size = 8 oz bowl
Olive oil	1 Tbsp
Onion, small dice	$1\frac{1}{2}$ c
Carrot, small dice	$\frac{3}{4}$ c
Celery, small dice	$\frac{3}{4}$ c
Mushroom, sliced $\frac{1}{4}$ inch thick	6 oz
Corn kernels	1 c
Peas	1 c
Tomato concassé	1 c
Vegetable Stock	60 oz
Barley	$\frac{1}{2}$ c
Thyme, fresh sprig	1 each
Parsley stems	2 each
Bay leaves	1 each
Peppercorn	6 each
Salt	To taste

Step 1: Calculate the conversion factor.

$$\frac{\text{New}}{\text{Old}} = \frac{150 \text{ portions} \times 6 \text{ oz}}{12 \text{ portions} \times 8 \text{ oz}} = \frac{900 \text{ oz}}{96 \text{ oz}} = 9.375$$

Step 2: Multiply each ingredient quantity times the conversion factor. Adjust units where appropriate.

Ingredient	Old Quantity	CF	New Quantity (Old × CF)	Unit Comparison Ratio (use to convert to new unit)	New Quantity, Units Adjusted and Rounded (New Quantity × OR ÷ Unit Comparison Ratio; then round)
Olive oil	1 Tbsp	9.375	9.375 Tbsp	16 Tbsp = 1 c OR 8 Tbsp = $\frac{1}{2}$ c	0.586 c OR $\frac{1}{2}$ c + 1 $\frac{1}{3}$ Tbsp
Onion, small dice	1 $\frac{1}{2}$ c	9.375	14.0625 c	4 c = 1 qt	3.516 qt OR 3 $\frac{1}{2}$ qt
Carrot, small dice	$\frac{3}{4}$ c	9.375	7.03125 c	4 c = 1 qt	1.759 qt OR 1 $\frac{3}{4}$ qt
Celery, small dice	$\frac{3}{4}$ c	9.375	7.03125 c	4 c = 1 qt	1.759 qt OR 1 $\frac{3}{4}$ qt
Mushroom, sliced	6 oz	9.375	56.25 oz	16 oz = 1 #	3.516 # OR 3 $\frac{1}{2}$ #
Corn kernels	1 c	9.375	9.375 c	4 c = 1 qt	2.344 qt OR 2 qt + 1 $\frac{1}{3}$ c
Peas	1 c	9.375	9.375 c	4 c = 1 qt	2.344 qt OR 2 qt + 1 $\frac{1}{3}$ c
Tomato concassé	1 c	9.375	9.375 c	4 c = 1 qt	2.344 qt OR 2 qt + 1 $\frac{1}{3}$ c
Vegetable Stock	60 oz	9.375	562.5 oz	16 oz = 1 # OR 128 oz = 1 gal	35.16 # = 35 # + 3 oz OR 4.395 gal = 4 gal + 6 $\frac{1}{3}$ c
Barley	$\frac{1}{2}$ c	9.375	4.6875 c	4 c = 1 qt	1.172 qt OR 1 qt + $\frac{2}{3}$ c
Thyme, fresh sprig	1 each	9.375	9.375 each	N/A	9 each
Parsley stems	2 each	9.375	18.75 each	N/A	19 each
Bay leaves	1 each	9.375	9.375 each	N/A	9 each
Peppercorn	6 each	9.375	56.25 each	N/A	56 each
Salt	To taste	9.375	To taste	N/A	To taste

Although this is a long problem, it is quite simple to calculate the conversion factor and to multiply each ingredient by the conversion factor. It gets complicated in the unit conversion, so let's look at a few rows individually.

- *Olive oil*, 9.375 Tbsp. Since we know that 16 Tbsp is 1 c, we can halve both sides to recognize that $\frac{1}{2}$ c is 8 Tbsp. Eight is significant because measuring 8 Tbsp as $\frac{1}{2}$ c leaves us only 1.375 Tbsp to measure (9.375 − 8 = 1.375). Since 1.375 is close to 1.33 or $1\frac{1}{3}$ and 1 Tbsp = 3 tsp, it is easy to measure 1.375 Tbsp practically as 1 Tbsp and 1 tsp.

- *Onion, celery, carrot, and mushroom* are all close enough to be rounded to the nearest 0.5 or 0.75 ($\frac{1}{2}$ and $\frac{3}{4}$, respectively).
- *Corn kernels,* Measuring 9.375 cups is particularly challenging. It converts to 2.344 qt, but 0.344 qt isn't close enough to round to anything else in quarts. In such a circumstance, calculate how many cups 0.344 qt is by multiplying by 4 (4 c = 1 qt). This gives us 1.376 c, which is very close to 1.33 or $1\frac{1}{3}$ c. So the answer is 2 qt + $1\frac{1}{3}$ c. While this may seem a bit unwieldy to measure, it is still faster than measuring $9\frac{1}{3}$ c. Fortunately, once the math is done for the corn kernels, the answer can be copied to the peas and to the tomato concassé, both of which also require 9.375 c.
- *Vegetable stock,* 562.5 oz. Because vegetable stock is almost entirely water, it can be treated like water, so 1 c = 8 oz or 128 oz = 1 gal. This gives us two options: Keep the measure in weight or convert it to volume. Both are shown here. To figure out how many ounces are represented by 0.16 # (the portion of 35.16 # that isn't obvious by sight), convert from pounds to ounces by multiplying 0.16 by 16 (16 oz = 1 #). The answer can be rounded to 3 oz. To determine how many cups are represented by 0.395 gal, multiply 0.395 by 16 (16 c = 1 gal). The answer is very close to 6.33 or $6\frac{1}{3}$ c.
- Note that when counting by "each", units are not converted. If the numbers were to become too impractical to count, a chef could do an experiment to see how many peppercorns fit in a quarter-cup, for example. In reality, a chef would probably estimate 56 peppercorns by sight rather than count them. Similarly, "to taste" is not converted but rather measured as instructed—by taste.

Example 3.12 is an example of a real-world problem. The math does not work out to nice round numbers, but they can be converted to practical units of measure. The process takes time, but the time spent saves money. A chef who converts recipes to adjust for different yields can minimize food waste from overproduction. Fortunately, a computer spreadsheet can be set up to calculate conversion factors and new quantities for each ingredient automatically with nothing more than the user inputting the new yield. Adjusting the units to something practical, however, sometimes requires a little "human" finesse as a computer may not know the most practical unit to which to convert for kitchen use.

One final note of advice: Always remember to label your units as you work. A number without a unit is meaningless. It can become quite confusing, on paper or on the computer, to convert back and forth between units in various steps and then to try to figure out which unit is the final one.

SUMMARY

In a professional kitchen, measurements are made primarily using units of weight or volume. Only water and substances that are composed almost entirely of water can convert easily between weight and volume without the aid of a chart. A cook can convert from one unit to another as long as he knows the comparative sizes of the two units. The cook simply multiplies or divides by the ratio between the two unit sizes. Whether to multiply or divide can be determined using the unit size–operation technique, the left/right-operation technique, or dimensional analysis. Recipe yields are adjusted using a conversion factor, which is calculated as new yield divided by old yield. Then, the quantity of each ingredient is multiplied by the conversion factor. If necessary, the resulting quantities are adjusted to new units and rounded for practical and efficient measuring. The process of converting a recipe takes time, but with practice, a cook can convert any recipe in just a few minutes. The benefit comes in reduced food cost from minimized production waste.

COMPREHENSION QUESTIONS

Fill in the blanks for questions 1–10. (For weight-to-volume conversions, assume you are measuring water.)

1. 6 qt = ___ c
2. 3 c = ___ tsp
3. 200 tsp = ___ pt
4. 2 oz = ___ Tbsp
5. 7 oz = ___ g
6. 2 gal = ___ L
7. 6 pt = ___ gal
8. 36 oz = ___ c
9. 1.5 gal = ___ qt
10. 3 c = ___ mL
11. A recipe yields 8 portions. The chef wants it to serve 14. What is the conversion factor?
12. A recipe yields six 2-oz portions. The chef wants to serve twenty-five 5-oz portions. What is the conversion factor?
13. Adjust the following recipe to yield 60 portions. Then, adjust the new quantities for practical measurement where necessary.

Tuna Salad			Yield = 4 servings		
Ingredient	Old Quantity	CF	New Quantity	Unit Comparison Ratio	New Quantity, Units Adjusted (Show both precise and rounded numbers)
Tuna, canned	14 oz				
Onion, diced	$\frac{1}{4}$ c				
Celery, diced	$\frac{1}{4}$ c				
Mayonnaise	$\frac{2}{3}$ c				
Lemon, juiced	$\frac{1}{2}$ lemon				
Parsley, chopped	3 Tbsp				
Salt/Pepper	To taste				

DISCUSSION QUESTIONS

1. Most baking recipes use only weight measurements for most ingredients. Why do you think this is? When would a volume measurement be more appropriate in baking?

2. A chef uses a hollandaise recipe that yields 12 servings. On most Sundays, he serves exactly 40 customers Eggs Benedict (the only dish on the menu that requires hollandaise). He has never taken the time to convert the recipe. For the sake of ease and speed, he simply quadruples the recipe. Is this a smart move? Is there a significant financial impact? A small one? Would your answer change if the hollandaise included truffle oil for an upscale signature Eggs Benedict?

3. In some operations, restaurants do not convert their recipe yields daily, which inevitably creates some underproduction and some overproduction day by day. Is this always a problem? For what kinds of dishes might this be a nonissue?

4. What kinds of foodservice operations are most likely to convert recipes daily? What kinds would never convert recipe yields (and not have waste)?

5. Think about a time you hosted and cooked for a large party in your home. Did you have to multiply any recipes to prepare enough food? Did you run out of food, overproduce, or have just the right amount? If you ran out, how did your guests react? If you overproduced, what happened to the leftovers? (If you had just the right amount, congratulations!)

4

Yields

A line cook typically only needs to understand enough cost control math to convert recipes. Once she earns a promotion to executive chef, however, her responsibilities increase significantly. She oversees purchasing, possibly in coordination with a purchasing manager. She may also become responsible for pricing menu items and controlling expenses so that the business remains profitable. While the journey to become an expert food-service manager is a long one, an important first step is to understand ingredient yields.

An ingredient yield is the quantity of useable product that results after an ingredient has been processed from its original delivered form. An executive chef recognizes that a one-pound bag of carrots, for example, does not provide 1 # of peeled, sliced carrots for a side dish. The same is true for most produce, meat, poultry, and seafood. There is almost always some loss with these types of ingredients as a result of preparing food for consumption. This loss impacts how much food a chef must order. It also impacts the true cost of an ingredient. A chef must be able to take this loss into account when calculating the cost of a recipe. But to do so, a chef or future chef must understand yield percentages, the difference between "as-purchased" and "edible portion" ingredients, and other forms of loss that occur during the preparation of food for consumption.

4.1 YIELD AND YIELD PERCENTAGE

Imagine that you are preparing a carrot cake, and the recipe calls for 1 # of shredded carrot. Would you go to a store to purchase a one-pound bag of carrots? If you did, you would find yourself short on carrots for the recipe. Why is that? First, as you prepare the carrots for shredding, you will lose some weight as you peel them and trim the ends. Second, you will likely have a small amount that is lost in the shredding process because it gets stuck in the grater. If you take the time to compare the useable amount you get from 1 # of purchased carrots, you might find that you get 13 oz of shredded carrots out of your original 16 oz. Not surprisingly, if you repeated this process several times, you would likely see that you get fairly consistent results each time–13 oz of shredded carrots from every 16-oz bag. That consistency allows a chef to predict how much shredded carrot to expect no matter how many pounds she starts with. This consistency is the foundation of the concept of yield percentages.

A yield percentage is the percentage of peeled, trimmed, and/or cut product that a cook gets out of a raw, unprocessed, "as purchased" ingredient. This percentage changes from product to product. Consider how little carrot is lost compared to the loss generated by trimming an artichoke just to get the heart. It changes with method of processing, too, and even slightly depending on the person doing the work. Carrots might have a slightly better yield if they are sliced rather than shredded because of the loss remaining in the grater. However, carrots will have a greater loss, because of their rounded sides, if the desired product is diced carrots. Add to the confusion that an experienced chef will probably get a better yield of diced carrots than a novice culinary student, who likely has a greater number of improperly cut, unusable dice. Charts and books are available that give approximate yield percentages for a range of products, but the most accurate yield percentages for a professional kitchen are conducted in person at that operation using the same employee who typically does the prep work.

4.1.1 Calculating a Yield Percentage

Before calculating a yield percentage, we must define two terms: "as purchased" and "edible portion." An as-purchased product is in the form an ingredient takes as it arrives to one's business. For example, raw potatoes often come whole and unpeeled; romaine lettuce probably comes in heads. This is how a company purchases it, thus, as purchased. Edible portion refers to the form that a product takes after a cook has removed the parts that will not be served. The edible portion is the part that remains for cooking and serving to guests. In some cases, such as with a russet potato that will not be cut before serving as a baked potato or with frozen vegetables that arrive already trimmed and ready to heat, as-purchased and edible portion products are identical. Other times, as with potatoes that must be peeled before making mashed potatoes or with green beans that must be trimmed before cooking, the as-purchased and edible portion products differ, and more importantly, weigh different amounts. As purchased is often abbreviated AP, and edible portion is generally abbreviated EP.

With the concepts of AP and EP quantity defined, it is now possible to calculate yield percentage—the percentage of useable product (EP) that remains from the as purchased (AP) ingredient after trimming. To determine a yield percentage for a product, you need the product, a scale, and any tools required to process the product the way you typically would for a given recipe. Then, follow this procedure:

Step 1: Weigh the uncut product and record the weight.
Step 2: Process the product as you would for a given recipe. (That is, peel, trim, cut, but do not cook it.)

Step 3: Weigh the processed product, and record the weight.

Step 4: Enter your results into the following formula:

$$\text{Yield \% (Y\%)} = \frac{EP}{AP}$$

In most cases, EP and AP are entered using weight. A volume measure here would only make sense if a product is purchased by volume and measured for service the same way. (The chapter "Beverage Control" describes how yield percentages work with alcohol, an example of EP and AP measured by volume.) No matter what measure is used, both EP and AP units must be the same to get an accurate yield percentage. So if AP is measured in ounces, then EP must be measured in ounces as well.

Example 4.1: If you process 4 # of eggplant for eggplant parmesan and get 3 # of peeled, sliced eggplant, what is the yield percentage?

In this case, the 4 # of eggplant is the AP weight, and the 3 # is the EP weight.

$$Y\% = \frac{EP}{AP} = \frac{3\ \#}{4\ \#} = 0.75 \text{ (or 75\% in percentage form)}$$

$$Y\% = 75\%$$

Example 4.2: If you process 4 # of artichokes and you get 1 # 14 oz of artichoke hearts, what is the yield percentage?

In this case, we must first convert the weights to the same units, either all pounds or all ounces. Since there are 16 oz in a pound, $4\ \# = 16 \times 4 = 64\ oz$.

For the hearts, $1\ \# = 16\ oz$. Added to the 14 additional ounces, $16 + 14 = 30\ oz$ total.

$$Y\% = \frac{EP}{AP} = \frac{30\ oz}{64\ oz} = 0.46875 \text{ or } 0.469 \text{ rounded. (In percentage form, this is 46.9\%.)}$$

$$Y\% = 46.9\%$$

(*Note:* Had you converted 1 # 14 oz to pounds, you would have 1.875 #, which divided by 4 # is still 0.46875 or 46.9%.)

There are a few things to note about the yield percentage formula. First, it is typically used for produce, which often creates a lot of unused waste, and for other products for which all the trim is tossed into the garbage. (Later in the chapter, we discuss a different formula for butchered meat, poultry, and seafood that generates useable by-products.) Second, the yield percentage should be recalculated for each type of preparation. For example, the yield percentage for Parisian potatoes (spheres or balls) will be very different from the yield percentage for potatoes prepped for mashing, assuming one trashes all of the scraps from making the potato balls. Chefs can save money by repurposing that "waste"—effectively increasing a product's yield—rather than throwing it away. If the scraps from one preparation are used in another recipe, the EP quantity for the ingredient is the combined total of all the used products, which results in a higher yield percentage. In the potato example, if a cook uses the peeled potato scraps from the Parisian potatoes to make mashed potatoes, then the only real loss is the peel; the EP quantity is the weight of the entire peeled potato. Finally, once calculated for a set of products prepared a certain way, cooks or chefs should not need to perform the yield test on those products again. The results are remarkably consistent from one day to the next as long as the AP products and the processing method remain the same. Cooks of different skill levels may get different yields, but with proper training and time, newer cooks should be able to achieve the higher yield percentages of more senior employees.

Whereas the yield percentage formula is crucial when working with weight and volume measures, it does not apply to items served by the "count" or by the "each." Consider the example of shrimp. If a shrimp stir-fry recipe calls for 4 oz of peeled, deveined shrimp, then when buying shell-on shrimp, a purchaser must buy more than 4 oz to account for the weight lost from peeling and deveining. However, the logic changes in the case of a shrimp cocktail for which the standard serving is "five-each" shrimp. After five AP shrimp have been peeled and deveined, there are still five EP shrimp left to serve. In effect, there is no loss in count, which is how this serving is measured.

A more important factor to consider for items sold by the count is the number of units packaged per pound. Shrimp are almost always sold to professional kitchens by the pound, no matter how the restaurants plan on portioning them for service. Additionally, shrimp are sold in a range of sizes, often described by the number of shrimp per pound. Thus, a package of 16/20 shrimp contains an average of 16 to 20 shrimp per pound. The size 21/25 shrimp have 21 to 25 shrimp per pound. (Bacon would be an example of another product typically purchased by weight and portioned or sold by count.) In all situations in which a product is sized in a range, like 21/25 or 16/20, always assume that the lowest number in the range is the count per pound. Why? Imagine that a restaurant serves shrimp cocktail as 4 shrimp per order and uses 16/20 size shrimp. If the chef assumes that there are 20 shrimp per pound, she might buy one pound for every five orders she expects to sell. However, since the shrimp could legitimately arrive at only 16 per pound, 1 # might only generate four orders; the chef would be short shrimp! Remember though, that these assumptions only apply to items portioned by count for service. If an item is portioned by weight, the yield percentage formula discussed earlier is the appropriate tool to calculate yield.

4.1.2 The Universal AP, EP, Yield Percentage Formula

The formula $Y\% = \dfrac{EP}{AP}$ can be manipulated to calculate any of the three variables, given the other two. Thus, there are two other formulas to consider:

$$AP = \frac{EP}{Y\%}$$

and

$$EP = AP \times Y\%$$

All three formulas can be expressed in a single diagram as follows:

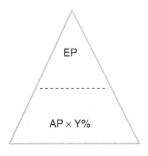

Figure 4.1
EP, AP, Y% Triangle

To use this graphic equation, simply cover up the variable that you wish to find, and what remains is the formula for finding it. Thus, if you cover Y% (yield percentage), you are left with EP ÷ AP. If you cover EP, you are left with AP × Y%, and so on. Note that in all cases, Y% must be written in its decimal form.

Why is it important to be able to calculate any of the variables? Yield percentage, as mentioned earlier, is calculated from measurements performed in the kitchen to allow for the accurate purchasing of ingredients. AP is the variable that a chef seeks when she needs to know how much to purchase to complete a given recipe. EP tells how much a chef can expect to yield from a given quantity of raw products. All are important bits of information in various circumstances.

Example 4.3: How many pounds of hulled strawberries can a cook get from 5 # of strawberries if the yield percentage for hulled strawberries is 91%?

Here, we know AP and Y%, but we are looking for EP.

$$EP = AP \times Y\% = 5\,\# \times 0.91 = 4.55\,\#$$

Note that the 91% is written in its decimal form, 0.91.

$$EP = 4.55\,\# \text{ or roughly } 4\tfrac{1}{2}\,\#$$

Example 4.4: How many pounds of onions should a chef purchase to get 84 oz of diced onions, if the yield percentage for diced onions is 82%?

$$AP = \frac{EP}{Y\%} = \frac{84\,oz}{0.82} = 102.44\,oz$$

Since the question asked for pounds, we must convert 102.44 oz to pounds.

$$16\,oz = 1\,\#$$

$$102.44\,oz \div 16 = 6.4\,\#$$

As onions are typically purchased in whole pounds, this number should be rounded. However, since we need an 84-oz yield, fewer than 6.4 # would leave us short on diced onions. Therefore, we must round up to 7 #, even though 6.4 looks like it should round down to 6. This leads to an important rule of thumb: When rounding AP quantities for purchase, always round up to make sure you yield enough product!

Example 4.5: A chef serves each guest 3.5 oz of green beans. She has 8.25 # of untrimmed green beans left in her walk-in. From experience, she knows that she can get a 93% yield on her green beans. How many guests can she serve before she runs out?

$$EP = AP \times Y\% = 8.25\,\# \times 0.93 = 7.6725\,\#$$

$$7.6725\,\# \times 16\,oz/\# = 122.76\,oz$$

$$EP = 122.76\,oz$$

But we're not done yet. The question asks, "How many guests can she serve?" We know that each guest gets 3.5 oz. So, we divide the total EP ounces by the number of ounces per guest to get the number of guests the chef can serve.

$$122.76\,oz \div 3.5\,oz/guest = 35.07\,guests$$

Since we cannot serve a guest anything less than a full serving, we automatically round down. Thus, another important rule relating to these formulas: When calculating the number of portions or guests that can be served from an EP product, always round down!

4.2 AS PURCHASED VERSUS EDIBLE PORTION COSTS

EP, AP, and Y% calculations have an obvious impact on product quantities. They tell a chef how much product to purchase and how much yield to expect after processing that ingredient. This becomes important when planning purchases and production needs. Yield percentages help chefs manage costs, too, since the true per-pound cost of a prepped ingredient is not necessarily the amount listed on the invoice.

Let's return to the carrot cake example from the beginning of the chapter. Assume that you paid exactly $1 for your one-pound bag of carrots. Do your shredded carrots cost $1 per pound? Considering that you would need to purchase part of a second bag to yield 1 # of shredded carrots, your shredded carrots bear the cost of the initial bag plus the additional portion of the second bag. How do we quantify this EP cost per pound?

$$EP\$ = \frac{AP\$}{Y\%}$$

where EP$ = Edible Portion Cost, AP$ = As-Purchased Cost, and Y% = Yield Percentage in its decimal form. This suggests another graphic equation. The relationship between EP$, AP$, and Y% can be expressed as:

Figure 4.2
AP$, EP$, Y% Triangle

As with the earlier triangle, simply cover the variable you wish to find to get the formula to calculate it. Thus, AP$ = EP$ × Y%, and EP$ = AP$ ÷ Y%. (Rarely, in the real world, would one use EP$ and AP$ to calculate a yield percentage, but it can be done using this graphic formula.)

Example 4.6: What is the EP cost for shredded cabbage if AP cabbage costs 0.99/# and the yield percentage for shredded cabbage is 88%?

$$EP\$ = AP\$ \div Y\% = \$0.99/\# \div 0.88 = \$1.125/\# \text{ or } \$1.13/\#$$

$$EP\$ = \$1.13/\#$$

We can confirm that the formula in Example 4.6 works by calculating AP and EP quantities. Assume we have 2 # of AP cabbage to process. That costs us, at $0.99/#, $1.98 total. Next, we calculate our EP quantity.

$$EP = AP \times Y\% = 2\# \times 0.88 = 1.76\#$$

After processing, we'll have 1.76 # of cabbage (EP), but it costs us $1.98 to get. So what is the EP cost per pound?

You can always calculate a cost per weight (or volume) by dividing total cost by total weight (or volume).

$$\$1.98 \div 1.76\# = \$1.125/\# \text{ or } \$1.13/\#$$

$$EP\$ = \$1.13/\#, \text{ just as we calculated earlier.}$$

Example 4.7: If our yield percentage for green beans is 93%, and our recipe cost assumes that a 4 oz EP serving costs $0.22, what is the maximum we can pay for green beans (AP) to remain in budget?

Here, we are given Y%, and we need to calculate AP$. But we aren't given EP$ directly. As stated earlier:

$$\text{Cost per Weight} = \frac{\text{Total Cost}}{\text{Total Weight}}$$

Our EP$ can be calculated as $0.22 ÷ 4 oz = $0.055/oz

$$\text{AP\$} = \text{EP\$} \times \text{Y\%} = \$0.055/\text{oz} \times 0.93 = \$0.05115/\text{oz}$$

Since green beans are typically charged by the pound, we need to convert this figure to cost per pound (using dimensional analysis . . .).

$$\frac{\$0.05115}{\text{oz}} \times \frac{16 \text{ oz}}{1 \#} = \$0.8184/\# \text{ or } \$0.82/\#$$

The budgeted AP$ is thus $0.82/#.

Note that if we spend less than this, the EP cost will be less, and if we spend more, then the EP cost will go over budget.

While calculating EP and AP costs may seem like a purposeless activity at this point, it is absolutely essential to calculating the cost of a recipe and consequently, the cost of a single serving of a recipe. Only once a chef determines the cost per portion for a dish, can she accurately determine a menu price that will bring in a profit.

4.3   BUTCHER'S YIELD TEST

The concept of a butcher's yield test is similar to that of a basic yield percentage test. As a large cut of meat (in this section, "meat" is used to refer to meat, seafood, or poultry) is fabricated, the quantity of edible product is less than what was purchased, and the cost of the edible product is more per pound than the original purchase price. The reason for a different test, however, is that large cuts of meat often yield by-products that a restaurant can use and would otherwise have to purchase. A large veal roast might provide veal bones for stock just as a whole fish yields bones. Whole chickens give not only bones but legs and wings in addition to their breasts. Beef and lamb may have trim, but some of that trim can be turned into ground meat for use elsewhere on the menu. (The same thing happens sometimes with produce, but since it is difficult to purchase produce by-products from a purveyor, it can be nearly impossible to assign a value to the by-products. For produce, the various by-products used are all assumed to have an equal value and thus are simply combined for a total EP weight.)

If a foodservice operation can salvage some of the butchery by-products and use them in other recipes rather than purchasing by-products separately, then the chef can "credit" or "refund" the by-products' value to the initial cost of the as-purchased price, thus reducing the edible-portion price somewhat. Here is how the process works:

4.3.1 Conducting the Butcher's Yield Test

A butcher's yield test begins just like a yield test on produce. It should be performed by the person who normally does the butchering with the same tools and large cut of meat that the operation typically uses. The test similarly requires the use of a scale.

As the employee butchers the meat, all of the pieces are saved and separated into piles: the main item sought from the large cut, useable by-products (which might include fat, scraps for grinding, chunks for stew, or bones just to name a few possibilities), and unusable scraps. In this test, any by-products that are not used in the operation (or otherwise sold) are considered unusable scraps because they end up in the trash whether they could have been used or not. All of the piles are weighed separately. Each type of by-product is scaled independently, so fat, bones, and chunks of meat, for example, would each be weighed separately. Those weights are then recorded on a chart or spreadsheet that might look like Figure 4.3a, which is a butcher's test on one beef tenderloin.

The top line of a butcher's test spreadsheet generally states not only the product's name, but its grade, weight, and price per pound. The grade is important as the percentages may be very different for products of different grades. The total cost can be calculated as the weight in pounds times the cost per pound. Additional information might include the name of the purveyor, the person performing the yield test, and any other specifications for the product being tested.

Item: Beef Tenderloin	Weight: 6 #, 2 oz		Total Cost: $50.41	
Grade: Prime	AP Price per #: $8.23/#			
Breakdown	Weight	% of Total Weight	Purchase Price/#	Total Value
Fat	1 # 9 oz			
Beef Chunks	15 oz			
Scraps	9 oz			
Trimmed Tenderloin	3 # 1 oz			
Total	6 # 2 oz			

Figure 4.3a
Butcher Test Spreadsheet (weight entered)

Once the weights are entered in the "weight" column, they are added together. The total weight should equal the initial weight of the whole item. If it does not, simply add the difference to the "scraps" row, or add a row labeled "loss" to account for any weight lost in the process. Once the weights are recorded, it is time to do some calculations to complete the spreadsheet.

Step 1: Calculate the percentage of total weight for each item by dividing each item's weight by the total weight. This will give the percentage in its decimal form. (For example, for the "fat" row, first convert 1 # 9 oz to 25 oz. Then convert the total weight from 6 # 2 oz to 98 oz. Divide the "fat" weight by the total weight. 25 oz ÷ 98 oz = 0.255 or 25.5%.) Perform this calculation for each row, and enter it in the "% of Total Weight" column. Then, total the percentages for the bottom row. The percentages should equal 100% or close to it, as a result of rounding.

Step 2: Locate the purchase price per pound for each by-product on a purveyor's database. This is the price a business would pay to purchase each of the by-products separately. Enter only the prices for the by-products that will be used in the foodservice operation; do not include the price for the main item being tested (in this case, the trimmed tenderloin). For this example, assume that the restaurant uses the fat in its Yorkshire pudding and the beef chunks in a tenderloin-mushroom vol-au-vent; the scraps go into the trash.

Step 3: Multiply the weight of each item, converted to pounds, by the purchase price per pound. (For the fat row, for example, 1 # 9 oz equals 1.5625 #. Assume the purveyor's price list reveals that beef fat costs $0.17/#. 1.5625 # × $0.17/# = $0.266 or $0.27 total.) Enter the total value for each row. Remember that items with no purchase price will have no total value and that the main item tested will be left blank at this point.

After these calculations, the Butcher's test spreadsheet might look like Figure 4.3b.

| Item: Beef Tenderloin | | Weight: 6 #, 2 oz | | Total Cost: $50.41 | |
| Grade: Prime | | AP Price per #: $8.23/# | | | |
Breakdown	Weight	% of Total Weight (Weight ÷ Total Weight)	(Weight converted to #)	Purchase Price/# (from a purveyor)	Total Value (Weight in # × Purchase Price/#)
Fat	1 # 9 oz	25.5%	1.5625 #	$0.17/#	$0.27
Beef Chunks	15 oz	15.3%	0.9375 #	$1.09/#	$1.02
Scraps	9 oz	9.2%	0.5625 #	No value	$0
Trimmed Tenderloin	3 # 1 oz	50%	3.0625 #		
Total	6 # 2 oz	100%			

Figure 4.3b
Butcher Test Spreadsheet (values entered)

With the values of the by-products entered, we can now calculate the value of the main item, in this case, the trimmed tenderloin. We know from the top row that the total cost of the AP beef tenderloin with all of its component parts is $50.41; we just need to make sure that all of the parts' values, when added separately, still equal $50.41. To ensure this, the value of the trimmed tenderloin (our main item) is set as the difference between the total cost and the value of the by-products. In this example, the value of the trimmed tenderloin is:

Total cost	$50.41
−Value of Fat	−$0.27
−Value of Beef Chunks	−$1.02
Trimmed Tenderloin	$49.12

The price of the trimmed main item is less than the AP total cost because the restaurant effectively received and paid for additional useable products in the initial purchase. Since the chef does not have to buy them separately, she can deduct their values here and charge them to the recipes where those by-products are ultimately used.

To make this information valuable beyond this particular piece of tenderloin, there are a few more bits of information to calculate: Cost per useable pound and ounce (for the main item) and the cost multiplier.

$$\text{Cost per Useable \#} = \frac{\text{Value of Main Item (determined in the yield test)}}{\text{Weight of Main Item in \#}}$$

In this example, cost per useable # = $49.12 ÷ 3.0625 # = $16.039 or $16.04/#. Cost per useable ounce can be calculated by putting the weight of the main item in ounces in the denominator or simply by dividing the cost per useable # by 16 (as 16 oz = 1 #). In this example, $16.039 \div 16 = \$1.002$ or $\$1.00$/oz. The cost per useable ounce is $1.00.

The cost multiplier is calculated by dividing this new cost per useable pound by the original AP cost per pound.

$$\text{Cost Multiplier} = \frac{\text{Cost per Useable \#}}{\text{AP Cost per \#}}$$

In this example, the cost multiplier is $\$16.04 \div \$8.23 = 1.949$ or 1.95.

Figure 4.3c illustrates the completed butcher's test spreadsheet, including cost per useable pound, cost per useable ounce, and the cost multiplier.

Item: Beef Tenderloin	Weight: 6 #, 2 oz				Total Cost: $50.41		
Grade: Prime		AP Price per #: $8.23/#					
Breakdown	Weight	% of Total Weight	Purchase Price/#	Total Value	Cost per Useable # (Total Value ÷ weight)	Cost per Useable oz (Cost per Useable # ÷ 16)	Cost Multiplier (Cost per Useable # ÷ AP Price per #)
Fat	1 # 9 oz	25.5%	$0.17/#	$0.27			
Beef Chunks	15 oz	15.3%	$1.09/#	$1.02			
Scraps	9 oz	9.2%	No value	$0			
Trimmed Tenderloin	3 # 1 oz	50%		$49.12	$16.04	$1.00	1.95
Total	6 # 2 oz	100%		$50.41			

Figure 4.3c
Butcher's Test Spreadsheet (complete)

Having a cost multiplier for a given product is a huge time saver to calculate future costs per useable pound when the purveyor's AP price shifts. Because the cost multiplier represents the ratio between the cost per useable pound and the AP cost per pound, a chef can simply multiply the cost multiplier times the new AP price to get the new cost per useable pound without having to conduct a whole new butcher's yield test.

Example 4.8: The AP price for Beef Tenderloin was $8.23/#. The cost multiplier was determined to be 1.95. Now, the purveyor is increasing the price of beef tenderloin to $8.97/#. What is the new cost per useable pound and cost per useable ounce?

Cost per Useable # = AP Cost per # × Cost Multiplier = $8.97/# × 1.95 = $17.49/#

Cost per Useable ounce = Cost per Useable # ÷ 16 (oz/#) = $17.49/# ÷ 16 = $1.09/oz

Costs per pound are useful to generate a cost multiplier for future price shifts. Costs per ounce are more helpful for calculating a cost per portion since portions are often stated in number of ounces. Both numbers have their place in culinary cost control.

Conducting a butcher's yield test is quite an undertaking, but thanks to the cost multiplier, it does not need to be performed regularly. There are generally only two reasons to repeat a butcher's yield test. The first is that the person who usually does the butchering has changed. Referring back to Figure 4.3c, if a new butcher could get a 55% yield instead of a 50% yield on the trimmed tenderloin, the useable cost per pound and the cost multiplier would change significantly. The other trigger for repeating a butcher's yield test is that the prices of the by-products increase or decrease greatly in comparison to the price fluctuations of the whole, unbutchered cut. While this does not happen too often, sometimes a by-product of little value becomes trendy and extremely valuable. Consider, for example, the low price of chicken wings before the popularization of Buffalo wings. Today, chicken wings cost much more in comparison to whole chickens than they did before the wing trend took flight.

There are a few remaining notes to stress before wrapping up the butcher's yield test. First, each test relates to a specific cut of defined specifications or "specs." For example, changing from an unpeeled to a peeled tenderloin would dramatically change the results of a yield test and require that a new test be performed. Next, in addition to providing a cost multiplier, the yield test also gives valuable information on weight yield percentages. A chef can safely assume that given the same product and the same employee, the product will yield approximately the same percentage of useable products, by-products, and waste as determined in the butcher's test. This information helps greatly for purchasing the proper quantity of meat.

Finally, a chef can use the cost information from a butcher's yield test to determine whether in-house butchering or purchasing purveyor-fabricated product presents the better deal. While a chef must still take into consideration the labor costs incurred from butchering in-house, a yield test lets the chef compare costs per useable pound rather than AP costs, which have little comparative value for differently fabricated products. Many foodservice operations today are moving toward the purchase of purveyor-fabricated products. Purchasing products that require no further preparation prior to cooking provides consistency as well as reduced labor costs. But operations with sufficient space and equipment, skilled staff, and the ability to use butchery by-products may find that their overall expenses go down by fabricating in-house.

4.4   COOKING AND TRIM LOSS

Unfortunately, a butcher's yield test does not account for all of the loss that meat, poultry, and seafood experience during the flow of food. The butcher's test only accounts for loss that occurs during the precooking fabrication process; it does not factor in any loss that takes place during cooking or, for large roasts, any trim lost during portioning. Fortunately, the process for calculating cooking loss is much simpler than is the butcher's yield test. Furthermore, cooking loss and trim loss only come into play for products sold by postcooked weight. For example, if a menu notes that its 14-oz steak is measured as "precooked weight," then it is irrelevant how much weight the steak loses during the cooking process. Since a steak is not normally fabricated any further after cooking, trim loss is immaterial for steaks as well.

Large roasts are the common products for which cooking loss is a relevant factor. If a restaurant advertises a 14-oz prime rib, it isn't portioning the meat prior to cooking. (That would make it a steak.) The same would be true for sliced turkey, ham, leg of lamb, or any other large cuts that are portioned fully cooked. Since a cook almost always has some shreds and, for bone-in cuts, bones that are not served to guests, there is generally trim loss for large roasts as well. Even a boneless prime rib roast will inevitably have a "remainder" portion that does not weigh a full serving.

4.4.1 Cooking Loss

To perform a cooking loss test, begin with the butchered or oven-ready weight and value of the item to be cooked. Unless the roast is purchased fully fabricated, the oven-ready weight and value come directly from the butcher's yield test. After the roast is cooked and has rested, weigh it again. The new weight is the cooked weight, and the difference between the oven-ready weight and the cooked weight is the cooking loss.

Example 4.9: A 7 # 8 oz roast is cooked in a 350-degree oven for 3 hours. When it comes out of the oven, it weighs 5 # 14 oz. What is the cooking loss?

First, convert everything to pounds.

Then, calculate Oven-Ready Weight − Cooked Weight = Cooking Loss.

$$7.5\,\# - 5.875\,\# = 1.625\,\#$$

Since $0.625\,\# \times 16\,\text{oz}/\# = 10\,\text{oz}$, the cooking loss is 1 # 10 oz.

Cooked weight and cooking loss can also be converted to percentages. While there is some value in seeing what percentage of weight is lost from the oven-ready roast, the percentages are typically calculated in relation to the AP weight (pre-butcher's yield test). Examples 4.10 and 4.11 illustrate the difference.

Example 4.10: A 12 # 4 oz roast loses 2 # 12 oz during the cooking process. What is the cooking loss percentage?

Both of these figures convert easily to pounds to get 12.25 # oven-ready weight and 2.75 # cooking loss.

$$\text{Percentage} = \frac{\text{Part}}{\text{Whole}} = \frac{2.75\,\#}{12.25\,\#} = 0.22449 \text{ or } 22.4\%$$

$$\text{Cooking Loss Percentage} = 22.4\%$$

To find out the percentage of the roast that remains (i.e., the cooked weight), subtract the cooking loss percentage (22.4%) from the total 100%. In this case, $100 - 22.4 = 77.6\%$, so the cooked weight of the roast is 77.6% of the oven-ready weight.

Example 4.11: A 15 # AP roast is butchered down to a 12 # 4 oz roast. During cooking, the roast loses 2 # 12 oz of weight. The cooked roast weight is what percentage of the original AP roast?

There are a couple of differences in this example from Example 4.10. First, the question asks the percentage of the weight of the cooked roast, not of the loss, so we need to calculate the final cooked weight of the roast. Second, the percentage is performed in comparison to the AP roast, not to the oven-ready roast. The solution is determined as follows:

$$\text{Cooked Weight} = \text{Oven-Ready Weight} - \text{Cooking Loss}$$
$$= 12.25\,\# - 2.75\,\# = 9.5\,\# \text{ cooked weight}$$

$$\text{Percentage} = \frac{\text{Part}}{\text{Whole}} = \frac{9.5\,\#}{15\,\#} = 0.6333 \text{ or } 63.3\%$$

The cooked roast is 63.3% of the AP roast's weight.

Note in both of the preceding examples that "part" and "whole" are defined by the question. Each question lets you know which part is being compared to which whole. The two types of percentages will be useful for different reasons. Calculating the percentage in terms of the oven-ready weight lets a chef know how much weight will be left (or lost) after cooking. A percentage in terms of the AP weight helps a chef to determine how much raw product to purchase to get a certain cooked yield. Because the percentages should remain fairly consistent for the same meats cooked the same way to the same degree of doneness, as long as a chef is comparing apples to apples (or prime ribs to prime ribs and turkeys to turkeys), she can predict quite accurately how much loss to expect during the cooking process even as the initial weight of the roast fluctuates somewhat.

While this text focuses on cost control, not cooking technique, it is appropriate to describe the reason cooking loss occurs. Through knowledge of cooking theory, a chef can help to minimize cooking loss and also recognize when to apply the cooking loss test. During the cooking process, proteins coagulate and squeeze out some of the moisture present in raw meat. Some of the moisture collects at the bottom of the pan (and can be used for sauces) while the remainder evaporates into the warm air of the oven. The hotter the proteins get, the tighter they bond, and the more moisture they force out of the meat. To minimize moisture loss, first a chef must be careful not to overcook meat. The more it is overcooked, the more moisture will be squeezed from the roast. Second, while a roast's doneness is measured by the internal temperature at the center of the roast (or its thickest part), not all parts of the roast will be the same temperature. The parts at the outer edge will be much hotter (and drier) than the parts at the center. Therefore, to reduce moisture loss, a chef can cook a roast at a lower temperature for a longer period of time to keep the temperature difference between the outer edge and the center of the roast to a minimum. Finally, to keep vast quantities of liquid from spilling out onto a cutting board, a chef should allow a roast sufficient time to "rest" out of the oven before carving. Resting allows a roast's juices to reabsorb partially into the protein structures of the meat. If the roast is cut too soon after it leaves the oven, the juices will end up on the cutting board rather than inside the meat.

Because cooking loss generally refers to moisture loss, an astute chef recognizes the applicability of the cooking loss test to noncooking processes. Two common ones merit mention. First, the curing of large fish, such as salmon, is somewhat trendy in restaurants today. Although the fish is not "cooked," the curing process removes moisture from the fish through the use of salt, and portion quantities are measured postcuring. Applying a cooking loss test to precured and postcured fish is extremely appropriate for accurate costing. Second, the brining of meat and poultry uses a saltwater solution to add moisture to a roast. While this is technically a gain rather than a loss, brining will impact the ultimate final cooked weight of any roast. Using the inexpensive ingredients of salt and water, a chef can increase the cooked weight of meat as compared with an unbrined roast.

4.4.2 Trim Loss

"Trim loss" differs from the loss that occurs during raw butchering only in that the meat is already cooked during the trimming stage. Otherwise, the concept is the same. Certain parts of the roast cannot be served to the customers. If that trim cannot be put to use elsewhere in the operation to save the chef from otherwise purchasing by-products, then the trim is considered a loss.

If all of the trim on a roast is tossed in the garbage, then the trim loss test is quite simple. Basically, weigh the product that is served to the customers, and then weigh the remaining scraps and bones. The two combined should total the initial cooked weight of the roast. The weight of the product that can be served is called the "saleable weight" or EP weight. Both saleable weight and trim loss can be converted to percentages. As with cooking loss, the percentages are typically calculated in relation to the AP weight of the roast, but they could be determined in comparison to the roast's cooked weight.

Example 4.12: An AP roast weighs 14 # 6 oz. After butchering, it weighs 9 # 12 oz. After cooking, it weighs 7 # 9 oz. And finally, after trimming, it weighs 6 # 15 oz. What is the saleable weight as a percentage of AP weight?

Of all the numbers provided here, we only need two—saleable or EP weight (6 # 15 oz) and AP weight (14 # 6 oz). After converting both to pounds, we can calculate the percentage.

$$\text{Percentage} = \frac{\text{Part}}{\text{Whole}} = \frac{6.9375 \,\#}{14.375 \,\#} = 0.4826 \text{ or } 48.3\%$$

Saleable weight is 48.3% of the AP weight.

The saleable weight finally allows a chef to determine the true EP cost per pound (or ounce) of a serving of meat from a large roast (or from anything else measured in postcooked weight). Since the value of the raw, butchered meat has not changed since it went through the butcher's yield test (*note:* the roast's total value comes from the butcher's yield test, not from the AP total cost), the chef can assume that the total cost of the roast cooked and trimmed is the same as it was before it lost all that weight. There is one exception to this assumption, but it will be discussed later in the chapter. To calculate the EP cost per pound, simply take the total value of the oven-ready roast and divide it by the saleable weight.

Example 4.13: A butcher's yield test determined that the total value of a 7 # 1 oz oven-ready leg of lamb was $24.17. After cooking and trimming, the saleable weight of the lamb dropped to 4 # 5 oz. What is the saleable (EP) cost per pound and per ounce?

$$\text{EP\$} = \frac{\text{Oven-Ready Value}}{\text{EP Weight}} = \frac{\$24.17}{4.3125 \,\#} = \$5.604 \text{ or } \$5.60/\#$$

To convert to price per ounce, divide by 16 oz/#.

$$\$5.604 \div 16 = \$0.35/\text{oz}$$

Example 4.14: A butcher's yield test finds that a 4 # 4 oz oven-ready roast costs $4.77/#. After cooking and trimming, only 2 # 12 oz remain. What is the EP cost per ounce?

First, calculate the total value of the oven-ready roast by multiplying its weight times its cost per pound.

$$4.25 \,\# \times \$4.77/\# = \$20.27$$

Next, divide this total value by the EP weight.

$$\$20.27 \div 2.75 \,\# = \$7.37/\#$$

To determine cost per ounce, divide by 16.

$$\$7.37/\# \div 16 = \$0.46/\text{oz}$$

The one exception to the simplicity of these formulas occurs when the trimming step yields by-products that are utilized elsewhere in the operation and save the chef from otherwise purchasing those ingredients. For example, a leg of lamb might yield scraps for a boutique pizza; a turkey might yield pieces for a soup. If these by-products have value, that value should be deducted from the total value calculated during the butcher's yield test. To determine the value of any by-products, multiply the weight of the useable by-products times their would-be prices if purchased from a purveyor—just as was done during the butcher's yield test. Deduct the value of the by-products from the total oven-ready value. Then, proceed to calculate EP cost per pound with this newly adjusted total value.

Example 4.15: A butcher's yield test determined that a prime rib roast had an oven-ready value of $76.78. After the roast is cooked, it weighs 8 # 8 oz. During the trimming process, 12 oz unusable trim and 3 # 4 oz of bone are lost as scrap. However, 7 oz of additional trimmed meat is saved for use in a soup. That salvaged meat saves the kitchen from paying $1.19/# for soup meat. What is the EP cost per pound for the prime rib?

There are a few steps to complete before using the formula:

$$EP\$/\# = \frac{\text{Total Value (In this case, the oven-ready value will be adjusted.)}}{\text{EP Weight}}$$

Step 1: Calculate the value of the salvaged meat. (7 oz = 0.4375 #)

$$\$1.19/\# \times 0.4375 \# = \$0.52$$

Step 2: Calculate the new total value as the oven-ready value minus the by-product's value.

$$\$76.78 - \$0.52 = \$76.26$$

(Now we have the "total value" part of the formula.)

Step 3: Calculate the EP weight. In this case, EP is cooked weight minus all loss during trimming.

$$8.5 \# \text{ (Oven-Ready Weight)} - 0.75 \# \text{ (Trim)} - 3.25 \# \text{ (Bones)}$$
$$- 0.4375 \# \text{ (Soup Meat)} = 4.0625 \# \text{ EP Weight}$$

Step 4: Now use the EP$/# formula.

$$EP\$/\# = \text{New Total Value} \div \text{EP Weight} = \$76.26 \div 4.0625 \# = \$18.77/\#$$

(*Note:* If the soup meat had not been deducted from the total value, the cost would have been $18.90/#, higher enough to make a difference in expenses and menu pricing.)

As example 4.15 suggests, there is a financial benefit to a foodservice operation to find a use for culinary by-products whenever possible. Saving a few pennies per pound on something so expensive may not seem significant, but when a restaurant serves hundreds of pounds of food each month, those savings add up quickly.

4.4.3 The EP Cost Multiplier

Fortunately, this unwieldy process of conducting a butcher's yield test, cooking loss test, and trim loss test has a valuable payoff that makes future cost calculations much easier. All of the data gathered during these tests can be placed in a summary spreadsheet (often called a cooking loss test) to determine an EP cost multiplier. As with the cost multiplier from the butcher's yield test, the EP cost multiplier allows a chef to calculate quickly the EP cost of a large roast even as the price from the purveyor fluctuates. This all assumes that the AP product, butchering, cooking process, and trimming process do not change significantly. However, as long as products with the same specs are purchased and the production processes remain the same (ideally, performed by the same cooks), the EP multiplier will provide accurate results. Figure 4.4 shows what a cooking loss test spreadsheet looks like with the summarized data included.

Food Item: Prime Rib		Cooking Technique: 6 hours at 150 degrees				
Breakdown	Weight	Yield % (Weight in # ÷ AP #)	Value/#	Total Value	EP$/# (EP Value ÷ EP Weight)	EP Cost Multi-plier/# (EP$/# ÷ AP Value/#)
AP Weight	14 # 3 oz (14.1875 #)	100%	$7.29/#	$103.43		
Butchery By-Products and Loss	3 # 14 oz	27.3%				
Butchered Weight	10 # 5 oz	72.7%	$8.18/#	$84.36		
Cooking Loss	1 # 2 oz	7.9%				
Cooked Weight	9 # 3 oz	64.8%				
Trim Loss	1 # 11 oz	11.9%				
EP Weight	7 # 8 oz	52.9%		$84.36	$11.25/#	1.54

Figure 4.4
Cooking Loss Test Spreadsheet

There are a few points to note in Figure 4.4. First, the total value of the butchered weight and its value per pound come directly from the butcher's yield test. Do not expect to calculate it from the information on this spreadsheet. Second, this example assumes there is no trim loss recovered for use elsewhere; that is, all trim gets tossed. As a result, the total value of the butchered or oven-ready roast is the same value as the EP or saleable meat. If there were a "rebate" for useable trim, the EP total value would be adjusted accordingly. Third, the yield percentages are calculated in reference to the total AP weight. Consequently, the butchery by-products and loss percentage and the butchered weight percentage both add up to 100%. The cooking loss and cooked weight percentages only add up to the percentage of the butchered weight since the combined cooking loss and cooked weight total the weight of the butchered meat, not the AP meat. The EP weight and trim loss percentages similarly add up to the cooked weight percentage.

To calculate the EP$/#, which is done only for the EP weight row, divide the total EP value by the EP weight.

$$\text{EP\$/\#} = \frac{\$84.36}{7.5\ \#} = \$11.25/\#$$

Finally, and most importantly, you can now calculate the EP cost multiplier per pound.

$$\text{EP Cost Multiplier/\#} = \frac{\text{EP\$/\#}}{\text{AP\$/\#}} = \frac{\$11.25/\#}{\$7.29/\#} = 1.54$$

This cost multiplier can be applied to any future AP costs per pound (for this specific AP prime rib processed and cooked in the same way) to generate an EP cost per pound. The formula is:

$$\text{EP\$/\#} = \text{AP\$/\#} \times \text{EP Cost Multiplier}$$

Remember that this formula only applies to the same product on which the butcher's, cooking, and trim loss tests were performed and with the EP cost multiplier that was generated from those tests.

Example 4.16: A whole, raw turkey costs $0.89/#. After conducting butcher, cooking, and trim loss tests, the chef calculates that the EP cost multiplier is 1.37. What is the EP Cost per pound for saleable turkey if the AP price for raw, whole turkey jumps to $1.03/#?

$$\text{EP\$/\#} = \text{AP\$/\#} \times \text{EP Cost Multiplier} = \text{\$1.03/\#} \times 1.37 = 1.411 \text{ or } \text{\$1.41/\#}$$

$$\text{EP Cost/\#} = \text{\$1.41/\#}$$

The process for calculating edible portion costs for large roasts can be more than a tad daunting. However, remember that once these tests are performed, they are not repeated very often. In fact, they are carried out extensively in the first place to allow for repeated accuracy in future EP costs without having to repeat the tests for every large roast that comes through the kitchen door. In-house butchered products require a butcher's yield test, but as long as they are portioned by precooked weight, there is no need to conduct a cooking and trim loss test on them. Produce is the easiest of them all, requiring only the most basic of yield tests.

Armed with the skills and techniques presented in this chapter, you are now able to learn how to cost a complete recipe and ultimately to calculate the food cost per portion for a dish. The ability to cost recipes accurately is one of the most important qualities of a professional executive chef. Without this ability, a chef has little chance of keeping a restaurant profitable.

SUMMARY

Yields allow a chef to account for the loss that occurs through trimming, peeling, and otherwise prepping a wide range of products. The relationship between as-purchased and edible portion quantities can be expressed as a yield percentage for a product prepared a certain way. The yield percentage describes the relationship between the as purchased cost and the edible portion cost, too. Conducting yield tests, called butcher's yield tests, for meat, poultry, and seafood is somewhat more complicated because the by-products may have different values by weight than the main, desired item. Cooking loss and trim loss come into play when the product being cooked is portioned after cooking rather than before. Fortunately, butcher's tests and cooking loss and trim tests generate a multiplier that allows a chef to determine an edible portion cost from an as-purchased cost in a single step. The process takes time, but it is the only way to determine a recipe's cost accurately.

COMPREHENSION QUESTIONS

1. A bunch of pears' AP weight is 3 # 4 oz. Their weight after peeling, coring, and slicing is 1 # 14 oz. What is the yield percentage for these pears?

2. What is the AP weight of 2 # 6 oz of peeled turnips if their yield percentage is 88%?

3. How many ounces of trimmed asparagus can you expect to get out of 1 # of purchased asparagus, if the yield percentage of asparagus is 79%?

4. What is the edible portion cost per pound for diced zucchini that costs $0.75/# and has an 86% yield?

5. What is the AP cost per pound for a butternut squash that has a 63% yield and an EP cost of $0.14/oz?

6. What is the EP cost per pound for lentils that require no precooking preparation and have an AP cost of $0.78/#? What is their yield percentage?

7. You paid $21.35 for 20 # of beets. After peeling and slicing, you have exactly 17 # of beet left. What is the EP cost per pound for the prepped beets?

8. A whole salmon, weighing 7 # 6 oz, costs $2.74/#. The fillets are removed, boned, and trimmed. The head, bones, and all trim is thrown into the trash. What is the total value of the remaining fillets, which now weigh only 4 # 15 oz? What is their price per pound? What is the salmon's yield

percentage? If the next salmon weighs 6 # 14 oz, how much boneless salmon fillet would you expect to yield from it after fabrication?

9. Complete the butcher's test spreadsheet that follows. Note, the boneless breast is the desired cut you are testing.

Item: Turkey		Weight: 14 #, 9 oz		Total Cost:	
Grade: A		AP Price per #: $0.37/#			
Breakdown	Weight	% of Total Weight	Weight converted to #	Purchase Value/# (from a purveyor)	Total Value
Legs/Thighs	2 # 7 oz			$0.41/#	
Wings	14 oz			$0.08/#	
Bones	4 # 13 oz			$0.07/#	
Scraps/Waste	6 oz			No value	
Breast	6 # 1 oz			X	
Total				X	

10. For the butcher's test given in question 9, calculate the cost per useable pound, cost per useable ounce, and cost multiplier for the oven-ready turkey breast.

11. Referring to question 9, you know from prior experience that the oven-ready turkey breast loses 12% of its weight during cooking. How much will the cooked turkey breast weigh? Calculate the cost per pound and cost per ounce for the cooked turkey breast.

12. The turkey described earlier is carved for guests. During the carving, 4 oz are lost as waste. What is the EP weight of the saleable turkey? Using the information you calculated in questions 9 to 11, what is the EP cost per pound, the EP cost per ounce, and the EP cost multiplier for turkey breast purchased and prepared this way from a whole turkey?

13. Enter the information you calculated in questions 9 to 12 into the following spreadsheet. Calculate the yield percentages.

Food Item: Turkey Breast from Whole Turkey						
Breakdown	Weight	Yield %	Value/#	Total Value	EP$/#	EP Cost Multiplier/#
AP Weight					X	X
Butchery By-Products and Loss			X	X	X	X
Butchered Weight					X	X
Cooking Loss			X	X	X	X
Cooked Weight			X	X	X	X
Trim Loss			X	X	X	X
EP Weight			X			

14. The price on turkeys has sky-rocketed to $0.83/oz, and you still have turkey breast on the menu. Using the information contained in question 13, what is the new EP$/oz for turkey breast?

DISCUSSION QUESTIONS

1. Many cuts of meat are readily available fully butchered to a chef's exact specifications. What might be the reasons that a chef chooses to butcher in-house? What might be the reasons that a chef chooses to purchase oven-ready meats? (Cost is only one possible reason, but it is a partial answer for both questions.)

2. This chapter has focused on produce, meat, seafood, and poultry. Why are dry goods such as flour, sugar, or honey not mentioned?

3. Do canned fruits and vegetables have a yield percentage less than 100%? Defend your position.

4. The chapter mentioned brining as a technique to help boost the cooked weight of a roast. What are

the pros and cons of brining meat? Why aren't all meats brined?

5. When all by-products from butchering and trimming are thrown in the trash, the cost per pound for a roast is higher. Since the higher cost can always just be passed along to the customer, why would a restaurant take the time to utilize "scraps"?

6. Assume that a chef normally purchases ground beef to make a meat sauce for her staff's family meal. Every day the staff has pasta with meat sauce, but on Sundays, the chef substitutes diced trim from the prime rib roast to make the meat sauce. Purchasing ground beef normally costs her $0.38/#; if she were to purchase cubed rib beef, it would cost her $1.07/#. When she tries to value the trim in her cooking loss test, which price per pound should she use? What is the reasoning behind your answer? (*Note:* There is logic behind either choice.)

7. Assume a restaurant cuts thick slices from the outside of some russet potatoes for its "potato nachos" appetizer (cutting off 65% of each potato) and reserves the centers (the 35% remaining) for making mashed potatoes. What yield percentage should the chef use to calculate how many potatoes (by weight) to order for her appetizer needs (assuming that it will leave her exactly enough "centers" for her mashed potato needs)? What yield percentage should she use to calculate her EP cost for the potatoes in the appetizer? Why?

5

Recipe Costing

For any chef, controlling food cost begins with a recipe. The recipe dictates what ingredients are to be used, how they are to be prepared, how much of them to have on hand and in what form. It also states the number of portions a recipe prepares. While some restaurants operate without recipes, it is virtually impossible to control food costs without them.

Using basic math or a computer spreadsheet, a chef can determine the cost that a recipe incurs as well as the cost for a single serving of that dish. However, costing a recipe becomes a fruitless exercise if the cooks do not follow the recipes. Standard recipes, recipes that every employee follows, are an essential element of cost control. When a cook's production differs from a recipe's instructions, food cost waivers from the chef's planned budget. Larger-than-expected portions drive up costs. Poor execution causes quality to suffer, and items returned by guests generate no income for their expense. In short, accurate recipe costing goes hand in hand with clearly worded recipes, employee management, and training. Completing the math is only half of the costing equation.

Objectives

By the end of this chapter, you will be able to:

- Calculate the cost of a recipe
- Calculate a recipe's cost per portion
- Define and utilize spice factors and Q factors in costing
- Describe the importance of using and following standardized recipes
- Describe the impact that portion and quality control has on food cost

5.1   COSTING A RECIPE

Figuring out the cost of a recipe is essential to the financial management of a foodservice operation. Recipe costs are used to determine menu pricing, to forecast food costs, and to monitor employee production for variation from the prescribed recipes. While a recipe's cost will fluctuate as ingredient prices change, creating computerized spreadsheets for each recipe allows a chef to recalculate costs simply by entering the new cost of an ingredient. That said, a chef cannot create a spreadsheet without first understanding how to cost a recipe by hand. To cost a recipe by hand or on a computer, a chef needs three pieces of information: the recipe itself, the results of yield tests for the recipe's ingredients, and invoices listing the AP (as purchased) costs of the ingredients.

5.1.1 The Costing Sheet: Entering Ingredient Quantities, Yield Percentages, and AP Costs

Most industry costing sheets begin with the quantities of each ingredient listed in a recipe. This data is transferred directly from one of the kitchen's recipes to the left-most column of a costing sheet. The next step is to list the yield percentages for each ingredient in the column immediately to the right. While the recipe's ingredient quantities (edible portion or EP quantities) and yield percentages could be used to determine AP quantity needs, the yield percentage will instead be used to convert AP costs to EP costs. Yield percentage was covered extensively in the previous chapter, but it is important to note that in a recipe, not every ingredient will have a yield percentage less than 100%. For example, if a cookie recipe requires butter, sugar, salt, eggs, and flour, none of the ingredients will experience any loss during preparation. All of these ingredients will have a 100% yield; in other words, their EP and AP quantities and their AP and EP costs are the same. Ingredients measured by count will also have a 100% yield. For those ingredients measured by weight or volume that do experience some loss during preparation, the yield percentage calculated during kitchen tests will be entered into the costing sheet. (Yield percentages calculated during butcher's tests or cooking and trim loss tests may be entered, but they will not be necessary for the purposes of the costing sheet because the EP cost has already been determined during the butcher's or cooking loss test itself.)

One other set of data can be entered into the costing sheet without any additional calculations. The AP cost for each ingredient comes directly from the purveyor's invoice. While this cost will ultimately be manipulated to get an EP cost, it is typically most efficient to first transfer the costs from the invoice to the appropriate recipe costing card and then to perform all of the mathematical calculations at once. A sample costing sheet with EP quantities, yield percentages, and AP costs is shown in Figure 5.1a.

A typical recipe costing sheet includes certain additional information. Not only a recipe's name but also the number of portions and the cost per portion are usually listed in the heading line. While the number of portions comes directly from the recipe, the cost per portion is what the chef will ultimately calculate by completing the costing sheet. Information such as spice factor and Q factor are discussed later in this chapter while food cost percentage (FC%) and selling price are covered in the next chapter.

5.1.2 The Costing Sheet: Converting AP Costs

While the AP cost of an ingredient comes directly from a purveyor's invoice, the information on an invoice is not always in a convenient form for use on a costing sheet. Consider, for example, an invoice that lists bread flour as $42/50 # bag. While we know how much a bag costs, we do not yet know how much a pound costs. If our recipe lists flour in ounces rather than in pounds, the cost per pound must be manipulated further to a cost per ounce. Many ingredients are priced on an invoice by their cost for a package or for a case, not by their cost per single pound. Thus, a chef must learn how to convert invoice pricing to a more useful format.

Recipe: Broiled Trout with Caper Butter				Spice Factor:	
No. of portions: 16				Q Factor:	
Cost per portion:		FC%:		Selling Price:	
Ingredient	Recipe (EP) Quantity (from recipe)	Yield % (from kitchen tests)	AP Cost (from invoice)	EP Cost	Extended Cost
Rainbow trout, fillet, 5 oz	80 oz	61%	$2.85/#		
Butter	1 #	100%	$80 for 36/1 #		
Capers	$\frac{1}{4}$ c	100%	$62 for 24/14 oz		
Parsley, fresh chopped	3 oz	48%	$0.59/bun[a]		
Lemon juice	1 oz	100%	$0.49 per lemon		
Salt	$\frac{1}{2}$ Tbsp	100%	$12.20 for 36/3 #		
White pepper, ground	$\frac{1}{2}$ tsp	100%	$6.48/#		
Total					

[a]Bunch.

Figure 5.1a
Costing Sheet—EP Quantities, Yield Percentages, and AP Costs

In the simplest of cases, cost per weight (or per volume) is determined by dividing the total cost by the total weight of the ingredient "pack." Mathematically, it looks like this:

$$\text{AP Cost/unit} = \frac{\text{Total Cost}}{\text{Total Unit Weight (or volume)}}$$

Example 5.1: Bread flour costs $42 for a 50 # bag. What is the cost per pound?

$$\text{AP Cost/\#} = \$42 \div 50 \# = \$0.84/\#.$$

$$\text{AP Cost} = \$0.84/\#$$

Not all cost determinations are so simple. For example, a case of oil might be listed as $80 for 6/32 oz. To make sense of this, one must recognize that 6/32 oz means 6 bottles each weighing 32 oz. In fact, a common way of expressing the quantity purchased on an invoice is "number of units in a case/weight or volume in one unit." So 12/1 L means 12 bottles of 1 L each. Similarly, 6/2 # means 6 units each weighing 2 #.

Interpreted this way, any item's cost on an invoice can be converted to a cost per unit by first calculating the total weight of a case or pack as follows:

Total Weight or Volume = Number of Units in a Case × Weight or Volume per Unit

Example 5.2: If a case of oil is listed on an invoice as $80 for 6/32 oz, what is the cost per ounce?

First, calculate the total weight.

$$\text{Total Weight} = 6 \text{ Bottles} \times 32 \text{ oz/Bottle} = 192 \text{ oz}$$

$$\text{AP Cost/Unit} = \text{Total Cost} \div \text{Total Weight} = \$80 \div 192 \text{ oz} = 0.416 \text{ or } \$0.42/\text{oz}$$

Example 5.3: A case of frozen pasteurized eggs is listed as $39.45 for 12/1 L. What is the cost per ounce?

First, calculate that the total volume as 12 units $\times$ 1 L = 12 L total

Next, AP Cost/Unit = Total Cost $\div$ Total Weight = $39.45 $\div$ 12 L = 3.287 or $3.29/L.

Finally, convert $3.29/L to ounces. Fortunately, eggs and water have the same weight per volume, so we can use the formula 33.8 oz = 1 L.

$$\$3.29/L \div 33.8 \text{ oz/L} = 0.097 \text{ or } \$0.10/oz$$

$$\text{Cost per Ounce} = \$0.10/oz$$

There are two final complications to calculating total weight or volume. First, sometimes the weight stated on a can is not the weight of the useable product inside the can. For example, canned pears packed in syrup will weigh less after the syrup is drained. (Some canned products list the drained weight of the main item inside the can, but even then, it is best to confirm that weight through a simple kitchen test.) Second, sometimes an item's quantity is stated in weight, and a recipe states its quantity in volume (or vice versa). If the item does not have the same density as water, the 8 oz = 1 cup conversion does not apply. In both of these cases, the easiest thing to do is to open the container and to measure the useable contents. Thus, if you open a 3 # can of pears in syrup and get $2\frac{1}{2}$ # of drained pears, the total weight should be calculated as number of cans times $2\frac{1}{2}$ # to account for the lost weight. Similarly, if your recipe measures capers in volume (e.g., tablespoon or cup), you can open a bottle of capers, which are likely labeled by the ounce, and measure the drained capers by volume. That will give you the volume per unit, which can be used to calculate cost per unit.

These kitchen calculations—using a drained weight or volume to calculate cost per unit—impact the yield percentage that should be listed on a costing sheet. For example, while the drained pears or capers may only be 70% of the original can's contents, by using the EP weight as the basis for the cost per unit, you have effectively already accounted for any yield percentage loss. In short, whenever you use the EP weight of an item as the basis for the converted AP cost, the yield percentage on that item—at least on a costing sheet—becomes 100%. (In the sample broiled trout recipe, this is the case not only with the capers but also with the lemon juice. The majority of the fruit is tossed away after the juice is removed, but the lemon juice is given a yield of 100%. Why? The cost is converted from dollars per lemon, an AP unit, to dollars per ounce of juice, an EP unit, through a kitchen test.)

Figure 5.1b shows the earlier sample costing sheet with the AP costs converted to useable units. By definition, for the units to be "useable," they must be expressed as dollars per the same units listed in the EP quantity column. For example, if the EP quantity is listed in ounces, then the EP cost must be expressed as dollars per ounce. To make the calculations simpler to conduct in future steps, a column for "converted AP cost" has been added to the earlier costing sheet. Example 5.4 illustrates how the converted AP costs are calculated. Note that some of the conversions rely on information that would be determined in the kitchen.

Example 5.4: Convert the AP costs in Figure 5.1b to useable costs per unit.

Rainbow trout   Convert $2.85/# to cost per ounce.

$$\$2.85/\# \div 16 \text{ oz/\#} = \$0.178/oz$$

Butter   Convert $80 for 36/1 # to cost per pound.

$$\text{Total Weight} = 36 \text{ Units} \times 1 \# = 36 \#$$

$$\text{Cost per Pound} = \text{Total Cost} \div \text{Total Weight} = \$80 \div 36 \# = \$2.222/\#$$

Capers Convert $62 for 24/14 oz to cost per cup. (*Note:* Since capers do not have the same density as water, we must measure the volume of a 14-oz container in a kitchen.) Assume that a kitchen test shows one 14-oz jar of drained capers measures $1\frac{1}{3}$ cups. Now, we can substitute 1.333 c for 14 oz in our calculations.

$$\text{Total Volume} = 24 \text{ units} \times 1.333 \text{ c/unit} = 31.992 \text{ or } 32 \text{ c}$$

$$\text{Cost per Cup} = \text{Total Cost} \div \text{Total Volume} = \$62 \div 32 \text{ c} = \$1.938/\text{c}$$

Recipe: Broiled Trout with Caper Butter					Spice Factor:	
No. of portions: 16					Q Factor:	
Cost per portion:			FC%:		Selling Price:	

Ingredient	Recipe (EP) Quantity	Yield %	AP Cost (from invoice)	Converted AP Cost (denominator units match EP quantity)	EP Cost	Extended Cost
Rainbow trout, fillet, 5 oz	80 oz	61%	$2.85/#	$0.178/oz		
Butter	1 #	100%	$80 for 36/1 #	$2.222/#		
Capers	$\frac{1}{4}$ c	100%	$62 for 24/14 oz	$1.938/c		
Parsley, fresh chopped	3 oz	48%	$0.59/bun	$0.118/oz		
Lemon juice, fresh	1 oz	100%	$0.49 per lemon	$0.218/oz		
Salt	$\frac{1}{2}$ Tbsp	100%	$12.20 for 36/3 #	SF		
White pepper, ground	$\frac{1}{2}$ tsp	100%	$6.48/#	SF		
Total						

Figure 5.1b
Costing Sheet—AP Costs Added

Parsley Convert $0.59/bunch to dollars per ounce. This calculation could only be done using a kitchen test to see how many ounces a typical bunch of fresh parsley weighs. Assume that the kitchen test shows 1 bunch weighs 5 oz. Now, we can substitute 5 oz for 1 bun.

$$\text{Cost per Ounce} = \$0.59/5 \text{ oz} = \$0.118/\text{oz}$$

Lemon juice Convert $0.49/lemon to cost per ounce. Again, this requires a test to determine how much lemon juice we get from 1 lemon. Assume that a kitchen test shows that 1 lemon yields 2.25 oz of juice. Now, we can substitute 2.25 oz for 1 lemon.

$$\text{Cost per Ounce} = \$0.49 \div 2.25 \text{ oz} = \$0.218/\text{oz}$$

Salt and White Pepper are simply listed as SF at this point. SF stands for "Spice Factor," which will be discussed later in the chapter.

In all cases, the units now match the EP units listed in the recipe. The prices are left rounded only to the nearest tenth of a penny to allow for greater accuracy in costing.

5.1.3 The Costing Sheet: EP Costs

There are two approaches that a chef could employ when creating a costing sheet. He could use the yield percentages to convert either the recipe's EP quantities to AP quantities or the AP costs to EP costs. While converting from EP quantities to AP quantities has the added benefit of generating a list of "purchase quantities" for the recipe's ingredients, the butcher's test and cooking and trim loss tests already provide the EP cost per weight. This text recommends converting the AP costs to EP costs.

To convert an AP cost to an EP cost, simply use the formula

$$EP\$ = \frac{AP\$}{Y\%}$$

For the AP cost (AP$), always use the AP cost converted to useable units. The formula will not provide useful information if the AP$ is entered as $42/50 # for an EP quantity listed in ounces. For those items that have undergone butcher's loss and/or cooking and trim tests, simply enter the EP cost per weight from those tests into the EP cost column. If the test results are not already in units that match the recipe's EP quantity, be sure to convert them to useable units. Figure 5.1c shows the sample costing sheet with the EP

Recipe: Broiled Trout with Caper Butter					Spice Factor:	
No. of portions: 16					Q Factor:	
Cost per portion:			FC%:		Selling Price:	
Ingredient	Recipe (EP) Quantity	Yield %	AP Cost	Converted AP Cost	EP Cost (converted AP Cost ÷ Y% in decimal form)	Extended Cost
Rainbow trout, fillet, 5 oz	80 oz	61%	$2.85/#	$0.178/oz	$0.292/oz	
Butter	1 #	100%	$80 for 36/1 #	$2.222/#	$2.222/#	
Capers	$\frac{1}{4}$ c	100%	$62 for 24/14 oz	$1.938/c	$1.938/c	
Parsley, fresh chopped	3 oz	48%	$0.59/ bun	$0.118/oz	$0.246/oz	
Lemon juice, fresh	1 oz	100%	$0.49 per lemon	$0.218/oz	$0.218/oz	
Salt	$\frac{1}{2}$ Tbsp	100%	$12.20 for 36/3 #	SF	SF	
White pepper, ground	$\frac{1}{2}$ tsp	100%	$6.48/#	SF	SF	
Total						

Figure 5.1c
Costing Sheet—EP Costs Added

costs calculated from the converted AP costs and the yield percentages. Note that for those items with a 100% yield, the EP cost is the same as the converted AP cost.

5.1.4 The Costing Sheet: Extended Costs

Now that the EP costs have been determined, the rest of the math is easy. To calculate extended costs, also known as the total cost for the quantity of that ingredient in the recipe, simply multiply the EP quantity by the EP cost. Yield does not come into play because it was already taken into account in calculating the EP cost. The results are shown in Figure 5.1d.

Recipe: Broiled Trout with Caper Butter					Spice Factor:		
No. of portions: 16					Q Factor:		
Cost per portion:			FC%:		Selling Price:		
Ingredient	Recipe (EP) Quantity	Yield %	AP Cost	Converted AP Cost	EP Cost	Extended Cost (EP quantity × EP cost)	
Rainbow trout, fillet, 5 oz	80 oz	61%	$2.85/#	$0.178/oz	$0.292/oz	$23.36	
Butter	1 #	100%	$80 for 36/1 #	$2.222/#	$2.222/#	$2.222	
Capers	$\frac{1}{4}$ c	100%	$62 for 24/14 oz	$1.938/c	$1.938/c	$0.485	
Parsley, fresh chopped	3 oz	48%	$0.59/bun	$0.118/oz	$0.246/oz	$0.738	
Lemon juice, fresh	1 oz	100%	$0.49 per lemon	$0.218/oz	$0.218/oz	$0.218	
Salt	$\frac{1}{2}$ Tbsp	100%	$12.20 for 36/3 #	SF	SF		
White pepper, ground	$\frac{1}{2}$ tsp	100%	$6.48/#	SF	SF		
Total						$27.02	

Figure 5.1d
Costing Sheet—Extended Costs Added

   To calculate the total recipe cost, simply add all of the extended costs together. In this case, the total is $27.02 before the spice factor is taken into account.

5.1.5 Spice Factor

Adjusting a recipe using a spice factor is a short-cut technique for adding ingredients such as spices, herbs, and seasonings to the total cost of a recipe. Each restaurant ultimately determines what ingredients it chooses to include in the spice factor, if any. It is possible to calculate the cost of spices, herbs, and seasonings separately for each recipe, but using a spice factor has several benefits. First, it is an obvious time-saver not to have to convert spices (typically measured in small volume units in recipes but sold by weight) to useable units. Second, by using a spice factor, a restaurant can account for ingredients measured "to taste" in a recipe. Third, the spice factor technique divides the cost of spices and herbs across all menu items, so items with lots of spices do not become inordinately expensive compared with lesser-spiced items. (Customers tend to judge plate value on their assumed cost for the main item on a plate, not for its spices.) Finally, since the spice factor can include any items the chef wishes it to include, some operations adjust the spice factor to account for garnishes or "lost" items that are ruined periodically by a cook's error or returned by an unsatisfied guest.

To determine an operation's spice factor, the chef must first determine those items to be included in the spice factor and then calculate their value for a period of time. If an item is used both as a primary ingredient and as a spice factor item, its value as a spice factor item must be determined separately. For example, if a chef wishes to include a strawberry garnish in the spice factor but the menu lists a strawberry tart, the chef must determine the value of those strawberries going just to the garnishes. If a chef wishes to include production waste in the spice factor, he must track the value of the lost items over a given period. Once these values are determined, the spice factor is calculated using the following formula:

$$\text{Spice Factor} = \frac{\text{Value of spice factor items (over a period of time)}}{\text{Value of total food purchases (over the same period)}}$$

Example 5.5: If the spice factor items cost $2,500 over a six-month period and the restaurant purchases $75,000 in food over the same time period, what is the spice factor for that operation?

Spice Factor = Value of Spice Factor Items ÷ Value of Total Food Purchases
= $2,500 ÷ $75,000 = 0.03333 or 3.33%.

To adjust a recipe's cost using a spice factor, simply increase the total recipe cost by the spice factor percentage. While this could be calculated by multiplying the spice factor times the recipe cost and adding the result to the recipe cost, it is much easier to multiply the recipe cost by 1 plus the spice factor (in its decimal form). Thus, if the spice factor is 3.33%, you would multiply the recipe cost by 1.0333 to get the spice-factor-adjusted recipe cost.

Example 5.6: A recipe's total cost is $47.88. The restaurant uses a spice factor of 4.25%. What is the spice-factor adjusted recipe cost?

Spice-Factor Adjusted Cost = Recipe Cost × (1 + Spice Factor) = $47.88 × 1.0425
= $49.91

The spice factor is 0.0425 in decimal form. Add 1 and it becomes 1.0425.
Adjusted Recipe Cost = $49.91 (a difference of over $2 for the entire recipe!)

The spice factor is always multiplied by (not added to) the recipe cost or, if preferred, cost per portion. If used, it should be applied to all recipes in the restaurant no matter what their level of spice and herb usage.

5.1.6 Q Factor

Unlike the spice factor, the Q factor only applies to entrées. The Q factor is a means to account for add-ons, side dishes, or other "freebies" that come with an entrée. For example, if a restaurant menu states, "Each entrée comes with your choice of soup or salad, your choice of potato, your choice of rolls or biscuits, and your choice of dessert," then all of those add-ons must be accounted for in the entrée cost and resultant menu price.

Unlike the spice factor, the Q factor is *added* to the entrée price. If a menu offers all items a la carte or if each entrée is paired with specific side dishes (read: no customer choice), then the Q factor might only cover the cost of the bread and butter given to the table. Bread and butter could be incorporated into the spice factor instead of into a Q factor, especially if the restaurant serves bread to guests ordering only appetizers. However, since most people order an entrée in a restaurant (and bread might not be served unless an entrée is ordered), bread is usually more aptly placed in the Q factor. The choice on accounting for bread is a chef's judgment call. Other than bread and butter, however, the add-ons given to a customer typically come only with the purchase of an entrée. For such add-ons, using the Q factor is the more appropriate approach.

To determine the Q factor value for a restaurant, first complete a recipe cost sheet for all of the possible add-ons. These might include soup, salad, side dishes, bread, butter, and even dessert, if they are all included with the purchase of an entrée. Next, select the most expensive choices for each add-on that a person could include. Thus, if an entrée comes with a choice of soup *or* salad, then the chef would select the most expensive cost per portion among the combined soup and salad options. On the other hand, if the entrée comes with both soup *and* salad, then the chef will select the most expensive soup and the most expensive salad for the Q factor. Next, total all of the most expensive add-on options. This total is the restaurant's Q factor. That way, if a guest orders all of the most expensive add-on choices, the restaurant has planned for that expense. If a guest orders some of the cheaper add-ons, the restaurant's expenses will come in under budget for that customer, making that customer's purchase more profitable.

Example 5.7: A restaurant includes a choice of soup or salad, choice of vegetable, choice of potato, and bread and butter with the purchase of an entrée. The costs of each add-on are calculated per portion as follows:

Clam Chowder—$1.02

Vegetable Soup—$0.78

House Salad—$0.98

Caesar Salad—$1.43

Corn side dish—$0.23

Carrot side dish—$0.18

Green bean side dish—$0.32

Baked potato—$0.27

Twice-baked potato—$0.57

Mashed potato—$0.43

Bread—$0.18

Butter—$0.10

What should the Q factor for this restaurant be?

First, select the most expensive choices that a customer could choose to add on. For this example, those are the Caesar salad, green beans, twice-baked potato, bread, and butter. (Bread and butter have no alternatives, so they are the most expensive in their category by default.)

Next, add up the costs for each of these items.

$$\$1.43 \text{ (Caesar)} + \$0.32 \text{ (green beans)} + \$0.57 \text{ (twice-baked)} + \$0.18 \text{ (bread)}$$
$$+ \$0.10 \text{ (butter)} = \$2.60$$

$$\text{Q Factor} = \$2.60$$

Once the Q factor is determined, it is added to every entrée's cost per portion, as long as all entrées offer the same add-on options. (Cost per portion will be covered in the next section.)

Example 5.8: A restaurant's Q factor is determined to be $2.60. What is the true cost per portion, once the Q factor is added, for an entrée that costs $5.12 per portion? Add the Q factor to the entrée's per-portion cost.

$$\$5.12 + \$2.60 = \$7.72$$

While calculating a restaurant's Q factor does take a little time, it dramatically cuts down on the time required to determine the true cost per portion for each entrée. There is one final note on Q factors and how they impact spice factors. Spice factors should be applied only once to any dish, so a chef should not use the spice factor on add-on dishes, add the Q factor to an entrée, and then use the spice factor again on that entrée. To do so would adjust for the spice factor twice on the add-on components. To avoid this predicament, this text recommends adjusting each recipe, including side dishes and other add-ons, for spice factor separately. Only then should the Q factor be added to an entrée's cost per portion.

5.1.7 Cost per Portion

Once a chef has completed (or nearly completed) a recipe costing sheet, he can finally calculate the cost per portion for a dish, which is the ultimate goal of costing a recipe. The process is simple and it requires only the recipe's total cost, its yield or number of servings, the operation's spice factor, and, if applicable, the restaurant's Q factor.

To calculate a cost per portion, follow this three-step process:

Step 1:   Divide the total recipe cost by the number of servings the recipe yields to get an unadjusted cost per portion. (If the restaurant does not use spice factors or Q factors, this is the sole step to calculate cost per portion).

$$\text{Cost per portion} = \frac{\text{Total recipe cost}}{\text{Number of portions}}$$

Step 2:   Multiply the unadjusted cost per portion times (1 + Spice Factor) to get the spice factor-adjusted cost per portion. (This is the true cost per portion for non-entrées.)

Step 3:   If applicable, add the Q factor to the cost per portion to get the true cost per portion.

Example 5.9: A recipe yielding 20 servings has a total recipe cost of $92.12. The restaurant uses a spice factor of 3.5% and a Q factor of $1.24. This particular recipe is an entrée, and the Q factor is applicable. What is the true cost per portion for this dish?

First, calculate the unadjusted cost per portion.

Cost per Portion = Total Recipe Cost ÷ Number of Portions = $92.12 ÷ 20 = $4.606/portion

Second, multiply the cost per portion × (1 + Spice Factor in decimal form) = $4.606 × 1.035 = $4.767

Finally, add the Q factor. $4.767 + $1.24 = $6.007 or $6.01
True Cost per Portion = $6.01

Using this series of steps, we can complete the Figure 5.1 series. Assume that the restaurant serving the broiled trout employs a spice factor of 1.4% and that the Q factor is $2.39. Figure 5.1e shows the completed recipe spreadsheet.

Recipe: Broiled Trout with Caper Butter					Spice Factor: 1.4%	
No. of portions: 16					Q Factor: $2.39	
Cost per portion: $4.10			FC%:		Selling Price:	
Ingredient	Recipe (EP) Quantity	Yield %	AP Cost	Converted AP Cost	EP Cost	Extended Cost
Rainbow trout, fillet, 5 oz	80 oz	61%	$2.85/#	$0.178/oz	$0.292/oz	$23.36
Butter	1 #	100%	$80 for 36/1 #	$2.222/#	$2.222/#	$2.222
Capers	$\frac{1}{4}$ c	100%	$62 for 24/14 oz	$1.938/c	$1.938/c	$0.485
Parsley, fresh chopped	3 oz	48%	$0.59/bun	$0.118/oz	$0.246/oz	$0.738
Lemon juice, fresh	1 oz	100%	$0.49 per lemon	$0.218/oz	$0.218/oz	$0.218
Salt	$\frac{1}{2}$ Tbsp	100%	$12.20 for 36/3 #	SF	SF	
White pepper, ground	$\frac{1}{2}$ tsp	100%	$6.48/#	SF	SF	
Total						$27.02

Figure 5.1e
Costing Sheet—Complete

The math behind the Figure 5.1e example is:

Recipe Cost ÷ Number of Portions = $27.02 ÷ 16 = $1.689 (unadjusted cost per portion)

$1.689 × (1 + Spice Factor in decimal form) = $1.689 × 1.014 = $1.713 (spice factor-adjusted)

$1.713 + Q factor = $1.713 + $2.39 = $4.103 or $4.10 (true cost per portion)

Once the true cost per portion is determined, it is written in the heading line of the costing spreadsheet. Food cost percentage and selling price are still missing, but those will be covered in the next chapter.

5.2 STANDARD RECIPES

While it is important for a chef to cost all of his recipes, it is a completely frivolous exercise if no one actually follows the recipes. What is the point of calculating the cost of a 5-oz portion of salmon if your cooks serve a 6- or 7-oz portion, right? That is why foodservice operations that take cost control seriously utilize standardized or "standard" recipes.

A standard recipe is simply a recipe written in sufficient detail that a range of cooks could each prepare the dish as written and the results would be the same. Consider the two recipes written in Figure 5.2.

Lasagna: Standard Recipe	Lasagna: Nonstandard Recipe
Yield = 8 servings	Ingredients:
Ingredients:	Lasagna pasta – 12 sheets
Lasagna sheets, dried Barilla, (3″ × 8″) – 12 sheets	Tomato sauce, canned – 1 can
Tomato sauce, canned, Hunt's – 10 oz	Ricotta cheese – 2 #
Ricotta cheese, part-skim, Polly-O – 2 #	Eggs – 2
Eggs – 2	Parsley, chopped – $\frac{1}{2}$ bunch
Parsley, fresh, chopped coarse – $\frac{1}{2}$ cup	Seasoning – to taste
Salt, kosher – 2 Tbsp	
White pepper, ground – 1 tsp	
Parmesan, fine grated – 2 oz	
Garnish: Parsley sprigs, 2 per plate (16 total)	
Procedure:	Procedure:
1. Parboil the lasagna sheets in salted boiling water until al dente, about 12 minutes. Drain and reserve.	1. Cook the pasta and reserve.
2. Mix the ricotta, eggs, parsley, salt, and pepper together in a large bowl until thoroughly combined. Reserve.	2. Combine the cheese, eggs, parsley, and seasonings.
3. In a 4″ deep half-hotel pan, spread a layer of 2 oz tomato sauce. Top with 4 sheets of pasta in a single layer. Top pasta with $\frac{1}{3}$ of the cheese mixture. Top with 4 oz tomato sauce, followed by 4 more pasta sheets in a single layer, followed by $\frac{1}{3}$ of cheese mixture. For top layer, add final 4 oz tomato sauce, then remaining 4 sheets of pasta in a single layer, and then the remaining cheese mixture. Sprinkle grated parmesan evenly on top.	3. Layer the pasta, tomato sauce, and cheese in a pan. Top with a liberal helping of parmesan cheese.
4. Cover with aluminum foil and bake in a 350° F oven for 50 minutes. Then, remove foil and bake for 20 minutes more. Top should have patches of light brown and a thermometer inserted into the center of the lasagna should read 165°F.	4. Bake in a 350°F oven until golden brown on top and warm in the middle.
5. Remove from oven and allow to cool for 10 minutes. Portion into 3″ × 5″ squares. (Yield will be 8 servings from a half-hotel pan.)	5. Cut into squares and serve immediately with a garnish of parsley.
6. Serve immediately centered on 8″ oval white plate with sprig of parsley on the side of the lasagna.	

Figure 5.2
Comparison of Standard and Nonstandard Recipes

A standard recipe includes a high level of detail, including the grades and brands of ingredients, garnish, type of pan, cooking methods, portion size, storage and preparation information, and plating instructions. It may include diagrams or photos of the final plate presentation to reduce possible misunderstandings of the written recipe's instructions. Most cooks following a standard recipe would create nearly identical dishes for customers. The nonstandard recipe in Figure 5.2 leaves enough opportunity for variation that two cooks following that recipe would likely serve two very different lasagnas.

If a customer visits a restaurant regularly and experiences great variation in the quality and quantity of a dish, he is less likely to return in the future. Guests prefer predictability in their restaurants. Even though the customer might be pleased the first time that he gets an oversized portion with extra garnishes, the next time if he gets a standard portion with the typical garnish, he will be disappointed. Consistency, assuming a restaurant's standards provide quality food and service, leads to customer satisfaction.

Furthermore, any disparity between a recipe and a cook's preparation invalidates the dish's cost per portion as the recipe used in a costing sheet is the standard recipe used in the kitchen. Assume that a chef completed a costing sheet for the lasagna described in the standard recipe in Figure 5.2. If a cook prepares the dish in a way that more resembles the nonstandard recipe, the quantity of tomato sauce and parmesan cheese might be much greater and the portion size might be much larger. In short, the dish could cost significantly more per portion to produce than the chef has budgeted. Such a discrepancy, left uncorrected, could drive a restaurant out of business in a matter of months.

Preparing a dish in such a way that it costs less than the standard recipe is no windfall for a restaurant either. As suggested earlier, a customer that leaves with his expectations for a restaurant unmet is less likely to return. Using the lasagna example again, if a cook were to serve a smaller portion or bake the lasagna to a chalky-white instead of to a golden brown, the guest may not return (or at least won't order the lasagna again). A dissatisfied customer also brings the potential for negative publicity. Guests who share their disappointing experience with friends influence the likelihood that others will not patronize that operation. In short, the best approach to maximize sales and to control costs is to ensure that all standardized recipes are written with no room for misinterpretation and that employees adhere to those standardized recipes.

To make certain that standard recipes not only exist but are also followed, a restaurant may provide employees with recipe cards or post recipes prominently in the kitchen. Recipes may be printed daily off a computer if the production quantities change regularly, so cooks will not make simple math errors in converting recipes. Most importantly, training and the watchful eye of a supervisor or expeditor can prevent nonstandard preparations from reaching a customer.

5.3 PORTION AND QUALITY CONTROL

Inextricably linked to standardized recipes are the concepts of portion and quality control. Without portion control a restaurant's food cost will likely be higher than expected. Guests may receive too large a portion, which drives up costs, or they may receive substandard quality or quantity food, which negatively impacts future business. Theoretically, standardized recipes should control this, but without proper management, occasional employee errors can become common variances from the kitchen's standards. While a chef does not typically monitor every single dish that leaves a kitchen, a properly trained expediter or sous chef can watch to ensure that only dishes that conform to the chef's standards make it to the customers.

Numerous tools help a chef control portion sizes. Most portions are measured by weight, by volume, or by count. The best devices for controlling portions measured by weight are scales. Spring scales and digital scales are both accurate and efficient (see Photo 5.1). A cook portioning 4-oz hamburgers should periodically weigh the burgers during production to ensure that they adhere to the 4-oz standard size. Since food does not come from a factory, most operations allow for some small variance in portioning, but anything outside of that variance is deemed unacceptable for service. For example, a restaurant that has its cooks prepare 4-oz hamburgers with a variance of $+/-0.25$ oz might serve a 3.75-oz burger or a 4.25-oz burger but never a 4.5-oz patty. Since these variances must remain small for a recipe's cost spreadsheet to have any value, variances are usually listed in a fraction of an ounce. A restaurant would never set a variance of $+/-1$ oz; otherwise, the largest and smallest portions might differ by as many as 2 oz!

When a portion is measured by volume, various tools can be used to yield consistent portion sizes. Measuring cups and ladles work well for liquids while portion scoops and ramekins are better for semisolid foods (see Photo 5.2). Kitchen spoons and slotted spoons are not all that precise, but they are better than nothing when working with certain vegetables or grains. Almost any container can be converted to a volume measure as long as it is used consistently by all cooks. For example, a coffee crème brulée might be portioned in a 6-oz coffee cup. As long as a chef calculates portion size as 6 oz, approves the presentation, and instructs all cooks to use the same cups for this particular dessert, the coffee cup becomes an effective measuring tool.

When an item is portioned by count, no tool other than the human eye is necessary. However, vigilance in quantity compliance remains important. A cook who serves every Greek salad with 5 olives instead of 3 will increase his restaurant's salad expense significantly over the course of a year. Unlike weight and volume measures, count standards

Photo 5.1
Spring Scale for Measuring Weight

Source: © Michael Flippo/Fotolia.

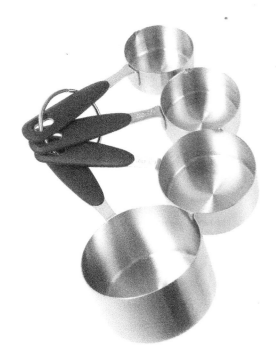

Photo 5.2
Measuring Cups for
Measuring Volume

Source: © Graphichead/Shutterstock.

may allow for no variance. One less shrimp on a shrimp cocktail, for example, would be a highly visible error that a regular guest would surely notice. Count, weight, and volume measures are all critical to maintain consistent portion sizes.

An expediter serves as a quality as well as a quantity control check for all food destined for the dining room. In addition to disappointing a customer, poor or inconsistent quality drives up a restaurant's food cost. Imagine that a restaurant sends an undercooked piece of swordfish out to a customer. Once the customer bites into it, he may be revolted by the thought of the raw fish and return the dish for a substitute—probably not fish. The kitchen is left preparing a second dish for this customer and at best earning the revenue for only one dish. On the other hand, if the expediter catches the mistake before the swordfish leaves the kitchen, he can ask the cook to return the same piece of fish to the heat until it is fully done. As long as the accompaniments do not lose their quality during the delay, the restaurant wastes no food in correcting this error. Even more importantly, the customer, unaware of the averted potential problem, leaves the restaurant satisfied.

Undercooked food is only one example of a potential quality control issue. A dish missing the right garnish should be corrected before it leaves the kitchen. Food that is wilting under a heat lamp or falling apart from its intricate plate presentation will look less appealing to the customer who receives it. Smudges on plates communicate sloppiness rather than elegance and cleanliness to the guest. Special customer requests should also be caught by the expeditor. For example, a consumer who notifies the server of an allergy might request a dish made in a modified fashion without certain components. Missing such an adjustment could have fatal results—literally—for the customer. Any one of these errors, left uncorrected, is cause for a guest to leave disappointed in a dining experience. Disappointed guests rarely return, which makes it difficult to grow future revenue. On the other hand, satisfied customers who return repeatedly, look forward to the restaurant's quality and quantity standards. Customers may not care that those standards also help the business's food cost to stay on budget, but a cost control manager surely does.

SUMMARY

Costing a recipe encompasses the concepts of both edible portion (EP) and as-purchased (AP) quantities and costs as well as yield percentages. As each ingredient quantity is paired with its respective cost on a costing sheet, a chef can determine the extended cost of each ingredient and as a result, the cost of the entire recipe. Armed as well with the number of portions that a recipe serves, the chef can determine a recipe's cost per portion. Since many operations do not bother to calculate spices and herbs individually in a recipe, the cost per portion may be adjusted using a spice factor. For those entrées that include meal components for no additional price, the Q factor helps determine the true cost per portion. For many of these computations, the greatest challenge is manipulating the units to ensure that the cost and quantity units match. (Otherwise, the math will not work.) A costing sheet is only valuable if cooks follow a standard recipe written in a clear and detailed manner. Lack of portion control and quality control will throw off the accuracy of a recipe's cost per portion as well. Proper training and supervisory oversight help to make certain that all food is prepared to the chef's standards.

COMPREHENSION QUESTIONS

1. Complete the following costing sheet using the information already included in the form.

Recipe: Grilled Chicken with Mango Salsa				Spice Factor: 3.0%		
No. of portions: 30				Q Factor: $1.88		
Cost per portion:			FC%: X	Selling Price: X		
Ingredient	Recipe (EP) Quantity	Yield %	AP Cost	Converted AP Cost	EP Cost	Extended Cost
Chicken breast, skinless, boneless, trimmed, 6 oz each	180 oz	95%	$1.47/#			
Mango, fresh, diced	2 #	61%	$10/8 #			
Red onion, diced	$\frac{1}{2}$ c	77%	$0.22/#			
Cilantro, fresh chopped	4 Tbsp	100%	$0.79/bun (1 bun = 5 Tbsp chopped)			
Lime juice, fresh	2 oz	100%	$0.39 per lime (1 lime = 1 oz juice)			
Salt	1 Tbsp	100%	$12.20 for 36/3 #	SF	X	X
Black pepper, ground	$\frac{1}{2}$ tsp	100%	$6.48/#	SF	X	X
Total	X	X	X	X	X	
Total with Spice Factor Adjustment						
Cost per Portion						
True Cost per Portion (Q factor adjusted)						

2. A chef tracks all of his spice factor items over a year and notices that their total value is $2,025. The total value of his food purchases was $80,750 over the same time period. What is the spice factor for this operation?

3. A restaurant offers each guest a cup of the soup du jour (which rotates daily), a house salad with their choice of dressing (vinaigrette, French, ranch, or blue cheese), choice of rice or baked potato, mixed vegetables, and bread sticks with the purchase of each entrée. Using the information that follows, what should the restaurant's Q factor be?

Costs per portions:
Beef barley soup—$0.28
Chicken noodle soup—$0.21
Manhattan clam chowder—$0.35
Cream of potato soup—$0.26
Plain house salad—$0.62

Vinaigrette dressing—$0.07
French dressing—$0.08
Ranch dressing—$0.09
Blue cheese dressing—$0.29
Rice—$0.10
Baked potato—$0.19
Mixed vegetables—$0.18
Bread sticks—$0.11

4. What is the likely impact to a restaurant that does not utilize standard recipes?

5. List five different tools that could be used for a portion measure.

DISCUSSION QUESTIONS

1. How might a restaurant attempt to control quality and portion sizes if it does not employ standard recipes?

2. One restaurant changes its menu daily to make use of seasonal products. Customers are rarely able to come back to the restaurant to experience the same dish twice. Is it important for this operation to employ standard recipes? How about standard portion sizes? Why or why not?

3. A mezze (Mediterranean tapas or small plates) restaurant serves "free" bread to all of its customers. Because of the nature of the menu, however, there is no entrée course; all dishes are essentially small tastings. How might this restaurant account for the bread in the true cost per portion of its dishes?

4. Chefs who research recipes in cookbooks written for homemakers typically rewrite them for their professional kitchen, if they add them to their menu. Why?

5. For most ingredients, a recipe costing sheet could adjust the EP quantity to an AP quantity, using each ingredient's yield percentage, and then multiply the AP quantity by the AP cost to get the extended cost. Why can't a large cut of meat that required a butcher's yield test simply use the yield percentage from the butcher's test and the AP cost from the invoice to determine the extended cost for that meat?

6. Assume that a recipe lists the quantity for fresh rosemary in tablespoons but the purveyor's invoice charges by the ounce. After a kitchen test, the chef calculates that 2 oz of fresh rosemary generates 4 Tbsp of chopped rosemary. A chart with yield percentages lists rosemary as having a 38% yield. In creating a costing spreadsheet for this recipe, what yield percentage should you enter after you calculate the cost per tablespoon for the rosemary?

6
Calculating Sales Price and Food Cost

Calculating and monitoring expenditures in a foodservice operation is only half of the prerequisite for operating a profitable business. Cost control managers must focus equally on revenue generation. While there are numerous ways to create and increase revenue, for most foodservice businesses the first step to bringing in money is to determine a fair sales price for each menu item.

For a restaurant to be successful long term, its food and beverage must sell at prices high enough to cover all expenses and profit but not so high that customers shun the business for a better deal elsewhere. While customers are generally attracted to a restaurant by more than value pricing, prices play an important role in customer psychology. Product differentiation provides a business some flexibility in what it charges as does the number of competitors in the market. These factors, along with food cost and other expenses, are taken into account when calculating a menu item's sales price.

While sales prices are calculated item by item, revenue, like food cost, can be viewed collectively as well. If a restaurant knows how many servings of each dish have been sold, it is possible to calculate the expected food cost and food sales revenue for the day. Of course, the actual costs and revenue may differ somewhat from the projected figures. A server may not charge a guest properly for all items served. Some ingredients may be lost through unanticipated waste, spoilage, or theft. Guests and employees may steal from the restaurant when they think they can get away with it. Because some uncollected "sales" and some food loss are inevitable over time, even under the best of circumstances some variance between standard (expected) and actual revenue and costs is inevitable. However, minimizing and controlling this discrepancy is one of the key functions of a foodservice manager.

6.1 MENU PRICING METHODS

While there are numerous methods for determining a menu item's selling price, all approaches center on the same logic—the menu price must cover the item's food cost plus an additional contribution margin that covers all other expenses, including some profit. *Contribution margin* is the portion of the sales price that is left over after a menu item's cost per portion is covered. For example, if a dish sells for $11.00 and the true cost per portion for that dish is $4.00, then the contribution margin is $7.00 ($11 - 4 = 7$). The contribution margin is required to cover non-food and -beverage costs, such as labor, rent, utilities, and other expenses. For this reason, a dish's selling price is never simply its cost per portion. That approach would not leave any money to cover the other costs of doing business. The next few sections will cover several common methods for calculating a menu item's sales price.

6.1.1 Calculating Menu Prices Using Food Cost Percentage

The most common industry approach to determining an item's selling price employs a ratio between food cost and food cost percentage. Several variations on this method exist, including the Overhead Contribution and the Texas Restaurant Association methods, but all are simply ways to determine an appropriate food cost percentage before using the *Food Cost Percentage* system.

Simply put, the food cost percentage method relies on the following formula:

$$\text{Sales Price} = \frac{\text{Food Cost}}{\text{FC\%}}$$

This formula can also be described graphically as follows:

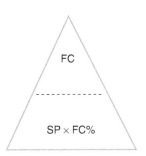

As with prior graphic formulas, simply cover up the variable you wish to find, and follow the remaining equation using the other two variables. In this case, FC = Food Cost, SP = Sales Price, and FC% = Food Cost Percentage.

Example 6.1: Determine the selling price for a tuna appetizer with a food cost of $2.12 if the restaurant aims for a FC% of 32%.

Sales Price = Food Cost ÷ FC% = $2.12 ÷ 0.32 = $6.625 or $6.63.

Sales Price = $6.63.

(How to adjust these awkward figures to more "comfortable" numbers like $6.95 is discussed later in the chapter.)

The food cost for a dish comes directly from the recipe costing spreadsheet. The figure a restaurant uses for its food cost percentage is somewhat less prescribed. Food cost percentages vary throughout the industry depending on the type of food served.

Because a selling price must cover labor cost, high-end establishments tend to have a lower food cost percentage, which leaves more money available to pay a highly trained staff. In some upscale operations, food cost may be as low as 20%. Fast food restaurants, on the other hand, which pay low wages to unskilled workers and which have high customer volume, often operate with a relatively high food cost percentage, sometimes in the 40% range. Generally speaking, the majority of mid-range restaurants have a food cost percentage in the low- to mid-thirties.

When a restaurant manager is trying to determine the proper food cost percentage to use, she may begin with a random number and adjust it over time. For example, she might begin with a 32% food cost, but if her executive chef consistently hits a 30% food cost, she may adjust her budget downward to plan for a 30% food cost. There are slightly more scientific approaches to selecting a target food cost percentage once a restaurant has some sales and expense history.

One approach to selecting a food cost percentage, the *Overhead Contribution Method,* uses a restaurant's financial history and upcoming budget to determine the total nonfood (and nonbeverage) expenses and desired profit. Those total expenses and profit must be achieved through the contribution margin percentage of sales. Thus, a manager can divide these combined "overhead" expenses and profit by the forecast sales to calculate the contribution margin percentage of each item's sales price. Since the contribution margin and food cost figures total 100% of the sales price, the food cost percentage is calculated as 100% minus the contribution margin percentage. This food cost is then used to determine sales prices from each recipe's cost per portion.

Mathematically, the overhead contribution method is interpreted as follows:

1. $\text{Contribution Margin\%} = \dfrac{(\text{Non-Food or -Beverage Expenses} + \text{Profit})}{\text{Sales}}$

2. $\text{FC\%} = 100\% - \text{Contribution Margin\%}$

(*Note:* Convert contribution margin from its decimal to its percentage form first)

3. $\text{Sales Price} = \dfrac{\text{Food Cost}}{\text{Food Cost\% (in decimal form)}}$

Example 6.2: A restaurant has budgeted for upcoming annual sales of $600,000. The combined overhead expenses (including labor, utilities, rent, etc.) are expected to be $400,000. The owners would like to realize a pretax profit of $20,000. Using the overhead contribution method, what is this restaurant's FC%? What should the restaurant charge for a steak entrée with a cost per portion of $3.74?

Step 1: To determine the contribution margin percentage, first add overhead and profit.

$400,000 + $20,000 = $420,000 (must be covered by contribution margin).

Step 2: Next, divide the contribution margin costs by total sales.

$420,000 ÷ $600,000 = 0.70 or 70.0%

Step 3: FC% = 100% − contribution margin% = 100% − 70% = 30%.

The restaurant's FC% is 30%.

Step 4: To calculate the sales price for the steak costing $3.74, use the formula
SP = FC ÷ FC%

$$SP = \$3.74 \div 0.30 = \$12.466 \text{ or } \$12.47$$

$$\text{Selling price} = \$12.47.$$

Some books refer to the *Ratio Method* of menu pricing. While the math appears different on the surface, the ratio method is essentially the same approach as the overhead contribution method. The ratio method generates a ratio of nonfood costs and profits to food costs to generate a price factor. The price factor is then multiplied times the cost per portion of a dish. However, the ratio is effectively the same figure, inverted, as the food cost percentage that is determined using the overhead contribution method. As both the ratio and overhead contribution methods yield the same results, there is no need to list alternate mathematical formulas for the ratio method here.

Another approach to selecting a food cost percentage is the *Texas Restaurant Association (TRA)* Method. The TRA method works just like the overhead contribution method with one major difference. The TRA approach calculates a separate FC% for each menu category on the basis of the profit desired from each menu category. Thus, a restaurant may factor 30% profit for appetizers and desserts but only 10% profit for entrees. The overhead and labor cost percentages remain the same across all categories, but the profit percentage changes, making the FC% different for appetizers versus entrées. For example, if a restaurant budgets 20% for nonlabor overhead and 40% for labor, that is 60% for all nonfood expenses. If the manager decides that desserts should be 30% profit, then 90% (60% + 30%) is the total contribution margin percentage for desserts. This leaves 10% for the food cost for dessert. If the manager determines that entrées only need to make 10% profit, then the entrée contribution margin percentage is 60% + 10% or 70%. This leaves a 30% (100% − 70%) food cost for the entrées.

The benefit of the TRA method is that it allows a restaurant to attract customers with value-priced entrées and make proportionately more profit on meal enhancers such as appetizers and desserts. Furthermore, the entrée category may be subdivided into popular versus slow-moving items. Items that do not sell well are effectively a burden on the restaurant. They require staff time and storeroom space, but they do not generate as many dollars of profit because they are sold so infrequently. To account for this imbalance, the TRA method suggests factoring a higher profit percentage into slow-selling items and a lower profit percentage into popular items. Other variables may be taken into account as well when determining the proper profit margin to use for each category of menu item.

As with the overhead contribution method, once the food cost percentage is determined using the TRA method, the food cost percentage is entered into the general Sales Price = Food Cost ÷ FC% formula to calculate the selling price for each menu item.

6.1.2 Calculating Menu Prices Using Prime Costs

Prime cost is defined as the combined total of food, beverage, and labor cost. When used to calculate a food menu price, prime cost specifically refers to the food cost per portion of a single dish and the direct labor cost needed to prepare that one dish in the kitchen. (In this case, direct labor cost does not include the support labor of dishwashers, service staff, or administrators; it only accounts for the preparation and cooking labor needed for that one dish.) Whereas the cost per portion is determined from a costing spreadsheet, the direct labor cost is calculated by tracking kitchen staff productivity over a given period of time and using each employee's hourly wages to determine the labor cost for each recipe and subsequently, for each dish. Because cooks often multitask during their work, calculating a precise direct labor cost for a dish can be difficult unless each cook is responsible for just one or two menu items.

Once the prime cost for each dish is determined, the manager who employs the *Prime Cost Method* selects a price factor that will be multiplied times every dish's prime cost to determine the appropriate sales price. A price factor, like food cost percentage, may be somewhat arbitrary at first, but it can be adjusted for greater accuracy as a restaurant gathers historical data on expenses and sales. Because the prime cost method includes direct labor cost in its approach, those dishes that are more labor-intensive command a higher selling price than simpler dishes with the same food cost. The one downside is that guests may not recognize or value the amount of labor it takes to prepare a dish. Consequently, customers may consider it gouging if a labor-intensive chicken dish costs as much as a simply grilled steak.

Mathematically, the prime cost method looks like this:

$$\text{Sales Price} = \text{Prime Cost} \times \text{Price Factor}$$

$$(\text{Prime Cost} = \text{Food Cost} + \text{Direct Labor Cost})$$

Example 6.3: A restaurant uses a price factor of 2.8 to determine its sales prices with the prime cost method. The cod in this establishment has a cost per portion of $2.82 and a direct labor cost per portion of $0.72. What should this restaurant charge for the cod?

Step 1: Prime Cost = Food Cost + Direct Labor Cost = $2.82 + $0.72 = $3.54

Step 2: Sales Price = Prime Cost × Price Factor = $3.54 × 2.8 = $9.912
 or $9.91
Sales Price = $9.91

The *Actual Pricing Method* uses the budgeted percentages for variable costs (other than food and direct labor costs), fixed costs, and desired profit to determine a price divisor to be applied to the prime cost for each dish. The variable costs, fixed costs, and profit are subtracted from 100% to determine the percentage of all sales that remains to cover prime cost; this is the price divisor. A dish's prime cost is then divided by this price divisor to get the dish's sales price. (*Note:* Fixed and variable costs will be defined in a future chapter, but for now, think of fixed costs as payments that don't change on a monthly basis such as salaries and rent, and think of variable costs as expenses that fluctuate, such as labor from hourly workers.) Mathematically, the actual pricing method looks like this:

1. Price Divisor = 100% − (Variable Cost% + Fixed Cost% + Profit%)

2. Sales Price = $\dfrac{\text{Prime Cost}}{\text{Price Divisor}}$

Example 6.4: A restaurant has a variable cost percentage of 28%, a fixed cost percentage of 13%, and a budgeted profit of 10%. Using the actual pricing method, calculate the sales price for an entree with a food cost of $2.97 and a direct labor cost of $1.12.

> *Step 1:* Price Divisor = 100% − (28% + 13% + 10%) = 100% − 51% = 49%
>
> *Step 2:* Prime Cost = Food Cost + Direct Labor Cost = $2.97 + $1.12 = $4.09
>
> *Step 3:* Sales Price = Prime Cost ÷ Price Divisor = $4.09 ÷ 49% (or 0.49 in decimal form) = $8.346 or $8.35
> Sales Price = $8.35

The prime cost and actual pricing methods both rely on similar principles. Both adjust a base cost that includes the food cost and direct labor cost. The actual pricing method is simply a more scientific approach to determining the price factor (or divisor) that the manager should use.

6.1.3 Calculating Menu Prices Using the Gross Profit Method

Unlike the previously described pricing methods that use multiplication or division, the *Gross Profit Method* employs addition to determine menu prices. The term "gross profit" means the money made from sales after food and beverage costs are deducted. It is essentially the same as contribution margin, though contribution margin refers to individual item sales whereas gross profit refers to collective sales over a given period. Gross profit can be manipulated to calculate a gross profit per customer. Gross profit per customer is nothing more than the business's total gross profit over a given time period divided by the number of customers for the same time frame.

To calculate a menu price using the gross profit method, simply add the item's cost per portion to the restaurant's predetermined gross profit per customer. Mathematically, the gross profit method looks like this:

$$\text{Sales Price} = \text{Food Cost per Portion} + \text{Gross Profit per Customer}$$

Example 6.5: A restaurant has a gross profit per customer of $4.15. A large salad costs $1.97 per portion. Using the gross profit method, what should the menu price for the salad be?

$$\text{Sales Price} = \text{Food Cost per Portion} + \text{Gross Profit per Customer}$$
$$= \$1.97 + \$4.15 = \$6.12$$

The gross profit method is most appropriate for operations with primarily low-cost items that are somewhat similar in their costs. A coffee shop is the best example for this method's benefits. In a coffee shop, most of the revenue comes from the sale of coffee beverages. While a coffee shop's food and beverage costs are relatively low compared with the food and beverage costs found in larger restaurants, the coffee shop still has to cover its rent, labor, and other overhead costs. This typically translates to a very low food cost (or in this case, beverage cost) percentage for a coffee shop. A cup of coffee might only cost $0.15 in ingredients, but the coffee shop might sell that cup for $1.50. While the beverage cost percentage is astoundingly low at 10%, the shop is still left with only a $1.35 contribution margin to cover all other costs. (Compare that with a larger restaurant that has a 33.3% food cost and sells a $3 per portion dish for $9. This restaurant does "worse" in percentages but much better in dollars, with a

$6 contribution margin in this case.) Thus, most coffee shops require exceptionally low beverage cost percentages just to survive.

Unfortunately, the food cost percentage method does not work well with extremely low percentages because small differences in costs magnify into large differences in sales prices. For example, a restaurant with a 10% food (or beverage) cost percentage might charge $1.50 for a drink that costs $0.15 and $2.50 one that costs $0.25 (only $0.10 more). Many customers won't tolerate such big price swings for such small increases in value. While the business would make substantially more money on the sales of the higher-priced items, most customers in this situation will purchase the cheapest item on the menu. The coffee shop, knowing roughly how many beverage sales to expect each week, is better off determining how much money it needs to make per sale to cover its overhead (gross profit per customer) and then adding each beverage's cost to that gross profit per customer. The result—menu prices that do not differ greatly from item to item—is a win–win. The customer focuses less on price and more on which beverage she will enjoy most. The restaurant makes the same contribution margin dollars no matter what drink the customer purchases. While the gross profit method is not ideal in all foodservice operations, it is generally the best choice when food and/or beverage cost percentages are extremely low.

6.1.4 Using the Base Price Method

Unlike the other pricing methods, the *Base Price Method* starts with a given menu price and then works backward to generate guidelines for each dish's permissible food cost. This is the approach most commonly used in corporate cafeterias with sales prices stipulated by the client company and in fast food restaurants that offer "dollar menus."

Essentially, the base price method first sets the desired sales price for each dish. Then, using the FC = SP × FC% formula, the manager takes the restaurant's food cost percentage and provides the chef the maximum food cost allowed for each dish. Rather than designing a dish first, the chef determines (or awaits from her boss) the food cost guidelines and then creates a dish that meets those guidelines. For example, a chef in a burger place with a $0.40 maximum food cost for a $0.99 burger will adjust the size of the bun, the quality and quantity of the meat, and the number and type of condiments to ensure that the burger does not cost more than $0.40.

Fast food operations employ this approach on their special-price menus. Corporate cafeteria chefs have a similar challenge as sometimes the company tells them how much to charge for a meal. For example, a software company may hire a foodservice provider to operate a cafeteria for its employees. As part of the arrangement, the company may require that its employees pay no more than $5 for a lunch entrée. If the foodservice company operates at a 40% food cost (40% of $5 is $2), then the cafeteria's chef will adjust all recipes such that none has a food cost higher than $2 per portion.

6.1.5 Matching Competitors' Prices

All of the aforementioned menu pricing methods are *internal* approaches in that they are solely based on the restaurant's own sales and cost history. However, some foodservice operations prefer the *external* approach of simply matching competitors' prices. While there is some logic to this technique, it can be extremely dangerous in the absence of any other pricing methods.

A restaurant that matches another business's prices and then uses the base price method to calculate food costs may find a way toward profitability. However, consider that most restaurants do not know the expenses of their competitors; they only know their sales prices. Thus, if a family-owned business uses the owner's retired parents, teenage children, and several other relatives as cheap or free labor, the business's labor costs will be extremely low. If the chef purchases its food from the owner's college roommate's company, she may get the best pricing in town for her ingredients and as a result, have a very low food cost. Similarly, large chains get bulk discounts on purchases that individual restaurants simply cannot access. In short, it may be impossible for one business to stay profitable at a competitor's sales prices.

6.1.6 Choosing the Right Pricing Method

Despite the multitude of pricing methods that exist, there is no "best" method. Each approach has its pros and cons. Prime cost techniques work well when there is great variation between the amounts of direct labor required for the different dishes on a menu. For example, if some menu items take 30 minutes of total labor and others only take 2 minutes, a prime cost technique will factor that disparity into the sales price. The base price approach is best when a business must hit a certain price point to survive in a highly competitive, price-sensitive market. Food cost percentage methods are probably the most common for their ease of use. A food cost percentage method works best when most menu items require roughly the same amount of labor and the food cost percentage is not extremely low (i.e., not much below 20%). Even a single business may employ different approaches for different parts of the menu. For example, a manager might use a prime cost method for entrées, a food cost percentage method for appetizers, and a base price approach for desserts. The right method to use is the one that gets the best profit results for the business, and that method will vary with each restaurant's concept, location, and market competition.

6.2 FACTORS THAT IMPACT FINAL MENU PRICING

Microeconomic theory suggests that in an open market with all players offering equivalent products, the market will eventually shrink to two suppliers. When there is only one business in the market (a monopoly), the business is likely to offer higher-than-necessary prices in its attempt to maximize its profits. A second business in the scenario keeps prices low as both must compete for customers. However, a third business divides the market even further, which makes it challenging for any of the three businesses to survive on reduced market share at competitive pricing.

This theory begs the question: How can more than two restaurants exist in the same city? The answer lies in the theory's base requirement that all businesses offer equivalent products. If three pizza parlors within walking distance of each other offer identical pizzas in identical environments with identical levels of service, one of those pizza parlors will surely fail. But if one of those pizza parlors offers only wood-fired, brick-oven pizza and the second offers only deep-dish Chicago-style pizza, and the third offers low-quality but really cheap pizza, there is a good chance that all three will survive in the marketplace. While all three serve "pizza", they are really selling three completely different products at different price points. Some people want high-end, thin crust pizza; some will only eat deep-dish, and still others think "pizza is pizza" and will go for the place that charges the least.

Creating differences between similar products so that they do not compete with each other is called *product differentiation*. While identical competitors, in their attempt to attract customers, drop their prices to the minimum necessary for survival, unique businesses can charge a premium for their products as a customer cannot purchase those products elsewhere. Product differentiation is only one of several factors that allows a restaurant to charge more than it otherwise might in a highly competitive industry.

Competition.   The number of competitors in a given market impacts the price a restaurant can charge for its food. For example, if a small city has three sandwich shops fairly near to each other, those sandwich shops must keep their prices low in order to attract customers. However, if a city has only one sandwich shop (and no other restaurants selling sandwiches), the shop can charge higher prices for its sandwiches.

A wise manager periodically conducts a competitive analysis to see the level of competition in the area. A *competitive analysis* looks at the number of competitors, what they charge, how similar or different they are from one's own business, and how to keep customers from choosing the competition over one's own operation. If a competitive analysis shows that a competing business attracts lots of customers and charges low prices, then a restaurant manager may not be able to charge more than the minimum for her food. On the other hand, if a competitive analysis shows only one competitor, and that competitor has poor service and little business, the manager may be able to charge much more for her products.

Price Sensitivity.   Some products are extremely price sensitive, while others are not. A product that is very price sensitive will see a severe drop in sales from a small menu price increase, while a product that is not price sensitive will show no change in sales as the menu price increases or decreases. Restaurant managers typically know which of their dishes are not price sensitive, and a manager has the ability to increase prices on those dishes slightly while holding the line on the price sensitive ones to increase overall revenue.

Perceived Value.   One of the biggest sales drivers is perceived value. Most customers do not compare actual food prices so much as they look for value for their dollar. For example, a restaurant may charge 20% more than their competitors but serve 50% larger portions; that restaurant may dominate the market even though it costs guests more to patronize that establishment. The impact of perceived value is one of the reasons that restaurant portion sizes have increased over the past few decades. A restaurant can bring in substantially more revenue by adding just a few pennies worth of extra ingredients to a plate.

Of course, as obesity rates in America have made consumers aware of the impact of huge portions, restaurants have turned to alternative means to portray "enhanced" value. One of the most common approaches is to list an ingredient's origin. After all, "XYZ Bay Diver Scallops" are surely worth more than plain old "scallops," aren't they? If they are not inherently better, the fact that they are "special" because they come from a specific location enhances their value. Today, various market segments attribute value to the knowledge of an ingredient's provenance. Products with higher quality grades, with specific places of origin (especially those of local origin currently), and of certain animal breeds are just a few examples of ingredients that garner higher pricing.

Product Differentiation.   As mentioned earlier, product differentiation is what a manager does to set her product apart from those of her competitors. In the restaurant industry, "product" includes many components beyond food. Restaurants provide service and ambiance in addition to edibles. A restaurant may differentiate itself through exceptional service, a unique dining environment, spectacularly high-quality food and drink, large (or in some cases, small) portions, and even signature items that cannot be found elsewhere. While a signature dish may merit a lower food cost percentage than other items on a menu, sometimes a unique décor or style of service justifies raising all menu prices over those of the competition.

In summary, restaurants with differentiated products, perceived value in their products, price insensitive products, and little competition (which comes partly as a result of highly differentiated products) can charge more for their menu items than can a similar restaurant with a fairly commonplace product, little perceived value, and lots of competition.

6.2.1 Psychological Pricing

While all of the calculations earlier in this chapter implied that a menu or sales price should be the exact result of a mathematical calculation, in reality, those figures are rounded further before they are printed on the menu. The reason for the rounding, quite simply, is customer psychology. Guests are more comfortable with prices that end in the following digits: $0.00, $0.25, $0.45, $0.49, $0.50, $0.75, $0.95, and $0.99. While there is nothing technically wrong with pricing a menu item at $11.47, because people are used to seeing prices that end in certain digits (and $0.47 is not one of them), it draws their attention to the price. The last thing a manager wants guests to focus on is the price.

Different pricing strategies fit better with different types of restaurants. For example, an upscale restaurant typically uses whole dollars rather than dollars and cents for its menu prices. These restaurants know that their guests expect to pay top dollar for high-end service, and fractions of a dollar are more representative of operations that want to imply "bargain" over "luxury." At the other extreme, prices ending in "9" suggest that the customer is getting a deal. Since most customers focus on the dollars rather than on the pennies, $14.99 feels like it is in the fourteen dollar range—a bargain considering its actual value is closer to $15. Menu prices listing cents ending in 5 or 0 represent a middle-range restaurant; the restaurant provides value but it isn't excessively "cheap."

Earlier in the book, we discussed that it is not always necessary to round up to the nearest penny when conducting culinary math calculations. A manager will almost always round up the calculations before placing the final price on the menu. For example, a calculated menu price of $14.92 will become $14.95, $14.99, or $15, depending on the image the restaurant wishes to portray. Rarely, would $14.92 drop to a lower price. There are occasions when a manager decides to round down, but even then, the manager would only round down a penny or two. For example, a calculated sales price that works out to $1.01 might be listed as $0.99 for psychological reasons, but if the calculation were $1.10, the manager would likely not drop the price down to $0.99.

Because customer psychology is a critical element to encouraging sales, the menu pricing methods described in section 6.1 only provide guidelines or estimates. The exact menu price takes other pricing factors into consideration. Listing numbers with which guests are comfortable is definitely one of those factors.

6.3 CONTROLLING TOTAL FOOD COST AND TOTAL SALES

Thus far, the chapter has discussed food cost, food cost percentage, and sales primarily in terms of individual recipes and portions. This perspective is essential to determine a sales price for a given dish. However, once a menu's pricing is in place, the manager next turns her attention to food cost and sales on a much larger scale—to how the restaurant's total food cost, food cost percentage, and sales change from one day, week, month, or year to the next.

While a restaurant may use the food cost percentage system to calculate all of its menu prices, the actual monthly food cost percentage may vary from month to month.

For example, a restaurant may price all of its dishes using a food cost of 32%, but a comparison of actual revenue and expenses may show a real food cost of 35%. Such variation may be the result of larger-than-expected food costs, uncollected revenue, or a combination of the two. It is the manager's job to track any variance between predicted and actual financial figures to correct any problems before they completely erode the company's profit.

6.3.1 Calculating Cost of Food Sold

The figures for total food cost and total sales are not as simple as they might seem. For example, one might assume that a restaurant's monthly food cost is simply the value of the food purchased that month. However, that amount does not account for any food purchased the month before that is pulled from inventory this month or for any remaining food that is not used before the month ends. It also does not account for any food prepared but not intended for sale (such as employee meals or promotional comps) or for any food received "for free" from another department in a multiunit operation. To calculate a more accurate total for the cost of food sold, a bit more math is required.

But before we delve into the mathematics, a discussion of some of the factors that contribute to the food cost formula is in order.

Total Purchases. For a given period—a month, for example—the purchases are simply the dollars spent on food. (Separate totals are generally kept for beverages to calculate the beverage cost and beverage cost percentage discretely.) The totals generally come from purveyor invoices.

Inventory Values. To account for any food already in inventory or leftover in inventory, the manager must know the value of the inventory at the opening of the period and at the closing of the period. These figures are referred to as "opening inventory" and "closing inventory." In order to generate the information, a storeroom manager or other employee conducts a physical inventory count at the end of the period and assigns each item on hand a value. (How to do this is discussed in a later chapter.) Fortunately, the inventory count is only required once per period since the closing inventory for one period is the opening inventory for the next period.

Employee Meals. As a restaurant may purchase some ingredients to feed its staff, that food should be removed from the restaurant's food cost. In reality, that food is an employee benefit and thus a portion of labor cost. There are various ways to calculate the food cost for employee meals. Some operations prepare a separate "family meal," so they simply total the cost of the meal's ingredients. Others allow employees to order off the menu. In these situations, the restaurant can track which dish each employee orders and deduct from total food cost the cost per portion for those meals. Still other businesses simply allot a dollar figure per employee or per meal period for staff meals. In these cases, the chef only provides meals to the employees that fall within that dollar guideline. The meals may be specially made for staff or may come from a limited set of choices off the menu.

Promotions. Sometimes a manager wishes to provide a customer food free of charge to attract business or to build good will. This food should be removed from the food cost and placed in the promotion or marketing section of the budget. Promotions may be small, like a free tasting experience for a bride and groom planning a large wedding reception, or large, such as a sampling booth at a community fundraiser. If a guest has an unsatisfactory experience and the manager wishes to comp her meal or another dish, this also falls under the category of promotion or good will. A similar expense, sometimes referred to as a "write-off," is the cost of the ruined meal that a customer does not eat, such as an overcooked steak or perhaps a meal that fell on the floor before making it to the guest's table. Since the food is not sold, it is deducted from the food cost and tracked separately, often as "waste" or as part of the spice factor.

Transfers. While not all restaurants track transfers, multiunit properties often do. A *transfer* is the giving or receiving of food from one department to another. For example, a hotel with a bakeshop may provide cakes to the hotel's upscale restaurant. The restaurant does not pay a purveyor for the food it will sell, but the bakeshop, which does not sell the cakes itself, has paid for the cakes' ingredients. To correct this imbalance, both departments transfer the cost of the cakes' ingredients. The restaurant transfers *in* the cost of the cakes' ingredients, while the bakeshop transfers *out* the same cost. A transfer in adds the cost to the operation's food cost; the transfer out deducts it from the department's food cost. Transfers may occur between identical restaurants as part of a larger chain, between two departments in a hotel, or even between separate areas of the same restaurant. For example, liquor used for cooking may be transferred from the restaurant's bar to the kitchen, and lemons and limes may be transferred from the kitchen to the bar.

Steward Sales. While not all restaurants permit steward sales, some do. A *steward sale* is the purchase of an item by an employee at cost or at a minimal mark-up. These are different from employee meals. An example of a steward sale might be an employee who buys from the restaurant 10 # of raw steaks for a summer barbecue at home. The restaurant may allow the sale to boost employee morale and loyalty, and the employee enjoys the perk of paying wholesale prices for her steaks. Steward sales should not factor into the cost of food sold, so they are deducted from the food cost total.

Grease Sales. Not all companies are able to sell their grease or animal fat, but some restaurants are able to make a small amount of money by selling fat to another business for rendering into other products. Because the fat is sold separately from normal restaurant sales and not used in the production of food at the restaurant, its value is deducted from the total food cost.

In short, when food is removed from inventory and not sold to customers as part of normal foodservice sales, the food's ingredient value or cost is deducted from the operation's total food cost. When food is added to production but is not paid for (typically through a transfer in), that food's value is added to the operation's total food cost. Now we are ready to review the following two-step formula for calculating food cost, a.k.a. cost of food sold.

1. Preliminary Cost of Food Sold = Opening Inventory + Purchases − Closing Inventory

   (*Note:* Preliminary Cost of Food Sold is sometimes referred to as "Cost of Food Available for Sale" or "Cost of Food Issued.")

2. Cost of Food Sold: Preliminary Cost of Food Sold
    + Transfers In
    − Transfers Out
    − Employee Meals
    − Promotions and Write-Offs
    − Steward Sales
    − Grease Sales
    _____

    Cost of Food Sold

Example 6.6: A hotel restaurant purchased $82,000 worth of food in January. Its opening inventory was $5,200 and its closing inventory was $6,100. It transferred out $420 worth of prime rib to the hotel's deli for its roast beef sandwiches, and it transferred in $95 worth of bread from the hotel's bakery. Employee meals for the month were valued at $382, and there were $696 worth of food comped for promotions. The restaurant permits steward sales, and sold $481 worth of semisweet chocolate to an employee. (There are no grease sales at this establishment.) What is the food cost (cost of food sold) at this restaurant?

> *Step 1:* Preliminary Cost of Food = Opening Inventory + Purchases − Closing Inventory = $5,200 + $82,000 − $6,100 = $81,100
>
> *Step 2:* Cost of Food Sold = $81,100 + $95 (Transfers In) − $420 (Transfers Out) − $382 (Employee Meals) − $696 (Promotions) − $481 (Steward Sales) = $79,216
> Cost of Food Sold = $79,216

6.3.2 Total Sales and Food Cost Percentage

Determining total sales is much simpler than figuring out the cost of food sold. *Sales* (in this case, food sales) is simply the amount of money charged to customers for the food they have purchased. It can be a combination of both food and beverage sales, but many places segregate the two to track food and beverage percentages separately. The only revenue collected that would be removed from sales is money earned from steward sales, grease sales, and any other ancillary sales of non-food or -beverage products (T-shirts, mugs, etc.).

Once sales totals have been summed from the sales records, the manager can calculate the food cost percentage. As with individual costs per portion and menu prices, food cost percentage lets the manager know the ratio between the food cost and the sales dollars. Under ideal circumstances, the food cost percentage used to determine menu pricing matches the food cost percentage at which the restaurant operates as a whole. However, there is likely to be some difference from the standard food cost percentage used for menu pricing.

One reason for a difference between actual and planned (standard) food cost percentages is that the menu prices have been rounded for psychological reasons. Second, the standard food cost percentage assumes no theft, no waste from overproduction, and no spoilage. Third, because purveyor prices fluctuate, ingredient costs may be higher or lower than when the recipe was originally costed. Finally, the sales totals may be less than expected if customers do not all pay their bills or if employees do not turn over all of the guest payments to the business. These variables aside, if a manager is doing her job, food cost percentages should not vary greatly from month to month. Food costs and sales volumes may change, but their sizes relative to each other (i.e., FC%) should remain the same.

To calculate FC% for a department or business as a whole, use the formula:

$$FC\% = \frac{\text{Cost of Food Sold}}{\text{Total Sales}}$$

The cost of food sold and total sales must cover the same time period (the same month, year, etc.).

Graphically, the formula looks like this:

FC

FC% × Sales

When considered collectively for a department or business (as opposed to a single dish), the FC in this formula refers to the cost of goods sold calculation described earlier in the chapter. As with our other triangular formulas, simply cover the variable you wish to find and follow the calculations given with the remaining two variables.

The goal of a foodservice manager is to keep the actual food cost percentage as close as possible to the standard food cost percentage. While there will be some variance or difference between the actual and the planned or standard food cost percentage, this difference should be slight and within the previously agreed upon limits set by upper management. A variance from the budgeted food cost has a direct effect on profit. For example, if a restaurant spends an extra $10,000 on food above what it forecast, with no additional sales revenue beyond the forecast, the restaurant will bring in $10,000 less profit. In other words, every excess dollar that contributes to an increase in standard food cost percentage represents a dollar that is lost from potential profit. When actual food cost percentage rises beyond an operation's acceptable variance, a manager must investigate the cause to preserve future profits.

There are several possible reasons for a higher-than-expected food cost percentage, and each cause requires a different tactic to resolve the problem. In the case of theft, the manager must tighten security or ensure that current controls are being implemented properly. To correct excessive production waste, the chef needs to monitor employee production more carefully and possibly provide additional training. Spoilage will require a conversation with the purchasing manager and possibly a process adjustment; spoilage may also be the result of poor product rotation by the kitchen or storeroom staff. If the variance occurs because of purveyor price increases, the purchaser may need to change purveyors or product choices. However, if the market prices for certain products have risen across the industry, the manager may need to increase menu prices or to adjust portion sizes to maintain a certain food cost percentage. Sometimes the change in food cost is the result of new government regulations to which the restaurant must adhere; in those cases, too, the manager may need to increase menu prices or adjust portion sizes. Finally, when the cause of a too-high food cost percentage is missing revenue, the manager must investigate the source of the theft and improve controls to ensure proper revenue collection for each and every sale. In short, wherever the problem lies, the manager must make sure that all employees are following preset standards and that the standards are still appropriate. The manager may need to retrain employees or adjust the restaurant's standards to keep food cost percentage and profit on target.

Sometimes an actual food cost percentage comes out much lower than expected. This surprise is not always cause for celebration. If the savings comes from better purveyor pricing, reduced production waste and theft, or better revenue collection, then the manager should expect the lower food cost percentage to be achievable every month. In this case, the target food cost percentage should be adjusted accordingly in future budgets. However, the lower food cost may just as easily come from a failure to meet minimum production quality and quantity standards. For example, if a kitchen staff were to reduce portion sizes by 10%, or if the purchasing manager were to switch to a lower-cost, lower-quality product, food cost percentage would most certainly decline. But over time, customers might begin to resent the reduction in the quality and quantity of their food. They might choose to patronize a competitor instead. While a lower-than-expected food cost percentage may appear to be an improvement, in the long run, it may result in lost revenue for the business. Since banks only accept dollars and not percentages, a lower food cost percentage is not a good thing if it results in fewer dollars coming in overall.

In summary, an operation's food cost percentage is simply a measure for tracking the business's consistency in meeting quality, quantity, and efficiency standards. Variances are not necessarily problems, only red flags that require further investigation. If a manager's research turns up evidence that her company is meeting all standards and just performing better, then a variance is a good thing, and the food cost percentage goal should be changed for the future. However, if an investigation shows that the variance is the result of operational problems, then the manager must correct those problems before they ruin the long-term viability of the business.

6.3.3 Controlling Revenue

While much of this section has focused on controlling food costs to maintain food cost percentages, the percentages can be skewed just as much when revenue controls are not in place. Because "sales" is part of the equation in calculating food cost percentage, even small amounts of uncollected revenue will dramatically increase a restaurant's food cost percentage. Dollars lost because an employee fails to collect them properly from a customer may never be recovered. Simple controls, implemented by a well-trained manager, help ensure that every dollar that should be collected from a sale ultimately makes it to the restaurant's cash register.

Perhaps the easiest and most effective tool for controlling revenue is the use of a POS or point of sales system. POS systems are computer programs that integrate all of the operations of a restaurant. Servers enter food orders into the system and a printer or screen transmits those orders to the kitchen. Servers use the same system to generate guest checks, and managers review the computer data to sort sales across a range of factors—by server, by hour, by dish, by day, or by almost any other data the computer collects (see Figure 6.1). As long as the kitchen only provides servers food that is entered into the system, all dishes will be accounted for. Personal security codes, electronic ID cards, or biometric readers (see Photo 6.1) incorporated into the POS system ensure that the data entered into the system is attributed to the correct employee. Controls may be implemented that allow only a manager to remove an item from a guest's check. Thus, servers must have a legitimate reason for not collecting payment for all food served. While credit cards may be processed through the system, managers may require that cash go through a single person (perhaps a manager or designated cashier), so no server can pocket cash and appear to close out a guest check. Finally, because managers can track data by server, a manager can see if any particular server has a history of nonpaying guests. In such instances, the server may need retraining or replacement, especially if there is evidence that the server is using the nonpaying guest excuse to steal from the business.

Photo 6.1
Micros POS Touch Screen
with Biometric Reader
Source: Printed with the permission of MICROS Systems, Inc.

Employee Sales Performance

Employee	Location	Net Sales	% Sales	Checks	Avg Check	Guests	Avg Dining Time	Table Turns	Voids	Discounts	Service Charges
Brooke	Potomac Mills	1,370.09	14.2%	70	19.57	144	51.7	68	(22.22)	(82.64)	149.85
Lili	Potomac Mills	866.57	9.0%	48	18.05	89	42.1	48	(3.69)	(45.43)	99.34
Gary	Potomac Mills	859.60	8.9%	34	25.28	84	41.0	34	0.00	(14.99)	76.42
Nyemade	Potomac Mills	818.42	8.5%	31	26.40	83	40.1	31	(5.49)	(58.84)	85.11
Robin	Potomac Mills	785.68	8.1%	33	23.81	87	41.2	33	(13.54)	(69.40)	100.63
Donte	Potomac Mills	730.62	7.5%	25	29.22	75	38.6	25	0.00	0.00	96.74
Amber	Potomac Mills	533.02	5.5%	22	24.23	56	39.3	22	0.00	(32.96)	54.24
Melissa	Potomac Mills	520.76	5.4%	14	37.20	39	46.7	14	(5.99)	(8.99)	63.11
Christen	Potomac Mills	473.14	4.9%	20	23.66	49	47.0	20	0.00	(10.99)	47.89
Toni	Potomac Mills	445.50	4.6%	20	22.28	45	41.6	20	(3.99)	(13.99)	38.93
Alante	Potomac Mills	428.85	4.4%	18	23.83	49	65.1	18	(14.55)	(38.95)	36.38
Brian	Potomac Mills	423.23	4.4%	17	24.90	38	43.9	17	(4.58)	(8.45)	19.04
Summer	Potomac Mills	337.54	3.5%	14	24.11	32	38.5	14	(11.17)	(8.58)	16.20
Tiffany	Potomac Mills	332.39	3.4%	14	23.74	32	43.0	14	(6.99)	(10.50)	31.54
Lauren	Potomac Mills	331.71	3.4%	12	27.64	36	49.8	12	0.00	(11.99)	25.58
AM DELI AM DELI	Potomac Mills	243.78	2.5%	30	8.13	0	0.0	0	(4.99)	(117.14)	1.51
PM DELI PM DELI	Potomac Mills	134.22	1.4%	17	7.90	0	0.0	0	0.00	(57.10)	0.00
Rosa	Potomac Mills	45.93	0.5%	1	45.93	0	0.0	0	0.00	0.00	0.00

Figure 6.1
Sample POS Employee Sales Performance Report
Source: Printed with the permission of MICROS Systems, Inc.

POS systems offer a wonderful approach to controlling revenue, but not all food-service operations utilize a POS system. In these instances, managers must employ other controls on the flow of food and money through the restaurant. Servers may be required to use duplicate check pads or "dupes" to generate two copies of each food order. One copy stays with the server and ultimately goes to a cashier with payment. The duplicate goes to the kitchen. As long as the chef or expediter ensures that no food leaves the kitchen without a dupe, then the cashier or manager can reconcile kitchen dupes with paid checks at the end of a shift. Managers can utilize check pads that are sequentially and uniquely numbered and record the check numbers that are given to each server. Thus, a dupe in the kitchen that never makes it to a cashier (to generate payment) can be tracked to the server assigned that check's unique number. A server must have a compelling reason when payment is not made for food she has ordered from the kitchen. Checks can also be reviewed for any errors in addition or pricing if the restaurant allows for handwritten math calculations by the servers on the checks. Even without the assistance of computers, managers can and should incorporate revenue controls into their operations.

SUMMARY

There are various techniques for calculating the menu price of a dish. Some are based on food cost percentage, some on prime cost, and some on gross profit. It is also possible to set the menu price first, determine a corresponding food cost, and then to design a dish within those cost parameters. There is no ideal method for pricing menu items, but each of the approaches works well in different situations. Menu prices are somewhat flexible in that they can be adjusted on the basis of several factors, including competition, price sensitivity, perceived value, and product differentiation. Additionally, most managers price their menus with comfortable numbers rather than with the exact numbers calculated from menu pricing formulas. An operation's food cost for a given period factors in inventory valuation, purchases,

employee meals, promotions, transfers, steward sales, and grease sales. That food cost or cost of food sold is then compared with sales to yield a food cost percentage. The actual food cost percentage for a business will vary slightly from the company's standard food cost, but if the variance is too great, a manager must investigate the cause to ensure that all employees are following effective standards. Uncollected revenue impacts a business's food cost percentage, too. Revenue is best controlled through a POS system, but controls can be implemented using check pads and dupes. No matter which menu pricing technique, what food cost percentage, or what revenue tracking system is used, an effective manager must control food cost and revenue to hit the desired profit goal for a foodservice operation.

COMPREHENSION QUESTIONS

1. Using the food cost percentage method, what should the sales price be for a dish with a food cost of $4.55 and a food cost percentage of 31%? What should the sales price be if the restaurant wants to hit a food cost percentage of 30%?

2. A restaurant budgets for overhead expenses of $430,000 and a profit of $65,000 on the basis of sales of $780,000. Using the overhead contribution method, what is this restaurant's food cost percentage? What should this restaurant charge for an entrée with a cost per portion of $3.97?

3. A cafeteria uses the prime cost method to price its food. The direct labor cost for the chicken entrée is $0.56 and the food cost per portion is $1.12. If the cafeteria's price factor is 3.1, what is the sales price for the chicken?

4. A hotel uses the actual pricing method to price its casual restaurant food. The hotel budgets the restaurant's variable cost at 34%, its fixed cost at 21%, and its profit at 3%. What is the sales price for an appetizer with a food cost of $1.46 and a direct labor cost of $0.97?

5. A coffee shop needs to make a gross profit of $1.82 per beverage to meet its budget goals. How much should the coffee shop charge for a cappuccino with a per portion cost of $0.57?

6. A fast food chain employs the base price method for its menus. If the chain operates with a 41.3% food cost and it wants to sell all of its sandwiches for $3.99, what is the maximum food cost per sandwich that the chef may have?

7. List four factors that impact a manager's ability to charge a premium for its product.

8. A very basic restaurant does not provide employee meals, use transfers, or permit steward sales. What is its food cost for a month that has no promotions or write-offs if the month's opening inventory is valued at $3,310, its closing inventory is $4,170, and its purchases for the month are $9,722?

9. A catering company records the following data regarding food cost for March: opening inventory is $378; closing inventory is $144; purchases are $12,706; employee meals are $588; promotions are $831; and steward sales are $701. What is the food cost for this business in March? (Assume no other variables impacting cost of food sold are in play.)

10. A restaurant has $312,500 in sales for the first quarter of the year. Its food cost for the quarter is $98,750. What is the restaurant's food cost percentage? If the owner allows a variance of +/− 0.5% on its standard food cost percentage of 32%, is the restaurant doing well in the first quarter or does the manager have a problem?

11. List three possible problems that may cause a food cost percentage to be higher than the restaurant's standard. List two possible problems that may cause a food cost percentage to be lower than the restaurant's standard.

12. A server is stealing from a restaurant. How might a manager identify the problem and the server if the restaurant has a POS system? How might the manager do this if the restaurant does not have a POS system?

DISCUSSION QUESTIONS

1. The chapter discusses some of the pros for each of the pricing methods. What do you think are some of the drawbacks or limitations of each of the methods?

2. Other than the factors listed in the chapter, what other factors might impact a restaurant's ability to charge a premium for its product?

3. Since a manager has flexibility in menu pricing, why does a manager need to cost out a recipe per portion at all?

4. Some restaurants offer the chef a bonus for coming in below the budgeted food cost percentage. Is this a good program for a restaurant? What are the risks? What are the rewards?

5. Most foodservice operations track food costs and sales separately from beverage costs and sales. Why do you think that is?

7
Beverage Control

Objectives

By the end of this chapter, you will be able to:

- Cost recipes and calculate cost per portion for beverages

- Calculate a beverage sales price given a beverage cost percentage and cost per portion

- Describe three techniques for reconciling actual versus standard beverage costs and sales

- Calculate the value of a bar's inventory

- List several methods for controlling beverage portions

- Describe the impact of ethics and liability laws on a manager's ability to grow revenue through alcohol sales

- List several ways that alcohol is commonly stolen from a bar and methods for preventing such theft

- List several categories of nonalcoholic beverages that are typical revenue generators for restaurants

While there are numerous differences between controlling beverages and controlling food, there are significant similarities. As with food, restaurants cost recipes for beverages, and they use that data to calculate an appropriate sales price. Beverage cost percentages, like food cost percentages, are monitored to gauge any variance between actual and standard costs and sales. Still, food and beverage are not identical. Alcohol is a highly regulated product that, unlike food, cannot be sold in infinite quantities to an individual simply because he wants more. Alcohol is also an easier target for theft, so it requires special controls to minimize pilferage (stealing) and to control portion sizes. Finally, whereas kitchen stations do not generally maintain large quantities of inventory outside of the storeroom, bars do. All of these factors merit a separate chapter focusing solely on beverage control.

The concerns over alcoholic beverages apply to all types of bars, even though hospitality businesses may serve alcohol from different kinds of bars. A *front bar* is a bar at which the customer sees the bartender preparing and serving the beverages. A *service bar*, on the other hand, operates behind the scenes primarily for servers, so customers do not see how service bar beverages are prepared. Catering departments or businesses may operate a *catering bar*, which typically has a smaller selection of beverages than the average front bar. Those selections may change, too, from one event to the next to meet the needs of different clients. Each of these types of bars has different constraints. For example, showmanship is a concern only when a customer can see the drink being made. High-tech equipment in place at a permanent bar may not be feasible for a caterer that needs a portable bar. However, for the most part, the control processes for beverages apply no matter what type of bar a foodservice business operates. While the biggest concerns surrounding beverages apply mainly to alcoholic drinks, beverage controls are extremely appropriate for nonalcoholic drinks as well.

7.1 SIMILARITIES BETWEEN FOOD AND BEVERAGE CONTROL METHODS

Food control and beverage control overlap in several areas. Both food and beverage utilize standard recipes. A standard recipe, whether for food or drink, includes an ingredient list with quantities, a procedure, a yield, a garnish (if there is one), and a serving vessel. For food, the "vessel" (plate, bowl, etc.) may not be given much thought. In some restaurants, for example, all entrées are placed on the same size and style of plate. However, beverages have a wide range of glassware options, and customers expect certain kinds of beverages to arrive in specific types of glasses. While some restaurants challenge tradition and experiment with various types of serving vessels, most serve a martini in a cocktail glass, sometimes called a martini glass. Wines are served in wine glasses, brandy in snifters, and whiskey shots (neat) in shot glasses. Guests would find it odd to see their shot of whiskey arrive in a beer stein, and a normal serving of wine would not fit in a shot glass. The type of glass in which a beverage is served is critically important to a standard beverage recipe.

A beverage standard recipe differs from its food counterpart in the flexibility of ingredient choices. A chef who lists russet potatoes in his mashed potato recipe would likely not permit new potatoes as a substitute. However, a beverage standard recipe calling for gin permits a bartender to use any brand of gin *that the customer requests*. Liquor is typically divided into two types: call and well. The *well* brand is the bar's standard go-to brand when a customer does not state a particular brand preference. A manager chooses the well brand in advance, and it does not change no matter who is mixing the drinks. It is called "well" because these liquors are commonly stored in a well behind the bar, below the sightline of the guests. Because the bottles in the well are not visible, a manager can use larger-format bottles, which are less expensive per ounce than their more common 750-mL versions. A *call* brand is one that a customer requests or "calls" by name. (Very expensive call brands are sometimes referred to as "premium liquors.") For example, when a customer asks for a "gin and tonic," the bartender uses the well gin, but if a customer asks for a "Tanqueray and tonic," Tanqueray, the call brand, must be used. The choice of liquor is determined by the guest, not by the bartender.

Because front bars are in the public's view, they often display their call brands to encourage sales of their high-end liquors (see Photo 7.1). In some operations, service

Photo 7.1

Bar with Call-Brand Liquors on Display

Source: © foto.fritz/Shutterstock.

bars stock only well brands, so a server in such a restaurant must go to the front bar to retrieve a call-brand drink. Catering bars with limited selections may have only one brand of a given kind of liquor, so guests may not have the option of requesting a call-brand drink.

Other than the flexibility in changing brands of ingredients, beverage recipes and food recipes look quite similar. This allows managers to use the same method to cost beverages that they use to cost food recipes.

7.1.1 Costing Beverage Recipes

To cost a beverage recipe, simply follow the process for costing a food recipe with one slight variation. Because beverages are not trimmed like vegetables or meats, one might expect beverages not to experience any yield loss. However, long-term storage of alcohol results in a small amount of evaporation loss, and the process of pouring drinks often results in some spillage even by the most experienced bartenders. The combined loss from evaporation and spillage is typically minimal—around 5%—for most drinks. Beer, when poured from a tap, is the one exception; it generally experiences a much greater yield loss. The appropriate percentage to use for loss due to evaporation and spillage is the one gleaned from each bar's individual experience. A manager must watch his bartenders carefully for a period of time to account for undue waste or theft, but if a two-week period shows that every keg of beer yields only 88% of servable beer, then the manager should use a yield percentage of 88% on its tap beer. Similar determinations can be made about liquor and wine. Just keep in mind that whole bottles or cans sold in their entirety do not experience any loss. A bottle of wine, even if it has lost 2 oz of liquid over decades of storage, is still sold as one bottle with no loss. A glass of wine, on the other hand, poured from a bottle and sold by the glass, experiences evaporation and spillage loss.

To calculate a yield percentage, divide the yield in ounces by the number of ounces in the original container. This provides the yield percentage in its decimal form, which can be converted to a percentage by moving the decimal two spaces to the right. This is effectively the same $Y\% = EP \div AP$ formula from earlier chapters.

Example 7.1: A manager observes over several weeks that, on average, a 750-mL (or 25.35 oz) bottle of wine yields 24.1 oz wine by the glass. What is the yield percentage for wine in this operation?

$$\text{Yield\%} = \frac{\text{Yield in Ounces}}{\text{AP Ounces (in container)}} = 24.1 \text{ oz} \div 25.35 \text{ oz} = 0.9507 \text{ or } 95.1\%$$

With a yield percentage determined, a manager can calculate the EP cost for a serving of any single-liquid beverage. To do so, use the following procedure:

Step 1: Convert the AP cost (from an invoice) to units that match the EP units. (EP units are most often ounces in the United States.)

Step 2: Convert the AP cost to EP cost by dividing by the yield percentage.

Step 3: Multiply the EP quantity (a.k.a. portion size) by the EP cost.

Example 7.2: Calculate the cost per portion for a 5-oz glass of wine, assuming the AP cost of the wine is $8/750 mL bottle and the yield percentage is 95.1%.

Step 1: Convert $8/750 mL to cost per ounce. (Recall, 1,000 mL = 1 L and 1 L = 33.8 oz)

$$\frac{\$8}{750 \text{ mL}} \times \frac{1{,}000 \text{ mL}}{1 \text{ L}} \times \frac{1 \text{ L}}{33.8 \text{ oz}} = \$0.316/\text{oz}$$

Step 2: Convert the AP cost ($0.316/oz) to EP cost by dividing by the yield percentage (in decimal form).

$$\$0.316/oz \div 0.951 = 0.332/oz$$

Step 3: Multiply the EP quantity by the EP cost.

$$5 \text{ oz} \times \$0.332/oz = \$1.66/glass$$

If the beverage involves more than one ingredient, it is best to use a recipe costing spreadsheet. The process is identical to the process for costing a food recipe, as Example 7.3 illustrates. Using the bold information in the martini recipe spreadsheet that follows, one can calculate all of the remaining information.

Example 7.3: Given the **bold** information for a martini recipe, calculate all remaining information.

Recipe: Martini						BC%: 15%
No. of portions: 1						Selling Price:
Cost per portion: $0.653						
Ingredient (with well brand specified)	Recipe (EP) Quantity	Yield %	AP Cost (from invoice)	Converted AP Cost (to match EP Quantity units)	EP Cost (converted AP Cost ÷ Yield % in decimal form)	Extended Cost (EP Quantity × EP Cost)
Gin (Beefeater)	$1\frac{1}{2}$ oz	95%	**$12.25/ 1.5 L**	$0.242/oz	$0.254/oz	$0.382
Dry Vermouth (Martini and Rossi)	$\frac{3}{4}$ oz	95%	**$6.80/1 L**	$0.201/oz	$0.212/oz	$0.159
Olive, garnish	2 ea	100%	**$1.40/14 oz (from kitchen test, 14 oz jar = 25 olives)**	$0.056/ olive	$0.056/ea	$0.112
Total						$0.653

As with a food recipe, the converted AP cost requires unit conversions. The keys to this conversion are the formulas 1 L = 33.8 oz and the given formula that 1 jar of olives contains 25 olives. (In fact, the jar size of 14 oz is irrelevant to the conversion.) The EP cost is determined by dividing the converted AP cost by the yield percentage (in decimal form, as always). Finally, the extended cost is the product of EP quantity times EP cost. The total is the sum of all extended costs. Since the recipe is for only one drink, the recipe cost is the cost per portion. The process is identical to that used for food recipes.

7.1.2 Determining Sales Prices

As with recipe costing, the price determination process for beverages is the same as that for food. While a manager can use any of the menu-pricing methods described in the

"Calculating Sales Price and Food Cost" chapter, the most common one to use for beverages is the food cost percentage method.

Using the graphic formula,

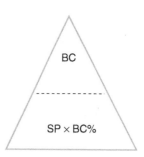

in which BC is beverage cost, SP is sales price, and BC% is beverage cost percentage, we can calculate sales price as BC ÷ BC%. The formula is the same as the food cost formula except that the term "food" has been replaced with the term "beverage."

Example 7.4: Using the data from Example 7.3, calculate the selling price for that martini. The beverage cost is $0.653 and the beverage cost percentage is given as 15%.

$$SP = BC ÷ BC\% = \$0.653 ÷ 0.15 = \$4.353 \text{ or } \$4.35.$$

On a menu, this drink price would likely be rounded up to $4.50, $4.75, or $5.00.

Although the advice for using standard recipes and a specific technique to calculate sales prices holds true, it presents a potential conundrum in the real world. In the typical bar, guests assume they can approach the bartender and ask for a drink made to any specification as long as the bar possesses the required ingredients. But if a guest asks for a made-up cocktail of say, Gran Marnier, rum, coffee-flavored vodka, and 7-Up garnished with a cherry, how much should a bartender charge? Without a standard recipe programmed into a computer, there is no set sales price that accounts for all of these ingredients in the ratio specified by the guest. To deal with this scenario, most operations have buttons in their POS systems for "well" and "premium" (or call) liquor. Sometimes those buttons lead to screens with more detailed choices; other times, they just provide a sales price on the basis of the number of ounces entered by the bartender. Assuming the aforementioned example contained a total of 2 oz of liquor, a bartender could simply enter 2 oz of premium liquor into the system to generate a sales price on the basis of the preprogrammed, estimated cost for the typical (or most expensive) premium liquors. The bar would simply write off the cost of the mixer and garnish, which is relatively cheap. If used too often, this function would be a red flag for managers to investigate potential theft by bartenders, but it is a useful tool for accommodating customers' special requests and for charging somewhat accurately and consistently.

7.2   BEVERAGE COST PERCENTAGE

Beverage cost percentages, like food cost percentages, are used to monitor compliance with production standards set by management. Unlike food, however, beverage cost percentages are almost always monitored separately for beer, wine, liquor, and nonalcoholic drinks. The reason for the category division with beverages is that most operations use different beverage cost percentages for different kinds of drinks. Restaurants price their beverages to maximize profits from beverage sales, and depending on the style of restaurant, each beverage category may have a different beverage cost percentage. (Tracking beer, wine, liquor, and nonalcoholic beverages separately also helps with government reporting. Some states require that costs and sales for each of these categories of beverages be reported separately to the state alcohol control board.)

In most cases, beverage cost percentages in a foodservice business are lower than the food cost percentages. Most guests who prefer an alcoholic drink with their meals will not switch to a nonalcoholic beverage for pricing reasons alone (as long as some reasonably priced options exist). For example, a restaurant that uses a 20% beverage cost for wine, can still offer some inexpensive wines well below $20 a bottle. Guests do not see the beverage percentage, only the sales price. Price-sensitive guests will purchase the lower-priced options, while others will opt for the more expensive bottles; all may pay the same percentage mark-up on the wine's wholesale cost. The same logic is true for beer and liquor.

[*Note:* Wine presents an unusual case generally not seen in other types of beverages. Wholesale wine prices can vary greatly from a few bucks for a cheap wine to hundreds or even thousands of dollars for a rare or boutique wine. If a restaurant operates with a 20% beverage cost percentage for wine, then each bottle's sale price is five times its wholesale price. This makes sense for a $2 bottle that sells for $10, but is a $200 bottle worth $1,000 simply because it is sold in a restaurant? To adjust for this potential problem, some restaurants operate with a dollar rather than percentage mark-up for wines over a certain price point. For example, a manager might decide that any wine over a $10 wholesale cost will simply sell for its wholesale cost plus $50 (or some other figure). This decision makes tracking by beverage percentage difficult, but it generates far more sales of higher-end wines, which at a profit of $50 or more per bottle is a better deal for the restaurant than selling several low-end bottles at a $10 profit.]

Cheap beverage pricing does not attract crowds for most business models (college-town beer and pizza joints and blue-collar bars excepted). For the majority of foodservice businesses, customers come for food quality and pricing, for atmosphere, for location, but not usually for cheap alcohol. With a low beverage cost percentage, a restaurant can make strong profits on each beverage sale without impacting business too greatly.

Monitoring employees through beverage cost percentage presents some challenges that do not arise with food cost percentage. Menus offer relatively few food choices when compared with the number of drink options in a typical bar. Counting the number of steaks left in inventory at the end of a kitchen shift is much easier than counting the number of ounces in each bottle at the end of a bar shift. Furthermore, a chef can observe and correct food portion errors much more easily than a manager can detect overpouring behind a bar. Cooks usually have their work double-checked by an expediter, while bartenders send their production to customers without a double-check. Finally, and perhaps most significantly, every time a server sells a 6-oz filet mignon, a manager knows how much money the restaurant should receive. When a bartender sells an ounce of liquor, the sales price will vary depending on whether the liquor is sold as a shot, with a mixer, or as part of a cocktail. Wine sold by the glass versus by the bottle and beer sold by the mug versus by the pitcher experience the same disparity. Because of all of these challenges, there are three common methods—the cost method, the liquid measure method, and the sales value method—for confirming employees' adherence to management standards and for identifying possible instances of theft.

7.2.1 The Cost Method

The cost method most closely resembles the process for monitoring food production via food cost percentages. Just as food cost is tracked by conducting an inventory each month, the cost of beverages sold can be calculated through a periodic inventory. Determining the value of an inventory for a bar is identical to that for food but for one exception—a bar actually maintains two inventories: one in the storeroom and one at the bar itself. Thus, to calculate the cost of goods sold for a bar, start with the formula:

Step 1:   Opening Inventory

+ Purchases

− Closing Inventory

+ Transfers In

− Transfers Out

− Promotions and Write-Offs
_____

Cost of Beverages Issued

This formula mirrors the cost of food sold formula without the components of employee meals, steward sales, and grease sales because none is applicable to a bar. In this case, the inventory, purchases, and transfers include not only the alcohol but also any mixers and garnishes used in the preparation of drinks. The inventory refers to the storeroom inventory, not the bar inventory, which requires a second step.

Step 2:   Calculate an adjustment for changes in the inventory at the bar itself as follows:

$$\text{Bar Inventory Differential} = \text{Opening Bar Inventory} - \text{Closing Bar Inventory}$$

Because purchases, transfers, and promotions are considered in the cost of beverages issued calculation, they are not included again here. The biggest challenge to valuing a bar's opening or closing inventory is determining partial-bottle value. It is easy enough to count bottles, but some bottles will be half full, some nearly full, and others nearly empty. Whether or not a manager chooses to estimate fractions of a bottle will determine the accuracy of the bar inventory's value. Modern establishments use electronic scales to determine the exact number of ounces in each bottle, which provides an extremely precise bar inventory. The value of the differential may be positive or negative as the bar may have more or less inventory at the end of the month than it did at the beginning of the month.

Step 3:   To complete the cost of beverages sold calculation, add the cost of beverages issued and the bar inventory differential. (If the differential is negative, you are adding a negative number—that is, subtracting the differential from the cost of beverages issued figure.)

$$\text{Cost of Beverages Sold} = \text{Cost of Beverages Issued} - \text{Bar Inventory Differential}$$

With the cost of beverages sold calculated, a manager can reference beverage sales figures to get a beverage cost percentage using the following formula, which corresponds to the food cost percentage formula:

$$\text{Beverage Cost Percentage} = \text{Beverage Cost (a.k.a. Cost of Beverages Sold)} \div \text{Beverage Sales}$$

To separate the cost percentages by beverage type (liquor, wine, beer, and nonalcoholic), a manager would need to determine the cost of goods sold for each of these categories. Wine and beer, unless the restaurant regularly mixes them with other ingredients, can be easily isolated. Separating the nonalcoholic costs from liquor mixers is a bit more challenging and requires extensive record-keeping, separate inventories for liquids to be used as mixers, or some other tracking mechanism. The sales value for each of these categories of beverage can be gleaned from sales records. Each percentage (e.g., beer percentage) can be determined by dividing that category's cost by its sales—for beer percentage, that would be Beer Cost ÷ Beer Sales.

Once a manager has calculated the beverage cost percentages, he can either compare this figure with historical data or with the standard cost percentage to confirm a bar's acceptable performance. Historical comparisons simply look from month to month to see if each beverage's cost percentages are consistent over time. For example, if a wine percentage for one month is 23%, it should be fairly close to 23% in subsequent months.

A more valuable but more time-consuming calculation is to compare the actual beverage cost percentage with the standard percentage that should result based on sales records. To do so, a manager begins with a list of total numbers of each drink sold over a given period (usually a week or a month). Then, using standard recipe costing spreadsheets, he calculates the cost that each drink sale represents. By totaling all of the costs expected from all of the sales, he then determines a standard beverage cost percentage. (Unfortunately, he cannot just assume the beverage cost percentage used to price drinks because rounding to make the menu prices comfortable throws off this figure.) Alternatively, he could compare the total standard cost, before converting it to a percentage of sales, to the actual cost of beverages sold as calculated from inventory. In either case, any variance between the actual and the standard should be minimal.

7.2.2 The Liquid Measure Method

A second method for confirming that the number of drinks prepared equals the number of drinks sold is to count ounces of liquor used. Using sales figures and recipe cards, a manager can determine the number of ounces of each liquor that should be "missing" from the previous day's or week's inventory. To conduct this calculation by hand is extremely time consuming and cost prohibitive, but a complete POS system makes it easier. Trying to measure the number of ounces that have been removed from a bottle of liquor typically requires a scale. However, if a bar uses computerized dispensers to pour the liquor for each drink, the computer can produce a daily record of the number of ounces of each beverage dispensed. That record should match sales quite closely except for spillage and promotional comps, which can also be tracked. Beer and wine ounces sold from bottles are easier to monitor by saving empty bottles, though computerized dispensers can be used for wine and beer as well.

7.2.3 The Sales Value Method

The third, and perhaps the most complex method for monitoring beverage sales variance is the sales value method. Using the logic that every bottle of alcohol represents a specific number of dollars in potential sales, a manager can calculate how much money should be realized when a given bottle of alcohol is consumed. By comparing inventory counts and purchases, a manager can track how many bottles of each beverage have been consumed over a given period and how much money should have been generated from the sales of those bottles. A comparison between anticipated sales and actual sales confirms how well the bar has performed.

Unfortunately, this theory has some complications when put into actual practice. Each ounce of liquor is not necessarily sold for the same price every time. For example, a straight shot of gin may sell for $4 when sold by the shot, for $6 when sold in a martini, for $5 when sold as a gin and tonic, and so on. Beer, sold at discounts by the pitcher versus by the glass, and wine, sold at a higher price by the glass than by the bottle, create similar problems. Happy hour specials make prices for the exact same drink vary based on the time of day they are sold.

One way to overcome this complication is to create a price adjustment for each type of beverage sold as it varies from a straight shot. Using gin as an example, if a gin shot sells for $4 and a gin and tonic sells for $5, then each gin-and-tonic sale requires that an additional dollar be added to the expected sales value. This adjustment must be made for each kind of drink, and the manager must make those adjustments on the basis of sales records for the entire period. The process can be a bit unwieldy.

Another way to overcome the challenge is to base the expected sales value from each bottle on the bar's historical average sales for that bottle. For example, if a closely supervised month reveals that every 100 oz of gin generates $350 in sales of gin-based drinks, then the manager can assume that each ounce of gin represents $3.50 in sales value ($350 ÷ 100 oz). As long as the sales mix remains fairly consistent over time, that average will be accurate. Once an average sales value is in place for each type of liquor, beer, and wine, a manager uses those figures to calculate expected sales from the consumed inventory.

One final approach to make the sales value method more accurate is to calculate a standard deviation from expected sales. Through this technique, a manager calculates the potential sales value of the inventory consumed assuming that all liquor sales are made as shots (or as bottles for wine or as glasses for beer). The total of all anticipated liquor sales dollars (beer and wine would each be calculated as separate categories) is added to yield a combined liquor sales value. This value is inevitably wrong because not all drinks are sold as shots. However, the percentage difference between the combined liquor sales value and the actual liquor sales value can be calculated. Assuming that the sales mix remains fairly consistent from month to month, the percentage difference from actual liquor sales will remain almost identical. Therefore, if the standard liquor sales value is 7% more than the actual sales value of liquor drinks during a test month, then the following month's anticipated liquor sales value should also be approximately 7% more than the actual sales value for that month. This same logic is followed for wine and beer.

Whether a manager uses a cost, liquid measure, or sales value method to confirm a bar's performance is irrelevant. What matters is that a method is used to ensure that alcohol poured generates the sales it should. When bartenders do not measure drinks properly or record sales accurately, a restaurant loses income that would otherwise go toward profit.

Unacceptable variances between actual and standard costs/usage/sales values are red flags for a manager to investigate. In most cases, the problem stems from employees not adhering to performance standards. Improper measuring of drinks may require retraining of bartenders. The unauthorized giving of free drinks or improper recording of sales may be viewed as outright theft and may require a more severe form of discipline.

7.3 BEVERAGE PORTION CONTROL

Portion control is one of a manager's greatest responsibilities. While *overpouring*, putting more alcohol in a drink than called for in a recipe, is not necessarily done with the intention of theft, it is no less costly to a business. Because liquor is used in relatively small amounts, a small increase in portion size can translate to huge increases in cost. For example, if a bartender pours $1\frac{1}{4}$ ounces of liquor into a drink that calls for only 1 oz, he is increasing the drink's alcohol cost by 25%. That quarter-ounce, only half a tablespoon's worth of liquor, may seem small, but it can decimate a bar's profits over time.

Some employees and many customers prefer for a bartender to *free-pour*. Free-pouring is simply dispensing alcohol from a bottle into a glass without the use of any measurement device. Experienced bartenders can be fairly accurate while free-pouring, but a manager has no way of confirming a free-pouring bartender's precision until the end of a shift, long after the drinks are sold. Through free pouring, a bartender can give a favorite customer a little extra and tailor a drink to a guest's tastes, but a manager cannot tell whether or not a bartender's overpouring is the result of an innocent heavy hand or an intention to steal. While customers like the showmanship involved in free-pouring, a manager has little control over portion sizes using this method.

The simplest, most low-tech way to control alcohol portions is to use a shot glass or a jigger to measure alcohol. Shot glasses may be purchased in various sizes for measuring to the rim or in one size with lines marking quarter-ounce intervals. These glasses work like measuring cups to help a bartender measure the correct amount of alcohol for each drink. A *jigger* looks like an hourglass (see Photo 7.2). It has two cups attached by their bases; each cup measures a different volume. Like a shot glass, a jigger functions as a measuring cup and can be purchased in a range of sizes, too. Shot glasses and jiggers, when properly used, help control portion sizes, and a manager can easily see whether a bartender is using these tools to measure every drink. Unfortunately, guests lose out on some of the showmanship of making mixed drinks when jiggers or shot glasses are employed.

Photo 7.2
A Jigger

Source: © Evgeny Karandaev/
Shutterstock.

Another tool to control portions is a pourer. A *pourer* fits on top of a bottle and, when used properly, clicks off once a certain amount of liquid has been dispensed. For example, if a liquor bottle is topped with a 1-oz pourer, the bartender can turn the bottle upside down and know that as soon as 1 oz is dispensed, the pourer will stop the flow of liquor. The pourer will not release another drop until the bottle is turned upright again. A pourer gives the guest the illusion of free-pouring even though the manager and bartender know that the portions are controlled. The one drawback to a pourer is that the mechanism usually only measures accurately if the bottle is held at the right angle. It is easy enough for a dishonest bartender to overpour if he wants to fool the system.

Automated dispensing systems and *integrated beverage control systems* take portion control completely out of the hands of the bartender. An automated dispensing system operates by connecting a series of tubes to a range of liquid ingredients (liquors, mixers, even other types of beverages if the management desires). When a bartender pushes a button to request a specific drink, the automated system dispenses the right amount of each liquid into a glass or other container per the preprogrammed recipe for that drink. In some operations, a *service gun* is used to deliver the beverage to the glass (see Photo 7.3). The gun is simply a handheld automated dispensing system that the bartender can move easily from one glass to another. An *integrated beverage control system* connects the automated dispensing system to a POS system. Thus, a bartender cannot get the machine to pour a drink until the drink has been ordered through the POS system and charged to a check. As long as only managers may delete an order from the POS system, a bartender will be unable to prepare drinks "off the record." Automated systems are an easy way for managers to ensure complete adherence to recipe standards and to minimize the possibility of theft. However, automated systems provide no showmanship whatsoever. As a result, some operations may use automated systems only for their service bar while using pourers in the front bar. Alternatively, a service gun may be used for making well drinks, while call brands are poured by hand to show the customer that the proper brand is being used.

Photo 7.3
A Service Gun for
Dispensing Beverages

Source: © Tana Lee Alves/Shutterstock.

Glassware plays a role in proper portioning, too (see Photo 7.4). If a bar only uses $1\frac{1}{2}$ oz shot glasses to serve shots to customers, then a bartender cannot serve more than that amount as long as he uses a shot glass. However, if a bartender were to serve shots in an 8-oz tumbler, it would be easy to overpour. In fact, the wrong glass might make a drink look small, while the right glass makes the portion look large. A martini served in a cocktail glass is typically filled to the rim, so the glass looks full. Beer dispensed into a 1-pt glass or mug helps the bartender and customer know that a proper portion has been served once the glass is filled. Wine is somewhat more challenging in that wine glasses are not meant to be filled to the brim. There must be sufficient empty space for the consumer to swirl the wine in the glass. Consequently, some businesses have taken to pouring wine into small glass vessels that resemble laboratory beakers and then pouring the wine from the beakers into the wine glass at the table. The beaker controls the portion size and the extra pouring at the table helps aerate the wine. Of course, a bartender could use any number of devices to measure the wine before or while pouring it into the service glass.

Photo 7.4
Various Glasses Matched
with Specific Drinks Can
Help Control Portions

Source: © Evgeny Karandaev/
Shutterstock.

7.4 ALCOHOL LAWS AND ETHICS

While purchasing for both food and beverage will be covered in later chapters, there are some parameters specific to alcohol that impact a manager's ability to buy and to sell alcoholic beverages. In the United States, these rules vary by state. Some states, called *license states*, issue licenses to purveyors to sell alcohol to bars, restaurants, and other retail operations. Restaurants may only purchase through licensed distributors, but the presence of multiple purveyors encourages competitive pricing. Even if only one distributor were to carry a certain brand of beer, wine, or liquor, a manager could just purchase a different brand elsewhere for a better deal. A *control state*, on the other hand, operates state-run stores. In these instances, a purchaser has only one option—purchasing from the state store. If the state store charges high rates, the manager must pay those rates or not carry those products at all. Some states allow for the purchase of wine and beer from purveyors, while liquor comes only from state stores. Depending on the state, a manager may be required to pay "cash on delivery" rather than to pay through a credit line for alcohol. These factors influence a manager's decisions in selecting brands and determining order quantities for alcohol.

Additionally, a restaurant or bar selling alcohol must possess an alcohol license. In some states, there are unlimited numbers of licenses available as long as the business owner qualifies and pays the license fee. In other states, only a limited number of licenses are permitted in circulation at one time. In these states, liquor licenses have a market value based on tight competition and may cost over $1 million. Restaurants in such situations may prefer a "bring-your-own" policy for guests to investing in a liquor license.

The selling of alcohol comes with significant legal and ethical responsibility. Legally, businesses may only sell alcohol to consumers of legal age (21 years or older); they may not sell alcohol to intoxicated guests either. Violation of these laws can result in the arrest of the server and the suspension of the business's alcohol license. Possibly more detrimental to a business are dram shop laws. *Dram shop laws* allow for an individual injured in an alcohol-related accident to sue not only the intoxicated offender but also the restaurant or bar that served him alcohol. If a customer is served large amounts of alcohol and then kills someone in a traffic accident on the way home, the restaurant will likely lose the lawsuit, its liquor license, and its ability to survive. For these reasons alone managers must monitor alcohol sales to ensure that guests are served responsibly. Minors and intoxicated guests must never be served. The proper portioning of drinks helps servers track a guest's consumption and avoid serving a guest to the point of intoxication.

From an ethical perspective, a manager must balance the need to generate profits from beverage sales with the need to serve customers safely. Rather than offering very inexpensive drinks and attempting to make large profits through volume, a business can increase its alcohol profits through upselling. *Upselling* is the encouragement of guests to purchase higher quality rather than larger quantities of alcohol. For example, if a customer orders a "vodka cranberry," the server can ask (by naming one or two premium brands), if he would like a call brand for the vodka. The call brand will generally garner a higher price and a bigger profit for the business. Through upselling, a manager can maximize beverage profits without compromising the safe environment of the bar or restaurant.

7.5   COMMON FORMS OF THEFT AT BARS

Unfortunately, bars are easy targets for theft from an unscrupulous employee. As control systems get more sophisticated, so do thieves. There is no foolproof system to ensure all sales are performed properly, but certain procedures and techniques help keep the honest people honest. Following are some of the more common means of stealing by bartenders:

Improper Measuring.   A bartender can steal from a business by overpouring or by underpouring. In overpouring, a bartender gives extra alcohol to a guest, perhaps to reward a friend or to get a bigger tip from a customer. Either way, the extra alcohol is not the bartender's to give away. Underpouring may be a way to avoid the detection of overpouring. If a bartender underpours some drinks to make up for other overpours, a manager may never catch the scheme. Alternatively, some bartenders underpour and later sell the extra, accumulated alcohol off the record to pocket the money from those sales. Pourers and automated dispensing machines, as well as the use of proper glassware, help keep portion sizes consistent from drink to drink, though truly determined thieves will find a way to disable pourers and automated systems.

Giveaways.   A bartender can give unauthorized free drinks to friends or customers, possibly to get a bigger tip. A manager may comp a beverage, but a bartender should not be permitted to make that decision alone. While the employee gets a bigger tip for no additional work, the restaurant loses alcohol for no compensation. Taking a free drink for oneself is no less of a crime, and it comes with the added problem of an intoxicated employee. Giveaways are often noticed when actual versus standard costs and sales are reconciled—too late to prevent them. However, once a problem is detected, a watchful manager may be able to spot the offending employee. Additional controls include the use of integrated beverage systems and computerized restrictions that only allow managers to remove a charge from a bill.

Inaccurate Charging.   Bartenders can steal from a business and from customers by charging improperly for drinks. If a guest is overcharged, the bartender may keep the difference in payment as an unauthorized "tip." Guests who are undercharged, on the other hand, may provide bigger tips in return. Just as with giveaways, the restaurant does not collect the revenue it should from that sale. The most brazen form of inaccurate charging is simply billing for drinks that the bartender did not serve with the hope that intoxicated guests will not notice the extra drinks on the bill. The payment for these "phantom" drinks is kept by the bartender without throwing off the expected beverage sales percentage. Point-of-sales systems, which list the drink's name and its charge, help control against inaccurate charging. Integrated beverage systems help as well. If electronic systems are not used, at the very least a bartender should be required to write down each drink on the guest check as it is sold to eliminate the excuse that a bartender "forgot" to charge for a drink.

Playing with the Cash Register.   A cash register is only effective in tracking sales if a bartender enters each sale correctly and consistently. Sometimes, a bartender may leave the register drawer open to transact a few unrecorded sales. In these instances, a bartender charges a guest properly but never enters the charge into the register; he puts the money into his pocket rather than into the cash drawer. (The drawer is left open just to make change.) Similarly, a bartender may charge a customer correctly but enter a cheaper drink into the cash register to pocket the difference. For example, he might pour and charge for a call-brand drink but enter only a well brand into the system while keeping the difference for himself. Of course, a bartender can always pocket payment from a customer and just claim that the consumer never paid. To reduce the risk of these forms of theft, a manager should monitor to ensure that the cash register drawer is never left open. Tip jars should be placed far from the cash register, so an attempt to make change from a tip jar is harder to conceal. Point-of-sales and integrated beverage systems keep a bartender from writing one price on a guest check and entering another into a cash register. When feasible, each bartender should have a separate cash drawer that only the manager closes out at the end of a shift. This allows the manager to catch any discrepancies between the cash drawer and the register tape that a thieving employee may have missed. Some employees use innocent-looking devices— toothpicks, paper clips, matches—to keep track of uncharged transactions in the register, which the bartender intends to remove before the cash drawer is reconciled. Swapping out cash drawers and reconciling a register before a shift ends allows a manager to catch such a scheme.

Playing with the Inventory.   Another form of theft occurs when a bartender sells an entire bottle off the record and keeps the revenue from those sales. One way to pull off this stunt is to bring a bottle of liquor from home and to keep all transactions from that bottle off the record. No alcohol is missing from inventory, and no record of extra sales occurs. A bartender can also break a bottle after selling its contents and claim that it broke before it was opened. Another way to mess with the inventory is to dilute a bottle with water. If a bartender sells 2 oz of liquor from a bottle and keeps the money from those sales, he can add 2 oz of water back into the bottle to return it to its original volume. Many guests might not notice the change in alcohol strength, and the bottle still generates the same number of drinks for the business. Dilution is difficult to catch, but a manager or customer familiar with a drink's standard strength may be able to detect a diluted bottle through tasting. Automated dispensing systems are the best prevention against dilution. To protect against employees bringing in their own bottles, managers can mark all issued bottles with a stamp that does not come off. Requiring a *par stock*, or set number of each bottle at the bar, allows a manager to check for extra bottles or bottles missing the proper mark during regular inventory counts. Restrictions against employees bringing bags or coats behind the bar make it more difficult for a thief to sneak a bottle from home into the inventory. A *bottle exchange system*, in which the storeroom manager only issues a full bottle of alcohol when an empty bottle is returned, also helps to keep the par stock consistent and to make any "extra" bottles easier to notice. Bottles can be stolen directly from inventory, too, so alcohol is best stored under lock and key with only certain employees authorized to access the inventory. Requiring an employee to sign a requisition sheet both when submitted and when beverages are picked up helps keep an employee from just walking off with a bottle to take home.

While no control system can prevent every form of stealing, a strong system of controls can reduce the number of thefts that occur and make them easier to detect.

7.6   NONALCOHOLIC BEVERAGES

Much energy is spent by cost control managers on controlling alcoholic beverages, but for some operations, nonalcoholic beverages make up the majority, if not the totality, of beverage sales. Some operations may choose to classify "beverages" as only alcoholic beverages and to treat nonalcoholic drinks as food and as a part of food cost. However, like alcoholic drinks, nonalcoholic beverages typically operate with very low beverage cost percentages and represent enormous profit centers for the business. Fountain sodas, even when offered with unlimited refills, cost pennies per customer. Breakfast operations may sell coffee or tea to nearly every guest. In short, cost control managers are wise to provide nonalcoholic beverages their fair share of attention to maximize profits.

Nonalcoholic drinks are seeing an increase in artisanal versions. Some trendy restaurants now offer both coffee and espresso drinks; a few even highlight the small batch production and source of their boutique beans. Tea, once available in most restaurants only as bagged black tea, is now commonly presented, whether in a tea box or in a ceramic dish, as a selection of black, green, herbal, and flavored options. This range of varieties can be sold iced, too. Swankier places may even serve tea in its loose leaf form. Sodas, while still dominated by Coca-Cola and Pepsi, are available in a wide variety of flavors from small-batch producers. Some restaurants have taken to brewing their own root beer or mixing their own flavored syrups with carbonated water. A restaurant may choose to sell apricot, sour cherry, and pomegranate juices alongside the traditional standbys of orange, apple, and cranberry. Even water, given away for free just a few decades ago, is now an opportunity for additional income. Some restaurants sell bottled still and sparkling options; a few even filter and sell their own. Any restaurant catering to children needs to stock a steady supply of milk as well.

While many bartenders think creatively only with alcoholic drinks, liquid creations can be made and marketed lucratively with or without alcohol. *Virgin drinks*, those made without alcohol, may resemble their alcoholic counterparts, such as margaritas, daiquiris, and piña coladas. However, a restaurant can create signature virgin drinks using combinations of sodas, juices, syrups, or any other range of ingredients. No manager should take these opportunities for additional revenue for granted as a unique, desirable product almost always garners a higher mark-up.

The control systems for nonalcoholic beverages are somewhat less stringent but no less important for keeping costs under control. Standard glassware and portion sizes should be consistent throughout the operation. When a restaurant permits free refills on certain drinks, a manager should calculate the average number of refills per customer and base each drink's cost per portion on that number of servings. Because coffee and tea typically come with cream, milk, sweetener, and/or lemon, these costs should be included as well. Beverages used as mixers in alcoholic drinks should be tracked separately from those sold as nonalcoholic drinks.

Beverages should be stored under appropriate conditions and issued, like food, with requisitions. Employees should be instructed on the proper preparation and storage of beverages to avoid variations in standards or spoilage. For example, tea and coffee should be made identically no matter which employee prepares them, and standards should be put in place for how long brewed coffee may sit before it is tossed. Milk must be stored under refrigeration and thrown out after its sell-by date. Fountain sodas may be purchased in *premix* (ready to serve or just needing carbonation) or *postmix* (as syrups in need of both water and carbonation) forms, and employees should know how to replace carbonation tanks and syrups when they run out.

When a foodservice operation allows its employees to consume beverages for free at work (and most do), guidelines must be in place as to which beverages are permissible.

For example, employees may have unlimited access to coffee, tea, fountain soda, and tap water but not to hot chocolate, bottled sodas, or bottled water. Beverages removed from the workplace should be treated as steward sales to keep employees from stocking their home refrigerators on the company's dime. When proper attention is paid to marketing and controlling nonalcoholic beverages, they can become highly profitable revenue generators for any foodservice business.

SUMMARY

Beverages require standard recipes, recipe costing methods, and sales price determinations similar to those used for controlling food. Comparisons between actual and standard beverage costs and sales are made using one of three approaches: the cost method, the liquid measure method, or the sales value method. Portion control for beverages is critical as overpouring can represent a significant financial loss to a bar. Shot glasses, jiggers, pourers, automated dispensing systems, and service glassware all help keep drink portions standard. Alcohol laws vary from state to state, but those laws impact a manager's decision making from what to purchase and where to source it to how to maximize profits from alcohol sales because minors and intoxicated guests cannot be served alcohol. Theft is a common problem in bars. Bartenders can steal from a business through improper measuring, giveaways, inaccurate charging, playing with the cash register, and messing with the inventory. Control systems help minimize the likelihood of such theft. Finally, nonalcoholic beverages represent a significant opportunity for revenue generation in any foodservice operation.

COMPREHENSION QUESTIONS

1. Fill in the blanks in the recipe spreadsheet below.

Recipe: Margarita						
No. of portions: 1				BC%: 22%		
Cost per portion: $				Selling Price: $		
Ingredient	Recipe (EP) Quantity	Yield %	AP Cost (from invoice)	Converted AP Cost	EP Cost	Extended Cost
Tequila	$1\frac{1}{2}$ oz	95%	$14.45/1.5 L			
Triple Sec	$\frac{1}{2}$ oz	95%	$8.30/750 mL			
Lime Juice	1 oz	100%	$.34/lime (1 lime yields 1 oz of juice)			
Total						

2. A beer keg contains $15\frac{1}{2}$ gal of beer. From that keg, the bar is able to serve 108 pt of beer. What is the yield percentage for this beer?

3. What is the cost of a pint of beer from question 2, if the keg costs $140?

4. Using the information in questions 2 and 3, what should a bar charge for a pint of this beer if it runs a beer cost percentage of 26%?

5. How does calculating the cost of beverages sold differ from calculating the cost of food sold?

6. List the three methods used for comparing actual versus standard costs and/or sales of bar products.

7. List three devices that can be used to help control portions when mixing and serving alcoholic drinks.

8. What two categories of guests must never be served alcohol?

9. Define upselling.

10. List and describe three ways that a bartender could steal from a bar without getting caught (if there are no control procedures in place).

11. List five categories of nonalcoholic beverages commonly served in restaurants.

DISCUSSION QUESTIONS

1. Guests can order any drink they want from a bar, assuming that the bar has the ingredients. A bartender can use generic call or premium buttons to charge properly for the alcohol. If 10% of a bar's drinks are "special requests" like this, what financial repercussions might the bar experience? What steps could a manager take to mitigate the financial impact of accommodating lots of special request drinks?

2. A front bar only uses 750 mL bottles while the service bar in the same hotel uses only the cheaper, large format bottles. Should the hotel charge different prices for the same drinks if they are made at different bars? How would you determine the right price(s) to use?

3. Of the three methods used to compare standard versus actual costs and sales data, which would you select to use as a manager? Why?

4. A college-town beer and pizza place advertises $0.25 drafts on Thursday nights. How might such a place generate enough profit to stay in business? Why would it offer such inexpensive beer?

5. A bar manager goes on vacation for a week and finds that his costs are higher than they should be for the level of sales recorded during his week away. The assistant manager swears that none of the inventory is unaccounted for. He also insists that the cash drawer was never left open between sales and that no one brought any large bags or coats behind the bar. Assuming the assistant manager is telling the truth, what form of theft might be the cause of the increased costs?

6. For a college-town bar/restaurant, what kinds of nonalcoholic beverages should be promoted on the menu? Are there any other benefits to a strong nonalcoholic beverage menu besides making nonalcoholic beverage sales?

8

Control through the Purchasing Process

The cost control responsibility for an executive chef extends beyond recipe costing and menu pricing for food and beverage. The ultimate cost of a dish or drink is inextricably linked to the purchasing process. The prices for costing a recipe come from a purveyor's price list, but chefs do not typically place orders with a purveyor until they have decided what to put on the menu. The interaction between chefs and purveyors occurs simultaneously with the process of recipe creation and cost control. In fact, many chefs rely on purveyors for information regarding new products to add to a menu. A purveyor who provides useful information on products and trends can help a chef to increase sales. However, chefs must recognize that purveyors are in business to sell their products. A good purveyor looks for a long-term relationship based on mutual trust and support; a purveyor who only wants to make a quick buck from a single sale is best avoided.

Selecting the right set of purveyors is only one element of purchasing control. A cost control manager or chef must also determine which products to purchase, the appropriate quantities to order, and from which purveyor to source each item. There is no best purveyor or product for all restaurants, so each chef must consider the needs and constraints of her operation when making a purchasing decision. By devoting sufficient attention to the purchasing process, a chef can avoid overpaying for product, purchasing the wrong kinds of ingredients, or maintaining too great an inventory. When purchasing is done without the proper controls, foodservice businesses are destined to lose potential profit.

Objectives

By the end of this chapter, you will be able to:

- List the factors that go into making a purchasing decision on a product
- Write a product specification
- List the variables to consider when selecting a purveyor
- Describe a bidding process to obtain purveyor pricing
- Calculate quantities to purchase given forecasted needs
- Describe and contrast periodic and perpetual inventory ordering systems
- Conduct a make/buy analysis

8.1   SELECTING THE RIGHT PRODUCT

Novices may think that a purchaser's sole job is to find the cheapest price for a product, but far more goes into purchasing than price comparisons. Consider the last time you went shopping for clothes. Was price the only deciding factor? Chances are you reflected on not only the article of clothing (shirt, pants, socks) but also on the style and size before factoring price into your decision. Before you went shopping, you probably put some thought into where to make your purchase. Perhaps you chose the stores to peruse based on location, but store quality, brand, reputation, return policy, and service may all have factored into your decision to select one retailer over another. Price may have been important, but it likely wasn't the only consideration in your purchasing decision.

Food purchasers operate in the same way. They have to decide which purveyors to patronize as well as which products to purchase. Unless the chef personally performs the purchasing functions in a foodservice business, the purchaser does not select products to buy on her own. A purchaser must follow the guidelines provided by the chef. Just because a chef needs peas for a recipe does not mean that a purchaser can find any product considered a green pea and assume it meets the chef's needs. Several variables must be accounted for with every product decision.

Quality.   Many ingredients are available in a range of quality levels. Beef, a common example, may be purchased in prime, choice, or select grades. But beef is not alone. Most products come in a range of quality levels. Will the chef require that her peas be picked that same morning and show no signs of sprouting or deterioration, or is a little variation in quality irrelevant to how those peas will be used?

Processing.   Peas, like many products, come in fresh, frozen, canned, and several other forms. They can be purchased shelled or in the pod, uncooked, cooked, pureed, or dried, just to name a few processing examples. The kind of processing desired depends on the ultimate use for the product. Will the peas be turned into split pea soup, minted pea puree, or simply buttered peas? The result impacts the type of processing required for an ingredient.

Equipment and Staff Skills.   The equipment a kitchen has, as well as the skill level of the cooks, also affects the level of processing a chef will require from each of her ingredients. For example, an upscale restaurant with a fully stocked kitchen and a highly trained workforce may want only fresh ingredients to make a pea soup while a very limited kitchen with untrained labor may be better off purchasing their soup already made. There is no point in purchasing ingredients that the staff cannot prepare properly whether from deficiencies in culinary ability or from inadequate equipment.

Storage.   A restaurant's storage space also limits a purchaser's range of ingredient options. For example, if a kitchen only has one single-door, reach-in freezer (and no walk-in freezer), the purchaser may not want to fill it with frozen peas, especially if canned peas would suffice for the chef's needs. When a product cannot change processing format because of the chef's requirements, a purchaser may need to select a smaller pack size to fit a limited storage space.

Shelf Life.   The lifespan of an ingredient also impacts the choice a purchaser makes. In many cases, a product with a short shelf life is purchased in a quantity small enough to be used before it spoils. But that may not be possible with all products. Consider yeast. A small, upscale bed and breakfast may bake its own bread for its guests. However, even small amounts of fresh yeast may spoil when this B&B only needs a few rolls each day. In this case, dried yeast would be a better choice.

Brand and Mission. In this case, brand refers to the restaurant's brand, not the product's brand. Some restaurants promote themselves as sustainable, "green," and local. For these restaurants, the source of the ingredient may be an overriding factor in its selection by a purchaser. In a "local food" restaurant, the chef may insist that only peas grown within 100 miles of the restaurant be purchased. An organic restaurant may require that its produce be grown organically. A restaurant known for scratch-cooking or upscale meals may need to purchase only fresh ingredients with no processing at all. These are not minor concerns, for a restaurant found to be untrue to its mission can lose its customer base overnight.

Cost and Value. Finally, though it is often subordinate to the other concerns listed earlier, a product's cost comes into play when deciding what to purchase. Sometimes cost affects whether a product is purchased or simply left off the menu entirely. For example, if blight causes the cost of peas to jump to $30/#, a chef might decide to remove peas from the menu. Other times, value is more the issue, and it impacts a product's pack size or processing format. If a chef plans a bacon and pea puree under her halibut, she may select whatever form of pea is cheapest, with the belief that the bacon will overwhelm the pea flavor anyway. Alternatively, she may insist on frozen peas but buy them in a large case size versus a smaller one because the cost per pound is lesser. As long as a chef has the flexibility to modify her menu, she can always work in reverse to adjust her recipes and menu items on the basis of the costs of available products.

8.1.1 Product Specifications

Once a chef or purchaser has considered all the factors that impact her selection of a product, she translates this information into a product specification. A *product specification* is a guideline specifying the acceptable parameters for a product (see Figure 8.1). Sometimes called a "spec," a product specification may list the product's quality or yield grade, size, level of processing, brand name, origin, degree of ripeness, color, pack size, and container type. When a spec is shared with a purveyor, additional information regarding delivery schedule and credit terms may be included as well. With this additional information, the spec is sometimes called a *purchase specification.*

Specifications help eliminate any miscommunication about a product between a purchaser and a purveyor. Products that are close, but not quite right, can significantly disrupt a kitchen's operation or a business's profitability. For example, if a restaurant wants frozen, peeled, sliced apples for making apple cobbler and the purveyor ships fresh, Granny Smith apples, the restaurant's production schedule will be thrown off severely, even though the fresh apples could be used for the cobbler. Alternatively, a purchaser may have wanted a 10 # choice boneless beef rib roast, but instead she receives a 16 # bone-in prime grade rib roast because she simply ordered a "beef rib roast." To use this product when a restaurant's menu price is based on the boneless choice roast is a financial risk that can cause a restaurant to lose money, especially if the cooks are not skilled in meat fabrication. In both examples, the miscommunication could easily have been avoided through the proper use of product specifications.

Using industry terminology helps to reduce misunderstandings. The National Association of Meat Purveyors prints *The Meat Buyer's Guide*, which allows a purchaser to order by product number. These numbers offer extremely precise guidelines for purveyors, so a chef will know exactly what to expect when the product arrives at her door. Using well-defined terms, such as "prime" or "grade A," is also more likely to yield the desired end product than simply asking for "good quality."

> Product Name: NAMP #1179B—Beef Loin, Strip Loin Steak, Special
>
> Intended Use: Grilled Steak
>
> Grade: Choice
>
> Size: 16 oz (+/− 0.5 oz) per steak
>
> Packaging: Cryovac each steak individually. Deliver in cardboard with ice packs.
>
> Origin: Cattle raised in Pennsylvania, Maryland, Delaware, or Virginia only.

Figure 8.1
Sample Product Specification

8.2   CHOOSING PURVEYORS

How does a purchaser decide which purveyors to patronize? Not all food suppliers are the same, and a purchaser must select the ones that best meet her company's needs. It is a rookie mistake to choose the purveyor that offers the cheapest pricing on the basis of that information alone. Many foodservice operations screen purveyors in advance to create a list of approved suppliers. A purchaser can then purchase only from this list of approved suppliers (or request that a new purveyor be added to the list). At a minimum, a chef or purchasing agent should consider the following factors when deciding to approve a purveyor.

Pricing.   Rarely will a single purveyor have the cheapest prices on every product in its line, but its pricing should be competitive in general. If a purchaser can get better pricing for similar quality and service elsewhere, she may choose to avoid the more expensive company. Keep in mind, though, that pricing is only one factor to consider.

Product.   There is no point in having a purveyor that does not carry any of the products a chef needs. The restaurant's product specifications will let a purchaser know if a purveyor can supply the required goods. For example, if a quick-service cafeteria wants to purchase only premade frozen foods that can be warmed and served, a fresh seafood purveyor will not be able to assist the cafeteria in its mission. Sanitation is a component of product. There is no point in receiving product that is not wholesome, so a purchaser should confirm that a purveyor's warehouse, suppliers, and delivery trucks all follow high standards for food safety. It is not uncommon for an unlicensed individual to show up to a restaurant trying to sell game meat or wild mushrooms. Chefs will want to consider potential safety risks before deciding whether to purchase from such a person.

Service.   The level of service that a purveyor provides is one of the most important reasons to choose one purveyor over another. A good salesperson can be one of the chef's greatest assets by sharing information and by helping the chef in an emergency. A poor salesperson simply waits for an order from the restaurant and offers no assistance when there are errors in a delivery. A chef's needs rarely fit perfectly with a purveyor's standard operating procedure. How flexible a purveyor is with the chef indicates the level of service. A purchaser should have a reasonable expectation that she can place an order without great difficulty, that the order will arrive accurately per her specifications during the delivery window she requests, that the salesperson or company will assist her to correct any errors in delivery (or in ordering), and that the purveyor offers acceptable payment terms. There is no one-size-fits-all purveyor. When ordering, some chefs want to place an order online while others prefer to order by phone. Some want a weekly visit from their salespeople, while others rarely want drop-in visits. Whether a chef provides a two-hour window or a six-hour window for deliveries, she has a right to expect delivery during that window (and may reject orders that arrive outside the window). Some restaurants are able to pay cash on delivery, but many require credit terms from their purveyors. Some chefs can operate with once-a-week deliveries based on orders placed four days in advance; others need to know that an order can be placed any day of the week and delivered the following day.

While prices may look good on a spreadsheet, a purveyor may make prices better or worse on the basis of its delivery policies. Some chefs only need small quantities of food. A salesperson that can "break" a case and supply small quantities may save a restaurant money in spoiled food and high inventory costs. Delivery charges will increase the cost of a purveyor's products. Thus, a purveyor with a minimum order or additional delivery charge may be the cheapest only if a purchaser places very large orders with that purveyor. Some purveyors offer discounts for good customers, too, so a chef who buys large quantities of products and pays her bills on time should expect better pricing for that behavior.

Finally, some chefs may prefer to deal with as few purveyors as possible. Some broadline distributors can supply every product that a restaurant needs (though not necessarily in the desired case size). Other suppliers carry limited lines, such as only seafood or only pastry products. Alternatively, some chefs choose to purchase only locally. They may select locally based distributors. Restaurants that focus on serving local food have begun to partner directly with farms, so purchasers at these restaurants may primarily purchase directly from farmers rather than from distributors. Once a chef or purchaser has considered all of these factors, she can create her list of approved suppliers and, using an order sheet of required ingredients, begin to solicit bids to get the best pricing she can.

8.3 SECURING PRODUCT PRICING

Although a purchaser may have already selected a set of approved suppliers on the basis of their normal pricing, the prices for any given item will fluctuate, sometimes daily. To get the best pricing on an order, a purchaser should solicit exact prices from a purveyor through either a bidding process or a contract. Several methods for securing prices are as follows:

Open Bidding. A commonly used approach to secure pricing, open bidding requires that a purchaser contact several purveyors with her food order quantities and specs. Each purveyor then quotes the purchaser a price. Once the purchaser has collected the bids on each item, she decides which purveyor offers the best pricing. Sometimes this process is conducted by phone; at other times, it is done online. Because the process is open, the purchaser may share the bid information from other companies to try to negotiate prices down. Sometimes, a purchaser will split the order between multiple companies to get the best pricing on each item. Other times, the purchaser will simply go with the one purveyor who has the best pricing for the majority of the food order, which saves time in dealing with multiple purveyors and potentially saves on delivery charges.

Sealed Bidding. Like the open bidding process, a purveyor using sealed bidding solicits pricing from several purveyors on a given food order. However, unlike in open bidding, in sealed bidding the purveyors do not know the bids of any other companies. While sealed bidding does not allow a purchaser to negotiate pricing on the spot, it is viewed as fairer and free of favoritism. Therefore, in large organizations or government agencies, it may be required to avoid steering business to the company that bids last in the open bidding process. One version of this approach is for purveyors to fax or e-mail their list of prices for the week to their customers. Alternatively, a purchaser may enter the food order into the purveyor's computer database to see the pricing for each item.

Cost-Plus Purchasing.   Rather than soliciting bids on every item, a purchaser may choose to set up a relationship with a purveyor to pay the purveyor's cost plus a percentage. If a low enough percentage is negotiated upfront, the relationship can be quite advantageous to a foodservice operation. However, documenting a purveyor's costs is a challenge, and there is no incentive for suppliers to keep their expenses low. Still, there is significant time saved by not soliciting bids each week.

Contract Purchasing.   A purchaser may contract with a purveyor to pay a set price for a certain range of products in exchange for a given level of business, usually over the course of a year. In some cases, the purchaser can adjust the quantities purchased during the year; in other cases, she is locked into buying a minimum quantity. Chefs that partner directly with farms may do so through contract purchasing to encourage farmers to plant products specifically for that restaurant. Contract pricing protects a purchaser from price fluctuation, but if the price goes down, the restaurant does not realize those savings.

Other forms of purchasing are made partly for convenience and partly for cost savings—on a business's reduced labor, through increased buying power, or via reduced delivery charges.

Co-op Buying.   Sometimes, foodservice operations partner with other companies to pool their orders and to get better pricing than each could get separately. Negotiating the best price is left in the hands of the co-op purchaser rather than with each kitchen's chef. To make co-op buying most effective, the cooperating businesses must have similar needs. Thus, a group of hospitals would make an effective co-op, but a BBQ shack, an upscale restaurant, a school cafeteria, and a hospital would not likely overlap in many of their purchases. When a single company with multiple outlets forms its own co-op, it is called *centralized purchasing*. Centralized purchasing is especially effective for franchises, which all carry the same set of ingredients. Each outlet submits its order to the central purchasing agent, who usually gets volume discounts for her large order.

Standing Orders.   A foodservice operation with consistent business levels may choose to have a standing order with a purveyor. For example, the restaurant may order two cases of frozen hamburger patties to be delivered every week until the purveyor is notified otherwise. Alternatively, the purchaser may permit the supplier's salesperson to come into the storeroom, take inventory, and place an order to increase the inventory to a set level or "par." For instance, a medical company representative may visit once each month to restock the kitchen's first-aid kit; the representative charges only for the supplies that are added to the kit.

One-Stop Shopping.   A purchaser may decide to make all of her purchases from a single, full-line supplier to save on dealing with multiple salespeople. These large companies can supply almost anything, and they offer low pricing, especially when they get all of a restaurant's business. Having just one delivery to receive may also be a time-saver. However, when a purveyor knows that it has all of a company's business, it has no incentive to negotiate its prices down. Without periodic price checks, the purchaser will not necessarily know if she continues to get good pricing. Furthermore, larger companies are often less willing to break cases or to adjust delivery times to meet a client's needs unless that client is an exceptionally large purchaser.

Warehouse Buying.   For small businesses that cannot store large purchases or justify high delivery charges for small orders, warehouse purchasing may be the best option. Warehouses, like Sam's Club or CostCo, allow a business to buy a membership to the warehouse and purchase food and drink quantities of less than a case at prices that beat typical retail pricing (and sometimes beat wholesale prices, too). Warehouses do not deliver, but for small foodservice operations, an entire week's order may fit comfortably in an employee's car or truck.

No matter how a foodservice operation chooses to purchase its products, the complete food order, including products and quoted pricing, should be compiled and saved for the receiving process, so an employee can confirm that the invoice and the order match. When an order is placed with a purveyor, the purchaser should include each product's specifications unless the purveyor already has them on file. When a purchaser uses a new company or orders a new product from a current company, the specs should be communicated then, too.

8.4 CALCULATING PURCHASE QUANTITIES

Determining how much of a given ingredient to purchase is based on a restaurant's forecasted guest count and on its menu mix. Forecasting and menu mix will be covered more thoroughly in future chapters, but for now know that a *forecast* is a prediction, based on history, reservations, and a range of other factors, of how many customers a restaurant can expect each day. A *menu mix* is a prediction of the number of sales of each dish a chef can expect. Menu mix is often discussed as a percentage, as in 12% of all sales will be prime rib, but the chef can easily convert those percentages to numbers of each dish sold once she has a forecast guest count (see Figure 8.2).

Sales Mix Summary

Item Group	Gross Sales	Item Discounts	Sales Less Item Disc	% Sales	Qty Sold	% Qty Sold	Average Price
Total Item Sales:	2,344,149.34	0.00	2,344,149.34	100%	806,159	100%	2.91
FOOD	1,900,568.98	0.00	1,900,568.98	81.1%	680,751	84.4%	2.79
CHK/BF/SEAFD	318,684.80	0.00	318,684.80	13.6%	23,220	2.9%	13.72
Chk/Bf/Seafd 308	253,908.29	0.00	253,908.29	10.8%	27,556	3.4%	9.21
Chk/Bf/Seafd 309	187,783.68	0.00	187,783.68	8.0%	24,509	3.0%	7.66
NON ALCOHOLIC	179,819.35	0.00	179,819.35	7.7%	120,948	15.0%	1.49
Sand/Burgers 507	161,754.30	0.00	161,754.30	6.9%	21,407	2.7%	7.56
App 107	78,720.51	0.00	78,720.51	3.4%	15,538	1.9%	5.07
App 108	78,277.87	0.00	78,277.87	3.3%	7,022	0.9%	11.15
LIQUOR	219,643.17	0.00	219,643.17	9.4%	58,455	7.3%	3.76
LIQ 1.25 OZ	72,548.90	0.00	72,548.90	3.1%	13,605	1.7%	5.33
LIQ 2.50 OZ	50,617.75	0.00	50,617.75	2.2%	6,583	0.8%	7.69
LIQ 1.50 OZ	38,352.35	0.00	38,352.35	1.6%	12,069	1.5%	3.18
LIQ 2.00 OZ	30,522.69	0.00	30,522.69	1.3%	5,100	0.6%	5.98
BEER	178,608.63	0.00	178,608.63	7.6%	58,924	7.3%	3.03
DOMESTIC OTHER	48,122.60	0.00	48,122.60	2.1%	10,251	1.3%	4.69
DOMESTIC PINT	47,401.07	0.00	47,401.07	2.0%	25,738	3.2%	1.84
IMPORT BOTTLE	27,271.79	0.00	27,271.79	1.2%	6,646	0.8%	4.10
DOMESTIC BOTTLE	24,838.93	0.00	24,838.93	1.1%	7,061	0.9%	3.52
WINE	44,692.63	0.00	44,692.63	1.9%	7,923	1.0%	5.64
GL PREMIUM WINE	31,714.16	0.00	31,714.16	1.4%	5,437	0.7%	5.83
GL HOUSE WINE	11,100.20	0.00	11,100.20	0.5%	2,381	0.3%	4.66
BOTTLED WINE	1,878.27	0.00	1,878.27	0.1%	105	0.0%	17.89

Figure 8.2
Sample POS Sales Mix Report

Source: Printed with the permission of MICROS Systems, Inc.

Because certain ingredients deteriorate quickly, a purchaser may need to order them daily or every other day. Fresh fish, for example, is commonly ordered several times per week. Each order requires that the purchaser conduct an inventory and compare the amount on hand with the amount needed to meet the forecast. That doesn't include the time that it takes the purchaser to solicit bids and to place orders. Fortunately, most purchasers do not need to order every product every day. Most foodservice businesses divide their supplies into perishables (those ingredients that spoil in just a few days) and nonperishables (those ingredients with long shelf-lives). The process for calculating an order quantity for a perishable ingredient differs greatly from the process for determining a nonperishable's order quantity. Having two separate processes also allows a purchaser to save time (and labor cost) by ordering the nonperishables infrequently.

8.4.1 Perishable Ingredients

Because perishable ingredients deteriorate quickly after purchase, it is imperative that a purchaser order only what the kitchen will need before the following delivery arrives. Thus, if an order will arrive on Monday and the next delivery can arrive as soon as Wednesday afternoon, the purchaser should order enough product to satisfy the needs for Monday, Tuesday, and the portion of Wednesday business that occurs before the scheduled delivery time. Many businesses will include a small buffer in case sales are larger than expected or in case a delivery truck is late. A purchaser also typically accounts for product currently in inventory and for the restaurant's expected use of that product before the upcoming delivery's arrival.

To calculate an order quantity, a purchaser must first know from a forecast how many guests are expected over the period the order covers. For example, a forecast may predict 120 guests on Monday, 135 guests on Tuesday, and 40 guests at lunch on Wednesday. If the food order must cover Monday, Tuesday, and Wednesday through lunch, this equals 295 guests (120 + 135 + 40). Next, the purchaser must know the menu mix for each menu item on a typical Monday, Tuesday, and Wednesday. For example, a restaurant's flounder served with green beans and carrots may consistently represent 14% of sales in the first half of the week. Using this percentage and the forecast number, a purchaser can predict how many flounder dishes the restaurant will sell. The formula for calculating the number of dishes sold from a forecast and menu mix is:

Predicted Item Sales = Forecast Guests × Menu Mix Percentage (in decimal form)

Example 8.1: A restaurant forecasts 295 guests. Generally, 14% of sales are flounder. How many flounder dishes should a chef expect to sell to 295 guests?

Item Sales = Forecast Guests × Menu Mix Percentage = 295 × 0.14 = 41.3

In this case, it is best to always round up to 42 servings of flounder, so a restaurant does not run short. In reality, the purchaser will probably increase the number by a couple of portions as a buffer anyway.

Once the purchaser knows the predicted number of sales for each dish, she uses the company's standard recipes to calculate total ingredient quantities. Those ingredient quantities are generally written as EP or edible portion quantities, so the purchaser will need to adjust them to AP or as-purchased quantities to place an accurate order. The purchaser or chef will use the AP = EP ÷ Y% formula to get those AP quantities.

Example 8.2: Given the simple recipe (from Table 8.1) that follows, which includes only the recipe's perishable ingredients, and the yield percentages, adjust the recipe to serve 42 portions. Then, calculate the AP quantities needed to prepare the adjusted recipe. (The flounder is purchased whole and filleted in-house.)

> *Step 1:* To solve this problem, create a chart that includes a conversion factor column (remember, CF = New Yield ÷ Old Yield), a new yield quantity column (so the recipe serves 42 portions), and an AP quantity column. The new quantity is the conversion factor times the old quantity. The AP

TABLE 8.1
FLOUNDER RECIPE

Flounder Entrée	Yield = 20 portions	
Ingredient	Quantity	Yield %
Flounder fillet	80 oz	44%
Green Beans, trimmed	60 oz	94%
Carrots, julienne	60 oz	71%

quantity is the new quantity (EP) ÷ Y%. Following is the new chart with the calculations performed.

TABLE 8.1a
USING FLOUNDER RECIPE TO CALCULATE AP QUANTITY FOR NEW YIELD

Flounder Entrée	Old Yield = 20 portions			New Yield = 42 portions	
Ingredient	Old Quantity (EP)	Conversion Factor (New Yield ÷ Old Yield = 42 ÷ 20)	New Quantity (EP) (Old Quantity × Conversion Factor)	Yield %	AP Quantity (New Quantity EP ÷ Yield %)
Flounder fillet	80 oz	2.1	168 oz	44%	381.8 oz
Green Beans, trimmed	60 oz	2.1	126 oz	94%	134 oz
Carrots, julienne	60 oz	2.1	126 oz	71%	177.5 oz

Step 2: If we convert our ounces to pounds (by dividing by 16 oz/#), our food order to prepare this recipe is 23.9 # flounder, 8.4 # green beans, and 11.1 # carrots. All of these quantities must be rounded up to the nearest pound when ordering by the pound as they are the minimum quantities needed to prepare this recipe. A purchaser might increase the quantities even more to create a buffer. For example, the correct answer to the problem is 24 # flounder, 9 # green beans, and 12 # carrots, but a purchaser might order 26 #, 10 # and 13 #, respectively.

For a one-day event run by a caterer, Example 8.2 might be the end of the problem. However, for a restaurant, the purchaser will need to take an inventory of ingredients on hand, to deduct from that total the expected usage before the next delivery arrives (to estimate how much will be left when the delivery arrives), and finally to deduct the predicted quantity left when the delivery arrives from the usage needs determined in Example 8.2. These calculations allow the purchaser to account for her current inventory when determining the proper quantities to order. If she does not perform these calculations, she will eventually build up a backlog of inventory that spoils faster than the chef can use it.

Example 8.3: Using the scenario from Example 8.2, calculate a food order to be placed on Saturday afternoon for Monday morning delivery to meet the needs of the flounder entrée. The following data is essential. The restaurant forecasts 120 guests for Saturday night (which does not include Saturday's lunch business). On weekends, the menu mix tends to adjust slightly, and flounder only represents 13% of total entrée orders. The purchaser conducts an inventory during lunch service on Saturday (after the lunch shift has pulled their mise en place to their stations but before the evening crew has had a chance to remove their ingredient needs from the storeroom); that inventory includes the following: 174 oz flounder, 90 oz green beans, and 68 oz carrots. The restaurant is closed for business on Sunday.

To calculate the food order, perform the following calculations:

1. Determine number of portions of flounder needed to get through until the next order arrives. The "need" is just to cover the Saturday evening service. To do so, use Predicted Item Sales = Forecast Guests × Menu Mix Percentage.
2. Using the flounder recipe and Y%, calculate how much AP product (the kind found in a storeroom before it is taken to stations) is needed to satisfy the predicted number of sales from step 1. You will need to create a chart similar to Table 8.1a.
3. Calculate: Predicted Quantity Left When Delivery Arrives = Each Ingredient's Inventory Quantity − Predicted Usage before Delivery (from step 2).
4. Calculate: Final Order = Forecast Needs for Next Delivery Period (from Example 8.2) − Predicted Quantity Left When Delivery Arrives.

Here's how this works with the numbers:

Step 1: Predicted Item Sales = Forecast Guests × Menu Mix Percentage = 120 (Saturday dinner guests) × 0.13 (menu mix) = 15.6 or 16 portions of flounder will likely be sold on Saturday night (after the food order is placed but before it arrives on Monday).

Step 2: Calculate the AP product that will be required to make the forecast 16 orders of flounder for Saturday. (The "16" comes from step 1.) This tells us how much inventory will be used between the time the order is placed on Saturday and the time it arrives Monday morning. (The **bold** information is given from the earlier examples.)

TABLE 8.1b
USING FLOUNDER RECIPE TO CALCULATE AP QUANTITY USAGE FOR NEW YIELD (PREDICTED USAGE)

Flounder Entrée		Old Yield = 20 portions		New Yield = 16 portions	
Ingredient	Old Quantity (EP)	Conversion Factor (New Yield ÷ Old Yield = 16 ÷ 20)	New Quantity (EP) (Old Quantity × Conversion Factor)	Yield %	AP Quantity (New Quantity EP ÷ Yield %)
Flounder fillet	**80 oz**	0.8	64 oz	**44%**	145.5 oz
Green Beans, trimmed	**60 oz**	0.8	48 oz	**94%**	51.1 oz
Carrots, julienne	**60 oz**	0.8	48 oz	**71%**	67.6 oz

Step 3: Predicted Quantity in Inventory When Delivery Arrives = Inventory Quantity − Predicted Usage (from Table 8.1b).

Inventory Quantity − Predicted Usage for each ingredient is:

Flounder: 174 oz − 145.5 oz = 28.5 oz

Green Beans: 90 oz − 51.1 oz = 38.9 oz

Carrots: 68 oz − 67.6 oz = 0.4 oz

Step 4: Forecast Needs (from Example 8.2) – Predicted Quantity in Inventory at Delivery (from step 3) = Final Order.

(All units must match, so convert ounces to pounds by dividing by 16 oz/#)

Flounder: 24 # − 28.5 oz = 24 # − 1.78 # = 22.22 #

Green Beans: 9 # − 38.9 oz = 9 # − 2.43 # = 6.57 #

Carrots: 12 # − 0.4 oz = 12 # − 0.03 # = 11.97 #

While these answers for Example 8.3 (22.22 # flounder, 6.57 # green beans, and 11.97 # carrots) are technically accurate, in reality there are a couple of reasons for adjusting the numbers up. First, any restaurant will want a small buffer in case Saturday's usage is larger than forecast or business is brisker on Monday, Tuesday, and Wednesday. Second, purveyors do not generally sell products like these in fractions of a pound. Therefore, any purchaser would need to round them up to whole pounds anyway. Finally, the purchaser may know of a price point at which it becomes a better deal to purchase a higher quantity—a judgment call that must balance savings value against risk of loss from spoilage. For example, if green beans cost less when ordered as a 40 # case, the purchaser must recognize that the time it takes to use up that quantity of green beans may exceed the shelf life of the beans; in other words, some beans will spoil, making the case more expensive overall. If, however, the price break occurs at 10 #, the kitchen can probably use up the beans quickly enough to justify the larger quantity purchase. In this particular example, a purchaser might order 25 # flounder, 10 # green beans, and 16 # carrots (assuming no other dishes use these ingredients). At a minimum though, the purchaser would need 23 # flounder, 7 # green beans, and 12 # carrots—the correct answer to the problem on paper.

There are a few things to note about the aforementioned process for calculating order quantities for perishable products. First, the process is a bit unwieldy to conduct by hand, but the calculations can be automated. (Of course, you need to know how to do it by hand to set up a spreadsheet that calculates everything for you.) Second, this process is complicated by the fact that the inventory is taken before the stations have gathered their mise en place for the full day. The chef could require that all cooks gather the ingredients for the full day's needs before the purchaser takes inventory. This would eliminate the need to account for usage between the order's placement and its receipt. However, such efficiency is not always possible. For example, if the restaurant is open on Sunday but the purveyor is closed, the purchaser will need to place a food order on Saturday that accounts for Sunday's forecast usage. Finally, in smaller operations, as purchasers gain comfort with their job and with the restaurant's typical business levels, they may intuitively know how much product normally is used between an order's placement and its receipt. For example, a purchaser may learn over time that every Saturday night she uses 8–10 # flounder, so unless there is something unusual about a particular Saturday night (i.e., a special banquet serving only fish or a particularly large or small forecast), she will simply look for her 8–10 # flounder in the storeroom during inventory. If it is there as she expects, she will likely not adjust her Monday order to account for current inventory and Saturday usage (again, assuming the place is closed Sunday). If the flounder quantity is particularly high or low, she may adjust her order in her head based on personal experience. While "skipping steps" in the purchasing process may be a time-saver for an experienced purchaser, keep in mind that it still requires a purchaser to check the forecast guest count, to look for special events, to adjust for menu mix changes as the seasons change, and to confirm the accuracy of her mental system regularly. In short, this type of purchaser is not skipping steps at all; she is just performing mathematical estimates in her head instead of on paper. Until a purchaser or chef becomes extremely knowledgeable in her business's usage patterns, it is best to perform the complete process for calculating order quantities—though a computer helps tremendously.

In summary, when calculating an order quantity for perishables, the purchaser (or chef) should always

a. calculate the forecast ingredient need for the order period,

b. calculate the expected inventory usage between the time the order is placed and the time the order is received,

c. conduct an inventory count to determine how much inventory is on hand when the order is placed,

d. calculate the amount of inventory expected on hand when the order arrives by subtracting the expected usage (step b) from the current inventory count (step c), and finally,

e. calculate the order quantity by subtracting the inventory expected on hand when the order arrives (step d) from the forecast ingredient need (step a).

8.4.2 Nonperishable Ingredients

Nonperishable ingredients require a very different process for calculating an ingredient's order quantity. These ingredients last for long periods of time, so a purchaser can save time and money by not ordering them more than once or twice per week (and sometimes as infrequently as once per month if storeroom space permits). Furthermore, a purchaser is better able to take advantage of discount pricing in return for large-quantity purchases. For example, if a restaurant only needs 200 # flour in a given week, but there is a price break at 300 # flour, the purchaser can save money and know that the flour won't spoil. For nonperishables, spoilage is less of a concern than is tying up dollars in inventory or having enough storage space.

There are two common approaches to determining order quantities for nonperishables, and they vary with the type of inventory that a purchaser conducts. Many purchasers conduct an inventory of nonperishables on a regular schedule on the basis of product usage and storeroom space. That schedule may be twice a week, once per week, once every two weeks, or once each month. When the purchaser only counts the inventory on this schedule, it is called a *periodic inventory* and requires one method for ordering. However, some operations maintain inventory sheets or cards that are updated every time a product moves in or out of the storeroom. Thus, at any given moment of time, a purchaser could consult the inventory sheets to find the exact inventory (assuming no errors) at that moment. Such an approach is called a *perpetual inventory*, and it utilizes a different approach for ordering nonperishables.

The *periodic inventory* approach begins either with a forecast of expected ingredient usage (using the approach described for perishable ingredients) or, more commonly, with a history of the business's typical needs for an order period (the number of days between orders). Nonperishable ingredients vary somewhat in their usage from week to week, but an experienced purchaser knows the usage pattern and adjusts based on upcoming weather, holidays, season or menu changes, and any major shifts in the business forecast. Whether through forecast usage calculations or via business history, the purchaser determines the quantity of each ingredient needed for the upcoming order period.

The purchaser also establishes, often with input from management, how much of each ingredient the storeroom should have left on hand at the end of the order period. This quantity operates as a safety net in case usage is higher than expected or in case the next delivery is delayed. This safety quantity may be stated in units or in percentages. Without a safety net, a kitchen assumes the risk of running out of an ingredient before the next delivery. Ingredient shortages make certain dishes unavailable on the menu and severely disrupt the dining experience of the guests. Finally, the purchaser gathers one last bit of information—the quantity of each ingredient currently on hand in the storeroom—through a physical count of the inventory performed on a regular schedule, just before placing the order (each week, two weeks, month, etc.).

With all of this information in hand, the purchaser calculates the quantity to order for each ingredient using the following formula:

> Quantity Needed for Upcoming Order Period
> − Quantity Currently in Inventory
> + Safety Quantity Desired in Inventory at End of Order Period
> _____
> Quantity to Order

This formula is used separately for each ingredient.

Example 8.4: A restaurant orders nonperishables every two weeks. It uses roughly 125 # all-purpose flour each week. Management wants to have one 50 # bag of all-purpose flour in inventory at the end of each order period in case a delivery runs late. The purchaser is doing her periodic inventory today, so she can place an order for nonperishables. If she has 75 # all-purpose flour currently in the storeroom, how much all-purpose flour should she order for the upcoming order period? How many bags is that if she only orders in 50 # bag quantities?

Step 1: Recognize that the 125 # usage is per week, but the order period is every two weeks. Therefore, she needs 250 # (125 # × 2 weeks) to get through the order period. Next, use the formula described earlier:

Step 2:   Quantity Needed for Upcoming Order Period (250 #)
> − Quantity Currently in Inventory (75 #)
> + Safety Quantity (50 #)
> _____
> Quantity to Order (225 #)

She should order 225 # flour. Since the flour comes in 50 # bags, she must divide 225 # by 50 #/bag to determine the number of bags she needs.

Step 3: $$225\ \# \times \frac{1\ bag}{50\ \#} = 4.5\ bags$$

Since she cannot order half of a bag, she must round up to ensure a sufficient supply of flour. Thus, she should order five bags. While this will give the purchaser 25 # more flour than she needs, that flour will be deducted out as current inventory in the next order cycle. The overpurchase does not tie up inventory dollars for long, and unlike with perishables, the excess flour will not spoil during that time period.

To utilize the *perpetual inventory* approach, a purchaser must maintain a perpetual inventory card or spreadsheet for each ingredient in the storeroom (Figure 8.3). For each ingredient, the inventory card includes not only the date and quantity of each unit added to or removed from the storeroom but also its par stock, reorder point, and reorder quantity. Depending on the operation, *par stock* may be thought of as a minimum or maximum quantity desired for each storeroom item, but in the perpetual inventory method, par stock is always defined as a maximum desired quantity to have on hand in the storeroom. The *reorder point* is the number of units an ingredient must fall to in inventory to trigger an order of that ingredient. For example, if the reorder point for boxes of quinoa is 6 boxes, then once the inventory falls to 6 boxes of quinoa or fewer, the purchaser will place an order for quinoa. The *reorder quantity* is the amount of an ingredient that a purchaser will order when that ingredient reaches its reorder point.

The concept is simple enough. Use the inventory spreadsheet to track the inventory and place an order whenever the quantity of a certain ingredient in inventory reaches its order point. The reorder quantity, determined well in advance, lets the purchaser know how much to order. However, for this system to work properly, the reorder points and quantities must be calculated carefully.

Item: Tomato Paste, 6 oz can			Par Stock:	30
Purveyor: Name and Contact Information			Reorder Point:	12
Cost: $7.90/24 can case			Reorder Quantity:	24

Date	Order Number	In	Out	Balance
2/1			4	14
2/2			2	12
2/3			3	9
2/4	377304	24	3	30
2/5			4	26

Figure 8.3
Sample Perpetual Inventory Card

Par stock, though not calculated through an equation, must take into account several factors. Par stocks must be high enough to get through an entire order period but low enough to fit into the storeroom's allotted space and not to tie up too much money in inventory. While a cost control manager may decide to increase the frequency of deliveries to keep par stocks low, she must have enough time between deliveries to build up an order that meets the purveyor's minimum order requirements. Determination of the proper par stock for each ingredient accounts for all of these variables.

To calculate the reorder point, the purchaser must know the typical daily usage of each ingredient, the time needed to receive a delivery once an order is placed, and the desired quantity to have on hand as a safety net when the delivery arrives. With this information, the purchaser can determine the reorder point by performing the following two calculations:

Step 1: Quantity Needed between Order and Delivery = Daily Usage × Days between Order Placement and Delivery Receipt
Step 2: Reorder point = Quantity Needed between Order and Delivery + Safety Net

(*Note:* If the safety net is described in percentages rather than in unit quantities, step 2 requires multiplication, as follows: (Quantity Needed between Order and Delivery) × (1 + Safety Percentage in Decimal Form) = Reorder Point.)

Example 8.5: What is the reorder point for canned chick peas if the par stock is 37 cans, the daily usage is 2 cans, and the management wishes to have 8 cans in inventory on each delivery date as a safety net? It usually takes three days for the delivery to arrive once the order is placed.

Use the two-step process to calculate the reorder point.

Step 1: Quantity Needed between Order and Delivery = Daily Usage × Days between Order Placement and Delivery

Quantity Needed between Order and Delivery = 2 cans/day × 3 days = 6 cans

Step 2: Reorder Point = Quantity Needed between Order and Delivery + Safety Net

Reorder Point = 6 cans + 8 cans = 14 cans

The reorder point is 14 cans.

Once a purchaser has calculated the reorder point, she can figure out the reorder quantity. The reorder quantity is determined using the following formula:

Par Stock

− Reorder Point

+ Quantity Needed between Order and Delivery

Reorder Quantity

Example 8.6: Using the information in Example 8.5, calculate the reorder quantity for chick peas.

Par Stock (37 cans)

− Reorder Point (14 cans)

+ Quantity needed Between Order and Delivery (6 cans)

Reorder Quantity (29 cans)

The reorder quantity is 29 cans. The actual order quantity may be slightly less depending on pack size. For example, if the chick peas are packed 12 cans per case, then the purchaser should purchase 2 cases or 24 cans. Because par stock is treated as a maximum rather than a minimum, the purchaser will almost always round down rather than up when adjusting for pack sizes. This increases the frequency at which products must be ordered, but it does not create a space shortage in the storeroom. (In case you are thinking that rounding down may result in a product shortage, such considerations are taken into account when determining the par stock. If a sufficiently high par stock is selected, the purchaser will be able to round down safely without fear of creating a supply shortage, even if the time between deliveries is as long as a month.)

Which inventory method a business chooses to use, periodic versus perpetual, depends greatly on the availability of staff to handle the inventory and purchasing functions. Smaller operations, which normally have an employee who does purchasing only as a small part of her normal duties, will likely utilize the periodic inventory approach. Larger companies, able to employ full-time storeroom staff, are better able to implement a perpetual inventory system. Perpetual inventory is better for controlling a storeroom, inventory flow, and as a result, costs; however, maintaining a perpetual inventory requires an employee to be present in the storeroom to record the ingredients flowing in and out of the storeroom. This significant labor cost means that perpetual inventory is typically used only in larger operations that already employ a full-time storeroom clerk.

8.5   MAKE–BUY ANALYSIS

One question that chefs and purchasers often face when making purchasing decisions is whether to make a product from scratch or to purchase it premade. Three major costs go into the production of any edible product—ingredients, labor, and energy. The cost of ingredients is assessed using a recipe costing spreadsheet exactly as it is used to determine a dish's food cost per portion. Labor cost is calculated by monitoring employees in their production of a given dish. How much time does each employee require to produce a given recipe? What does each employee earn per hour, and do the employees receive benefits? Multiplying the number of hours an employee spends producing a recipe times the employee's hourly wages (including any additional benefits percentage, if applicable) yields the labor cost for the production of that recipe. Finally, if any additional energy costs (gas, electric, etc.) are incurred in producing a dish, those costs must be factored in as well. Divide the sum of all three costs—food, labor, and energy—by the number of portions the recipe produces to get the cost per portion.

Example 8.7: Calculate the cost per portion (labor, food, and energy) for a bowl of cream of asparagus soup. The recipe yields 20 portions and costs $37.07 for the entire recipe. The employee who makes the soup gets paid $9/hour (no benefits) and spends 45 minutes preparing the soup. The energy costs for the recipe are estimated at $2.00.

Step 1: Labor: $\frac{3}{4}$ hour $\times$ $9/hour $=$ $6.75 labor to produce the recipe

Step 2: Total Recipe Cost: $6.75 (labor) + $37.07 (food) + $2.00 (energy) $=$ $45.82

Step 3: Cost per Portion $=$ $45.82 $\div$ 20 portions $=$ $2.291 or $2.29

The cost to produce this dish from scratch can be compared with the cost of purchasing cream of asparagus soup, already made, from a purveyor. In this manner, a purchaser can determine which approach, to make in-house or to buy, offers better pricing.

Example 8.8: A purchaser can order frozen cream of asparagus soup from a purveyor. The purchased soup yields 12 servings and costs $25.90 per package. An employee, getting paid $9/hour (no benefits), can get the soup from frozen to ready-to-serve using only 10 minutes of her time and $1.75 worth of energy. What is the cost per portion for this cream of asparagus soup? Is it cheaper or more expensive than the soup made from scratch in Example 8.7?

Step 1: Labor: $\frac{1}{6}$ hour $\times$ $9/hour $=$ $1.50 labor to produce the recipe

Step 2: Total Recipe Cost: $1.50 (labor) + $25.90 (food) + $1.75 (energy) $=$ $29.15

Step 3: Cost per Portion $=$ $29.15 $\div$ 12 portions $=$ $2.429 or $2.43

Since the soup made from scratch in Example 8.7 is only $2.29 per portion, the frozen soup is more expensive than the scratch soup.

As shown, it is possible to compare costs to see whether it is cheaper to make a product from scratch or simply to purchase it. However, cost is not the only factor that should go into the make-or-buy decision. The first and most important consideration is quality. A restaurant would rarely want to replace its current product with something of noticeably lower quality. Customers may detect the difference, and some will stop purchasing that dish or cease patronizing the restaurant altogether. Any change that drives away business is seldom a good one. In addition to cost and quality, a manager should consider space and equipment availability. For example, a restaurant might be able to make a higher quality chicken stock at a lower price than the purchaser can source from her purveyors. However, to do so requires the chef to purchase a 30-gal pot and to tie up at least two burners for half of the day. The chef would also need to create space in the freezer for stock as well as for chicken bones. After considering all of these factors, some chefs will conclude that it makes more sense to purchase the stock already made while others will opt to make the stock from scratch.

In a make-buy analysis, a chef or purchaser should compare costs between scratch and premade products and should account for the variables of quality, space, and equipment. If a product can be sourced that meets the quality standards of the business at a comparable cost to the same product made in house, a chef may or may not choose to use the premade ingredient or dish instead of the in-house version. As with most other cost control topics, the right answer lies partly with the mathematics and partly with the manager's consideration of other factors.

SUMMARY

Food purchasers select products on the basis of quality, type of processing, equipment and staff skills, storage space, shelf life, the restaurant's brand and mission, and cost and value. To ensure that a purveyor provides the right product, a purchaser creates product specifications or "specs." Specs are given to the approved purveyors, which are chosen based on their pricing, product lines, and service. Exact pricing for each product is secured through one of several approaches including open bidding, sealed bidding, cost-plus purchasing, or contract purchasing. Some operations will source products through co-op buying, standing orders, one-stop shopping, or warehouse buying. Deciding how much of a product to buy depends on whether that product is perishable or nonperishable.

Perishable ingredient quantity determination is based on forecast, menu mix, recipes, and yield percentages in order to purchase just the quantity needed for a short period of time plus a small safety buffer. Nonperishables, with their longer shelf life, can be purchased less frequently using the periodic inventory method or the perpetual inventory method. Finally, through the use of a make-buy analysis, a chef can determine if it is better to prepare a product from scratch or to purchase a premade product from a purveyor. By paying sufficient attention to purveyor and product selection and to product quantity determination, a purchaser is better able to control costs directly related to the purchasing function in a business.

COMPREHENSION QUESTIONS

1. List seven factors that should be considered when making a decision on product selection.
2. Pick a food ingredient (your choice) and write a product specification for it.
3. What three factors are most important when selecting a purveyor?
4. Describe the difference between open bidding and sealed bidding.
5. A restaurant forecasts 150 guests for a given period of time. The menu mix typically shows that 19% of guests order chicken skewers and 23% order rib-eye steak. Both are served with baked potato and steamed broccoli florets. The chicken breast, which needs to be trimmed and cut into cubes, has a 91% yield. Guests are served a 5 oz portion of the chicken (precooked weight). The steak, on the other hand, comes in completely trimmed, portioned, and ready-to-cook. Broccoli is served as a 4 oz portion and has a 38% yield. Using this information, calculate how many pounds of AP chicken breast and broccoli must be ordered. Also, calculate how many units of steak and baked potato must be ordered to serve the guests during this time period. (None of these ingredients are used for any other dishes.)
6. A purchaser uses the periodic inventory method and orders food every two weeks. Her chef needs 220 # sugar for the next two weeks and, per company policy, she must target to have 50 # sugar left in inventory at the end of the two weeks. If she currently has 70 # sugar on hand, how many pounds of sugar

should she order? If the sugar comes in 25 # bags, how many bags does she need to order?

7. A purchaser uses the perpetual inventory method. Her chef requests a par stock of 200 # sugar because the chef uses 23 # of it each and every day. The purchaser needs to place an order two days in advance of delivery with her dry goods purveyor. Her chef also requests a one-day supply of all nonperishables be treated as a safety net—that's a 23 # safety net for the sugar. From this information, calculate the reorder point and reorder quantity for sugar.

8. A chef locates a premade tuna salad that is nearly identical to the one she makes from scratch in her sandwich shop. To make it from scratch, an $8.25/hour employee needs 20 minutes to prepare the tuna salad. The ingredients cost $12.18 and yield ten 4-oz servings. The chef can purchase the premade tuna salad at $26.99 for a 5 # tub. Calculate the cost per portion for the scratch-made and the premade versions. If cost were the only factor, should the chef make or buy this product?

DISCUSSION QUESTIONS

1. Imagine you are a purchaser for a large foodservice company. Two potential purveyors want your business. Both offer similar product lines and similar pricing. How do you handle this situation to get the best results for your company?

2. As a purchaser, you have a very good working relationship with a purveyor. In fact, it is so good, that the purveyor never complains about taking back an item you don't want and replacing it with the right product. For this reason, you haven't written well-defined product specifications; you know you can always correct an error later. Is there any potential risk or problem with this situation? What is the possible cost(s) to the restaurant for this relationship?

3. Imagine you are the purchaser for a mid-size, Mediterranean bistro. Of the many ways to go about purchasing and getting best pricing, which one would you prefer most? Why?

4. Which approach, the perpetual or periodic inventory method, appeals more to you? Why?

5. The chapter noted that with the perpetual inventory method, "the purchaser will almost always round down rather than up when adjusting for pack sizes." In what situation(s) might it make sense to round up? Are there any potential problems that may occur with rounding up?

6. A fine-dining restaurant has been making everything from scratch for the five years it has been open; it is the only operation in the area known for scratch-cooking. The management hires a new chef who does a make–buy analysis only to discover that she can get much better pricing on many of her products if she buys them premade. After a tasting comparison, she discovers that the premade products are of high quality and taste only slightly different from her own. Should she switch to the premade products? Would your answer be different if this decision took place when the restaurant first opened?

9
Receiving, Storage, and Issuing Control

All of the work that a chef or purchaser does to source the right products in the right quantities are for naught if the business does not follow proper receiving procedures. Most, though not all, purveyors are honest in their business dealings, but all of them make mistakes from time to time. Consider the following three examples. 1) A purchaser orders fresh spinach leaves for the restaurant's spinach salad, but the purveyor accidentally delivers frozen spinach. 2) The chef needs 2 pt of beautiful raspberries to use as a garnish on dessert. Knowing that some of them will not be pretty enough to use as a garnish, he orders 3 pt, but when the raspberries arrive, over half of them are squashed, molded, or otherwise unattractive. 3) A purchaser negotiates a yearlong contract to purchase boneless rib roasts at $7/#. Three months into the year, the order arrives as bone-in rib roast at a cost of $8/#. In each of these examples, whether the purveyor has delivered inappropriate products accidentally or purposely is irrelevant. What truly matters is that the business will suffer if the error is not caught immediately upon delivery. In the preceding examples, if the product is accepted, the kitchen may have to remove the spinach salad from the menu, serve a dessert with a nonstandard garnish, or lose time and money by boning out a rib roast that costs more per portion than the restaurant can afford. These challenges can result in increased labor and food costs as well as in dissatisfied customers and lost business. Such problems are more easily overcome if they are noticed and corrected during rather than after the receiving process.

Receiving is the method through which a foodservice operation verifies that what is delivered to the kitchen matches the quantity, price, and product specifications of what was ordered. Storage and issuing also play a role in cost control. Proper storage of ingredients helps to ensure that the business suffers minimal product loss from spoilage. A well-planned and executed requisition and issuing system further helps to control loss. While alcoholic beverages are highly susceptible to theft, a few additional controls specific to beverages help protect that inventory as well.

Objectives

By the end of this chapter, you will be able to:

- Identify the resources needed for a proper receiving area
- List the required steps for a thorough receiving process
- Describe the paperwork requirements for the receiving process
- List the storage procedures and locations for the proper storage of delivered food
- Describe the importance of FIFO product rotation
- Describe a controlled issuing system using a closed storeroom
- Calculate the value of storeroom inventory using one of several methods
- List several techniques for preventing theft from inventory
- List several controls specific to beverages that should be implemented in a complete receiving and issuing system

9.1   THE RECEIVING PROCESS

Depending on the size of an operation, receiving may be the responsibility of a full-time receiving clerk, or it may be a task given to an employee who has myriad other duties elsewhere in the kitchen. It may take all day long or less than an hour. It may be performed in a vast space reserved just for receiving or in a small section of the kitchen. Regardless of the form that it takes, proper receiving always requires the same functions: verifying the delivered items' quantities against the purchaser's order, confirming each product's quality against the operation's specifications, and making sure that the prices on the invoice match the prices quoted to the purchaser.

9.1.1   Required Resources for Receiving

To receive product in a foodservice business properly, a cost control manager must ensure that certain resources are in place. Perhaps the most important requirement is a well-trained employee to handle receiving. While larger operations may have a full-time receiver, many smaller businesses assign the job to a kitchen employee with other responsibilities. The receiver need not be the chef, sous chef, or even a line cook. A dishwasher or steward can handle receiving as long as he has training in the process and a strong knowledge of the restaurant's quality standards. A receiver must be able to identify foods that do not meet the chef's quality standards, to weigh products properly, and to complete the paperwork. The only person who should not handle receiving is the purchaser. Allowing a purchaser to both order and to receive products gives that individual too great an opportunity to steal products while fudging paperwork to avoid being caught. Having two employees—one to purchase and one to receive—reduces the ability of either to collude with the purveyor.

To do his job well, a receiving agent requires certain resources beyond training. Sufficient space to receive food is a must. The ideal receiving area is separate from the kitchen, close to the storeroom as well as to the loading dock or back door, clean and well lit, and secured from unauthorized employees. In reality, larger operations tend to do a better job meeting these requirements than do smaller ones. When a small restaurant permits receiving in the kitchen, the receiving agent must take extra care to ensure that the delivery driver does not meander through the kitchen and that the kitchen staff does not remove delivered food until the receiving process has been completed. Kitchen staff who interfere with the receiving process can cause costly errors.

A receiving clerk needs tools to check each item's quantity and quality. Accurate scales are essential. One scale should be able to weigh the heaviest delivered items within a fraction of a pound; a second scale should be able to weigh smaller items to a fraction of an ounce. To check an ingredient's wholesomeness, the receiving agent needs a thermometer as well as a table on which to work. He also requires a knife for cutting into product and a ruler for measuring items as part of the quality confirmation process. Hand trucks, dollies, and in larger operations, pallet jacks and forklifts are essential to aid receiving clerks as they move product from the receiving area to storage. Needless to say, basic cleaning supplies should be available to help avoid cross-contamination of products.

As paperwork completion is an essential component of the receiving process, a well-equipped receiving area will also have pens, paper, clipboards, and calculators. Large operations will even provide receiving clerks with a desk, computer, and file cabinets in the receiving area. In addition to these generic supplies, the receiver will need copies of the purchaser's order sheets, bid sheets (if they are used), and the restaurant's product specifications. A daily list of deliveries allows the receiving clerk to know which purveyors to expect each day, so he may contact an absent company. Any forms the receiving agent must complete should also be available.

9.1.2 Checking Products and Invoices

With the proper space, equipment, and paperwork, a receiving clerk is ready to begin the receiving process. The process shifts from purchasing to receiving the moment the purveyor arrives to the property. The purchaser should have already scheduled the delivery for a window of time during which the receiving agent has the time to check in all products properly. If the delivery arrives outside of that window, the receiving agent is within his rights to decline the delivery and to request it later in the day. The restaurant may be desperate for the product, so the receiver may need to accept it whenever it arrives. However, if the receiving clerk is too busy with other duties to perform the receiving job accurately, it is risky to accept the delivery and to hope that it will be accurate. Businesses may opt to seek replacement purveyors for those that miss their delivery window regularly.

When the delivery arrives, the receiving clerk gets an invoice (often in duplicate or triplicate) theoretically listing all of the products delivered with their quantities and prices (see Figure 9.1). That invoice is the bill to be paid by the foodservice business; confirmation of the invoice's accuracy is the responsibility of the receiving agent. The receiver goes through the invoice and places a checkmark next to a product listing after he has verified three things about that product: 1) that its quality meets the restaurant's specification standards, 2) that it is present in the quantity listed on the invoice, and 3) that the price and quantity on the invoice match the price and quantity from the purchaser's order and bid sheets.

Invoice			Invoice #: 3832		
Fay's Produce			Customer #: 199302		
111 W. Astor St.			Date: February 12, 2011		
Washington, DC 20002					
Phone: (800) 555-0789					
Fax: (202) 555-0790					
Deliver to:			Bill to:		
Hamachi Rama			Hamachi Rama		
717 F St. SE			717 F St. SE		
Washington, DC 20003			Washington, DC 20003		
			(202) 555-1762		
Quantity	Unit	Item	Unit Price	Extension	
2	case	Apples, cameo, 60 ct.	31.72	63.44	
1	12/1 Qt	Lemon Juice	38.22	38.22	
3	lbs.	Mushroom, Portabella	7.18	21.54	
3	case	Potato, russet 80 ct.	19.97	59.91	
1	case	Zucchini	21.15	21.15	
Total				204.26	
Received by: _____			Date/Time: _____		
Credit Terms: Net 60				Rep: Carla Ulsine	

Figure 9.1
Sample Invoice

To test quality standards, the receiving clerk should visually scrutinize products throughout a package. Produce, for example, is often packed to hide the worst-looking pieces at the bottom of the container. Pints of berries that look acceptable from the top may not pass muster when viewed from the bottom. In some cases, tasting or cutting into product may be appropriate. For example, receivers may need to cut into pieces of meat to confirm quality grades or to taste melons to verify ripeness levels. The receiving clerk should also check the temperatures and packaging of products. Potentially hazardous foods received in the temperature danger zone may not be safe to use; a receiving agent who accepts such products puts the business at risk of facilitating a food-borne illness outbreak. Damaged packaging provides clues to a product's quality as well. For example, damp cases of frozen foods suggest thawing and refreezing, which impact quality. Dented cans may have broken seals, making the food within them unsafe. Any food that does not meet the quality standards of the operation should be rejected. If a receiving agent has any questions on the quality of a product, he should consult the chef or manager rather than accepting a product of questionable quality.

(In the real world, sometimes a restaurant is desperate for ingredients, and the purveyor delivers a product that does not meet the operation's standards. What should the receiving clerk do? Ideally, he would return the product, but the chef or manager may overrule that decision. Unfortunately, the situation is a lose–lose for the business. If the kitchen serves substandard food, guests may notice, and the reputation of the restaurant will suffer. If the kitchen rejects the ingredient, some dishes may be unavailable for sale, again resulting in disappointed customers. The decision is rarely made lightly, but it is also a decision that the receiving clerk should never make alone.)

To verify quantity standards, the receiver should weigh any and all products sold by weight. Expensive items, such as meat and fish, are typically sold this way. While some operations allow their receiving clerks to weigh the entire shipment of meat for comparison against the total weight of all the meat ordered, the only truly accurate measure is to weigh only like items together (e.g., all strip loins together). If the packaging is minimal, the clerk may simply verify that the weights are close. If packaging is substantial, the clerk is wise to remove the packaging and to weigh the ingredient by itself. Fish packed in ice, for example, weighs much less once the ice is removed.

In addition to weight, the receiving agent should verify items sold by the count or by volume. An item listed as two cases of twenty-four 12-oz boxes should be present in exactly that format and count. Two cases containing twelve 24-oz boxes are not the same. Cream ordered by the quart can create challenges if accepted in half-pint containers. Cooks are slowed in their production if they must open four containers rather than one to get a quart of cream. In some situations, counting items is impractical. For example, a purchaser may order several cases of 80-count potatoes (i.e., 80 potatoes per case). The receiver and the purveyor's driver likely do not have time to count each case of potatoes while the driver waits, but a periodic spot-check helps to ensure that purveyors remain honest. Once the quantities of delivered products are confirmed against the invoice, they should next be checked against the purchaser's order sheets. If a purchaser orders ten cases of tomatoes and only two arrive, the restaurant may need to get an immediate supplemental delivery of tomatoes to get through service that day. (If the invoice lists more than two cases of tomatoes, the receiving clerk must correct that error, too.) Quick notification of shortages will help the purchaser or chef to take corrective action before the shortage creates a crisis.

When checking pricing, the receiving clerk compares the prices on the invoice with the prices on the purchaser's order form or bid sheet. They should match. While computerized invoices generally calculate extension pricing (quantity times price per unit) accurately, handwritten extensions should be verified by the receiving agent before approving the invoice.

9.1.3 Invoice Adjustments and Approvals

Unfortunately, rarely will a receiver's job go off without a hitch. Sometimes, a product is rejected for quality reasons. Sometimes, the quantity listed on the invoice is not what was ordered or what was delivered. Occasionally a price is not listed accurately. Each of these situations requires a different remedy.

When a product does not meet an establishment's standards, the receiving clerk should notify the driver of the issue. In most cases, the driver will complete a credit memo listing the item being returned, the reason for its rejection, and the dollar amount to be credited to the invoice (see Figure 9.2). The credit memo includes the restaurant's name, the date, and the invoice number. The receiving clerk should also make a note of the rejection on the invoice and ask the driver to initial it. A copy of the credit memo and of the invoice remains with the receiving agent. This is also the process that occurs if the product quantity is listed improperly on the invoice, or in industry terms, if the product is "short" the listed quantity. (Sometimes, a company does not issue credit memos but rather makes the corrections on the invoice alone. In these instances, it is critical to get the driver's signature next to each adjustment on the invoice.)

Fay's Produce 111 W. Astor St. Washington, DC 20003 Phone: (800) 555-0789 Fax: (202) 555-0790			**Credit Memo** Customer Name: Hamachi Rama Invoice Number: 3832 Date: 2/12/11		
Item	Quantity	Unit	Unit Price	Extension	Reason
Zucchini	1	cs	21.15	21.15	Quality
Driver's Signature:_____ Receiver's Signature:_____			Total: $21.15		

Figure 9.2
Sample Credit Memo

If the price on the invoice is not correct, again, the receiver should notify the driver. Typically, either the driver or the receiving agent calls the purveyor to sort out the problem. The purchaser may need to get involved as well. Until the dispute is resolved, the receiving agent should not sign off on the invoice. Doing so implies that the restaurant accepts the price as listed on the invoice. Once the parties have agreed to a resolution, the receiving agent may receive a credit memo for the adjusted price, or the restaurant may agree to accept the product at the higher price. Sometimes, the receiving agent may return the product, leaving the purchaser to source that ingredient elsewhere.

Finally, in those situations where a product's quantity is accurate for the delivery but does not match the purchaser's order form, the purchaser or chef must be alerted to the discrepancy. Sometimes, the purveyor is able to send out a supplemental delivery later in the day. Other times, the purveyor just doesn't have that product available.

In either case, the kitchen presumably needs the product, so finding an immediate source for it becomes a priority for the chef or for the purchaser. As long as the invoice is correct against the delivery, no credit memo needs to be issued, but the receiving agent will want to make a note of it on his report. Such tracking alerts a purchaser to a purveyor who routinely shorts products, which may necessitate a move to a different purveyor.

Once the invoice is confirmed and any credit memos issued, the receiving agent signs the invoice acknowledging his acceptance of the delivery and his verification of the invoice. A copy of the invoice stays with the receiver, and a copy leaves with the purveyor. Some operations employ an invoice stamp, which provides spaces for the receiver to sign, date, and confirm that all checks on the delivery and invoice have been completed. An invoice stamp may display a separate line to verify that price extensions have been confirmed and another line to sign once the invoice has been paid. Such a process allows a cost control manager to track the progress and control procedures for invoices through the entire accounting process.

In some companies, receiving clerks are required to complete a Receiving Clerk's Daily Report (see Figure 9.3). This report lists, item by item, all of the supplies that have arrived on a given day. The report includes quantities and prices for each item as well as columns to sort the products into one of three categories: direct purchases, storeroom purchases, and sundries. Direct purchases or "directs" go straight to the kitchen for immediate use; these are typically highly perishable products. Storeroom products or "stores" go to their proper location in the storeroom for issuing at a later

| Receiving Clerk's Daily Report | | | | | Date: 2/12/11 | | | | |
| | | | | | Prepared by: Josephine Hammond | | | | |
Quan.	Unit	Item	Rec.	Unit $	Ext.	Total	Direct	Stores	Sundries
		Fay's Produce							
2	cs	Apples, cameo	✓	31.72	63.44		31.72	31.72	
1	12/1	Lemon Juice	✓	38.22	38.22		38.22		
1	cs	Portabellas	✓	21.54	21.54		21.54		
3	cs	Russet Potato	✓	19.97	59.91		39.94	19.97	
1	cs	Zucchini		21.15	21.15				
						183.11			
		Rural Meats							
27	#	Pork Loin	✓	7.08	191.16				
						191.16		191.16	
		Paper and Soap Bros.							
2	cs	Paper Towel	✓	9.09	18.18				
1	cs	Degreaser	✓	49.97	49.97				
						68.15			68.15
Totals						442.42	131.42	242.85	68.15

Figure 9.3
Sample Receiving Clerk's Daily Report

(*Note:* If an entire invoice is going to one area, such as cleaning supplies all going to sundries, the total, rather than each individual item's cost, can be written in the proper column.)

date. Sundries are simply non-food or -beverage items, such as paper goods or cleaning supplies. By dividing deliveries in such a way, the cost control manager is better able to track food and beverage costs by the day. This daily report, along with all invoices and credit memos, is delivered to the accounting department, so proper payment to suppliers can be made.

Fortunately, many purveyors are interested in a long-term relationship with a foodservice business and thus, want to deal honestly with their customers. For many of these purveyors, the receiving agent can call his salesperson to report a problem in quantity or quality after the driver has left the premises. Sometimes, the salesperson will drive out personally with a replacement product when he arrives to pick up the return. Other times, the purveyor sends a driver to pick up the product and to issue a credit memo. However, for the establishment's own protection, it is best to locate these problems before the original driver departs. Some items cannot be returned for food safety reasons, and few products can be returned after a day or two has elapsed. The purveyor is never obligated to take back an ingredient once the receiver has signed the invoice and accepted the product.

9.2   FOOD STORAGE

Much effort goes into purchasing the right quantity and quality of ingredients and ensuring that those products are received properly. However, all of that work is wasted if the products are not quickly and properly stored after receipt. Seafood that arrives at 34 degrees loses its wholesomeness after sitting out on a warm loading dock for four hours. Liquor left unsecured for hours is begging to be stolen. Proper storage of received product is the next immediate concern of the receiving agent as soon as, if not before, the driver leaves the premises.

Refrigerated and frozen items should be the first to go into storage. Frozen products left at room temperature begin the slow thawing process immediately and can lose quality if left out too long. Refrigerated products, too, grow bacteria at an accelerated rate when left in the danger zone, so they must be moved quickly to a refrigerator. Depending on the ambient temperature, thirty minutes on a loading dock may be enough to ruin delicate greens. The faster refrigerated and frozen products are moved to their proper storage locations, the better.

To understand how to set up a freezer or refrigerator, it is important to know how these machines work. Simply put, these are enclosed compartments or boxes in which cold air (made cold by a compressor) is circulated by a fan to cool the entire enclosure. Every time the box is opened, cool air leaves the box and warmer air replaces it. Warm items placed inside the box work like little coals to heat the unit, while the compressor and fan work to cool it. The hotter and larger the quantity of items put in the box, the longer it takes for the compressor to cool everything back to refrigerator or freezer temperature. Most importantly though, culinary professionals must recognize that the only way an item in the refrigerator or freezer is kept cold is by contact with this chilled air. The most common way to ruin the effectiveness of a refrigerator or freezer is to block the circulation of air, either by obstructing the fan or by compacting items against the wall behind other items. Thus, to make a cooling unit as efficient as possible, keep shelves 6" off the floor and 6" away from the walls to allow air to move freely around all items. Do not store products on the floor. Never place anything directly in front of the fan, so the air can circulate around the entire enclosure. Finally, avoid placing large quantities of extremely hot items in the refrigerator or freezer lest they raise the ambient temperature into the danger zone for lengthy periods.

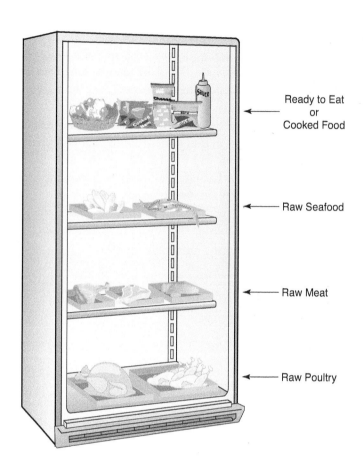

Figure 9.4
Diagram of Properly
Organized Reach-in
Refrigerator

A receiving clerk must store refrigerated products in a way that minimizes the risk of bacterial cross-contamination between ingredients. The clerk or other employee storing the food must place cooked ingredients over raw meat, seafood, or poultry to minimize the risk of dangerous liquids, like raw chicken juice, dripping onto something that will not be cooked again, such as roast turkey breast. In large operations, potentially hazardous foods may be stored in separate refrigerators from produce. ServSafe guidelines provide plenty of information on the proper locations for various ingredients in a refrigerator or freezer (see Figure 9.4).

Refrigerators should be kept in the 33°F–40°F range. Freezers should be set at or below 0°F. To minimize theft, cooling units should have locking capability, so they can be locked when unmonitored. Keys should be controlled, so only authorized personnel can unlock the units.

Products destined for dry storage should be stored after refrigerated and frozen products have been safely put away. As with refrigerators, dry storage areas should be arranged to allow for proper air circulation and to make it difficult for insects and rodents to contaminate the food. Consequently, shelving should be placed at least 6" off the floor and 6" away from the wall. Nothing should be sitting directly on the floor. Storeroom managers may wish to set up bins with tight-fitting lids to hold products shipped in rodent-penetrable packaging, such as bags of flour. Dry storage should be kept at a cool room temperature, 60°F–70°F, and at low humidity. Operations in very humid climates may require dehumidifiers. As with refrigeration units, dry storage areas ideally should have lockable doors to secure them when a storeroom worker is not present.

Chemicals and cleaning supplies should be stored last. These products must be kept separate from foodstuffs to avoid the risk of cross-contamination. Cleaning supplies must remain in their original, well-labeled containers, so employees do not accidentally confuse a chemical for an ingredient.

9.2.1 Storage Guidelines for All Products

One of the main causes of spoilage in a storeroom is improper stock rotation. Rarely will a new shipment of an ingredient arrive at exactly the moment the previous delivery's quantity is consumed. To ensure that every ingredient spends as little time as possible in storage, the receiving agent or other storeroom employees should rotate stock according to the *first-in, first-out* (or FIFO) method. To use the FIFO method properly, employees should store the newest shipments of products behind older shipments, so the oldest products (now located at the front of the shelf) are used first. They arrived first, so they should be used first—first-in, first-out. Products should be labeled with the date they arrived, in case there is any question as to which product is older. Ideally, items are also labeled with their price. This allows management to more easily value inventory.

A best practice for storage is to keep products in the same general location/shelf in the storeroom. This approach makes it easier for employees to locate products in a hurry. Additionally, inventory sheets can be organized in the order in which products are located on the shelves, making the counting of inventory far more efficient. When a storeroom is reorganized, the inventory sheets should be reorganized as well. In some operations, shelves are labeled, so storeroom workers know where to place each ingredient.

In some companies, management may require a storeroom clerk to complete a spoilage report, listing any ingredients (and their quantities) that have spoiled in storage. Such a form alerts a cost control manager to potential storeroom problems. Significant losses from spoilage may be a sign that products are not properly rotated or that the same ingredient is located in multiple locations, again resulting in newer products being used before older ones. Of course, excessive spoilage could also be the result of overpurchasing, poor forecasting, poor receiving, or an unethical purveyor. When spoilage reports demonstrate an increase beyond acceptable levels of spoilage, a cost control manager should investigate the cause and work with employees to solve the problem.

9.3 REQUISITIONS AND ISSUING

Once ingredients have been placed in the storeroom in their proper locations, they need to be transferred, at certain points, to the kitchen for ultimate use in food preparation. There is no single best approach to controlling this process. Some operations simply leave the storeroom open for all employees to gather ingredients as they need them. This system saves on the cost of a storeroom manager's wages, but it leaves the storeroom more susceptible to theft and, more commonly, disorganization. Other companies have a closed storeroom and require employees to make a written or electronic request for ingredients from the storeroom. The storeroom manager then fills the order and issues it to the kitchen (or other appropriate department). The product request is called a *requisition*, whether it is handwritten or communicated electronically (see Figure 9.5). The process of releasing the order to the employee who requested it is termed "issuing." While a formal requisition and issuing system allows for far greater inventory control, it comes at a price—specifically, the cost of employing a storeroom manager or clerk to issue products. Larger operations with extensive inventories are better able to justify this labor cost than a small restaurant can.

Requisition Form			
Department: Café			Date: 12/18/11
Quantity	Item	Unit Price	Extension
4 #	Cooked Ham, sliced	$2.74/lb.	$10.96
2 jars	Deli Mustard	$0.85 each	$1.70
6 each	Romaine heads	$0.79 each	$4.74
Total			$17.40

Requested by: _____   Order Filled by: _____

Received by: _____   Pricing completed by: _____

Manager approval: _____

Figure 9.5
Sample Requisition Form

Of course, small businesses are not entirely without storeroom control options. Chefs may open the storeroom only during certain times; outside of that time window, employees must request items from a manager. When the storeroom is open, the chef or other manager may keep a watchful eye on the storeroom to see what ingredients an employee is taking from storage. Monitoring product leaving the storeroom not only reduces the opportunity for an employee to steal but also helps a chef to catch possible overproduction before it starts. Finally, a chef may leave some parts of the storeroom open and other parts closed. Typically, only a few products are targets for theft, and they are the expensive ingredients, such as meat, seafood, or alcohol. A foodservice operation could allow employees to take personally most of the ingredients they need from the storeroom but require them to request, informally or in writing, the more expensive ingredients from a manager.

When an open storeroom is employed, conducting regular inventory counts becomes extremely important to catch theft or waste. An unusually high food or beverage cost for a week or month may be a sign that someone is stealing from the open storeroom. When this occurs, the chef may need to pay closer attention to the food leaving the storeroom. He may need to install surveillance cameras or review camera footage. While it is harder to prevent theft from occurring in the first place with an open storeroom, it is possible to recognize when it has happened and then to take steps to keep it from occurring repeatedly.

A requisition and issuing system is more complex than the open storeroom approach, but it makes it easier to protect an inventory against theft and spoilage. It also makes it easier to track daily food cost. In this system, an employee completes a written requisition. The requisition lists the products needed as well as the quantities requested for each ingredient. The form typically requires the signature of a chef or manager to ensure that the employee is ordering appropriate quantities of food. In some cases, employees are required to submit their requisitions in advance, so the storeroom clerk can organize his day efficiently. Conducting inventories, rotating stock, and cleaning the storeroom all take much longer when constantly interrupted to fill last-minute requisitions.

Once a requisition form is delivered to the storeroom, the storeroom clerk fills the order. He takes care to use the oldest products first to minimize spoilage risk. He also records on the requisition form (or computer) the per-unit and extended costs for each item provided. Since the form includes the date and department to which the products are being issued, a cost control manager can use the forms to calculate the food cost easily for each department each day. (*Note:* A department's food cost for a given day includes the issues from the storeroom *and* the directs sent from that day's delivery.) Depending on the operation, the per unit food cost may be taken from the prices written on the products or from the most recent invoices. While the food cost is not exact because the kitchen may use some products stored at a cook's station from the previous day, the cost is typically close when averaged over several days.

Once a completed requisition is ready for pickup, the employee picking it up from the storeroom should sign the requisition form to acknowledge receipt of the product. In a perpetual inventory system, the storeroom clerk will also deduct the issued products from the current written inventory or bin cards. (In a periodic inventory system, this step is eliminated.) When a physical storeroom inventory is conducted, it should reflect the products received from deliveries and the ingredients sent to departments through requisitions. The inventory is periodically conducted and reconciled whether a business uses the perpetual or the periodic inventory system. Significant differences between the physical inventory and the written, predicted inventory are cause for concern and may suggest a problem with theft or spoilage that needs to be corrected.

Not every item leaving the storeroom is slated for kitchen production. Sometimes, ingredients are being transferred to another department or to another company unit. When this occurs, the process is similar to the standard requisition and issuing system. The storeroom manager receives a form—in this case, it is called a transfer request—listing ingredients and their quantities to be transferred. It lists both the department receiving and the one issuing the products. The form also includes space for each product's unit and extended cost. Finally, the form requires the date and signatures from the employee issuing and from the one receiving the product. While this form looks remarkably similar to a requisition form, it should be used whether the business otherwise requires written requisitions (closed storeroom) or not (open storeroom). It becomes impossible to calculate a kitchen's food cost or a bar's beverage cost accurately if products move untracked between the two departments.

At the end of each day, all of the day's completed requisitions and transfer requests are sent to the cost control manager, who can use them to calculate approximate food and beverage costs for the day. Variations in food cost percentages (food cost as a function of sales) from day to day are normal because the kinds and quantities of products carried over on a kitchen station will vary daily, but when viewed across a longer stretch of time, like a week, food cost percentages should remain relatively consistent. Large fluctuations in weekly food costs or beverage costs are warning signs that a cost control manager should investigate the cause of the cost spike before it gets out of control. A jump in food cost could be the result of increased business, but it could also be the consequence of malicious employee behavior or of poor storeroom management.

9.3.1 Conducting and Valuing Inventory

Conducting a physical inventory on a regular schedule is one of the best ways for a cost control manager to assess the effectiveness of controls against spoilage and theft. Theoretically, a foodservice operation using a closed storeroom could assume that any purchases allocated to the storeroom and not yet issued to the kitchen are still in the storeroom. Of course, such an assumption is rarely accurate even in the best-controlled operations because inevitably some ingredients are lost to spoilage. Regularly conduct-ing an inventory alerts management to inordinately large product losses as well as to potential problems caused by carrying excessive inventory.

To conduct an inventory is a simple but time-consuming process. Typically, an operation enlists two people for the job—one to count and one to record. These employees may work from blank sheets or from preprinted inventory lists; some opera-tions utilize handheld computers or scanners to make data entry more efficient. A properly completed inventory sheet should include not only each item's name and quantity but also its unit and extended price. Every item in storage should be tallied and recorded. Many businesses require that items in production but yet unsold be counted as well. Consequently, it is best to conduct inventory when the restaurant is closed and when no deliveries are scheduled, so the counting can be done without dis-ruption to other workers.

Valuing the inventory is not as straightforward as counting each ingredient's quantity. The total extended cost of any product is:

$$\text{Extension} = \text{Number of Units} \times \text{Price per Unit}$$

But the price per unit is not always easy to determine. Imagine that a restaurant buys cans of diced tomatoes four times over the course of a month. If the price for canned tomatoes changes over that time period, how much is one can in inventory worth at the end of the month? Is it the value paid for the most recent canned tomato purchase? What if the inventory was not properly rotated? Should the price be based on the cost paid for that specific can or by some other method? There is no correct answer. The business's accountant will most likely require one approach to valuing inventory. Five of the most common techniques to value inventory are:

FIFO (First In, First Out).   This method assumes that the employees rotate the inven-tory properly. As a result, the cost for inventory is based on the most recent invoices and only progresses earlier in time if there is more product in inventory than can be accounted for with the latest invoice.

Example 9.1: A restaurant has 18 cans of tomatoes in stock. The restaurant pur-chased 12 cans at $0.95/can on June 5, 12 more cans at $0.98/can on June 17, and 12 more cans at $1.02/can on June 28. No other cans of tomatoes were purchased during June. Using the FIFO method of pricing, what is the value of the 18 cans currently in inventory?

The FIFO method requires that you start with the most recent invoice and work backwards. Thus, 12 of the 18 cans are valued at $1.02/can (June 28) and the remain-ing 6 cans are valued at $0.98/can (June 17). To calculate the total cost of the cans, you calculate two sets of extended costs.

$$\text{Extension} = \text{Number of Units} \times \text{Price per Unit}$$

$$12 \text{ cans} \times \$1.02 = \$12.24 \text{ (for assumed June 28 cans)}$$

$$6 \text{ cans} \times \$0.98 = \$5.88 \text{ (for assumed June 17 cans)}$$

Total extended cost is the sum of all the can costs or $12.24 + $5.88 = $18.12.

LIFO (Last In, First Out).   Sometimes, an accountant will prefer that the inventory is valued based on the earliest purchases in the inventory period rather than on the most recent ones. (*Note:* This accounting method has nothing to do with the actual product rotation; for food safety purposes, all food should always be rotated using the FIFO method.) In this case, the unit cost is based on the first invoice in the period and only progresses forward once the entire inventory on that invoice has been accounted for.

Example 9.2: Using the data in Example 9.1, employ the LIFO method to value the 18 cans of tomatoes.

Since LIFO starts with the earliest invoice, 12 of the cans are presumed $0.95/can (June 5) and the remaining 6 are presumed $0.98/can (June 17).

$$12 \text{ cans} \times \$0.95/\text{can} = \$11.40$$

$$6 \text{ cans} \times \$0.98/\text{can} = \$5.88$$

Total extended cost is the sum of all the can costs or $11.40 + $5.88 = $17.28.

Weighted Average.   To calculate the weighted average cost of an ingredient, a restaurant must add the total amount it has spent on that ingredient over the inventory period and divide that total by the number of units purchased during the same period. That calculation provides the weighted average price per unit for the extension formula. As Example 9.3 illustrates, the weighted average method requires a great number of steps and lots of data, so it is typically used only when an operation employs a completely computerized invoice and inventory accounting system.

Example 9.3: Using the data in Example 9.1, calculate the value of the 18 cans of tomatoes with the weighted average method.

Weighted Average = Total Cost over the Period ÷ Total Number of Units over the Period

Total Cost is:

$$\text{For June 5, 12 cans} \times \$0.95 = \$11.40$$

$$\text{For June 17, 12 cans} \times \$0.98 = \$11.76$$

$$\text{For June 28, 12 cans} \times \$1.02 = \$12.24$$

Total for the month is $11.40 + $11.76 + $12.24 = $35.40, which is the total for all 36 cans purchased.

$$\text{Weighted Average} = \$35.40 \div 36 \text{ cans} = \$0.983/\text{can}$$

Extension for the 18 cans still in inventory is 18 cans × $0.983 = $17.69.

Actual Cost.   The actual cost method is extremely accurate, but it requires that the receiving or storeroom clerk write each item's unit cost on the item itself as it arrives to the storeroom (i.e., each individual can or box, not just the case). This technique also necessitates multiple lines per item on an inventory sheet; six cans of the same product with six different prices would need to be entered on six different lines. Once each ingredient is listed on an inventory sheet with each quantity paired with its corresponding price, the extensions are calculated and totaled to get the extended price for the entire quantity of that ingredient. While the actual pricing method may be necessary for operations that do not rotate their stock properly, in a business with properly rotated inventory, the actual pricing method gives the same results as the FIFO method.

Most Recent Price.   The most recent price method simply uses the unit price listed on the latest invoice as the unit price for the entire quantity of that ingredient in inventory. Using the data from Example 9.1, the entire 18 cans of tomatoes would be valued at $1.02/can, the most recent price for tomatoes. This method is easy to use, but with highly volatile prices for a given product, the most recent price approach distorts how much was actually paid for the inventory. Still, proponents of this system note that it would cost the most recent price to replace those products in inventory. After all, if you paid $5 for a Picasso at a yard sale and found out that it was worth millions, is it fair to say that your "collection" is only worth the $5 you paid?

Once a pricing method is selected and an inventory conducted, a cost control manager can calculate the value of the entire inventory simply by adding all of the extension prices together. That total inventory figure becomes the closing inventory (or opening inventory, depending on one's perspective) value for formulas such as Preliminary Cost of Food Sold (Opening Inventory + Purchases − Closing Inventory). Without the completion of a physical inventory, a cost control manager would be unable to track food cost accurately or to evaluate and control potential problems in the storeroom. Even those operations that utilize a perpetual inventory system conduct periodic physical inventories to confirm the accuracy of the bin cards and inventory sheets.

9.3.2 Preventing Inventory Theft

Whether a foodservice operation employs a closed or an open storeroom, there are certain precautions that every business can take to reduce the risk of theft from inventory.

People.   Make sure that trustworthy, honest people are placed in positions of power. While a dishonest line cook can steal hundreds of dollars of product each month from an open storeroom, a clever storeroom clerk could wreak even greater havoc from his position of power. Assigning managers to monitor products leaving the storeroom helps reduce the risk that an individual, acting alone, will steal from the storeroom.

Locks and Cameras.   In most companies, foodservice or not, a determined thief will find a way around any security system. Most people just need a small reminder to remain honest. Placing high-priced items under lock and key are enough of a deterrent to keep the honest employees from helping themselves to a steak or a bottle of wine. Keys should be given to only a few trusted managers who can open the secured areas when necessary. Security cameras also help discourage theft. Knowing that they are likely to be caught on tape, most employees will not steal from the storeroom.

Paper.   While a paper trail does not usually prevent a theft, it can alert a manager that a theft has occurred. Major changes in food cost percentages are red flags that a spoilage or theft problem may exist. Employees who sign their names on requisitions should expect to be questioned by a manager should a loss occur.

Inventory Quantity.   One final way to control inventory more easily is to minimize the quantity of inventory on hand. When a storeroom goes through its inventory quickly, a stolen or spoiled item is sorely missed and noticed with the inevitable ingredient shortage. However, a restaurant that stocks months of supplies may not notice when a single ingredient is taken. A good rule of thumb is to track inventory turnover and to aim to turn over the inventory every one or two weeks. The method for calculating inventory turnover is as follows:

Step 1:   Calculate: Average Inventory $= \dfrac{\text{Opening Inventory} + \text{Closing Inventory}}{2}$

Step 2:   Calculate: Inventory Turnover $= \dfrac{\text{Cost of Food Sold}}{\text{Average Inventory}}$

(Recall that Preliminary Cost of Food Sold = Opening Inventory + Purchases − Closing Inventory. For the simplification of this example, we will assume no other costs from employee meals, transfers, etc.)

Example 9.4: A restaurant has an opening inventory value of $2,800 and a closing inventory value of $3,100 for the month of April. The purchases for April are $7,300. Calculate the Inventory Turnover for this restaurant.

Step 1:   Cost of Food Sold = Opening Inventory + Purchases − Closing Inventory

$$= \$2,800 + \$7,300 - \$3,100 = \$7,000$$

Step 2:   Average Inventory $= \dfrac{\text{Opening Inventory} + \text{Closing Inventory}}{2}$

$$= \dfrac{\$2,800 + \$3,100}{2} = \dfrac{\$5,900}{2} = \$2,950$$

Step 3:   Inventory Turnover $= \dfrac{\text{Cost of Food Sold}}{\text{Average Inventory}} = \dfrac{\$7,000}{\$2,950} = 2.37$

In this example, the restaurant turns over the inventory 2.37 times in April.

How does a manager determine if the inventory turnover rate falls within the guideline of turning over inventory every one to two weeks? Simply divide the number of days in the month by the turnover rate to see how many days pass before the inventory turns over.

Example 9.5: If the April inventory turnover rate for a restaurant is 2.37, does this fall within the one- to two-week inventory turnover recommendation?

Number of Days to Turn Over Inventory $= \dfrac{\text{Number of Days in the Month}}{\text{Inventory Turnover}}$

$$= \dfrac{30 \text{ days}}{2.37} = 12.7 \text{ days}$$

Since 12.7 days is between one and two weeks, this is an acceptable inventory rate.

Having too small an inventory can create problems as well. Trying to turn over an inventory daily will prevent a restaurant from taking advantage of bulk pricing. Still, maintaining smaller inventories that turn over every week or two helps to reduce spoilage and to deter theft that is more likely to occur when larger inventories are kept on hand.

As one final note, recognize that the calculation of inventory turnover is based on the inventory's dollar valuation and not on each item's time spent in storage. Some products will spend weeks in storage while others will turn over in a day. By using an average based on dollars rather than on numbers of items, the more expensive items carry more weight. Therefore, if the most expensive items (which are also the most likely to be stolen) are turned over quickly, a business will have a better turnover rate than one in which the expensive items languish in storage. A quick turnover rate allows a foodservice operation to get by with less money tied up in inventory and with less space reserved for storing ingredients. Throw in the fact that less time in storage means less chance of spoilage and theft and a cost control manager is sure to recognize the value of an appropriate inventory turnover rate.

9.4   SPECIAL CONCERNS FOR BEVERAGES

While most of the processes for proper receiving, storing, and issuing apply equally to food and beverages, there are a few special concerns regarding beverages that a cost control manager should consider. Some of these issues and recommended procedural adjustments are as follows.

Receiving Alcohol.   Because alcohol is such a magnet for theft, it is critically important that extra precautions be taken in receiving. In those states where liquor must be picked up at an ABC store (rather than delivered to the foodservice establishment), the alcohol should be checked in twice—once by the person picking it up at the ABC store and once by another individual when the alcohol arrives at the business's storeroom. The check conducted at the ABC store ensures that there is no purveyor error. The second receiving check makes sure that the employee picking up the purchase did not conveniently leave some of it in his car.

When alcohol is delivered to a storeroom or loading dock, the receiving clerk should never leave it unattended. It is simply too easy for a person to walk by unnoticed and to swipe a bottle of alcohol. Large pallet jacks or hand trucks help a receiving clerk transport deliveries quickly without leaving alcohol unsecured in an open area. If necessary, a manager may request a second person to assist, so no alcohol is ever left unattended. To prevent a receiving clerk from making the difficult decision to store alcohol or perishables first, purchasers should always schedule alcohol deliveries when no other food deliveries are expected.

Finally, since a receiving clerk should not open bottles to taste or to smell any arriving alcohol, the quality inspection for alcohol relies heavily on label reading. A receiving clerk must check labels for brand names, and if applicable, for vintage and freshness dates. One brand of liquor may cost many dollars less than another brand of the same product. A wine from one vintage may cost twice the price of the same wine from another vintage. Beer that arrives well past its freshness date is likely to be rejected by customers and to result in a financial loss for the establishment. All bottles of alcohol should have proper fill levels. An underfilled bottle of liquor represents lost quantity of product; an underfilled bottle of wine may suggest a completely spoiled, oxidized beverage.

Storing Alcohol.   While some businesses may choose not to lock up their expensive meats or seafood, all operations should keep alcohol under lock and key and limit the number of managers with key access. An open storeroom is never appropriate for alcohol. Storing each type of bottle separately in its own bin makes inventory and issuing much faster. Imagine trying to locate one bottle from a thirty-page wine list in a cluttered storeroom while a customer waits for his wine order to arrive. By assigning each type of wine a bin number and by ordering bins (or shelves) (see Photo 9.1) in numerical order, a manager is able to locate each bottle quickly.

Photo 9.1
Wine in Storage Bins

Source: © Michael Klenetsky/ Shutterstock.

Alcohol also has specific storage requirements. Still wine should be stored on its side to keep the corks moist. Wine and beer are sensitive to light, humidity, and fluctuations in temperature. Ideally, wines should be stored in a low-light room with controlled humidity and a temperature somewhat below room temperature—roughly 55°F for red wine, slightly cooler for white. Beers may be stored in their original cases, but once chilled should remain refrigerated. Kegs should be stored between 40°F and 50°F. Both wine and beer should be handled and moved minimally and gently.

Issuing Alcohol. Many foodservice operations require a bottle exchange system in which bottles are released from storage only when empty bottles of the same beverage are returned. This system helps management track usage and catch possible theft. Whether or not a bottle exchange system is employed, no alcohol should leave the storeroom without a written requisition. Providing a single manager with a key to the alcohol storeroom and the right to issue alcohol further reduces the ability to steal alcohol.

With properly trained and responsible employees controlling alcohol through receiving, storage, and issuing, a foodservice establishment is less likely to lose alcohol through theft or spoilage. Still, upper management must regularly cross-reference paperwork and inventories and verify procedures in action to ensure that all alcohol is secure. No system is foolproof, but a thoughtfully planned and executed control system will deter all but the most determined and brazen criminals.

SUMMARY

With proper receiving, storing, and issuing procedures in place, a foodservice operation can save lots of money on otherwise stolen or spoiled products. Receiving requires a knowledgeable employee with access to sufficient space, equipment to measure and transport ingredients, and office supplies to approve or document errors in a shipment. Invoices are the main communication means between the purveyor and the restaurant, so a receiver must verify every invoice's accuracy. Invoice errors require credit memos or other written adjustments to the invoice, so a manager can pay the purveyor accurately. A receiving clerk's report aids both in the proper payment to purveyors and in the accurate tracking of daily food cost. Suitable storage facilities include areas and equipment for frozen, refrigerated, and dry goods as well as a separate area for cleaning supplies. When properly organized and maintained, these spaces keep ingredients wholesome for their entire anticipated lifespan. Rotation of product according to the FIFO method further reduces the likelihood of spoilage. To transfer ingredients from storage to production, a restaurant can employ an open storeroom where employees gather their own products or a closed storeroom to which employees must supply written requisitions for their ingredients. In a requisition and issuing system, storeroom workers issue only those products for which they have requisitions; managers can use those requisitions to track daily food cost more easily. Conducting and valuing an inventory periodically further helps managers to control inventory and to monitor food costs. Theft from the storeroom is always a possibility, but security measures can be put in place to reduce the risk of loss from theft. Keeping a good inventory turnover rate helps prevent stealing and spoilage as well. Beverages generally follow the same receiving, storing, and issuing procedures as foods, but a few extra precautions help protect this expensive and desirable inventory.

COMPREHENSION QUESTIONS

1. List five resources needed to operate a receiving area properly.
2. List the steps in the receiving process.
3. In addition to an invoice, what paperwork is typically collected or completed by a receiving clerk?
4. Describe the proper set-up for a refrigerator to operate efficiently.
5. What is FIFO and why is it important?
6. Describe how a requisition and issuing system works.
7. List three ways in which a business can limit theft from a storeroom.
8. List three controls specific to beverages and related to receiving, storing, and issuing.
9. A restaurant purchases chicken breast four times each week and conducts an inventory weekly. The most recent week's deliveries have been:

Monday—20 # chicken at $1.87/#

Wednesday—25 # chicken at $1.86/#

Friday—20 # chicken at $1.92/#

Saturday—45 # chicken at $1.93/#

Calculate the possible values for 30 # of chicken left in inventory on Sunday afternoon using the FIFO, LIFO, weighted average, and most recent price methods. Assuming the restaurant rotates stock properly, provide the value using the actual price method as well.

10. Calculate a business's inventory turnover rate if the opening inventory is valued at $1,800 and the closing inventory is valued at $1,400 for the month. There are $6,200 in purchases for the month. Assume that the restaurant has no adjustments to the cost of food sold from employee meals, promotions, etc.

DISCUSSION QUESTIONS

1. If you were the manager of a small restaurant, which approach would you prefer, an open or a closed storeroom? Why? Does your answer change if you are managing a multiunit resort?
2. Imagine that you are a receiving clerk for a caterer. You have ordered two flats of fresh berries for an event the next day. (They are the "fruit" sitting on top of pastry cream for a fresh fruit tart.) The berries that arrive in the morning have lots of soft spots and do not look attractive. The tarts must be completed today, but the delivery person states that all of his company's berries are in this condition. What do you do?

3. Two receiving clerks work together on a loading dock for a large hotel. They are expecting a large delivery with nearly two tons of food. How might these two workers divide up and organize the work to keep the food wholesome and fresh without sacrificing proper receiving checks?

4. A cost control manager notices that the quantities of spoiled food in storage have increased in the past three months. What might be the cause of the increase?

(There are many possibilities, so suggest at least five.) If the purveyor changed three months ago but all other systems are exactly as they have been for years, what adjustments should the manager make to bring spoilage rates back in line?

5. If you were a cost control manager in a large hotel with three foodservice outlets, which method for valuing inventory would you use? Why?

6. A manager has a theft problem from his storeroom. He is frustrated because he uses a requisition and issuing system, keeps expensive products under lock and key, only supplies two managers with those keys, and even has security cameras. What steps might such a manager take to discover the source of the problem?

7. As a manager, you have found a great source for employees by hiring recovering alcoholics who have gone through a culinary training program. Do you need to change your control procedures regarding alcohol? Why or why not?

10
Employee Organization and Scheduling

Objectives

By the end of this chapter, you will be able to:

- Explain the cost of high turnover
- Compare the pros and cons of salaried versus hourly employees
- List the components and purpose of a job description, a job specification, and an organizational chart
- Describe performance standards and state how they are determined
- Schedule employees efficiently given a forecast hourly labor need and production standards

Cost control can be thought of as the management of resources and revenue. A company's labor force is often its most valuable resource. However, unlike other resources, human beings are more than just objects with fixed value. People produce more or less, depending on how they are managed. A person can generate far more output when given proper training, clear direction, and a quality work environment than when given no training, vague instructions, and a poorly designed workspace. Idle workers cost far more money than idle equipment or stored product waiting to be used. Making sure that employees are as productive and efficient as possible is one goal of labor cost control.

To extract every possible penny of efficiency out of a labor force, a cost control manager must attempt to schedule employees in alignment with the production needed hour by hour each day. Work has a way of expanding to fill the time allotted, so surplus employees may look busy but cost more money than necessary. Paying as little as possible to minimize labor costs is not the best approach either. There are huge costs to high employee turnover, so paying employees competitively to retain them often generates long-term cost savings over paying minimum wage. Efficiency in labor management comes from how a manager organizes and controls the staff and their work environment. Equipment, facility layout, scheduling, ingredient format, organizational charts, job descriptions, production standards, and training all impact how cost effective a labor force is.

10.1 THE ROLE AND VALUE OF LABOR

Of the many resources in a foodservice establishment, only labor has the ability to think. This fundamental difference gives labor a far greater potential value over all other resources in a business. One can speak about a piece of equipment "doing" something, but in reality, it is only a tool operating as the extension of a person. Without a human being to turn it on and to manipulate it, it does nothing. All other resources are similarly controlled by human beings. Human beings, however, are never truly under the complete control of another person, even in an employee–manager relationship. How a manager treats her employees greatly impacts the value that she gets from those workers.

Historically, factory managers often thought of employees as easily replaceable, interchangeable "machines" that had little value beyond their physical production capacity. Because a chef or manager typically designs the recipes and kitchen processes for all employees to follow exactly and consistently, one could think of a kitchen as a factory environment. It is tempting to assume that a cook, given a set of ingredients, equipment, and recipes, contributes nothing beyond the manipulation of food to generate the chef's creation—the kitchen factory's output. However, because of their ability to think, cooks also have the ability to perform basic managerial functions as well—problem-solving, process analysis, ingredient evaluation, and new product innovation, to name a few—if the formal managers allow them this leeway. (*Note:* This theory applies equally to servers, dishwashers, stewards, receiving clerks, and all other hospitality industry employees as well; the example of the cook is only one of many that could be described here.)

Imagine a restaurant kitchen in which the chef has the cooks square off all four sides of a potato before they make their cuts for diced potato. In a traditional environment, most cooks would keep their mouths shut and follow instructions. However, in a modern kitchen environment, a cook might feel empowered to recommend that everyone begin by squaring only two sides of the potato since the final slices to make the planks and sticks are rarely exactly the right size and are tossed out anyway. Such a suggestion might save only one penny per potato, but in a large-volume restaurant, that could represent hundreds of dollars each year. This example illustrates the enhanced value that an average employee provides if only a manager would treat her as more than a cog in a machine.

While this is a cost control and not a supervisory management text, suffice it to say that labor costs are reduced in a work environment in which employees are treated as team players who want the business to succeed rather than as laborers forced to follow instructions because they need an income. A valued, respected, and well-treated worker is more likely to work hard, to suggest or to create efficiencies, to reduce errors, and to stay with the company longer than an ill-treated employee. The remainder of the chapter focuses on the more traditional means through which managers control labor costs, but a wise manager recognizes that an inspired, empowered, well-led workforce often aids rather than undermines a manager in the pursuit of her company's cost control goals.

10.1.1 The Cost of Turnover

A manager's primary function is to maintain company standards in both the short-term and the long-term. Those standards include both quality and financial goals. For example, a restaurant known for exquisitely flavored dishes presented with precision and artistry would lose its clientele if some plates left the kitchen with sloppy presentations or bland food. While this lapse in quality could be the result of any number of factors, it is one predictable consequence of a low-caliber staff incapable of meeting the company's standards.

How does a restaurant end up with a low-caliber staff? It could be the result of poor training, insufficient pay to attract and maintain better workers, or poor treatment by the line workers' supervisors. Whatever the cause, the result is financially devastating in the long run, even if it results in a short-term financial gain. Imagine a scenario in which a manager fires all current employees to replace them with others earning half as much money. In the present, the manager realizes a huge cost savings and may end up with a lower labor cost. But in the long run, a low-caliber staff may fail to meet enough quality standards to keep customers returning; future revenue will decline. When this occurs, labor costs not only become a larger percentage of revenue, but all other costs become a larger percentage of revenue, too. In short, it puts the business's survival at risk.

This is not to say that a manager should always hire the highest-caliber workers available. Instead, the business should employ the right worker for the job—not over-qualified, not under-qualified. A line cook in charge of seafood will likely need a stronger skill set than one hired to make toast. Attracting a person with better skills typically requires higher wages. Paying enough to get the right worker and treating her well enough to stay helps to control costs by reducing turnover.

A business's turnover rate is the ratio of the number of employees lost in a given period (usually a year) compared with the average number of employees working during that period. The formula for calculating a company's turnover rate is:

$$\text{Turnover Rate} = \frac{\text{Employees Who Worked That Year} - \text{Employees Still Working There}}{\text{Average Number of Employees on Staff During the Year}}$$

Example 10.1: A company averages 50 employees throughout the year. If it has 48 employees at the end of the year and sends out 97 W-2 forms to workers who were employed there that year, what is the company's turnover rate?

$$\text{Turnover Rate} = \frac{\text{Employees Who Worked That Year} - \text{Employees Still Working There}}{\text{Average Number of Employees That Year}}$$

$$= \frac{97 - 48}{50} = 0.98$$

Converted to its percentage form, the turnover rate is 98%.

Turnover is not just an inconvenience for a manager; it is a financial drain on the business. Many organizations require an exit interview and other paperwork from each departing employee, which costs time for the administrators performing those tasks. When an employee's position is vacant, the restaurant typically pays other workers overtime to get the job done, or product quality suffers from insufficient staffing. Hiring a new employee incurs even greater costs, including money spent on advertising to recruit applicants for the position, time spent interviewing candidates, wages for the new employee and a trainer during a training period, and time spent by administrators processing the new employee's paperwork. Considering that a new employee may take weeks to become as productive as a past employee, a smart manager recognizes that a reduction in turnover saves on expenses.

Able to calculate her operation's turnover rate, a manager can take steps to improve the turnover rate and to track her progress. Taking the time to hire an employee who will be a good fit for the company helps with the long-term retention of that employee. Proper orientation and training are critical, too. Finally, a manager who motivates and empowers employees to make them feel successful and valued typically prevents turnover from getting out of hand. This is not to say that a business should never lose an employee. An employee who is unqualified for the job or a poor fit should be terminated and replaced quickly before she generates larger problems for the organization. New employees can bring fresh ideas into a long-term workforce, but in general, a business with a low turnover rate saves greatly on the cost of labor replacement.

10.2 FORMS OF COMPENSATION AND EMPLOYMENT

Workers can be categorized in several ways. One common division is based on the number of hours worked. A full-time employee typically works a forty-hour week (though some companies define full-time slightly differently). A part-time employee works less than full-time most weeks. (*Note:* It is possible for a part-time employee to work more than forty hours in a week, but when this occurs regularly, the employee is effectively a full-timer and should be treated as such with regard to benefits.)

Workers are also often classified by the form of compensation they receive. A salaried employee receives a salary or set amount of compensation regardless of the number of hours she works. An hourly employee receives wages, which are monies paid at an hourly rate in exchange for the worker's time. Some companies offer benefits to their employees beyond a paycheck. Whether a company extends benefits to all employees or only to certain employees is up to the management. It is not uncommon for only salaried managers to receive benefits in the culinary industry, but some progressive foodservice businesses now offer benefits to hourly laborers who meet a minimum number of hours (not necessarily full time) each week.

Employees who work over forty hours per week are sometimes entitled to overtime pay. Overtime pay is equivalent to $1\frac{1}{2}$ times the employee's regular hourly rate. Whether an employee must legally receive overtime pay or not has nothing to do with whether the person receives a salary or hourly wages. Instead, it is based on the U.S. Department of Labor's definition of an exempt (from overtime pay) or nonexempt worker. Because the laws vary by state as well, a manager should consult her state's laws. While not an exact definition, often a salaried manager performing "white-collar" work is exempt from receiving overtime pay, but a salaried manual laborer with minimal supervisory responsibility is entitled to overtime compensation. (This is an overly simplistic definition that would not hold legal muster, but it helps give readers a general idea of the difference between those who do and do not receive overtime pay.)

There are pros and cons to having full-time versus part-time or salaried versus hourly employees. Full-time employees generally make up the core of workers in a business. As full-timers, they are the most committed to the company and are usually available to work a full schedule each week. Their forty-hours per week (or more) of practice in their jobs keeps their skills honed. Exempt salaried workers may work dozens of extra hours when necessary for no additional compensation. However, full-time, salaried employees are paid the same weekly amount no matter how low business drops. If they receive benefits, the company incurs the costs for benefits as well. In some companies, full-time hourly employees must be scheduled for forty hours of work before other employees receive hours and regardless of business levels.

Part-time employees, on the other hand, fill voids when a company needs extra staff for a few hours but not for an entire day. For example, a part-time cook might assist with special events or cover for absent workers but not receive any hours during slow weeks. A part-time server might work 5:00–9:00 p.m. and not worry that she only gets four hours of work per day as her employer only needs her help during the actual dinner service. Part-time workers, though, may not always be available when the manager needs them. For example, a full-time student might work part-time at a restaurant, but she may not be able to work during her class hours, during finals week, or at all during summer break. An efficient company often has a balance of full-time and part-time workers on staff.

10.2.1 Benefits

In addition to a paycheck, some workers receive benefits as part of their compensation. Most employee benefits are not required by law, but they are typically valued by workers and can attract a higher caliber, long-term employee. A full range of benefits can add an additional 30%–40% of expense to a worker's pay, so each organization must decide what benefits it will provide and which employees are eligible for them. Some common benefits are as follows:

Vacation.   Most workers only get paid when they are at work. This penalizes the employee for taking the day off from work. Paid vacation allows an employee to take time off from work while still collecting a paycheck. There are many ways to implement a paid vacation system. Some companies allow workers to earn vacation hours for each week they work, while others simply give employees a bank of vacation time to use for the year. Some give all employees the same number of days off each year while others adjust the benefit based on years of service with the company. Most have a limit to the number of hours that an employee can carry from one year to the next. There are good reasons to have such a limit. First, one of the values to the company for offering vacation is to allow workers to recharge and to come back energized for work. The threat of losing vacation days encourages workers to use them and to refresh themselves. Second, most companies must pay workers for their unused vacation time when the worker separates from the company. An employee with years of saved vacation time can create a cash-flow problem if she leaves and requires a huge vacation payment all at once. For a foodservice company, vacation can be a costly benefit as each employee's position must be covered by another worker during her absence.

Holidays.   While paid time off on holidays is common in many fields, most foodservice establishments are open on holidays. That said, some companies pay a small bonus or higher wages for working on a major holiday.

Sick Leave.   Similar to paid vacation, some businesses pay a worker her wages when she is out sick. As with vacation, the number of sick days a worker may take each year is limited. Encouraging sick employees to stay home helps keep the staff from infecting each other and from making customers sick. Unlike vacation time, unused sick leave is not generally compensated when a worker leaves the company. Some companies have begun providing workers a single set of days to use for either sick leave or vacation. This approach not only removes the incentive for workers to call out sick just to take an unused sick day but it also encourages employees to work while sick to take longer vacations.

Health Benefits.   Some companies offer their employees subsidized medical, vision, and/or dental insurance. In these programs, the company pays a portion of the monthly premium, while the employee pays the balance. The cost to a company for health care can be staggering, but it is an enormous benefit to employees. It helps to keep employees healthy and loyal. With the federal health care legislation of 2010, there is government aid for some companies to provide health care and penalties for certain ones that do not offer it.

Bonuses.   Sometimes a company will provide financial incentives to managers to achieve certain goals. For example, a chef could receive a 2% salary bonus for keeping the food cost below 30% for the year. Bonuses are excellent, cost-effective ways to incentivize workers toward cost-savings. If the goal is not reached, the company saves on the bonus, but if the goal is calculated properly, the company will save or earn more through achieving the goal than it spends on the bonus. Potential downsides to bonuses include unethical behavior, poor decisions made to reach the goal at all costs, or low morale for a hard-working employee who fails to earn her bonus. While bonuses are often thought of as cash payments, they can come in the form of gift cards, sporting event tickets, free meals, or other cost-effective recognitions for employees.

Retirement. Many companies offer 401(k) retirement plans for their employees, and some match a portion of each employee's contribution. Pensions are less common today, but they do still exist as a possible retirement benefit a company could offer.

Meals. In foodservice, the provision of meals, either free or at a reduced cost, is a common benefit. A "family meal" is a great outlet for leftovers or other ingredients that are perfectly edible but not appropriate for service, such as tenderloin tips in a restaurant that only does filet mignon. Giving food to employees for meals not only improves morale, but it also reduces theft. With so much food around her, a hungry employee will likely grab whatever she can steal without getting caught. By serving a family meal or allowing the selection of only certain menu items, a manager encourages employees to eat lower-cost foods rather than to steal the most expensive ones.

Legally Required Benefits. By law, businesses must participate in the workers' compensation and social security programs. In both cases, the company adds its own contribution to an amount deducted from the employee's compensation and sends the total to the government. (*Note:* Some state workers may be exempt from federal social security because they participate in a state-run version.) Social security benefits retirees, individuals disabled before age 22, and certain family members of deceased workers. Workers' compensation takes care of injured workers. Workers' compensation is a state-run program, so the laws vary by state; however, employers should challenge fraudulent employee claims. A company's rates go up with an increase in work-related injuries. Job safety programs that reduce on-the-job accidents can help to reduce the cost of workers' compensation.

Other Benefits. While the aforementioned benefits are some of the most common, they are far from a complete list. Businesses can administer pretax savings accounts for childcare or medical expenses for employees. A company can offer life insurance for its employees. Many offer short- and/or long-term disability insurance in case of a disability that keeps an employee out of work. Some companies offer subsides for employee transportation (parking spaces or bus/rail passes), and a few companies have maternity/paternity benefits—often paid or unpaid leave. A great benefit to offer is tuition or professional development subsidies to encourage employees to grow professionally; this benefit usually returns value to the company in the form of a more productive worker or one better able to handle greater responsibility. Progressive companies offer health and wellness programs to keep their employees healthy and productive. A wellness program could be as simple as a gym membership or as complex as counseling for drug and alcohol abuse and programs for smoking cessation. Finally, some food service organizations allow for profit sharing. Profit-sharing gives employees a stake in the success of the company and encourages them to work harder to help the business to flourish.

There is no end to the list of possible benefits that a business could offer. The challenge for the cost control manager is to determine which benefits provide the best return to the company in terms of productive, loyal, and happy employees. Because the restaurant industry is so risky, many smaller foodservice companies offer few benefits to the majority of their employees.

10.2.2 Fixed and Variable Costs

The discussion of salaries, wages, and benefits leads to a discussion of fixed versus variable costs. Simply put, a fixed cost is one that does not change with business volume. A variable cost, on the other hand, fluctuates as business changes. For example, a salaried worker receives the same amount of money and benefits each week whether her company sees one customer or one million; this is a fixed cost. If a cost control manager normally has four hourly cooks to handle 500 covers and she can cut their hours by 20% when the restaurant is only forecasting 400 covers, the labor cost for the cooks is considered a variable cost. The total amount spent for cooks goes up or down as the business shifts.

Fixed and variable costs are not specific just to labor. Food and beverage are variable costs as more food and drink is consumed with greater numbers of customers. Rent and insurance are fixed costs; they don't change from month to month. The reason to discuss fixed and variable costs amid a discussion on labor is that labor is a combination of fixed and variable costs. There will always be some minimum number of cooks and servers needed no matter how low business drops, but the cost can be controlled to some degree. Salaried employees are most definitely a fixed cost, but they are in the same labor pool as those variable hourly workers. The semivariable nature of labor makes it one of the most difficult expenses to control.

10.3   DEFINING A JOB

Long-time workers sometimes joke that their job is to do "whatever the boss wants." While every foodservice company needs their workers to be flexible when emergencies arise, asking employees to shift their duties daily at the whim of a supervisor is not an efficient means of conducting business. Such employees do not get enough ongoing practice at a single task to improve their performance over time. And how would a manager evaluate such an employee's performance? If the worker never does the same thing twice, can her boss truly measure her progress?

To foster an efficient workforce, a company should outline certain information for each employment position—specifically, a job description, performance standards, a job specification, and a reporting hierarchy (or from a grander perspective, an organizational chart).

The data necessary to generate these documents typically comes from a job analysis. To conduct a job analysis for a specific job, a manager observes and interviews the employees performing that job as well as the employees' supervisors. This in-depth analysis yields information on the specific tasks that these employees perform, how much work they can reasonably handle while maintaining the company's quality standards, and what skills, knowledge, and other qualifications they need to perform their jobs well. The interviews also help a manager understand each employee's reporting structure and any possible conflicts that exist from the current reporting hierarchy. In an existing organization, nearly all of the information needed to conduct a thorough job analysis can be found within the company's workforce. In a new company, the start-up managers must rely on their own experience and judgment, possibly supplemented by advice from other industry professionals.

10.3.1 Job Descriptions

With a job analysis completed, a manager can create an accurate job description. A job description is simply a document that outlines the tasks an employee is expected to perform on the job. It includes the job title, the supervisor's title, a paragraph summarizing the position, and a set of bullet points listing the specific duties for that position.

When done properly, a job description also describes the employee's working conditions and lists the order in which tasks are to be performed if they must be done sequentially. It may include the position's job specifications (to be described later) and the scheduled hours for that job.

Using a well-written job description (Figure 10.1), a new employee can read exactly what she is expected to do on her job. Because it is based on a job analysis, the job description should be realistic and complete. It should include every task and responsibility for which the employee will be held accountable, and it should be reasonable in its expectation of employee productivity. In other words, an average employee should be able to perform every task on the job description to the company's quantity and quality standards within the scheduled work hours.

JOB TITLE: Prep Cook   **SUPERVISOR**: Sous Chef

SUMMARY: The prep cook washes, peels, cuts, and inventories all produce to be used at the line cook, salad, and dessert stations. All tasks are performed in the main kitchen or in the food storeroom.

DUTIES:
1. Conducts a mise en place inventory of all stations upon arriving and provides that inventory to the sous chef.
2. Prepares the fruit and vegetable mise en place for each station to bring the total inventory up to the chef's requested daily kitchen production quantity.
3. Peels potatoes, cuts them into rough 2" chunks, and stores them in cold water before delivering them to the cook stations.
4. Washes, dries in a salad spinner, and hand-tears all lettuces. Delivers them to the salad station in a lexan container covered with damp paper towels.
5. Peels carrots, onions, garlic, and eggplant. Cuts them to the sizes listed on the kitchen production schedule, stores them separately in 4" one-sixth pans, and delivers them to the cook stations.
6. Washes and cuts tomatoes, celery, broccoli, and zucchini to the sizes listed on the kitchen production schedule, stores them separately in 4" one-sixth pans, and delivers them to the cook stations.
7. Washes and cuts all berries to the sizes listed on the kitchen production schedule, stores them separately in 2" one-sixth pans lined with dry paper towel, and delivers them to the dessert station.
8. During service, prepares supplemental produce and assists the salad cook per the instructions of the sous chef as needed.
9. After service, conducts an inventory of produce in the walk-in and storeroom; delivers the inventory list to the executive chef.
10. Maintains a clean and sanitary work environment.
11. Adheres to company uniform and dress code policies.

Figure 10.1
Job Description

10.3.2 Performance Standards

A job description provides a foundation on which employees can be evaluated, but this document is incomplete without a set of performance standards (Figure 10.2). A performance standard is an observable, measurable definition outlining the quality and quantity standards for each bullet point on a job description. For example, a job description for a lunch cook may state (as one bullet point) that the cook is responsible for preparing all mise en place for her station. The performance standard for that single task may read "Between 9:00 and 11:00 a.m., prepares sufficient mise en place to handle up to 200 covers from the station." This standard is both observable and measurable,

Job Title: Prep Cook	Shift: Morning, 7:00 a.m.–3:30 p.m.
Tasks:	Standards:
1. Conducts a mise en place inventory of all stations upon arriving and provides that inventory to the sous chef.	1. Inventory is delivered to sous chef by 7:30 a.m. Inventory form is 100% complete with no more than 1 quantity error.
2. Prepares the fruit and vegetable mise en place for each station to bring the total inventory up to the chef's requested daily kitchen production quantity.	2. All produce mise en place is delivered to the stations by 10:30 a.m. in the correct quantity to bring the station inventory up to the kitchen production schedule quantity for up to 200 forecast guests.
3. Peels potatoes, cuts in rough 2" chunks, and stores them in cold water before delivering them to the cook stations.	3. Potatoes are skin free and delivered by 10:00 a.m. Chunks are of consistent size and not discolored from air exposure.
4. Washes, dries in a salad spinner, and hand-tears all lettuces. Delivers them to the salad station in a lexan container covered with damp paper towels.	4. Lettuce is torn into pieces no larger than 2" square. Lettuce is free of dirt and excess water; no browning or rotting is evident on lettuce.
5. Peels carrots, onions, garlic, and eggplant. Cuts them to the sizes listed on the kitchen production schedule, stores them separately in 4" one-sixth pans, and delivers them to the cook stations.	5. Vegetables are free of peel. Cuts are of consistent size and shape and 90% are no greater than $\frac{1}{8}$" deviation from size standard listed on production schedule.

Figure 10.2
Production Standards (for portion of prep cook position)

so a manager can fairly evaluate an employee. If the mise en place is either not completed by 11:00 or runs out after 100 covers, the manager will know that the employee is not performing properly. However, the standard is also reasonable and fair to the employee. If the restaurant is swamped with 300 lunch reservations, the supervisor will know to provide additional help to the cook in the preparation of mise en place.

Without performance standards, the employee has room to argue that her performance addresses all of the tasks outlined in a job description. With the standards, however, the employee can predict exactly how her annual evaluation will go. The use of performance standards also helps to ensure that all employees are assessed fairly and without favoritism. Finally, performance standards help determine the number of employees needed to meet the business's quality and quantity standards. Using the example in which a cook is expected to handle 200 covers at her station, once this restaurant grows to the point that it regularly exceeds 200 sales from that station, the supervisor knows that she will need to add an additional employee to aid that station. As another example, if a server is expected to handle twenty guests at once and the restaurant forecasts a constant flow of eighty seated customers at a time during service, then the manager knows to schedule four servers during that period.

Managers, sometimes, adjust the work environment in order to increase the staff's productivity levels beyond what is described in a performance standard. A facility's layout or its set of tools can greatly impact how much a worker can reasonably get done in a given time period. For example, if servers are hampered because of the distance they walk to retrieve beverages, a manager may decide to relocate the beverage station.

If a cook spends hours peeling potatoes by hand, her supervisor may decide that it is worth the investment to purchase an automated potato peeler (or to purchase prepeeled potatoes). Training also impacts the productivity an employee exhibits as an untrained employee may not know the steps to take to improve her job performance. By making some adjustments to the work environment or to a training program, a manager can sometimes make productivity improvements permanent. When productivity consistently remains high, the production standards should be amended to reflect the new productivity levels.

Of course, improvements in productivity must always adhere to the operation's mission and brand. For example, purchasing peeled potatoes might undermine the brand of a restaurant that promotes its food as made 100% from scratch. Well-considered changes may improve workers' productivity, but they should never come at the expense of company standards. Otherwise, short-term improvements may result in a long-term loss of business.

10.3.3 Job Specifications

Job specifications (Figure 10.3) relate directly to the job description. Simply put, a job specification lists the required abilities and qualifications needed to perform a job. Job specifications may include a degree credential (such as a high school diploma or a culinary school degree), an experience requirement (such as a minimum number of years in a similar position elsewhere), a physical requirement (e.g., must be able to lift 50 #), or even an age requirement (e.g., must be 18 years of age or older). Job specifications must relate directly to the requirements of the job description to avoid potential legal trouble. For example, if it is illegal for a minor to use an electric slicer and the job requires the use of a meat slicer, then a job specification can include a minimum age of 18. However, if the job specification listed a minimum age of 30 or a maximum age of 50, the company would be open to discrimination lawsuits.

The purpose of a job specification is to provide a set of criteria for screening job applicants. When reviewing résumés or in first-round interviews, the manager or human resources director may eliminate candidates that do not meet the job specification requirements. If the requirements are, in fact, necessary for the performance of the job description, anyone not possessing them will not likely perform well on the job. However, if the job specifications are written too narrowly and are not necessary for the employee to meet performance standards, then the pool of "qualified" applicants will be artificially limited, making it much more difficult to find a qualified employee.

Position Title: AM Sous Chef
Education: Culinary associate degree or higher
Experience: Minimum 2 years in line cook positions at mid-range to high-caliber restaurants
Physical: Must be able to lift 40 #.

Figure 10.3
Job Specification

10.3.4 Organizational Charts

Organizational charts are visual depictions of the reporting hierarchy in a company (Figure 10.4). When done properly, the chart shows not only to whom each employee reports directly but also any "dotted line" relationships or positions designed to coordinate and communicate regularly with each other, even though they may not technically be equals or peers in terms of responsibility. An organizational chart illustrates each employee's supervisor, which is also listed on a job description. Any inconsistencies between the organizational chart and the job description may be a sign of communication problems within the company. An organizational chart also reveals any situations in which a person reports to more than one boss—a potential problem within a business. When this occurs, management must decide who has ultimate authority over the employee, so the employee is not given conflicting instructions from various supervisors.

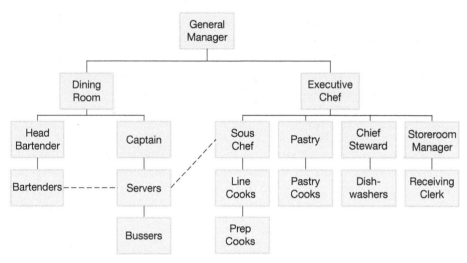

Figure 10.4
Organizational Chart

10.4   SCHEDULING EMPLOYEES

How a manager schedules employees is perhaps one of the greatest opportunities for labor cost savings (or for a bloated budget). In factory-type production, the task is simpler. For example, in a catering company, a chef might schedule 80% of her hourly staff to arrive every day at the same time to the commissary and to work until the day's production is complete. If all employees are notified in their job descriptions that their shift ends when the work is done and that no one is guaranteed forty hours per week, then the scheduler's only task is to determine which employees get which days off. Fewer people might be given a day off on those days with the most parties, but the time at which everyone arrives and departs is simple—everyone arrives at the same time, and everyone leaves when the work is complete. (Scheduling the on-site workers for the catered event itself is a different scenario more akin to a school cafeteria, described later.)

Foodservice businesses with consistent business levels over a given time period add another layer of complexity but are still relatively simple. A school cafeteria is one example of this type of operation. A manager in a school cafeteria knows exactly how many students she serves daily and at what times they arrive throughout the day. In a school cafeteria, business is typically a consistent flow of students from the first customer to the last. As long as the manager knows how many employees are needed to handle customer volume during service, she can schedule that number of employees to work during the service period. What makes this scenario more complex than a factory is that not all of the workers are needed for advance preparation or for cleanup. Therefore, a scheduler may have three people arrive at 8:00 a.m. to cook, two more arrive at 10:00 a.m. to set up service lines, and still two more to aid with the service itself. All but a couple may leave at the end of service as cleanup can be completed with a smaller staff. After a brief testing period, a manager will know exactly how many people are needed for each task throughout the day. The testing period is critical as it is unlikely that a manager will schedule staff perfectly the first time. Because the business levels do not change from one day to the next, a refined, post-testing phase schedule can be duplicated throughout the school year.

Restaurants and hotels are perhaps the most challenging businesses in terms of scheduling employees efficiently. In a restaurant, business levels change dramatically from one hour to the next and from one day to the next. Saturday night is likely busier than Monday night, and far fewer customers are probably in-house at 3:00 p.m. than are present at 7:00 p.m. For this reason, a restaurant manager must schedule employees weekly based on forecasts. Some restaurants keep an employee or two on call in case of last-minute increases in business. As it provides the greatest scheduling challenge, the upcoming section on scheduling will focus specifically on restaurants.

10.4.1 Business Volume and Variable Staffing Needs

To determine the number of hourly workers needed to handle a given volume of business, a manager first turns to each position's performance standards. Because these standards state the amount of business (in customers, plates, etc.) that an employee can handle, a manager can correlate the forecasted business levels to the number of employees needed at each position. Mathematically, just divide the total number of customers by the number of customers one employee on a given task can handle to calculate how many employees in each job position are needed. The formula must be performed separately for each position with the same job title and set of responsibilities, and the production standards provide the information on how many customers the employee in each position can handle.

$$\text{Number of Employees} = \frac{\text{Number of Guests}}{\text{Production Standard (in number of guests) for That Position}}$$

For example, if a server is expected to handle twenty customers at once and eighty customers are forecast for a given hour of service, then four servers are needed to handle the volume of business ($80 \div 20 = 4$). A manager will need to use some judgment as the numbers rarely work out exactly. For example, if business were forecast at 75 customers, the manager would still need four servers. But if it is forecast at eighty-five customers, the manager might opt to hold at four servers and to assist personally with the extra few guests to avoid the cost of an additional server. However, exceeding production standards always comes with a risk. Managers with a broad range of responsibilities may be unable to drop everything to assist employees with excess customer volume. If the employees cannot handle the extra business in stride, quality standards and thus, customer satisfaction, may suffer.

Example 10.2: A manager has a catered event upcoming with 400 guests. She knows that 1 cook can finish and plate food for 80 during the event; 1 server can serve 30 guests; 1 bartender can handle 100 guests, and 1 dishwasher can clean dishes for 150 guests in the time frame set for the event. How many workers in each position does the manager need to schedule?

$$\text{Number of Employees} = \frac{\text{Number of Guests}}{\text{Production Standard (in number of guests) for That Employee}}$$

$$\text{Number of Cooks} = 400 \div 80 = 5$$

$$\text{Number of Servers} = 400 \div 30 = 13.3$$

$$\text{Number of Bartenders} = 400 \div 100 = 4$$

$$\text{Number of Dishwashers} = 400 \div 150 = 2.7$$

Unless the decimal is extremely small (0.1 or less), these numbers should always be rounded up. Otherwise, the staff is likely to be overwhelmed, and quality standards may suffer. In summary, this manager needs five cooks, fourteen servers, four bartenders, and three dishwashers.

Service Performance Summary

Day Part	Net Sales	% Sales	Guests	Sales per Guest	Checks	Avg Check	Table Turns	Avg Minutes
Service Totals	10,151.35	100%	1,836	5.53	1,879	5.40	0	0
Breakfast	3,317.01	32.7%	742	4.47	754	4.40	0	0
Lunch	4,515.54	44.5%	678	6.66	702	6.43	0	0
Dinner	2,318.80	22.8%	416	5.57	423	5.48	0	0

Hour	Net Sales	% Sales	Guests	Sales per Guest	Checks	Avg Check	Table Turns	Avg Minutes
6:00 AM	146.80	1.4%	47	3.12	51	2.88	0	0
7:00 AM	799.74	7.9%	206	3.88	209	3.83	0	0
8:00 AM	1,034.63	10.2%	206	5.02	207	5.00	0	0
9:00 AM	748.38	7.4%	173	4.33	174	4.30	0	0
10:00 AM	587.46	5.8%	110	5.34	113	5.20	0	0
11:00 AM	997.21	9.8%	146	6.83	151	6.60	0	0
12:00 PM	1,263.87	12.5%	173	7.31	180	7.02	0	0
1:00 PM	703.35	6.9%	150	4.69	156	4.51	0	0
2:00 PM	1,009.70	9.9%	116	8.70	120	8.41	0	0
3:00 PM	541.41	5.3%	93	5.82	95	5.70	0	0
4:00 PM	664.05	6.5%	107	6.21	110	6.04	0	0
5:00 PM	411.93	4.1%	77	5.35	77	5.35	0	0
6:00 PM	528.92	5.2%	95	5.57	96	5.51	0	0
7:00 PM	385.32	3.8%	73	5.28	75	5.14	0	0
8:00 PM	235.71	2.3%	44	5.36	44	5.36	0	0
9:00 PM	96.07	0.9%	20	4.80	21	4.57	0	0
10:00 PM	(3.20)	-0.0%	0	0.00	0	0.00	0	0
All Fixed Periods								

Figure 10.5

Sample POS Sales and Guest Counts by Hour

Source: Printed with the permission of MICROS Systems, Inc.

With production standards in hand, a manager next needs to analyze sales history to forecast business volume by the hour (see Figure 10.5). Because restaurants (unlike catered events) see business fluctuations every few minutes, it is not enough to know that a restaurant saw 400 customers in a given day. The manager needs to know how many came at lunch versus dinner, what are the peak periods for each meal, and so on. Thanks to modern technology, managers can easily glean this data from their POS systems. Those companies without computerized systems can gather similar information by time stamping guest checks or dupes as they go to the kitchen. The best way to view the business volume data is through a chart or graph tracking the number of guests each hour (or even each quarter-hour) over the course of the day. Once a manager has determined a pattern over several weeks for a given day of the week, she can use that pattern to forecast hourly sales volume in the upcoming weeks. It is important to recognize that due to the nature of the restaurant business, it is best to compare several weeks of the same day of the week (e.g., consecutive Fridays) rather than comparing the most recent days of the past week. People's eating habits tend to change dramatically on weekdays versus weekends but remain fairly consistent from one day to the corresponding day the following week. Figure 10.6 shows a chart of guest counts by the hour comparing the same day of the week, Tuesday, across several weeks.

Time Slots	Tues, June 4	Tues, June 11	Tues, June 18	Tues, June 25	Tues, July 2
11:00 a.m.–Noon	27	31	44	18	20
Noon–1:00 p.m.	77	83	90	69	80
1:00–2:00 p.m.	68	77	88	57	61
2:00–3:00 p.m.	21	24	22	17	14
3:00–4:00 p.m.	4	6	7	2	6
4:00–5:00 p.m.	19	22	25	12	20
5:00–6:00 p.m.	45	48	51	33	45
6:00–7:00 p.m.	80	87	99	65	82
7:00–8:00 p.m.	102	110	117	88	99
8:00–9:00 p.m.	59	61	71	50	60
9:00–10:00 p.m.	33	35	43	24	31
10:00–11:00 p.m.	20	22	31	17	20
11:00 p.m.– Midnight	12	18	21	9	14

Figure 10.6
Business Volume per Hour Chart—Number of Guests vs. Time and Date

Guest counts by the hour can be depicted in graph form for those who prefer visual images. Figure 10.7 illustrates the data from Figure 10.6, which normally comes directly from a POS system report. The graph shows the extremes—the high and low counts—for each hour as well as the median count. The median, rather than the average, is used to measure a typical service. The median is simply the

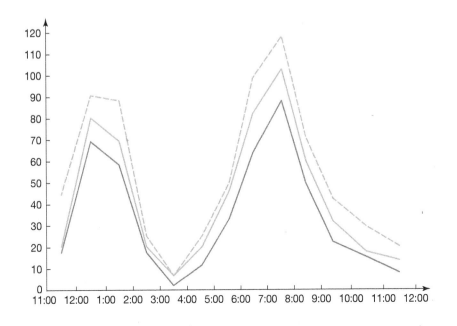

Figure 10.7
Business Volume by Hour Expressed Graphically

middle number in the sequence. For example, if the first hour of service each week in Figure 10.6 is ordered by guest count into 18, 20, 27, 31, and 44, the median is the middle number in the sequence—27. This keeps an unusually large or small day from skewing the numbers. When the guest forecast is average, the manager would use the median line. When the guest count is forecast to be extremely high or extremely low, the manager would refer to the outer lines to determine her employee needs by the hour for that day.

Time Slots	Forecast Guests	Servers Needed (Company Standard = 20 Guests/Server). Calculate as Guests ÷ Performance Standard
11:00 a.m.–Noon	27	2
Noon–1:00 p.m.	80	4
1:00–2:00 p.m.	68	4
2:00–3:00 p.m.	21	1
3:00–4:00 p.m.	6	1
4:00–5:00 p.m.	20	1
5:00–6:00 p.m.	45	3
6:00–7:00 p.m.	82	4
7:00–8:00 p.m.	102	5
8:00–9:00 p.m.	60	3
9:00–10:00 p.m.	33	2
10:00–11:00 p.m.	20	1
11:00 p.m.–Midnight	14	1

Figure 10.8
Employee Scheduling Worksheet—Servers
(Based on an Average Guest Count Forecast for a Tuesday, so Uses Median from Figure 10.7)

Using production standards and business volume history, a manager can effectively determine how many people she needs at each position, hour by hour, throughout the day. The manager can use this information to generate an employee schedule that minimizes excess staffing and inactive employees. In order to schedule most efficiently, a manager will need to utilize all of the tools at her disposal—part-time employees, split-shift scheduling, and staggered start times. It would not make sense for a manager to bring in all of her servers at 10:00 a.m. to set up for lunch if business does not really pick up until noon, but bringing a few people in early to set up and having others start their shifts just before the peak times allows the servers to handle the guest load comfortably without lots of idle time. When business slows, the number of employees scheduled for that hour should similarly drop. On the basis of the data in the Employee Scheduling Worksheet in Figure 10.8, Figure 10.9 illustrates how a manager might schedule employees. Notice that some are part-timers and that the full-timers work a split-shift schedule.

Another tool to help managers schedule efficiently is a scheduling guide (see Figure 10.10). A scheduling guide tells each employee when she should perform her tasks at each moment of the day. With these guides, a manager can ensure that every required job function is completed at its appropriate time. Scheduling guides help a scheduler to notice blocks of time where an employee would be idle and

Server No.	Time Slots														
	9:00–10:00 a.m.	10:00–11:00 a.m.	11:00–Noon	Noon–1:00 p.m.	1:00–2:00 p.m.	2:00–3:00 p.m.	3:00–4:00 p.m.	4:00–5:00 p.m.	5:00–6:00 p.m.	6:00–7:00 p.m.	7:00–8:00 p.m.	8:00–9:00 p.m.	9:00–10:00 p.m.	10:00–11:00 p.m.	11:00 p.m.–12:00 a.m.
1		■	■	■					■	■	■				
2			■	■	■										
3				■	■			■	■	■	■	■			
4					■	■	■		■	■	■	■			
5									■	■	■	■			
6										■	■	■	■		
7											■	■	■	■	

Figure 10.9
Employee Schedule—Derived from Server Scheduling Worksheet (Figure 10.8)

otherwise not needed. It also helps management to identify possible crunch times where an employee is asked to do too much in the allotted amount of time, which suggests the need for additional staffing during that period. These guides are particularly useful for organizing the hours of prep time and cleanup when handling customers is not the immediate priority.

Job Title: Prep Cook	Work Schedule: 7:00 a.m.–3:30 p.m.
Time Slot	Tasks
7:00–7:30 a.m.	Inventory station mise en place; deliver to sous chef. Retrieve kitchen production schedule.
7:30–8:15 a.m.	Peel and cut potatoes. Deliver to line cook station.
8:15–9:00 a.m.	Prep carrots, onions, garlic, and eggplant. Deliver to line cook station.
9:00–9:30 a.m.	Prep tomatoes, celery, broccoli, and zucchini. Deliver to line cook station.
9:30–10:15 a.m.	Wash, tear, and dry lettuces. Deliver to salad station.
10:15–10:30 a.m.	Wash and prep berries. Deliver to dessert station.
10:30–11:00 a.m.	Lunch break.
11:00 a.m.–2:00 p.m.	Prepare supplemental mise en place per sous chef instructions. Assist salad cook as needed.
2:00–2:30 p.m.	Conduct storeroom inventory of produce. Deliver inventory to executive chef.
2:30–2:45 p.m.	Communicate with PM prep cook to determine PM prep list.
2:45–3:30 p.m.	Clean prep area and walk-in refrigerator. Assist PM prep cook as needed.

Figure 10.10
Scheduling Guide—Prep Cook

While charts and graphs can tell a manager how many employees in each position are needed each hour, they still leave many challenges unaddressed for the scheduler. The scheduler must take into consideration other concerns, such as the hours that an employee is available to work, the skill level of each employee, vacation requests, and each employee's wage rate. For example, a manager could opt to pair newer and senior employees during the same shifts to facilitate on-the-job training, or she could schedule her strongest employees for the busiest days. Similarly, a manager can choose to give more hours to the lower-wage workers to save money, or she can give the heavier work schedule to the most senior employees (often, the highest paid ones). She can weigh whether to have an employee work an hour of overtime or to bring in an additional employee to avoid anyone receiving overtime. While scheduling to avoid idle or overwhelmed workers should be a universal goal across businesses, there are no right answers regarding how to choose which employees to put in each time slot. Those choices are left to the manager based on the company's values and policies.

The final step in the scheduling process is to evaluate the schedule's real-world efficacy. If a manager notices that her staffing levels are unable to handle the level of forecast business, she may need to adjust her performance standards, her scheduling choices, or even her training program for the staff. Likewise, if she observes too many workers to handle a given business volume, she should adjust future schedules accordingly. In time, a manager who fine-tunes her skills based on constant feedback will become an expert scheduler.

10.4.2 Fixed Staffing Needs

Unlike hourly wage staff, the scheduling of salaried workers is based rarely on business volume. Instead, salaried workers are scheduled to cover their specific duties during the times that those tasks must be performed (Figure 10.11). For example, if there are two employees who work as assistant dining room managers, it would make sense to schedule one for lunch service and one for dinner, but definitely not to schedule both for one meal and none for the other. The storeroom manager may work when the storeroom is open or when deliveries arrive, but her hours will not change on the basis of forecasted business volume. The chef and sous chef, too, will work when their expertise is needed, which likely does not correlate to fluctuations in sales. For example, while customer levels typically drop off mid-afternoon, a chef may be required to work then to oversee dinner preparation, to meet with purveyors, or to interview job applicants. That same chef may be required to oversee dinner execution, or she may be comfortable leaving that task to her sous chef. In short, salaried positions should be scheduled based on their job responsibilities, not on the customer flow.

Supervisors overseeing a given area should not be scheduled to perform the same task at the same time. Two servers can both work side by side without creating conflict, but two equal managers overseeing the dining room at the same time can cause trouble. This is not to say that managers cannot both be present to participate in meetings together, but they should not perform supervisory duties over the same group at the same time. It is possible that an employee would get different instructions from each manager. Having just one direct report at a time helps eliminate this potential conflict for employees. (Note: A manager and an assistant manager play different roles and are not equals, so they may be scheduled together without causing problems.) Similarly, at least one manager should be available when guests are present and for the most part, when employees are on site. Imagine a scenario in which a guest has a complaint and there is no dining room manager scheduled. If the cooks preparing for lunch service run out of an ingredient, whom would they consult for direction if neither the chef, sous chef, nor purchasing manager were present? Someone with the authority to make decisions must always be available. Even overnight, hotels always have at least one manager on duty to answer questions from any department. Small bakeries might have an hourly worker arrive in the morning to open the shop, but they generally have access to a manager by phone should an emergency arise.

Because salaried workers generally receive the same compensation whether they work forty hours or less, schedulers should always plan on giving salaried employees a full forty hours (or more) unless the employee has requested time off. To do otherwise pays the employee for doing nothing—a model of inefficient scheduling.

Employee	Monday	Tuesday	Wednesday	Thursday	Friday	Saturday	Sunday
Asst. Dining Room Manager (Jones)	9 a.m.–6 p.m.	9 a.m.–6 p.m.	Off	Off	9 a.m.–6 p.m.	9 a.m.–6 p.m.	9 a.m.–6 p.m.
Asst. Dining Room Manager (Smith)	3 p.m.–1 a.m.	3 p.m.–1 a.m.	3 p.m.–1 a.m.	3 p.m.–1 a.m.	Off	Off	Off
Asst. Dining Room Manager (Alvarez)	Off	Off	9 a.m.–6 p.m.	9 a.m.–6 p.m.	4 p.m.–1 a.m.	4 p.m.–1 a.m.	4 p.m.–1 a.m.
Server (Brooks)	10 a.m.–2 p.m.; 5 p.m.–9 p.m.	10 a.m.–2 p.m.; 5 p.m.–9 p.m.	10 a.m.–2 p.m.; 5 p.m.–p.m.	10 a.m.–2 p.m.; 5 p.m.–9 p.m.	10 a.m.–2 p.m.; 5 p.m.–9 p.m.	Off	Off
Server (Hackett)	Off	Off	Off	Off	5 p.m.–12 a.m.	11 a.m.–12 a.m.	10 a.m.–5 p.m.
Server (Bachmann)	11 a.m.–2 p.m.	11 a.m.–2 p.m.	11 a.m.–2 p.m.	11 a.m.–2 p.m.	11 a.m.–2 p.m.	Off	11 a.m.–3 p.m.
Server (Lee)	Off	Off	5 p.m.–11 p.m.	5 p.m.–11 p.m.	5 p.m.–1 a.m.	5 p.m.–1 a.m.	5 p.m.–11 p.m.
Server (Dominguez)	Off	Off	11 a.m.–9 p.m.	11 a.m.–9 p.m.	11 a.m.–9 p.m.	11 a.m.–9 p.m.	Off
Server (Benoit)	4 p.m.–10 p.m.	4 p.m.–10 p.m.	Off	Off	4 p.m.–10 p.m.	4 p.m.–11 p.m.	11 a.m.–9 p.m.
Busser (Collo)	6 p.m.–11 p.m.	6 p.m.–11 p.m.	Off	6 p.m.–11 p.m.	6 p.m.–11 p.m.	6 p.m.–1 a.m.	Off
Busser (Appres)	Off	Off	6 p.m.–11 p.m.	6 p.m.–11 p.m.	6 p.m.–1 a.m.	6 p.m.–11 p.m.	11 a.m.–3 p.m.
Bartender (Yona)	11 a.m.–7 p.m.	11 a.m.–7 p.m.	11 a.m.–7 p.m.	11 a.m.–7 p.m.	11 a.m.–7 p.m.	Off	Off
Bartender (Lutz)	Off	5 p.m.–Midnight	5 p.m.–Midnight	5 p.m.–Midnight	5 p.m.–1 a.m.	5 p.m.–1 a.m.	Off
Bartender (Jemina)	Off	Off	Off	Off	7 p.m.–1 a.m.	4 p.m.–Midnight	11 a.m.–8 p.m.
Bartender (Abbot)	5 p.m.–Midnight	Off	Off	Off	Off	11 a.m.–5 p.m.	Noon–Midnight

Figure 10.11
Employee Schedule—Front of the House

For all workers, whether salaried or hourly, their schedules should be posted at least one week in advance to provide employees with sufficient notice to plan their personal responsibilities around their work schedule. Last-minute schedule notifications may lead to employees with personal conflicts, and in such situations, work is not always made the top priority. Advance notice also gives the scheduler time to make adjustments should an error be made regarding an employee's request for time off. While business volume in the restaurant industry can change dramatically in the course of a week, such changes do not usually occur regularly. Employees will understand last-minute changes once or twice a quarter from unexpected events, but managers who make last-minute changes weekly to the same employees typically find themselves with disgruntled employees in search of work elsewhere.

SUMMARY

Labor is one of the most valuable resources in any foodservice operation. Employees, under the oversight of management, maintain the business's quality and quantity standards. Loss of employees through turnover increases the cost of doing business for a company. Employees can be classified as part-time or full-time, hourly wage or salaried workers. Benefits, of which there are many possible options, also contribute to the cost of maintaining a labor force. Some costs in a business are fixed, meaning they do not change with shifts in sales volume, while others, termed "variable costs," fluctuate with sales. Labor is typically part fixed and part variable. Jobs are defined through job descriptions, performance standards, job specifications, and organizational charts. To control costs effectively, managers schedule their variable cost workers according to business volume. Peak periods require the greatest number of laborers, while slower hours call for a smaller staff. Salaried staff, on the other hand, are scheduled for the hours during which those employees can best perform their specific duties. When managed properly, a company's labor force can meet all of the organization's quality and quantity goals with little wasted time or expense.

COMPREHENSION QUESTIONS

1. A restaurant averaged 40 employees over the course of a year. What is the turnover rate for that restaurant if it employed 112 employees over the course of the year but only has 36 employees on staff at year's end?

2. List six benefits commonly given to at least some employees in a foodservice business. Are any benefits required for all employees?

3. Explain the difference between a fixed cost and a variable cost.

4. What is the difference between a job description and a job specification? Write an example of a performance standard for a prep cook who peels carrots and cucumbers and washes lettuce for a restaurant's salads.

5. A museum is open from 10:00 a.m.–5:00 p.m. The chart on the next page shows forecast business volume each hour for a given day in the museum's cafeteria. You are in charge of scheduling variable cost employees. Production standards suggest that 1 cook can handle up to 60 people in an hour, 1 server can handle 80 people in an hour, 1 cashier can handle 90 people in an hour, 1 busser can handle 120 people in an hour, and 1 dishwasher can handle 70 people in an hour. The manager also knows from experience that 2 cooks can work 2 hours each to complete the day's mise en place (separate from their cooking duties during service). Set-up for the other areas is negligible, but every area requires 1 person to perform 1 hour of cleanup after customers have left for the day. Enter in the following chart the number of people needed to staff each position for each hour of the day based on business volume and assuming that every employee operates exactly at their production standard.

Time	Business Volume	Cooks	Servers	Cashiers	Bussers	Dishwashers
8:00–9:00 a.m.	0					
9:00–10:00 a.m.	0					
10:00–11:00 a.m.	30					
11:00 a.m.–Noon	95					
Noon–1:00 p.m.	180					
1:00–2:00 p.m.	150					
2:00–3:00 p.m.	40					
3:00–4:00 p.m.	15					
4:00–5:00 p.m.	5					
5:00–6:00 p.m.	0					

6. Using the chart you completed in question 5, create a work schedule for your staff. Each type of position has one full-time employee who must be scheduled for an eight-hour shift. The rest of the workers are all part time. For the sake of simplicity, only the full-time employees will need a break (which will count as one paid hour out of their eight-hour workday). Mark in the schedule which hour each full-timer will take as her break, and remember that another employee must cover the full-timer's work during her break.

DISCUSSION QUESTIONS

1. Imagine you own a restaurant. Which positions would you make salaried and which hourly? What benefits would you offer to all of your staff and which benefits only to some? Why?

2. Which type of employee would you prefer to manage, a part-timer or a full-timer? Why? What challenges would you face if you hired 90% of your staff in that format (part-time or full-time)?

3. A business is co-owned by two people equally. The organizational chart shows that the front-of-the-house staff reports directly to one owner while the back-of-the-house staff reports directly to the other owner. There are no management levels between the employees and the owners, and the owners themselves are peers with neither reporting to a higher position. What problems might you anticipate with this organizational structure if the company has 40 employees?

4. You have worked your way up to the executive chef position in a restaurant. Your duties now include a range of management functions; cooking food for customers is no longer a required task for you. If the restaurant is open from 11:00 a.m. to midnight, six days a week, what hours do you feel you should work on the days the restaurant is open? Give a rationale for your answer.

11

Labor Management and Control

Objectives

By the end of this chapter, you will be able to:

- Calculate standard and actual labor costs given employee wage rates and work hours
- Calculate labor cost percentage
- Describe multiple methods for measuring employee efficiency and work quality
- List several ways to increase employee efficiency and thus to reduce labor costs
- Calculate prime cost and prime cost percentage

A manager who wishes to schedule employees efficiently must be able to track his labor costs to ensure that the costs remain under control and at an appropriate percentage of the budget. Earlier chapters dealt with food and beverage costs and cost percentages. Labor cost and labor cost percentages are similar concepts; controlling them is equally important to the financial health of a business. Calculating food or labor cost requires a summation of the expenses of each individual unit cost, whether an ingredient or employee. Labor cost percentage, like food cost percentage, is a comparison of the total cost to sales.

Still, there are differences in the process for calculating and evaluating costs when those costs are workers' earnings rather than ingredient expenses. While a set of tomatoes in a case all cost roughly the same amount, an hour of work from one cook may not cost the same as an hour of labor from another cook being paid a different hourly rate. Having one cook substitute for another may change the kitchen's labor cost even though both cooks do the same job. Furthermore, wage rates are not the only form of compensation for employees as the company pays benefits and taxes, too.

Because foodservice workers typically work in teams but may earn different wage rates for doing the same job, it is important to measure a group's work quantity and quality in ways that go beyond looking at labor cost alone. To assess the efficiency of a group's output, a manager may choose to calculate sales per person-hour or covers per person-hour. To evaluate a team's quality of work, a manager may measure the workers' errors per cover. Making a labor force as efficient as possible, which helps to control labor costs, is as critically important as controlling food and beverage costs is. Together, food, beverage, and labor costs make up the vast majority of all expenses in nearly every foodservice business. If they are properly controlled, a manager gives himself the best chance of generating a profit.

11.1 CALCULATING LABOR COSTS

Since a department manager knows the hourly wages or salaries of his employees, with a weekly schedule he can calculate the anticipated or standard labor cost for his department for a given day or week (Figure 11.1). (Recall that "standard" cost is the cost that is planned or budgeted while "actual" labor cost is the cost that is incurred after someone has earned his salary or wages.) Upper-level management can do the same for the company as a whole. The calculation could be made over a month or year, too, but long-term forecasts and planned annual employee schedules are typically less accurate than are the ones prepared one week out.

To calculate the standard labor cost for a single hourly employee before benefits, multiply the worker's hourly rate by the number of hours scheduled, as follows:

(For Hourly Workers)

Preliminary Labor Cost (for one employee before benefits) = Hours Scheduled (or worked) × Hourly Rate

Notice that the formula states "Scheduled or Worked." For standard labor cost, the scheduled hours are used. Once an employee has actually worked those hours, the total hours worked will provide the actual labor cost rather than the scheduled standard labor cost.

Example 11.1: An employee earns $9.50/hour and is scheduled to work 38 hours this week. How much standard labor cost does he represent before benefits?

$$\text{Preliminary Standard Labor Cost} = \text{Hours Scheduled} \times \text{Hourly Rate}$$
$$= 38 \text{ hours} \times \$9.50/\text{hour}$$
$$= \$361.00$$

Job Code Employee Detail

Job Codes	Total Pay	Total Hours	Avg Hourly Pay	Regular Pay	Regular Hours	Overtime Pay	Overtime Hours
Server	70,935.57	22,030.42	3.22	70,935.57	22,004.85	0.00	25.57
Albany NY	802.38	174.43	4.60	802.38	174.43	0.00	0.00
OMAIRA O OCASIO	51.43	11.18	4.60	51.43	11.18	0.00	0.00
JESSICA ROMANO	41.58	9.04	4.60	41.58	9.04	0.00	0.00
JESSICA HADDEN	40.66	8.84	4.60	40.66	8.84	0.00	0.00
TINA B BRISSON	40.30	8.76	4.60	40.30	8.76	0.00	0.00
BETH K KELLY	32.25	7.01	4.60	32.25	7.01	0.00	0.00
KIM B BRADLEY	31.42	6.83	4.60	31.42	6.83	0.00	0.00
RICHARD VALENTINE	31.23	6.79	4.60	31.23	6.79	0.00	0.00
MATTHEW CROSS	31.10	6.76	4.60	31.10	6.76	0.00	0.00
KATIE L LOCKWOOD	30.91	6.72	4.60	30.91	6.72	0.00	0.00
MICHAEL MOAK	29.58	6.43	4.60	29.58	6.43	0.00	0.00
MARY W WESTPHAL	28.61	6.22	4.60	28.61	6.22	0.00	0.00
HEATHER SECOR	28.47	6.19	4.60	28.47	6.19	0.00	0.00
AMY B BURGER	27.69	6.02	4.60	27.69	6.02	0.00	0.00
KAELIN C COLTRE	27.55	5.99	4.60	27.55	5.99	0.00	0.00
ELIZABET BRAMAH	27.42	5.96	4.60	27.42	5.96	0.00	0.00
SAMANTHA BOWIE	27.23	5.92	4.60	27.23	5.92	0.00	0.00

Figure 11.1

Sample POS Labor Report by Employee, No Benefits

Source: Printed with the permission of MICROS Systems, Inc.

Once the preliminary labor cost (the employee's pretax paycheck) is determined, management can next calculate the labor cost with benefits. But first, a discussion of preliminary labor cost for salaried employees is in order.

While the aforementioned formula works for hourly workers, salaried workers require a different approach. Since salaried employees earn a set amount on the basis of a year, their salary can be reduced to a cost per day by dividing their annual salary by 365 days in a year. Since the salaried worker gets paid the same amount for working five, six, or seven days in a week, calculating the preliminary labor cost for a given period of time requires that the cost per day be multiplied by the number of days in the period, not the number of days worked in that period.

(For Salaried Workers)

Preliminary Daily Labor Cost (for one employee before benefits)
= Annual Salary ÷ 365 days

This figure can be adjusted to cost per week by multiplying by seven days per week or to the cost for a given month by multiplying by the number of days in that month.

Preliminary Weekly Labor Cost = Preliminary Daily Labor Cost × 7

Example 11.2: A salaried worker earns $48,000 per year. What is the labor cost before benefits each week for this employee?

Step 1: Preliminary Daily Labor Cost = Annual Salary ÷ 365 days = $48,000 ÷ 365 = $131.507

Step 2: Preliminary Weekly Labor Cost = Preliminary Daily Labor Cost × 7 = $131.507 × 7 = $920.55

Both of the "preliminary" formulas for hourly and for salaried workers are not the complete picture but rather an intermediate step toward calculating a worker's labor cost. Benefits, too, must be taken into account. Even workers thought of as receiving no benefits incur some additional cost through social security and worker's compensation. Each employee's benefit package may be different, so the business's accountant may have to itemize each benefit separately to determine its cost for each employee. For salaried workers, that cost should remain constant until the employee earns a raise or until a benefit's cost changes. For an hourly worker, the benefits will likely change each time the employee works a different number of hours. For this reason, benefits are calculated as a percentage added to the preliminary labor cost.

Standard (or Actual) Labor Cost = Preliminary Labor Cost × (1 + Benefits Percentage as decimal)

Example 11.3: If the benefits for hourly workers cost an additional 12.4% of the worker's income, what is the standard labor cost for a worker scheduled to work 40 hours at $11.00/hour?

Step 1: Preliminary Labor Cost = Hours Scheduled × Hourly Rate = 40 hours × $11/hour = $440.00

Step 2: Standard Labor Cost = Preliminary Labor Cost × (1 + Benefits Percentage as decimal) = $440 × (1 + 0.124) = $440 × 1.124 = $494.56

Example 11.4: A manager earns $80,000/year and receives an additional 37% in benefits. What is his standard labor cost for a week?

Step 1: Preliminary Daily Labor Cost = Annual Salary ÷ 365 = $80,000 ÷ 365 = $219.178

Step 2: Preliminary Weekly Labor Cost = Preliminary Daily Labor Cost × 7 = $219.178 × 7 = $1534.25

Step 3: Standard Weekly Labor Cost = Preliminary Weekly Labor Cost × (1 + Benefits Percentage as decimal) = $1534.25 × (1 + 0.37) = $1534.25 × 1.37 = $2101.92

Calculating an individual's standard labor cost for a week is tedious, but computerized spreadsheets make the process quite easy to complete (Figure 11.2). With each worker's name, title, hourly rate or daily rate, and benefits percentage remaining constant from week to week, a manager only needs to enter each employee's scheduled hours for the period (or, in the case of salaried workers, simply the length of the period) to determine each worker's standard labor cost. To determine the standard labor cost for the department as a whole, the manager merely needs to total the standard labor costs for all employees. This process can be used to predict standard labor costs for the day, week, month, or year. The only caveat is that changes in wage rates, salaries, or benefits during the period will throw off the actual figures a bit even if the employees work exactly the number of hours scheduled. The longer the period, the less accurate the standard labor cost is likely to be compared with the actual labor cost.

Weekly Payroll Budget Worksheet			Week of: 8/19			
Name	Position	Wage Rate or Weekly Salary	Work Hours	Overtime Hours (earns $1\frac{1}{2}$)	Total Earnings
Salaried Employees (*Note:* These workers get a weekly salary that has nothing to do with how many hours they work in the week)					
Hoban, Jack	Chef	$1153.89	65	N/A	$1153.89
Lee, Kwan	Asst. DR Mgr	$673.21	50	N/A	$673.21
Mubutu, Ali	DR Manager	$1346.80	60	N/A	$1346.80
Yoaz, Leah	Sous Chef	$718.02	55	N/A	$718.02
Subtotal					$3891.92
Total including Benefits Percentage, 38.2%—Social Security, Medical, Taxes, etc. (Calculate as Subtotal Earnings × (1 + benefits percentage as decimal)					$5378.63
Hourly Employees					
Aya, Uma	Server	$6.00/hour	32		$192.00
Chron, Tai	Cook	$9.50/hour	40		$380.00
Ewer, Joe	Cook	$8.75/hour	40	2	$376.25
Felder, Eve	Server	$6.00/hour	38		$228.00
Kohr, Bob	Dishwasher	$7.00/hour	35		$245.00
Qup, Will	Dishwasher	$7.00/hour	40		$280.00
Shen, Ella	Server	$6.30/hour	40		$252.00
Subtotal					$1953.25
Total including Benefits Percentage, 21.9%—Social Security, Medical, Taxes, etc. (Calculate as Subtotal Earnings × (1 + benefits percentage as decimal)					$2381.01
Total All Employees (Salaried + Hourly)					$7759.64

Figure 11.2
Payroll Budget Worksheet (Weekly)

11.1.1 Standard versus Actual Labor Costs

Using the same formulas for determining standard labor cost, a manager can calculate actual labor cost by entering the hours worked instead of the hours scheduled. In an ideal situation, the two would be identical, but that rarely happens in the average foodservice organization. An emergency may occur and the staff may need to work a slightly longer shift than planned. One worker may call out sick and a higher-paid worker may be asked to take his place, possibly earning overtime in the process. Sometimes, business may be so slow that a few workers are sent home early to save on labor cost. (Because salaried managers do not typically earn extra income for working additional hours, a manager can cut labor costs during slow periods by performing some of the frontline tasks himself.) In all of these situations, the standard labor cost will differ from the actual labor cost. Figure 11.3 illustrates how the standard weekly labor cost from Figure 11.2 might differ from the actual labor cost. Notice that some employees have had to work additional hours beyond their scheduled shifts, and a lower-paid cook, who calls out sick, is covered by a higher-paid cook. Salaried workers earn the same amount no matter how their actual hours differ from their scheduled hours.

Weekly Payroll Worksheet					Week of: 8/19				
Name	Position	Wage Rate or Weekly Salary	Work Hours (Budget)	Overtime Hours (Budget)	Total Earnings (Budget)	Hours (Actual)	Overtime (Actual)	Earnings (Actual)	Variance
Salaried Employees									
Hoban, Jack	Chef	$1153.89	65	N/A	$1153.89	70	N/A	$1153.89	0
Lee, Kwan	Asst. DR Mgr	$673.21	50	N/A	$673.21	52	N/A	$673.21	0
Mubutu, Ali	DR Manager	$1346.80	60	N/A	$1346.80	64	N/A	$1346.80	0
Yoaz, Leah	Sous Chef	$718.02	55	N/A	$718.02	65	N/A	$718.02	0
Subtotal					$3891.92			$3891.92	0
Total including Benefits Percentage, 38.2%—Social Security, Medical, Taxes, etc. (Calculate as Subtotal Earnings × (1 + benefits percentage as decimal)					$5378.63			$5378.63	0
Hourly Employees									
Aya, Uma	Server	$6.00/hour	32		$192.00	34		$204.00	12.00
Chron, Tai	Cook	$9.50/hour	40		$380.00	40	8	$494.00	114.00
Ewer, Joe	Cook	$8.75/hour	40	2	$376.25	36		$315.00	(61.25)
Felder, Eve	Server	$6.00/hour	38		$228.00	38		$228.00	0
Kohr, Bob	Dishwasher	$7.00/hour	35		$245.00	40		$280.00	35.00
Qup, Will	Dishwasher	$7.00/hour	40		$280.00	40		$280.00	0
Shen, Ella	Server	$6.30/hour	40		$252.00	40		$252.00	0
Subtotal					$1953.25			$2053.00	99.75
Total including Benefits Percentage, 21.9%—Social Security, Medical, Taxes, etc. (Calculate as Subtotal Earnings × (1 + benefits percentage as decimal)					$2381.01			$2502.61	121.60
Total All Employees (Salaried + Hourly)					$7759.64			$7881.24	121.60

Figure 11.3
Payroll Actual Worksheet (Weekly)

While emergencies do happen, proper planning and quality management help to keep the differences (variances) between standard and actual labor costs to a minimum. Many of the side effects of poor management come across in labor cost variances. High turnover may result in new employees working at less than 100% efficiency or in senior employees working overtime to cover open positions. Unhappy workers may have higher rates of absenteeism, which again makes controlling overtime difficult. Poor training may cause employees to work slower than anticipated or to make multiple errors that take time to correct. In short, while managers can learn to schedule employees to make their operations and standard labor cost as cost-effective as possible, actually hitting the budgeted labor cost target comes from management skills well beyond scheduling ability.

11.2 LABOR COST PERCENTAGE

Reviewing variances between standard and actual labor costs is important, but a better measure of management and scheduling effectiveness is to analyze labor cost percentages. If a restaurant is unusually busy one night and does an extra 20% in sales, management may need to call in additional staff to handle the business. If sales are 20% higher, then labor cost should be 20% higher as well to keep budget percentage projections in line. If labor cost goes up 30%, management will have to explain its poor performance. If labor cost only goes up 10% (and quality standards do not suffer), management will be commended for its increased efficiency and higher profits. In both cases, the labor cost in dollars will vary from the standard, scheduled cost, but this alone is not a measure of management performance. The percentages tell the true story.

Labor cost percentages describe labor cost in comparison with sales revenue. To calculate labor cost percentage, simply divide the total labor cost by the total sales and convert the resulting decimal to its percentage form.

$$\text{Labor Cost \%} = \frac{\text{Labor Cost (in dollars)}}{\text{Sales (in dollars)}}$$

The labor cost and the sales totals must cover the same period, so that the percentage reflects the costs incurred to generate those exact sales. For example, the labor cost for the month must be compared with the sales for the same month. Otherwise, the resulting data is meaningless. Labor cost percentage can be calculated as standard labor cost percentage using standard labor cost and forecast sales for a given period or as actual labor cost percentage using actual labor cost and actual sales figures for a given period.

Example 11.5: Calculate a business's labor cost percentage for April if the labor cost for that month was $24,874, and the sales for April were $83,577.

$$\text{Labor Cost \%} = \frac{\text{Labor Cost}}{\text{Sales}} = \frac{\$24,874}{\$83,577} = 0.2976 \text{ or, in its percentage form, } 29.8\%$$

Comparing percentages rather than dollars allows management to evaluate its performance when sales volume differs significantly from the forecast (see Figure 11.4). Management can sometimes adjust schedules on the fly to mitigate loss from lower than predicted sales or to expand profits during busier-than-expected periods.

Job Code Summary

Job Codes	Total Pay	Total Hours	Avg Hourly Pay	Regular Pay	Regular Hours	Overtime Pay	Overtime Hours
Server	70,935.73	22,030.42	3.22	70,935.73	22,004.85	0.00	25.57
Broiler	55,082.16	4,374.01	12.59	55,082.16	4,374.01	0.00	0.00
Saute	40,957.02	3,573.89	11.46	40,957.02	3,573.89	0.00	0.00
Fry	37,900.46	3,511.70	10.79	37,900.46	3,511.70	0.00	0.00
Plate,	35,749.91	3,257.21	10.98	35,749.91	3,257.21	0.00	0.00
Host/Hostess	28,569.95	4,871.24	5.87	28,569.95	4,871.24	0.00	0.00
Dish	23,696.23	2,570.26	9.22	23,696.23	2,546.23	0.00	24.03
Svc Bartndr	14,485.32	4,406.47	3.29	14,485.32	4,398.95	0.00	7.52
Bartender	14,159.37	3,678.49	3.85	14,159.37	3,678.49	0.00	0.00
Clean Crew	12,934.67	1,302.11	9.93	12,934.67	1,302.11	0.00	0.00
Busser	10,957.66	2,021.26	5.42	10,957.66	2,017.02	0.00	4.24

Net Sales	Total Labor	Total Time	Avg Hourly Pay	Labor Cost (% Net Sales)	Sales Per Labor Hour
2,244,991.94	417,001.71	64,197.99	6.50	18.6%	34.97

Figure 11.4
Sample POS Labor Cost Report by Job Title, Including Labor Cost Percentage

Source: Printed with the permission of MICROS Systems, Inc.

Example 11.6: A manager forecasts $18,000 in sales for the week in his department. His department's labor cost, as scheduled, is $6,188. By the end of the week, sales are only $17,050, but the manager sent a couple of employees home early on certain days to reduce labor costs. As a result, actual labor cost for the week is only $5,942. Compare the standard and the actual labor cost percentages for the department.

$$\text{Labor Cost \%} = \frac{\text{Labor Cost}}{\text{Sales}}$$

$$\text{Standard Labor Cost \%} = \frac{\$6,188}{\$18,000} = 0.3437 \text{ or } 34.4\%$$

$$\text{Actual Labor Cost \%} = \frac{\$5,942}{\$17,050} = 0.3485 \text{ or } 34.9\%$$

The actual labor cost percentage at 34.9% is slightly higher than the standard labor cost percentage, which is 34.4%.

Because labor cost, unlike food cost, is only a semivariable expense, it is difficult to evaluate a manager's performance by simply comparing actual labor cost percentage with the standard labor cost percentage. In Example 11.6, note that the question does not ask whether or not the manager has done an appropriate job. There is just not enough information here to make such an assessment. For example, he cannot reduce salaries for the week, which likely includes his own pay. Thus, it would have been difficult to reduce hourly workers' wages enough to compensate for his unchanged salary. That he reduced the labor cost at all is a good sign. The only way to know whether or not the manager reacted appropriately (unless the actual labor cost percentage ends up lower than the standard labor cost percentage without causing quality to suffer) is to delve deeper into the choices he made in cutting hours to see if he could have cut hourly staff even further. Similarly, when sales are larger than forecast, the labor cost percentage should end up lower than the standard labor cost percentage; after all, the salaried employees do not receive more money when sales volume increases. Salaries are fixed expenses.

The concept that labor cost percentages should improve when business volume increases (or worsen when business decreases) is part of the reason why managers must devote attention to increasing revenue as well as controlling costs. Since fixed costs do not change with business volume, an increase in sales beyond the budget should translate to greater profits as long as management controls variable costs appropriately.

Consider a simplistic restaurant example in which there is only one short-order cook working at a time. Because there is only one cook's position, the kitchen is always fully staffed whenever the restaurant is open. In effect, the cook is a fixed cost even though his wages may be hourly. The same is true for the other work areas if there are only one server and one dishwasher working at a time, which is the case in this example. Let's assume for the sake of simplicity that these three workers earn a combined $300 for their eight-hour shift (and that there are no other employees to speak of other than an owner who does not take a salary). If the restaurant typically does $1,000 in sales during that eight-hour period, then the labor cost percentage will be 30% ($300 ÷ $1,000). If the sales drop to $800, labor cost percentage will increase to 37.5% ($300 ÷ $800). Alternatively, an increase to $1,200 in sales reduces the labor cost percentage to 25% ($300 ÷ $1,200). This is one reason why labor cost is considered only semivariable. Since staffing levels can only be cut so far (to a minimum of one employee per position or per work area), labor cost percentages depend heavily on actual sales hitting their forecast goals.

There are, of course, other factors beyond sales volume that greatly impact labor cost percentages. A restaurant's design and equipment limit how efficiently an employee can work. When a kitchen includes many laborsaving devices, fewer cooks are needed to complete the required prep work. An automatic dishwasher will allow a large restaurant to operate with fewer human dishwashers than a similarly sized restaurant with only one three-compartment sink does. A facility in which the kitchen is located close to the dining room allows servers to take fewer steps to retrieve food than they would in a facility in which the kitchen is a long distance from the dining room. Requiring fewer steps for servers translates to more efficient service staff and thus, to fewer servers needed to handle a given number of customers.

Outsourcing (paying another company rather than one's own employees to perform a given task) and menu selections also impact labor cost. A manager may discover that it is cheaper to hire an outside company to clean the kitchen and dining room each night than it is to pay his own staff to do it. A restaurant that buys more of its food preprocessed will require fewer labor-hours to produce meals than does a similar restaurant with a fully scratch-cooked menu. A limited, easy-to-prepare menu requires fewer laborers than does a menu with a larger number of extravagant offerings. Case in point, two cooks could probably handle 250 customers for lunch in a restaurant with only five dishes, all fried; a restaurant with ten multicomponent entrees, each using a different cooking technique, might require five cooks to handle 250 lunch customers.

As many variables influence labor cost and labor cost percentage, a manager must consider all pertinent information when making decisions that affect labor cost. After all, profit, not labor cost, is the ultimate goal. Outsourcing bakery and dessert production may reduce labor cost but increase food cost. Limited menus and minimal service styles cost less in labor but command lower prices than a higher-end restaurant does. Laborsaving devices can cut costs, but a small facility may not have the space to accommodate them. In short, managers must be able to calculate their labor costs and labor cost percentages while realizing that the data only highlights potential problems; the solutions are for the managers to determine.

11.3 MEASURING AND IMPROVING PERFORMANCE

Since increased revenue typically translates to lower labor cost percentages (or at least to labor cost that is easier to control), there are measures that management can use for the ongoing assessment of employee performance irrespective of labor cost. Some of these tools are also effective in evaluating a team of employees when attributing a team's output to a single worker is impossible.

Sales per Person (Employee).   Thanks to POS systems, managers can determine exactly how many dollars in sales each server generates. A computer can calculate this data per hour, per shift, or per guest. Servers can be compared to see if one is better able to coax higher sales out of his customers than are other servers. Cross training in effective sales techniques typically helps increase sales overall for an operation. While cooks and dishwashers can be evaluated by sales per person, too, their performance is better measured collectively. Depending on how the kitchen operates, it may be impossible to tie each back-of-the-house employee to a specific set of dollars, so sales per person for cooks or dishwashers is generally calculated as sales per person-hour. *Person-hours* are the sum of work hours completed by the people in a group for a given period. The formula is:

$$\text{Sales per Person-Hour} = \frac{\text{Total Sales for a Period}}{\text{Number of Person-Hours during That Period}}$$

In other words, if $1,000 in sales occurs during a one-hour period and four kitchen employees are working during that hour, the sales per person-hour are $1,000 (sales) ÷ 4 (person-hours) = $250 per person-hour for the kitchen staff. Again, total person-hours are calculated as the number of hours worked by all persons during the considered period.

Example 11.7: A restaurant grosses $2,892 between 11:30 a.m. and 2:00 p.m. In the kitchen, there are 3 cooks and 2 dishwashers who work that lunch shift. Calculate the sales per person-hour for the combined cooks and dishwashers team for this particular meal period.

Because the period being evaluated goes for 2.5 hours and each employee in the group works for that entire period, the total number of person-hours is 2.5 hours × 5 employees = 12.5 person-hours.

$$\text{Sales per Person-Hour} = \frac{\text{Sales}}{\text{Person-Hours}} = \frac{\$2,892}{12.5} = \$231.36$$

Covers per Person. A POS system can also measure the number of covers each server handles in an hour or in a shift. Again, a server who can handle more covers per hour is more valuable. As with sales per person, covers per person can be modified into covers per person-hour for evaluating the output of certain employee groups (or, if desired, for all employees in the operation).

$$\text{Covers per Person-Hour} = \frac{\text{Total Covers for a Period}}{\text{Number of Person-Hours during That Period}}$$

Example 11.8: A restaurant serves 308 guests (covers) between 5:00 and 9:00 p.m., the restaurant's dinner service hours. While 6 employees work in the back-of-the-house for the entire dinner service, 2 others work in the kitchen for just 2 hours of the service. Calculate the covers per person-hour for the back-of-the-house for this dinner shift.

To calculate the covers per person-hour, first recognize that 6 employees work the full 4 hours of dinner while 2 other employees only work 2 hours each. Multiply the number of employees by the number of hours they work separately and then add the totals together:

Step 1: 6 employees × 4 hours = 24 person-hours
Step 2: 2 employees × 2 hours = 4 person-hours
Step 3: Total Person-Hours = 24 + 4 = 28 person-hours
Step 4: Now, use the covers per person-hour formula:

$$\text{Covers per Person-Hour} = \frac{\text{Covers}}{\text{Person-Hours}} = \frac{308}{28} = 11$$

For both sales per person-hour and covers per person-hour, the goal is to establish a baseline and then to work on improving efficiency. Since each operation is different, 23 covers per person-hour may be a lot for a high-end restaurant or a small amount for a fast food establishment. Once a business establishes a pattern, management should work to maintain or to improve the dollars and customers per person-hour. These figures, which are calculated "per person-hour" measure employee efficiency better than labor cost percentage, which is impacted by variations in employees' wage rates. Both are ultimately necessary to determine where a cost-saving opportunity exists (in improved employee output or in more cost-effective scheduling based on employee wage rates).

Errors per Cover. While increased employee output (higher sales per person-hour or covers per person-hour) typically results in better labor cost percentages, it is all for naught if quality goes down as a result. After all, twice as many guests per hour getting low quality food and service can result in no return customers the following week. Consequently, quality standards must be maintained as efficiency increases. But humans are not infallible, so some errors are to be expected. To measure quality, a manager can track the number of errors (or voids) per cover, which should be a decimal well below 1. To calculate errors per cover, simply record the number of errors that occur during a period, usually in an hour or in a shift. Then divide the number of errors by the number of covers served during the same period. An error might be a dropped plate, a returned entrée, a burned food item, or some other mistake that results in an unsellable dish.

$$\text{Errors per Cover} = \frac{\text{Number of Errors in a Period}}{\text{Number of Covers Served in That Period}}$$

Example 11.9: A restaurant maintains a void sheet of all the errors that result in unsalable food. During one particular dinner, there were 3 dropped dishes, 2 misorders, and 2 burnt entrées out of 241 total covers served. Calculate the number of errors per cover for this particular dinner.

There are a total of 7 errors (3 dropped dishes + 2 misorders + 2 burnt entrées).

$$\text{Errors per Cover} = \frac{\text{Errors}}{\text{Covers}} = \frac{7}{241} = 0.029$$

When calculated by the hour, a manager can see if the number of errors grows as business increases during a service period. While the number of errors in an hour may increase proportionally to the number of covers, ideally the ratio will remain consistently low. For example, if a restaurant has one error when it serves hundred customers and two errors when it serves 200 customers, the number of errors per cover remains the same, 0.01. However, if the number of errors grows to six when 300 customers are served, then the ratio has actually doubled to 0.02 errors per cover. Normally, this would be an unacceptable increase in errors for management. In such an instance, a manager should investigate the cause of the increase to see what corrective action the employees or the manager must take to bring quality back in line. The same process can be followed across service periods to compare errors per cover on a slow business day versus on a busy day.

11.3.1 Additional Factors That Impact Performance

Some of the factors that impact production quality and quantity—turnover, scheduling, facility layout, equipment, menu, and outsourcing through purchasing prefabricated products—have already been discussed elsewhere in this book. However, a manager has the power to do many other things to improve labor costs.

Training.   Perhaps the best way to improve employees' productivity is through proper hiring and training. Untrained or poorly trained employees are likely to make more mistakes and work more slowly than their counterparts. Training costs money upfront, but it usually leads to reduced labor costs down the road as long as the operation does not have high turnover. If a manager hires a bad "fit" for the company, that employee may never perform at the desired quality and quantity levels. Ideally, a good manager will filter out most of the poor choices during the interview process and quickly dismiss any bad fits before they become too great a burden on the company.

Motivating and Managing Employees Effectively.   A good manager inspires his staff to come to work and to meet their goals every day. An abusive manager causes increased absenteeism or high turnover rates. When employees do not show up for their scheduled shifts, managers are forced to adjust schedules on the fly, often at a higher cost than planned. Consequently, a manager with good supervisory skills often has an easier time keeping labor costs in check than does a poor manager. Through good personnel management, a supervisor can keep the actual labor costs close to the standard labor costs.

Forecasting Accurately.   When a manager forecasts accurately, his presumably cost-effective work schedule should not require last minute adjustment. If he regularly makes major errors in forecasting, he may need to ask employees to work overtime to cover greater-than-expected business volume. Similarly, if he forecasts too high, he will have too many employees being paid for the sales levels actually generated. In either case, the only way a manager's schedule is effective at controlling labor cost is through accurate forecasting.

Reducing Injuries and Illness.   A sick or injured employee cannot and should not work. These employees cause the same problems with on-the-fly scheduling that unmotivated, no-show workers do even though sick or injured workers represent a very different management challenge. Additionally, when an employee receives workers' compensation, the business's payment for the workers' compensation program may go up. The best way to keep motivated employees on the job is to ensure a safe working environment. Including safety instruction as part of training and maintaining a safe facility help reduce the number of employee injuries. Wellness programs may also help employees to require fewer sick days—another cost saver.

Labor cost is a major expense for a foodservice company, and a manager impacts labor cost in many small ways every day. The better a manager keeps employees on the job as scheduled, the more likely he is to control labor costs effectively.

11.4   PRIME COST

With all of this discussion on controlling labor cost, it is important to acknowledge that labor cost and food cost do not function in isolation from each other. When a purchaser buys more prefabricated ingredients, labor cost goes down but food cost goes up.

A manager who pushes staff to work beyond their reasonable production levels may reduce labor cost only to find more food production errors and thus, higher food costs. A labor cost savings that is offset by an equal increase in food cost (or vice versa) results in no additional gain in profit.

Prime cost is the sum of food and beverage costs (a.k.a. cost of goods sold) and labor costs including benefits. To calculate prime cost, use the formula:

$$\text{Prime Cost} = \text{Cost of Goods Sold} + \text{Labor Cost}$$

Example 11.10: If the cost of goods sold in a restaurant is $37,800 for a month and the labor cost for the same month is $48,200, what is the prime cost for that month?

$$\text{Prime Cost} = \text{Cost of Goods Sold} + \text{Labor Cost} = \$37,800 + \$48,200 = \$86,000$$

Like food cost, beverage cost, and labor cost, prime cost can be expressed as a percentage of sales.

$$\text{Prime Cost \%} = \frac{\text{Prime Cost}}{\text{Sales}}$$

Example 11.11: If the restaurant in example 11.10 earns $155,000 in sales during that month, what is the prime cost percentage for that month in the restaurant?

$$\text{Prime Cost \%} = \frac{\text{Prime Cost}}{\text{Sales}} = \frac{\$86,000}{\$155,000} = 0.5548 \text{ or } 55.5\%$$

An improved prime cost percentage is the ideal goal for a cost control manager as this typically translates to higher profits. To achieve this goal a manager must reduce labor, food, or beverage costs without increasing the other costs beyond the realized savings. The caveat, of course, is that cost savings must not come as the result of a reduction in quality standards either. Doing so may save money in the short run only to undermine long-term revenue through customer dissatisfaction.

Example 11.12: A manager has a food cost budget of $41,000, a beverage cost budget of $19,000, and a labor cost budget of $46,000 for a month. At the end of the month, the actual food cost is $42,300 and the actual beverage cost is $18,600. Actual labor cost is $46,500. Sales were budgeted at $300,000, but actual sales were $305,000. Did the manager do a good job controlling costs or not? To find out, compare standard and actual prime cost percentages.

Step 1: Calculate budgeted prime cost and actual prime cost.

$$\text{Prime Cost} = \text{Food Cost} + \text{Beverage Cost} + \text{Labor Cost}$$

$$\text{Budgeted Prime Cost} = \$41,000 + \$19,000 + \$46,000 = \$106,000$$

$$\text{Actual Prime Cost} = \$42,300 + \$18,600 + \$46,500 = \$107,400$$

Step 2: Calculate budgeted and actual prime cost percentages.

$$\text{Prime Cost \%} = \frac{\text{Prime Cost}}{\text{Sales}}$$

Budgeted Prime Cost % = $106,000 ÷ $300,000 = 0.3533 or 35.3%

Actual Prime Cost % = $107,400 ÷ $305,000 = 0.3521 or 35.2%

Since the actual prime cost percentage is slightly lower than the budgeted prime cost percentage, the manager has done a great job controlling costs. Even though the actual prime cost in dollars is higher than budgeted, the increase is likely the result of higher sales volume. The prime cost percentages reveal the best measure of the manager's performance in controlling costs.

SUMMARY

A department's or business's labor cost can be calculated both as a standard labor cost (according to the employees' scheduled hours) and an actual labor cost (based on the hours employees actually work). Labor cost percentage allows a manager to evaluate labor management effectiveness across periods of varying sales volume. Labor cost percentage (rather than standard versus actual labor cost variance) becomes a better measure of labor management when sales volume has changed significantly after a schedule has been posted. Since labor cost can only be cut so low, maintaining or increasing sales volume is one of the best ways to control labor costs. Employee productivity can be measured in other ways, including sales per person-hour and covers per person-hour, which allow a

manager to evaluate the performance of a team collectively. The value for errors per cover reflects the team's adherence to quality standards. Turnover, scheduling, facility layout, equipment, menu, purchasing, training, management's motivational approach, forecasting, and employee safety all impact the labor cost in a foodservice business. Prime cost, the sum of labor cost and cost of goods sold, measures a manager's ability to control the largest variable costs at the same time. Monitoring prime cost helps to ensure that a manager is not cutting costs on labor only to raise the company's food expense or vice-versa. By effectively controlling labor cost and prime cost, a cost control manager can help a company to reach its profit goals.

COMPREHENSION QUESTIONS

1. A worker earns $12.25/hour and is scheduled to work a thirty-eight-hour week. What is the preliminary standard labor cost for this worker? If the benefits percentage for the company is 18.2%, what is the standard labor cost including benefits for this worker?

2. Using the information from question 1, what is the actual preliminary labor cost and actual labor cost for this worker if he works a forty-hour week? If he works a forty-two-hour week?

3. A salaried worker earns $42,000 a year. His company provides him with benefits worth 34.5% of his salary. What is his preliminary daily labor cost and his daily labor cost with benefits?

4. Using the information from question 3, what is the worker's weekly labor cost? How much does he get paid if he works a forty-hour week? If he works a fifty-hour week?

5. Using the chart below, calculate the standard labor cost for the department assuming that cooks earn $10/hour, servers and cashiers earn $9/hour, and bussers and dishwashers earn $8/hour. You are the only manager, and you earn a $48,000 annual salary. Benefits for all employees, including you, are an additional 16% of wages.

Position	Work Hours	Overtime Hours	Wage Rate/Weekly Salary	Total Earnings
You/Manager	50			
Cook 1	40	8		
Cook 2	40			
Server 1	30			
Server 2	37			
Cashier	40			
Busser	40			
Dishwasher	40	8		
Subtotal				
Total including Benefits Percentage				

6. A bakery has an actual labor cost of $2,780 the same week it earns $8,240 in sales. What is the labor cost percentage for this week at the bakery?

7. The bakery in question 6 was scheduled to have a standard labor cost of $2,600 with forecast sales of $8,100. Did the actual labor cost percentage from question 6 beat, meet, or fall below the standard labor cost percentage? State the standard labor cost percentage in your answer.

8. Of the measures of sales per person-hour, covers per person-hour, and errors per cover, which ones measure employee quantity output and which measure employee work quality?

9. A restaurant serves 180 guests and earns $5,760 in sales during a three-hour dinner service. Five back-of-the-house employees work during the entire dinner service. Calculate the sales per person-hour and the covers per person-hour for the back-of-the-house team.

10. The same restaurant from question 9 serves 220 guests and earns $7,260 in sales during the following day's three-hour dinner service. However, it takes six back-of-the-house employees to handle the workload. Calculate the sales per person-hour and the covers per person-hour for the back-of-the-house team on this day. On which day is the team more efficient in its output?

11. A restaurant handles 180 customers but has 6 errors during service on Monday. The same restaurant handles 220 customers but has 8 errors during service on Tuesday. Calculate the errors per cover for each day. Assuming each error results in a guest having to wait for a dish to be remade, on which day did the restaurant staff provide higher quality service to its guests overall, as measured solely by the errors per cover rate?

12. List five factors within the control of management that impact labor cost.

13. Calculate the prime cost for a restaurant that has a cost of goods sold of $36,000 and a labor cost of $66,000 for the month of March.

14. Using the information from question 13, calculate the prime cost percentage if the restaurant has sales of $161,000 in March.

15. The restaurant from questions 13 and 14 sees an increase of $2,000 in its cost of goods sold and an increase of $1,000 in its labor cost in April. Sales for April are $165,000. Calculate the prime cost percentage for April. Did the restaurant control costs better in March or in April?

DISCUSSION QUESTIONS

1. When a restaurant operates exactly on budget, its labor cost (including hourly wages, salaries, and benefits) is 30% of sales. If sales do not meet their targets, should an owner still expect the management to hit a labor cost percentage of 30%? Why or why not?

2. Why does absenteeism (for any reason) impact labor cost so much? In other words, if one employee is

out (and not getting paid) while another employee works his job for him, why isn't that essentially an equal swap in labor cost?

3. A chef earns an additional bonus for every percentage point he reduces the food cost percentage. There are no other bonuses. Is this a good bonus system from management's point-of-view? What possible problem exists with this system?

4. Your company's sales volume is projected to decline significantly in the upcoming year due to a poor local economy. You employ full-time senior workers with high wage rates, part-time workers with low wage rates, and salaried managers who earn benefits.

You need to cut your labor cost. How would you do it? What are the possible downsides of your choices?

5. You have two different teams of back-of-the-house workers in your restaurant. One group works Monday through Thursday. The other works Friday through Sunday. You notice that the Friday through Sunday group consistently has a higher sales per person-hour and covers per person-hour ratio than the other group does? Should this be a concern? How would you address it, if at all, if the difference in ratios between the two groups is relatively small? How would you address it if the difference is extremely large?

12

Revenue Prediction

Be it planning purchase quantities, kitchen production, or employee schedules, a manager relies heavily on an accurate forecast. Imagine trying to control costs without knowing if you will see 10 or 1,000 customers for dinner service. Some businesses lend themselves to easy forecasting. Hospitals, schools, and prisons have nearly exact counts of the number of people who will be eating on a given day. Their captive audiences have no alternative dining locations, so forecasting meal counts is a bit easier than it is in a restaurant. Restaurants, some of which do not take reservations, have to rely almost entirely on historical data and on a manager's proficiency in educated guesswork. Even restaurants that do take reservations cannot assume that the number of reservations represents the exact number of people who will dine there. Inevitably, there will be no-shows and walk-ins to skew the total count. However, the more accurately a manager predicts customer counts, the easier it is to control costs.

Forecasting people is only half of the challenge. A manager must also divine exactly what number of each dish will be sold. What percentage of the population will order dessert? How many will want chicken instead of fish? Wedding caterers sometimes ask the bride and groom to poll their guests in advance, so they can have an exact count of each entrée choice. Restaurants do not have that luxury. Most guests don't even know what they will order until they sit down and look at a menu. Fortunately, behavior patterns for a discrete market population tend to be stable and predictable over time. Managers can use tools, such as a guest check average, to estimate sales dollars expected for a given day. They can also forecast how many of each dish will be required of the kitchen. As a manager's predictions become more accurate over time, she can tweak the menu in small ways to manipulate customer food selections and thus, to increase a restaurant's profitability. Developing the skills to predict and to monitor business levels is essential to a manager's ability to generate profit.

Objectives

By the end of this chapter, you will be able to:

- Forecast customer counts given a set of variables and historical data
- Calculate guest check average and use it to calculate forecast sales dollars
- Calculate seat turnover
- Calculate menu mix percentages given a set of historical data
- Conduct a menu analysis and use the data to suggest menu adjustments to increase profitability
- Write a kitchen production schedule based on a given menu mix and forecast
- Reconcile kitchen production with sales to account for any missing or unrecorded food

12.1 FORECASTING CUSTOMER COUNTS

It is difficult for a brand new restaurant to predict its business level accurately for its first day. However, each day thereafter provides a manager the most important information for forecasting—historical data. With historical data, a manager has a basis on which to predict future customer behavior. For example, a manager might expect to see 200 customers on their opening Tuesday, but only 100 show up. Armed with this bit of historical data, the manager will know to plan for a number closer to 100 than to 200 for the second day of business.

Customer counts, however, are not the sole variables needed to predict business levels accurately. In time, managers amass a large store of data and how it impacts business. Holidays, local events and festivals, weather reports, days of the week, and current trends all inform how tomorrow's business will differ from today's levels. The process for forecasting, though difficult to master, is straightforward.

1. Collect as much historical data as possible to initiate a forecast.
2. Adjust prior data using rolling averages or trends.
3. Make further adjustments on the basis of qualitative factors to create a final forecast.
4. Record actual counts and other data to evaluate the forecast's accuracy and to adjust for future forecasting.

12.1.1 Collecting Historical Data

Each foodservice operation can and should keep track of its sales history. Managers must be able to look back at any prior business day to see exactly how many customers were served. In addition to knowing the customer counts, the manager should know what number made reservations, how many were walk-ins, and what the group collectively ordered. This sort of data is readily available through the restaurant's POS system, but it could be compiled by hand if necessary.

In addition to the quantitative data, managers should record other qualitative data about each business day. Commonly recorded facts include the weather, special events or conventions in the area, holidays, local construction projects, local business competition changes, marketing promotions by the business or by its competitors, and any other data that is a possible cause for business fluctuations from the previous day or week. Managers (or other employees) may record this information in the restaurant's computer system, or they may simply maintain a handwritten logbook.

12.1.2 Rolling Averages and Trends

Depending on how long an establishment has been in business, a manager will typically reference the same day of the week last week or last year as a starting point. New businesses may not have a year of historical data, and major menu or concept changes may invalidate last year's data, but in general, the third Tuesday in March last year is a great starting point to forecast customer counts for the third Tuesday in March this year. (The same days of the week are used rather than the immediately preceding day because people's dining habits typically change dramatically with the day of the week. Business for a fine dining restaurant in a residential area is likely to be much higher on the weekends than it is on the weekdays, while a luncheonette in a business district may be busy during the week but completely empty on weekends. Trying to use Sunday's numbers to predict Monday's business levels is an exercise in futility.)

With that starting point in hand, a manager must now adjust it on the basis of business trends. First, the manager checks to see if business levels have been changing up or down at a consistent rate. For example, if the last three weeks' customer counts have all been 5% higher than last year's counts, the manager can safely assume that next week's counts will also be 5% higher than last year's numbers. Trends may be used from week to week as well. If a new business has experienced a 2% increase in customers each week, a manager may assume that next week's business will continue to grow by 2%.

To calculate a percentage increase or decrease, use the following formula:

$$\text{Percentage Change} = \frac{\text{Current Customer Count} - \text{Prior Customer Count}}{\text{Prior Customer Count}}$$

This will provide the percentage in decimal form. Multiply by 100 to convert it to its percentage form. If the number is negative, then the trend is a decrease in business. If it is positive, then the business is growing.

Example 12.1: A restaurant saw 212 customers last Friday and 218 this Friday. What is the percentage increase this week over last?

$$\text{Percentage Change} = \frac{\text{Current Customers} - \text{Prior Customers}}{\text{Prior Customers}}$$

$$= \frac{218 - 212}{212} = 0.028 \text{ or } 2.8\% \text{ increase}$$

A single week's percentage change is only significant if it is supported by similar trends; however, if each of the past several weeks has shown a percentage increase between 2% and 3%, the manager may choose to adjust next week's forecast by 3% over this week's count.

Once a manager knows the trend, she can adjust an historical guest count to generate an initial forecast. To adjust a customer count up or down according to a trend, use the following formula:

New Customer Count = Prior Customer Count × (1 + Percentage Change in decimal form)

Remember that the percentage change will be a negative number if the trend is headed downward.

Example 12.2: A business has demonstrated a consistent decrease in business of 3.4% over last year's customer counts. If last year's Memorial Day saw 188 customers, how many customers might the manager forecast for this year's Memorial Day?

New Customer Count = Prior Customer Count × (1 + Percentage Change in decimal form)

Note: Since this is a decrease, the percentage change is actually −3.4% or −0.034 in mathematical terms.

New Customer Count = 188 × [1 + (−0.034)] = 188 × (1 − 0.034)

= 188 × 0.966 = 181.6 or 182 customers

While trends work quite well for forecasting, some operations may not have a clear-cut trend. For example, if a restaurant sees a 0.4% increase in business one week, followed by a 1.2% decrease the following week and a 4.2% increase the week after, it is nearly impossible to guess how business will change in future weeks. In such cases, a manager may prefer to forecast on the basis of a rolling average, which is simply the average number of guests over a multiday period. Using a rolling average allows a restaurant to approximate guest levels from historical data while reducing the impact to the forecast of anomalies (unusually high or low business levels).

Before computing a rolling average, one must first decide how many weeks' worth of data to use to generate the average. A manager might choose to go back two, three, four weeks, or more. Averaging over longer time spans reduces the impact of anomalies, but it tends to mask any newly emerging trends. For that reason, businesses with clear trends are better off using the trend approach than the rolling averages approach.

To calculate a rolling average, use the following formula:

$$\text{Rolling Average Customer Count} = \frac{C_1 + C_2 + C_3 + \cdots + C_N}{N}$$

in which each C is the customer count for that period (day, week, month) and N is the total number of periods counted. For example, if a manager conducts a rolling average over four Tuesdays, C_N is the customer count on the fourth Tuesday and $N = 4$.

Example 12.3: A business forecasts using a rolling average over three weeks. If the company saw 376 customers three Saturdays ago, 322 two Saturdays ago, and 401 last Saturday, what is the rolling average customer count to use for the upcoming Saturday forecast?

$$\text{Rolling Average} = \frac{C_1 + C_2 + C_3}{N} = \frac{376 + 322 + 401}{3} = \frac{1099}{3}$$

$$= 366.3 \text{ or } 366 \text{ customers}$$

It should be noted that even restaurants that accommodate guests by reservation only would need to forecast beyond simply counting reservations. Since forecasts are used for everything from scheduling labor to determining food orders, neither of which can be done effectively on four hours' notice, a restaurant must first forecast its business and then make last-minute adjustments one or two days out if its reservations suggest that the forecast is inaccurate. Neither trend adjustments nor rolling averages are 100% accurate, but they provide the manager a foundation on which to build the final forecast.

(*Note:* There are other approaches to calculating an initial forecast. Hotel restaurants may forecast based on the number of room reservations in the hotel. Caterers typically use client guest count guarantees to forecast their staff and production needs. Rolling averages and trends are not the only way to generate an initial forecast, but they do tend to provide the longest lead time for businesses that forecast weeks or months in advance. Other techniques may be employed to refine an early forecast's accuracy as the date in question nears.)

12.1.3 Adjusting for Qualitative Data

With an initial forecast calculated, a manager (or often, a management team) modifies the forecast even further based on available qualitative data. With copious amounts of historical qualitative data, a manager may be able to pinpoint the exact forecast with near 100% accuracy, but most of the time, the forecast is an educated guess based on a manager's experience with the qualitative data. In time, a manager may learn that a forecast for light rain will decrease her initial forecast 2%, while heavy rain will cause it to drop 8%, but many managers use their gut to determine how much to adjust their initial forecast up or down.

Consider the following scenario. A manager has an initial forecast of 380 customers for Saturday night. She knows, however, that this Saturday the city is hosting a 2,000-person medical conference in the new convention center. (The convention center didn't exist last year.) Because her restaurant is located only four blocks from the convention center and serves generally healthy cuisine, she anticipates an increase in business beyond the 380 prediction. How large of a jump should she plan for? She knows that business has been off this week thanks to the repaving project on her block, and the weather forecast calls for rain on Saturday. Still, she has countered by advertising in the conference's program. How many guests to plan for is anyone's guess, but it is the manager's responsibility to make that guess as accurate as possible. If she decides that she should plan for 470 and only 450 customers come, the business will perform much better than it would with a forecast of only 380.

The types of qualitative data that a manager may consider are numerous. Some common ones include weather reports, major local events, and planned construction projects (see Figure 12.1). Managers can account for some of these variables one week in advance, but others must wait until the day before for final adjustment. Why? While a local festival is typically publicized months in advance, weather reports are notoriously inaccurate the further out they are. The best weather reports are those given within 24 hours of the day being considered, not seven days in advance. Therefore, an experienced manager continues to make guest forecast adjustments almost until the service itself.

Weather by Location Report

Date	Weather Condition	High Temp	Low Temp	Guests	Checks	Sales
Chesapeake						
10/26/2007	Thunderstorms	77	71	498	266	5,145.33
10/27/2007	Thunderstorms	76	68	813	380	8,330.81
10/28/2007	Partly Cloudy	66	60	846	377	8,900.69
10/29/2007	Partly Cloudy	61	52	302	196	3,099.56
10/30/2007	Sunny	65	40	389	223	3,891.27
10/31/2007	Sunny	71	43	354	222	3,598.01
11/1/2007	Partly Cloudy	76	54	420	277	4,742.33

Figure 12.1
Sample POS Weather Log with Sales History
Source: Printed with the permission of MICROS Systems, Inc.

12.1.4 Evaluating the System

The final step in forecasting is recording data to see how accurate the forecast was. Managers review their predictions against actual results to improve their forecasting abilities for the future and to spot new trends as they emerge. If actual business is 3% higher than forecast for a week straight, perhaps business is picking up more so than expected. If forecasts are too high every time it rains, perhaps the manager should adjust future forecasts even lower when rain is predicted. In short, constant evaluation of forecast accuracy is required to improve the precision of future forecasts.

12.2 FORECASTING AND SALES

Forecasting can be made not only in terms of anticipated customers but also in terms of expected dollars. While knowing how many customers to expect facilitates employee scheduling and ingredient purchasing, forecasting revenue allows a manager to budget and to control costs properly. There are many formulas and concepts needed to forecast revenue, but perhaps the simplest and most powerful is guest check average.

12.2.1 Average Check

The guest check average or average check is defined as the amount of revenue the average person generates on a check. While this information is useful on its own, it can be subdivided into a range of other categories, too. A manager can calculate the average check by server and thus compare which servers generate more sales. Using such a tool, a manager might decide to have the servers with the highest check averages train the weaker ones to improve food and beverage sales overall. Check average can also be calculated by month, week, day, or meal period. Knowing the days of the week with the highest and lowest check averages may inform the type of promotions that a manager offers those days—upselling beverages versus encouraging appetizer purchases, for example.

Perhaps the most important use for the average check number is forecasting revenue for a given period. While a POS system can generate a check average for a given period, the math is simple enough to do by hand.

$$\text{Average Check} = \frac{\text{Revenue for a Period}}{\text{Guests for That period}}$$

Example 12.4: A restaurant has $227,487 in revenue for the month of March. It served 6,192 customers in March. What is the restaurant's average check for March?

$$\text{Average Check} = \frac{\text{Revenue for March}}{\text{Customers for March}} = \frac{\$227,487}{6,192} = \$36.74$$

In other words, on average each customer spent $36.74.

Once an average check is known, it can be used to forecast as well as to monitor ongoing performance. To monitor ongoing performance, a manager simply conducts an average check calculation each week, month, or year. If the check average drops each month, the manager will want to investigate why and to correct that pattern. Perhaps servers are getting lax in pushing dessert sales, or perhaps a recent increase in appetizer portion sizes has encouraged guests to skip entrees and to purchase only appetizers. Whatever the reason, there are only a limited number of seats in the dining room, so the manager will want to make as much money as possible each time a guest occupies one of those seats.

To use the average check figure to forecast sales dollars is quite simple once a manager has forecast a guest count. Just use the following formula:

$$\text{Forecast Revenue} = \text{Forecast Customers} \times \text{Average Check}$$

Example 12.5: A manager forecasts 1,881 customers for next week. The restaurant consistently runs an average check of $27.69. How much revenue should the manager expect next week?

$$\text{Forecast Revenue} = \text{Forecast Customers} \times \text{Average Check}$$
$$= 1,881 \times \$27.69 = \$52,084.89$$

Forecast revenue for a given period is the foundation upon which a budget can be built. If a manager knows her targets for food cost percentage and beverage cost percentage, she can use the forecast revenue to generate her food and beverage budget. She can do the same with her labor cost percentage as well. In short, calculating a revenue forecast allows a manager to budget for controlling costs.

12.2.2 Seat Turnover

While seat turnover does not directly deal with dollars as average check does, it is the other means for squeezing more revenue out of an operation with limited seating. There are generally only two ways to increase revenue: bring in more money per customer (increase the check average) or serve more customers (increase the seat turnover). The seat turnover or "turns" is the number of customers each seat in the restaurant serves in a given period. Mathematically, it looks as follows:

$$\text{Seat Turnover} = \frac{\text{Customers Served in a Period}}{\text{Total Seats Available in the Dining Room}}$$

Example 12.6: A restaurant has 56 seats in its dining room. It serves 85 people at lunch. What is the restaurant's seat turnover for lunch?

$$\text{Seat Turnover} = \frac{\text{Customers Served}}{\text{Seats Available}} = \frac{85}{56} = 1.52$$

In other words, each seat serves an average of 1.52 customers during lunch.

Seat turnover may not seem significant. After all, if a restaurant has many empty seats, attracting new customers, not turning tables multiple times, is the imminent challenge. However, not all restaurants have empty seats available to serve more customers. When a restaurant cannot add more seating to accommodate additional guests, it must turn tables more quickly to increase business volume. In other words, servers must seat guests, serve them, clear, and reset the table in a shorter span of time to get customers through the door faster—that is, increase the seat turnover.

The variables that impact seat turnover are many, and management oversees all of them. Slow service from the kitchen reduces the seat turnover for a busy restaurant. An understaffed dining room can result in tables left dirty for extended periods, rendering them unavailable for new customers. Guests waiting for a table often get frustrated and leave if they observe several empty tables waiting to be cleared. In short, the more efficiently a manager operates her restaurant, the more customers she will be able to serve in a given period.

The one caveat to increasing seat turnover is that it must be done without reducing the check average. Tables can be turned much faster by not offering guests appetizers or desserts, but to do so would reduce the average check and possibly the overall revenue for the establishment. Tables should be served efficiently to increase seat turnover, but customers must not be short-changed on their dining experience as a result.

For restaurants that do not have a shortage of seats, seat turnover becomes a tool for efficient dining room management. Some dining rooms have multiple sections that can be opened or closed to accommodate guests. If a manager knows that her main dining room can comfortably turn tables three times during dinner, she may choose to leave the other dining rooms closed except on those nights where the forecast is more than three times the number of seats in the main dining room. Besides giving the room a feeling of liveliness instead of emptiness, keeping all of the servers in one room can facilitate more efficient service. If a restaurant manager, instead, finds that she cannot increase the seat turnover rate no matter what she tries, she might use it as evidence that the establishment needs to consider expanding its dining room. Turnover rate alone cannot justify a restaurant expansion, but it is one of the variables to consider in determining a restaurant's future customer capacity.

12.3 MENU MIX AND KITCHEN PRODUCTION

Knowing how many customers and dollars to expect over a given period is essential for a manager, but wouldn't it be wonderful and much easier to control costs if a manager could predict exactly what those customers are going to order? To some degree of accuracy this is achievable. The concept is called *menu mix;* it lets a manager calculate what percentage of sales come from each menu item. In most foodservice operations, the percentages remain relatively consistent from week to week as long as certain other variables remain the same—same day of the week, same time of year, same weather. Consequently, the historical menu mix can be used to predict the number of each item on the menu that will be sold in the coming days.

The menu mix can be derived from a POS system easily, but it is still important to understand the concept and the math for use in those operations that do not employ a POS system. While it is simple enough to determine the percentage of guests that ordered each menu item, for the sake of conducting a menu analysis (forthcoming in this chapter) a manager is well served to first divide the menu into categories (appetizers, entrées, desserts, etc.) and to work with each category separately.

To calculate the menu mix percentages, the manager collects the sales data for each category of items sold. From this sales data, she can see the number of each menu item sold during a given period (a week, a day, a meal). Because eating habits change with the day of the week and by meal period, it is best to calculate the menu mix for a meal period on a given day. Table 12.1 illustrates how such sales data might look for a set of entrées.

The "number sold" comes directly from sales data. The percentages are calculated using the concept that a percentage is a part divided by the whole. In this case, the "part" is the number of a given item sold and the "whole" is the total number of items sold. Mathematically, it looks as follows:

$$\text{Menu Mix\%} = \frac{\text{Number of That Item Sold}}{\text{Total Number of Items Sold}}$$

TABLE 12.1
MENU MIX DATA

Wednesday Dinner—Entrée Category		
Entrée Item	**Number Sold**	**Percentage (Number Sold ÷ Total Sold, in this case, 81)**
Filet Mignon	17	0.210 or 21.0%
Chicken Breast	25	0.309 or 30.9%
Salmon	9	0.111 or 11.1%
Trout	5	0.062 or 6.2%
Leg of Lamb	11	0.136 or 13.6%
Pork Chops	14	0.173 or 17.3%
Total	81 (sum of all items sold)	100% (off slightly due to rounding)

Example 12.7: A restaurant sells 266 entrées one night. Of those, 40 are duck breast. What percentage of entrées sold does the duck breast represent?

$$\text{Menu Mix\%} = \frac{\text{Number of That Item Sold}}{\text{Total Number of Items Sold}} = \frac{40}{266} = 0.1503 \text{ or } 15.0\%$$

The second step to making the menu mix data useful for forecasting is to determine what percentage of people ordered food from that category. While one might expect every guest to order at least an entrée, this is not necessarily the case. In most restaurants today, at least some customers will arrive just for drinks, some just for dessert, and some just for appetizers. It is never a good idea to assume that all customers will make a purchase of something out of a given category. To calculate the percentage of guests buying a certain category of food, use the part-divided-by-whole approach; only this time, the part is the number of guests buying that category and the whole is the total number of guests. Mathematically it looks as follows:

$$\text{Percentage Buying a Category of Food} =$$

$$\frac{\text{Number of Guests Buying That Category (entrée, dessert, etc.)}}{\text{Total Number of Guests}}$$

Example 12.8: Referring to Table 12.1, 81 guests bought entrées Wednesday night. If there were 88 guests in the restaurant that evening, what percentage bought entrées?

$$\text{Percentage Buying Entrees} = \frac{\text{Number Buying Entrees}}{\text{Total Number of Guests}} = \frac{81}{88} = 0.920 \text{ or } 92.0\%$$

If a manager knows both the percentage of guests who will buy food from a certain category and the menu mix percentages for that category, she can use her guest forecast to predict how many of each item will sell on a given night. To convert this data into actual counts for each dish, use the following process:

Step 1: Guest forecast × percentage buying a category of food = number of dishes in that category forecast to be sold.

Step 2: Number of dishes in a category of food forecast to be sold (from step 1)× menu mix percentage for an item in that category = number of that item forecast to be sold

Don't forget, in both cases, to use the decimal form of the percentage when multiplying.

Example 12.9: From Wednesday's historical data, 92% of guests typically buy entrées, and usually 13.6% of the entrées sold are leg of lamb. If the forecast for next Wednesday is 120 guests, how many leg of lamb entrées should the manager expect to sell?

Step 1: Multiply total guests by the percentage ordering entrées = 120 × 0.92
= 110.4

Step 2: Multiply 110.4 (from step 1) by the menu mix percentage for lamb
= 110.4 × 0.136 = 15.0

The manager should expect to sell 15 leg of lamb entrées.

As with forecasting total guest counts, these mathematical results are subject to revision based on the manager's experience and instinct. For example, if a manager knows that there has been a story in the news about the health benefits of lamb, she may choose to increase the forecast for the number of lamb dishes. Similarly, she may add a few orders or a given percentage increase to each category as a buffer. That way, she protects against any fluctuations in the mix and reduces the chance that a dish will run out before service ends. Managers may not always wish to have a buffer. For example, if the leftovers from a certain dish cannot be held from one day to the next, management may deliberately aim to run out of the dish near the end of service. In such cases, the manager would not add a buffer to the forecast.

Being able to predict the number of each dish to be sold on an upcoming day empowers a manager to control costs incredibly well. She can use the forecast and menu mix to create a kitchen production schedule that minimizes purchases and leftovers while reducing the risk of shortages. Running an efficient inventory and limiting leftovers controls production waste and inventory spoilage. It also allows a manager to schedule the right number of employees to the right work assignments. In short, combining the information in a forecast and in a menu mix allows a manager to control food and labor costs efficiently.

12.4   MENU ANALYSIS FOR INCREASED PROFITABILITY

Menu mix is valuable not only for its ability to forecast sales and to control kitchen production but also for its role in conducting a menu analysis. *Menu analysis* is a process through which managers compare each menu item's profitability and popularity. Ideally, everything on the menu would be popular and highly profitable, but mathematically, some items are always going to be less profitable. Finding ways to make the most profitable items the best sellers maximizes a restaurant's overall profitability. Conducting a menu analysis is not the simplest of managerial functions, but computers help speed up the process. This section takes the process step by step to make it as easy to understand as possible.

It should be noted that while a menu mix can be conducted by the meal or by the day, a menu analysis is best performed over longer periods. Since the ultimate goal of a menu analysis is to make adjustments to the printed menu for improved profitability, a manager should take a long-term view of sales. After all, the manager is not likely going to offer different menus by day of the week. Typically, buying patterns over the course of a month work much better for a menu analysis than those on any given day.

12.4.1 Popularity

The first step in conducting a menu analysis is to determine each menu item's popularity. Effectively, the manager begins with the menu mix. As with the earlier discussion on menu mix, it is best to work with each menu category separately. Knowing that all of the entrées are more popular than all of the appetizers is less valuable than knowing which entrées are top-sellers and which appetizers are the most popular. The steps that follow will use the appetizer category as an example, but they work the same way with any menu category.

Step 1:   Starting with the number of each item sold, add the total number of items (in this case, appetizers) sold and divide the total by the number of appetizers offered on the menu. Table 12.2a provides an example. In Table 12.2a, 492 appetizers are sold, and there are six different appetizers available for sale: $492 \div 6 = 82$. This represents the average number of each item sold.

TABLE 12.2a
MENU ANALYSIS—CALCULATING POPULARITY

Menu Item	Number Sold	Menu Mix% (Number Sold ÷ Total Sold, in this case 492)
Calamari	117	23.8%
Oysters	58	11.8%
Beef Carpaccio	51	10.4%
Chicken Skewers	102	20.7%
Potato Skins	129	26.2%
Vegetable Napoleon	35	7.1%
Total	492	100%
Average Number of Each Item Sold (Total ÷ Number of Offerings)	82 (492 ÷ 6)	

Step 2: Multiply the average number of each item sold (from Step 1) by 70% or 0.7 to create a popularity benchmark. The goal in menu analysis is not to work simply with the mathematical average but rather with something statistically significant. If all of the menu items were relatively close in sales, it would be inaccurate to call something popular because it sells two units above the average and to label its counterpart unpopular because it sells two units below the average. Therefore, the industry standard in this procedure is to consider a menu item popular as long as it sells at a level that is at least 70% of the mathematical average. Using the example from Table 12.2a, multiply 82 (average number of each item sold) by 0.7 to get a popularity benchmark of 57.4.

Step 3: Determine which items are "high popularity" and which are "low popularity" by seeing whether they sell more or fewer units than the popularity benchmark. See Table 12.2b for a comparison.

TABLE 12.2b
MENU ANALYSIS—CALCULATING POPULARITY

Menu Item	Number Sold	Menu Mix%	Popularity (H/L) (number sold above or below 57.4)
Calamari	117	23.8%	H
Oysters	58	11.8%	H
Beef Carpaccio	51	10.4%	L
Chicken Skewers	102	20.7%	H
Potato Skins	129	26.2%	H
Vegetable Napoleon	35	7.1%	L
Total	492	100%	
Average (Total ÷ Number of Offerings)	82 (492 ÷ 6)		
Popularity Benchmark (Average × 0.7)	57.4		

12.4.2 Profitability

Now that each item has been classified as having a high or low popularity, it is important to know which items are more profitable and which are less profitable. Ideally, all items are profitable to some degree, but the ones that make the most difference in covering labor and other overhead costs are the ones that the manager will want to sell most often. In short, the menu items with the highest contribution margins are the ones that will be the most profitable.

Recall from earlier discussions that the contribution margin is the money left from the sale of an item after its food (or beverage) cost has been covered. The contribution margin is the money from a sale that goes toward labor, fixed and other costs, and ultimately profits. Mathematically, contribution margin is:

Contribution Margin = Item Sales Price − Item Food (or Beverage) Cost

In the discussion of menu analysis, contribution margin will be viewed from a menu perspective to take into account all sales and all costs together.

Step 4: Add each item's sales price and food cost to the menu analysis chart. Then, calculate each item's contribution margin using the formula: Item Contribution

Margin = Item Sales Price − Item Food Cost. Table 12.2c illustrates this step. (Menu mix percentage and the popularity column are dropped here only for ease of instruction. Typically, they would be left in the chart.)

TABLE 12.2c
MENU ANALYSIS—CALCULATING PROFITABILITY

Menu Item	Number Sold	Item Sales Price	Item Food Cost	Item Contribution Margin (Sales Price − Food Cost)
Calamari	117	$7.95	$2.88	$5.07
Oysters	58	$10.00	$4.12	$5.88
Beef Carpaccio	51	$7.95	$2.47	$5.48
Chicken Skewers	102	$5.95	$1.69	$4.26
Potato Skins	129	$5.50	$0.96	$4.54
Vegetable Napoleon	35	$6.45	$1.92	$4.53
Total	492			
Average (Total ÷ Number of Offerings)	82 (492 ÷ 6)			
Popularity Benchmark (Average × 0.7)	57.4			

Step 5: Multiply the number of each item sold by that item's contribution margin to create a menu contribution margin. Then, add all of the menu contribution margins together to get a menu contribution margin total. Mathematically this looks as follows:

$$\text{Menu Contribution Margin} = \text{Number Sold (for an item)} \times \text{Contribution Margin (for that item)}$$

Table 12.2d illustrates the calculation of the menu contribution margin.

Step 6: Determine the average weighted menu contribution margin as follows:

$$\text{Average Weighted Menu Contribution} = \text{Total Menu Contribution Margin} \div \text{Total Number of Items Sold}$$

From Table 12.2d, this is $2392.44 ÷ 492 = $4.86.

Step 7: In the final step, decide whether each item is "high profitability" or "low profitability." To make this decision, compare each item's individual contribution margin to the average weighted contribution margin. For our ongoing example, the average weighted contribution margin is $4.86. Those items with an item contribution margin above $4.86 would be listed as high; the others will be listed as low. See Table 12.2e. (To create a single summary table, the popularity column has been added back in as well.)

12.4.3 Menu Analysis Categories

Now that each menu item has been classified in terms of popularity and profitability, it is time to decide what to do about it. This is where a manager's instinct and expertise really come into play. The novice might decide to eliminate all items that are not highly profitable. However, a manager has a great many ways to adjust an item's popularity and profitability. To increase popularity or the number of sales that an item receives, a manager might relocate that item to a more prominent place on the menu or

TABLE 12.2d
MENU ANALYSIS—CALCULATING PROFITABILITY

Menu Item	Number Sold	Item Sales Price	Item Food Cost	Item Contribution Margin	Menu Contribution Margin (Number Sold × Item CM)
Calamari	117	$7.95	$2.88	$5.07	$593.19
Oysters	58	$10.00	$4.12	$5.88	$341.04
Beef Carpaccio	51	$7.95	$2.47	$5.48	$279.48
Chicken Skewers	102	$5.95	$1.69	$4.26	$434.52
Potato Skins	129	$5.50	$0.96	$4.54	$585.66
Vegetable Napoleon	35	$6.45	$1.92	$4.53	$158.55
Total	492 (total number of items sold)				$2392.44 (total menu contribution margin)
Average (Total ÷ Number of Offerings)	82 (492 ÷ 6)				
Popularity Benchmark (Average × 0.7)	57.4				

TABLE 12.2e
MENU ANALYSIS—COMPLETE

Menu Item	Number Sold	Item Sales Price	Item Food Cost	Item CM	Menu CM (Number Sold × Item CM)	Popularity (H/L)	Profitable (H/L)
Calamari	117	$7.95	$2.88	$5.07	$593.19	H	H
Oysters	58	$10.00	$4.12	$5.88	$341.04	H	H
Beef Carpaccio	51	$7.95	$2.47	$5.48	$279.48	L	H
Chicken Skewers	102	$5.95	$1.69	$4.26	$434.52	H	L
Potato Skins	129	$5.50	$0.96	$4.54	$585.66	H	L
Vegetable Napoleon	35	$6.45	$1.92	$4.53	$158.55	L	L
Total	492				$2392.44		
Average (Total ÷ Number of Offerings)	82 (492 ÷ 6)						
Popularity Benchmark (Average × 0.7)	57.4						
Average Weighted CM (Total Menu CM ÷ Total Number of Items Sold)					$4.86 (2392.44 ÷ 492)		

ask servers to sell that item more aggressively. To make an item more profitable, a manager could increase that item's sales price or reduce its portion size or food cost. It might be appropriate to remove or to replace a menu item that is low in both popularity and profitability, but if that menu item serves a very specific need (such as accommodating vegetarians), it might be better to adjust the item instead to make it more popular and more profitable.

The two variables of profitability and popularity allow for four categories of menu items. Many industry professionals use more colorful names for these categories than simply calling them high and low.

Star.   A star is an item that is both highly popular and highly profitable. In general, managers tend to leave these items alone as they are doing their job—making lots of profit and selling often. In the aforementioned example, the calamari and oysters are both stars.

Plowhorse.   A plowhorse is high in popularity but low in profitability. Depending on the role a plowhorse plays on the menu, a manager might decide to increase its sales price or to reduce its food cost. In doing so, a manager must be sure that she will not cause sales of the plowhorse to drop in the process. A plowhorse may sell well because customers recognize it as a value. If customers come to the establishment in large part to buy the plowhorse, making it a signature dish by default, it may be best to leave the plowhorse alone. This is especially true if the plowhorse sits only slightly below the average weighted contribution margin. In the aforementioned example, the chicken skewers and potato skins are plowhorses.

Puzzle.   A puzzle is low in popularity but high in profitability. A manager's goal should be to increase sales of puzzles to make them more popular. This can sometimes be achieved by relocating the puzzle on the menu to draw customers' attention to it or by having servers push puzzles in their sales pitches. A puzzle might need nothing more than a better menu description. For puzzles, a manager might decide to survey some customers to find out why they do not choose these items and then to adjust the puzzles accordingly. In the aforementioned example, the beef carpaccio is a puzzle.

Dog.   A dog is low in both popularity and profitability. It requires a change of some sort. Increasing its sales price can turn a dog into a puzzle. Suggestive selling a dog can convert it into a plowhorse. In some cases, it is just easier to replace a dog with a new dish that will sell well with a higher contribution margin. Keep in mind, however, that some dogs serve specific purposes. Perhaps a few regular customers come to an establishment just to order the dog every day. Perhaps the dog is the only vegetarian option on the menu; replacing it with another vegetarian option might just create another dog, but one necessary to serve the restaurant's vegetarian clientele. A manager should know whether a dog is best changed or removed. In the aforementioned example, the vegetable napoleon is a dog.

In summary, menu analysis provides a manager the information she needs to make informed decisions on menu changes. Engineering a menu is not as simple as eliminating unpopular dishes or replacing less profitable ones. Both popularity and profitability must be taken into account. Managers who look at both factors for each menu item and make adjustments accordingly are best prepared to maximize the profitability of their restaurant's menu.

12.5   RECONCILING KITCHEN PRODUCTION WITH SALES

A cost control manager who employs forecasting and menu mix has the ability to control costs in relation to sales. Using her forecast and the menu mix, she can generate a kitchen production schedule to eliminate waste from overpurchasing and overproduction. However, kitchen production sheets can be used as a control in other ways. A kitchen production sheet can be reconciled against sales receipts (guest checks or POS reports) to confirm that all food produced either has been sold or remains in the kitchen as leftovers. Inevitably, discrepancies will arise, but they, too, can be tracked using a mishap form to account for any dropped, incorrectly ordered, customer rejected, or otherwise unusable food that has been removed from the production inventory. The first step in this control process is to create the kitchen production sheet from the forecast and the menu mix.

12.5.1 The Kitchen Production Sheet

As discussed earlier in the chapter, a single item's forecast sales can be determined by multiplying the forecast guest count first by the percentage of guests who typically buy that category of food and then by the menu mix percentage for that item. By performing this calculation for each menu item, a manager can forecast the sales and thus, needed production, for each menu item.

Example 12.10: Using the chart that follows, forecast the number of each menu item that will be sold if the company is forecasting 270 guests for tomorrow and 49% of customers typically buy appetizers.

Menu Item – Appetizers	Menu Mix%	Forecast Sales Quantities
Calamari	23.8%	
Oysters	11.8%	
Beef Carpaccio	10.4%	
Chicken Skewers	20.7%	
Potato Skins	26.2%	
Vegetable Napoleon	7.1%	

The first step is to determine what number of people will purchase appetizers. To do so, multiply 270 guests by 49% (or 0.49): $270 \times 0.49 = 132$ guests.

Next, multiply each menu mix percentage in the chart by 132 to generate a forecast sales quantity for each item. The result is the chart that follows.

Menu Item – Appetizers	Menu Mix%		Forecast Sales Quantities
Calamari	23.8%	× 132 =	31.4
Oysters	11.8%	× 132 =	15.6
Beef Carpaccio	10.4%	× 132 =	13.7
Chicken Skewers	20.7%	× 132 =	27.3
Potato Skins	26.2%	× 132 =	34.6
Vegetable Napoleon	7.1%	× 132 =	9.4

While the chart created in Example 12.10 is a good first step, it is not yet ready to serve as a kitchen production schedule for a restaurant's appetizers. In addition to the fact that it asks for fractions of a portion, it needs to account for several other variables. First, the preliminary numbers should be adjusted by a manager both one week in advance and again the day before service to account for weather and for any other qualitative factors. Second, the kitchen production schedule should factor in any prior leftovers as well as a "buffer" in case the forecast or menu mix is slightly off. Prior leftovers to use up are often referred to as "portions on hand" in order to distinguish them from the leftovers that result from the current service. A proper kitchen production sheet might look like Figure 12.2.

For a kitchen production sheet (and in Figure 12.2), the manager makes the adjusted forecast the day before service, so the kitchen may adjust its production according to the most recent information. The chef or kitchen manager, who monitors

Menu Item – Appetizers	Forecast	Adjusted Forecast	Portions on Hand	Buffer	Portions to Prepare (Adjusted Forecast + Buffer – Portions on Hand)	Total Available (Portions to Prepare + Portions on Hand)	Leftovers
Calamari	31	35	0	10	45	45	
Oysters	16	20	0	5	25	25	
Beef Carpaccio	14	16	2	5	19	21	
Chicken Skewers	27	27	5	10	32	37	
Potato Skins	35	35	0	10	45	45	
Vegetable Napoleon	9	14	7	5	12	19	

Figure 12.2
Kitchen Production Sheet (Appetizers)

the reusable leftovers from the previous shift, records the portions on hand. The chef or cost control manager determines the buffer in advance to ensure that the kitchen can handle most services without running out of menu items. "Portions to prepare" is calculated by adding the adjusted forecast and the buffer and then subtracting the portions on hand. "Total available" is the sum of Portions to Prepare and Portions on Hand; it should also correspond to the sum of the adjusted forecast and the buffer.

The "leftovers" column is completed at the end of a shift. It is used as a record to confirm that the leftovers at the end of one shift do not disappear and are still available as portions on hand in the next shift. Not every restaurant reuses leftovers from one shift to the next, but leftover quantities should still be tracked. If too many leftovers end up in the trash each day, the manager will need to reconsider her forecast or to confirm that the stations are not overproducing beyond the kitchen production sheet. Each dish that ends up in the garbage represents an unnecessary increase in food cost.

If a kitchen gets slammed harder than expected and cooks must prepare additional portions during service beyond their initial production, such extra production should be recorded and noted on the production sheet. Some managers will include a column for "additional production" on their forms while others will just make a note on the form and adjust the numbers of portions to prepare and total available. In some kitchens, managers will simply eighty-six a dish (make it unavailable for sale) once the initial production runs out. Regardless of management's policies on additional production, the manager should always record the time at which a dish runs out or at which additional production is needed. Such information is vital for revising future forecasts. For example, a dish that runs out five minutes before service ends might be considered perfect forecasting, while eighty-sixing a dish two hours before service ends represents a serious flaw in forecasting. Recording this information allows a manager to improve her future forecasting as no kitchen wants to run out of food early in the service or to have their line cooks performing prep work in the middle of service.

12.5.2 Mishaps and Sales Reconciliation

If used properly, a kitchen production schedule not only tells a manager how many of each item are available for sale, it also notifies managers of any discrepancies between food produced and food sold. Imagine a scenario in which a server feels like having a free lobster dinner. She could order the lobster "for a table" and eat it out of the sight of her coworkers without anyone knowing. If no one ever checks to see that all of the food produced by the kitchen actually generates sales, she might easily get away with her scheme. If questioned about it, she could simply say that the customer rejected the lobster and that she threw it in the garbage. Foodservice establishments must have a system in place to guard against such theft.

If no errors occur during service, the number of each dish sold (as recorded via guest checks or a POS system) should equal the total number available for sale minus any leftover portions. However, rarely does a service go off without a hitch. For this reason, there is often some amount of product loss because of employee errors. All of these errors should be recorded on a food mishap report or void sheet.

A void sheet, sometimes called a food mishap report, is merely a report of all items rendered unusable during service (Figure 12.3). For each lost item, it includes the name of the server, the item name, and the reason for the void. Some companies also list the check number or the date and time of the mishap. Food items become voids for many reasons. A server may drop a dish on the floor. The customer may reject the food as improperly cooked or simply as unappetizing. The cook may burn the dish during the cooking process and remove it from circulation before it even gets to the server. Whatever the reason, every voided dish must be accounted for to ensure that it is not being stolen by a server, cook, or customer.

The void sheet should be completed by a trusted employee, such as a manager, to verify that items listed on the form have been legitimately lost. Typically, a server will bring the ruined food back to the manager to have it listed on the report; otherwise, the server might enjoy her free lunch and just tell her boss that she threw the food out. The report is useful in identifying the source of the mishaps as well. If one server is responsible for many of the misorders, perhaps she needs training to avoid errors in ordering. If most of the mishaps come from one particular cook's station, that cook may need retraining as well. Many problems evenly distributed across the kitchen may suggest that the kitchen is understaffed. In short, every operation will have some quantity of mishaps, but they should be kept to a minimum and not all stem from a single employee.

Void Sheet		Day/Date: Tuesday, March 4	
Food Item	Reason for Void	Server Name	Time
Scallop App	Rejected—"Off" taste	Alison	11:47 a.m.
NY Strip	Overcooked	Eve	12:03 p.m.
Mixed Grill	Misordered	Stewart	12:20 p.m.
Chocolate Mousse	Dropped on floor	Stewart	12:35 p.m.
Manager's Signature:_____			

Figure 12.3
Void Sheet or Food Mishaps Report

At the end of a service or day, a manager should complete a food and sales reconciliation form to confirm that all portions prepared by the kitchen are accounted for. Because all food should end up as sales, voids, or leftovers, the reconciliation form reflects all of this data in one location. Figure 12.4 illustrates a sample reconciliation form.

Most of the information on the reconciliation form comes from the kitchen production sheet and the void sheet. The remainder comes from guest checks (or the POS system) and a physical inventory of leftovers at the various kitchen stations. In larger operations that issue precut, individually portioned meats and seafood from the storeroom or butcher shop, "additional preparation" can be confirmed through requisition sheets. Because there is no waste from trimming or fabrication at a cook's station in these

Food Sales Reconciliation Form					Day/Date: _____
Kitchen Production					
Food Name	Portions on Hand	Portions Prepared	Additional Preparation	Total Available (On Hand + Prepared + Additional Prep)	Leftovers	Portions Consumed (Total − Leftovers)
Lasagna	6	24	0	30	2	28
Filet Mignon	0	30	3	33	0	33
Sea Bass	0	20	0	20	5	15
Sales Accounting					
Food Name	Portions Sold	Voids	Total Output (Sold + Voids)	Portions Consumed (from above)	Difference (Consumed − Total Output)	Notes
Lasagna	28	0	28	28	0	
Filet Mignon	29	2	31	33	2	Stewart missing check
Sea Bass	14	1	15	15	0	
					Manager's Signature:_____	

Figure 12.4
Food Sales Reconciliation Form

instances, portions requisitioned should match portions prepared exactly. This is not the case when a cook fabricates her own meat, poultry, or seafood on her station.

Since the purpose of a reconciliation sheet is to ensure that all dishes prepared are accounted for, the total output (Portions Sold + Voids) for the restaurant should match the portions consumed, the number of servings of each dish sent out by the kitchen. When a discrepancy occurs, it should be investigated immediately before the cooks and servers forget the details of the service. Sometimes, a server forgets to report a mishap on the void sheet. A server who forgets to enter voids regularly requires retraining or discipline. In nonelectronic systems, a paper check may be missing, which shortchanges the number of sales recorded. While not direct evidence of theft, missing checks are red flags that a theft may have occurred and should be sought and investigated. When missing checks become common, especially for a single server, theft is the likely cause. Fortunately, operations that employ POS systems typically require that a server enter an order into the computer system for food to be prepared in the kitchen. Thus, while the food may not make it to the table, a record of the check and the server who ordered the food is always available for management to review.

SUMMARY

Proper forecasting allows a manager to predict revenue and to plan accordingly for controlling costs. Forecasting relies on historical data, including both quantitative and qualitative information. A customer count forecast is commonly determined through the calculation of rolling averages or by analyzing trends and then by adjusting preliminary numbers on the basis of qualitative data. Forecast customer counts can be converted to forecast sales dollars using a guest check average. Seat turnover

allows managers to measure efficiency in customer service as well as to spot opportunities for increased revenue. Menu mix allows a manager to predict the quantities in which each dish will be sold. Menu mix assists with the creation of kitchen production sheets, and it plays a role in menu analysis. By measuring contribution margin and popularity simultaneously, menu analysis helps a manager adjust a menu for increased profitability. A manager reconciles kitchen production with sales to ensure that all food leaving the kitchen is accounted for in some way. The kitchen production sheet tracks food preparation and leftovers, while a void sheet monitors any food that leaves the kitchen but does not generate revenue. By reconciling food production with sales, a manager is better empowered to spot problems, such as understaffing, needed training, or theft, and to ensure that all of the hard work that goes into forecasting and menu analysis results in controlled expenses and greater profit for the business.

COMPREHENSION QUESTIONS

1. A restaurant serves 2,118 customers for lunch in June, 2,202 customers for lunch in July, and 2,290 customers for lunch in August. What is the current trend, as expressed by monthly percentage increase, for this operation? How many customers might the restaurant expect for lunch in September?

2. Over a four-week period, a cafeteria sees 384, 471, 402, and 399 customers respectively. Using a rolling average approach that considers guest counts from the past four weeks, how many customers should the cafeteria forecast for next week?

3. List four pieces of qualitative data that might cause a manager to increase or to decrease her forecast guest count for an upcoming service.

4. A restaurant generates $189,030 in revenue for a given period. During that time, it serves 5,983 customers. What is the guest check average for this restaurant during that period?

5. A luncheonette has a consistent guest check average of $9.14. The manager forecasts 1,372 customers for the upcoming week. How much revenue should the manager expect next week?

6. An upscale restaurant typically serves 88 customers on a Sunday evening. The restaurant only has 60 seats. What is the seat turnover rate for this operation?

7. A restaurant sells 371 entrées on a given night. Of those, 48 entrées are the seared salmon. What is the menu mix percentage for the salmon entrée that night?

8. Complete the following chart:

Menu Item	Number Sold	Menu Mix%	Popularity (H/L)
Cheeseburger	243		
Fried Chicken	187		
Spaghetti/Meatballs	99		
Tuna Steak	74		
Seafood Pasta	89		
Pork Chops	110		
Total			
Average Number Sold			
Popularity Benchmark			

9. Complete the following chart:

Menu Item	Number Sold	Item Sales Price	Item Food Cost	Item Contribution Margin	Menu Contribution Margin	Profitability (H/L)
Cheeseburger	243	$6.95	$2.01			
Fried Chicken	187	$8.95	$2.87			
Spaghetti/Meatballs	99	$6.25	$1.44			
Tuna Steak	74	$9.50	$3.27			
Seafood Pasta	89	$8.95	$2.98			
Pork Chops	110	$7.95	$2.75			
Total						
Average Weighted Contribution Margin						

10. Combining the information in questions 8 and 9, label each entrée as a star, plowhorse, puzzle, or dog.

11. Using the menu mix information in question 8, forecast the quantities of each entrée to prepare assuming the guest forecast for the next day is 245 customers and 97% of customers order entrées. Use that information to complete the chart that follows:

Menu Item	Menu Mix%	Forecast	Portions on Hand	Buffer	Portions to Prepare	Total Available
Cheeseburger			0	10		
Fried Chicken			0	10		
Spaghetti/ Meatballs			7	10		
Tuna Steak			2	5		
Seafood Pasta			0	5		
Pork Chops			10	5		

12. Describe the purpose of a void sheet (or food mishap report). List four "acceptable" reasons for a food mishap that might end up on a void sheet.

13. The food sales reconciliation form that follows is missing some information. Complete the form and then list (in the notes column) which dishes, if any, require further investigation for potential theft.

Food Sales Reconciliation Form				Day/Date: _____		
Kitchen Production						
Food Name	Portions on Hand	Portions Prepared	Additional Preparation	Total Available	Leftovers	Portions Consumed
Beef	6	57	3		0	
Chicken	7	87	9		0	
Fish	0	28	0		8	
Sales Accounting						
Food Name	Portions Sold	Voids	Total Output	Portions Consumed	Difference	Notes
Beef	66	4				
Chicken	103	0				
Fish	18	2				
				Manager's Signature: _____		

DISCUSSION QUESTIONS

1. A restaurant owner comes into her restaurant to review the books. She notices that the daily reports for two straight weeks show a forecast that matches the kitchen production and sales exactly—in other words, no voids, no leftovers. Should the owner be thrilled or concerned that the manager on site appears able to forecast guest consumption exactly? What might be the real world effect on the restaurant if, in fact, the reports are accurate; that is, what might be the guest experience in a restaurant in which there are never leftovers or food removed from service?

2. A novice manager starts her first management job at an established restaurant and wants to make a good impression on the owners. She notices that the guest counts seem to bounce around from one day to the next. She begins by setting up a forecasting process using rolling averages. Her process is to take the average guest count over the past 14 days to generate a forecast guest count for day 15. Will her system be effective at getting accurate forecasts? Why or why not?

3. The owners at two different restaurants wish to increase their revenue. Restaurant A has a seat

turnover rate of 0.78. Restaurant B has a seat turnover rate of 3.81. Both restaurants have advertised dinner hours of 5:30–9:30 p.m. What suggestions should the managers at each restaurant propose to the owners to increase revenue? Do the restaurants effectively have the same problem? Why or why not?

4. In conducting a menu analysis, you notice that your upscale restaurant menu has only one "dog"—the steak tartare. The dish is your least profitable and least popular, but you have been written up in the local paper as the only place in town to get steak tartare. Additionally, the local dining critic has remarked in print that your steak tartare is excellent. Given these circumstances, what would you do with this dish? What are the possible consequences, both positive and negative, of your decision?

5. Your restaurant's void sheet tends to list 10 to 20 mishaps each day, but you never have any discrepancies on the food sales reconciliation sheet. You typically serve 80-100 customers on a given night. What is going right and what is going wrong in your restaurant? How would you deal with such a situation?

6. You have noticed that over the past few months, sales have decreased in the restaurant you manage. The average guest check has dropped by over a dollar and the customer counts are flat from a year ago. Because your kitchen has so few cooks, you decide the only place to cut labor cost is in the service staff. You call a meeting with your servers. During the meeting, the staff begs you to reconsider cutting their hours or terminating one of them altogether. One employee astutely notes that the servers have been pushing sales of the burgers and pasta dishes (both with high contribution margins but low sales prices). That employee suggests that by pushing the seafood and steak dishes (both expensive menu analysis "dogs") instead, they could raise the average check and thus the overall revenue. Another employee suggests keeping the entrée sales the way they are and pushing to sell more desserts instead. You know that none of the desserts has a contribution margin as high as the entrées. A third states that by rushing people quickly through the meal, the team can get more customers through the door. She points out that guests sometimes have to wait 5–10 minutes for a table. You know that your seat turnover rate is 1.38. You decide to give the service staff one more week to improve their numbers. Which server's approach do you endorse? Why?

13

Revenue Management

Objectives

By the end of this chapter, you will be able to:

- Describe the importance of conducting a cost/volume/profit analysis

- Calculate an operation's break-even point in sales dollars and in number of customers

- List ways to improve a foodservice business's break-even point

- List several ways that a manager can increase revenue through marketing

- Describe the role that point-of-sales systems play in supporting revenue growth and cost control

Forecasting and tracking business levels are critical for a cost control manager to plan and control his labor and ingredient needs appropriately. However, no amount of cost control can compensate for severely low business volume. Fixed costs always exist, and some amount of money must be earned to cover those costs, even if no profit is made. Working actively to generate, drive, and manage revenue is just as important a responsibility for a manager as is controlling costs. When variable costs are properly controlled, higher levels of business make the job of covering fixed costs and of generating profits easier.

Even those culinary businesses with missions other than making a profit (supporting a hotel, serving schoolchildren, feeding patients, etc.) must know the point at which they break even in order to guide a manager toward certain revenue goals. In these types of operations, a profit of zero might be acceptable, but a loss is not usually welcome news. Skilled managers not only calculate their business's break-even point in a cost/volume/profit analysis, but they also encourage or direct a range of marketing activities to increase (or at least to maintain) revenue. Modern technology, specifically POS systems, further aids a manager in reaching his sales goals. While earlier chapters have shown that POS systems are excellent tools for controlling costs, this chapter demonstrates that they are extremely helpful for pinpointing ways to grow revenue, too.

13.1 COST/VOLUME/PROFIT ANALYSIS

In the typical foodservice establishment, revenue comes in exclusively through sales dollars. (Corporate cafeterias may receive a set fee or subsidy for servicing a business's staff, which would require a different analysis system, but caterers or school cafeterias, which receive monies from a single client or government agency, respectively, still get a dollar amount per customer—essentially sales dollars.) Because foodservice businesses must cover all of their costs, including profit, from sales dollars, sales are effectively the sum of all variable costs, all fixed costs, and all profit. The mathematical interpretation is as follows:

$$\text{Sales} = \text{Variable Costs} + \text{Fixed Costs} + \text{Profit}$$

Rearranged,

$$\text{Profit} = \text{Sales} - \text{Variable Costs} - \text{Fixed Costs}$$

This text has discussed fixed and variable costs elsewhere, but to review, fixed costs (employee salaries, rent, insurance and licenses, etc.) do not change as sales go up or down. Variable costs (food costs, beverage costs, hourly wages) do change as sales fluctuate. What shouldn't change with variable costs is the percentage of sales that they represent. If a $1.00 soda costs $0.20 to make, then the beverage cost for that soda is $0.20 ÷ $1.00 = 0.20 or 20%. If 100 or 1,000 sodas are sold, the variable cost percentage will remain the same. Similarly, a foodservice establishment will usually find that its variable costs represent approximately the same percentage of sales from month to month. Exceptions to this rule occur either in an uncontrolled environment (think: rampant waste, ongoing product loss, and uncontrolled labor), during a month with unexpected severe shifts in ingredient costs (think: crop loss due to frost), or during a period when a manager is deliberately adjusting the menu mix or introducing a new menu.

As long as the variable cost percentages fluctuate only slightly across weeks and months, a manager can calculate an average *variable rate*—the percentage of sales that go toward covering variable costs. (An average variable rate can be calculated when monthly variable cost percentages fluctuate wildly, but it is relatively valueless information for forecasting future variable costs.)

$$\text{Variable Rate} = \frac{\text{Variable Costs}}{\text{Sales}}$$

Expressed graphically,

VC represents Variable Costs, and VR represents Variable Rate. As in earlier chapters, cover up the item you wish to solve for, and do what the graphic tells you to do with the remaining data. The variable costs and the sales must cover the same period (a week, a month, a year). Because the variable rate is an average that changes slightly over short periods, it is best calculated over a period of a month or longer.

The remaining money that doesn't cover variable costs goes toward fixed costs and profit. The percentage of each sales dollar that goes toward fixed costs and profit is called the *contribution rate*. Because there are no other places to divert sales dollars other than to variable expenses, fixed costs, and profit,

$$\text{Contribution Rate} = 1 - \text{Variable Rate}$$

The contribution and variable rates are expressed in their decimal forms in this equation. In other words, the variable rate plus the contribution rate represents 100% of costs and profit; the "100%" is the "1" in the formula.

Example 13.1: A foodservice business has variable costs of $58,000, fixed costs of $33,000, and a profit of $4,000 for a month. Calculate the total sales dollars, the variable rate, and the contribution rate for this operation.

Step 1: Sales = Variable Costs + Fixed Costs + Profit = $58,000 + $33,000 + $4,000 = $95,000

Step 2: Variable Rate = Variable Costs ÷ Sales = $58,000 ÷ $95,000 = 0.611 (or 61.1% of sales)

Step 3: Contribution Rate = 1 − Variable Rate = 1 − 0.611 = 0.389 (or 38.9% of sales)

A manager can also use the aforementioned formulas to predict the amount of profit that a given sales volume should generate.

Example 13.2: A cafeteria has a variable rate of 0.644 and monthly fixed costs of $32,000. Calculate the forecast profits if sales are $121,000.

Step 1: From the earlier triangle graphic, Variable Costs = Variable Rate × Sales = 0.644 × $121,000 = $77,924

Step 2: Profit = Sales − Variable Costs − Fixed Costs = $121,000 − $77,924 − $32,000 = $11,076

Unfortunately, in the foodservice industry it is not uncommon to find a business that is operating at a loss. In such a situation, the business is not earning enough money to cover its fixed costs. There are really only two ways to rectify this problem: increase the contribution rate (by raising prices or by cutting variable costs) or increase sales volume.

Consider a scenario in which a restaurant has a variable rate of 0.741 and fixed costs of $47,000. The top half of Table 13.1 illustrates how profit changes with adjustments to the variable rate, while the bottom half shows how profit changes with increases in sales volume.

TABLE 13.1
PROFIT CHANGES AS VARIABLE RATES AND SALES CHANGE

	Sales	Variable Rate	Contribution Rate (1 − VR)	Fixed Costs	Variable Costs (VR × Sales)	Profit (Sales − Var. Costs − Fixed Costs)
A	$150,000	0.741	0.259	$47,000	$111,150	− $8,150
B	$150,000	0.641	0.359	$47,000	$96,150	$6,850
C	$150,000	0.541	0.459	$47,000	$81,150	$21,850
D	$150,000	0.741	0.259	$47,000	$111,150	− $8,150
E	$175,000	0.741	0.259	$47,000	$129,675	− $1,675
F	$200,000	0.741	0.259	$47,000	$148,200	$4,800

There are several lessons to take from Table 13.1. First, the negative numbers in the final column represent a loss; in other words, there is not enough money to cover the fixed costs. Second, there is a minimum sales volume needed to generate a profit with a given variable rate and fixed cost. Although $150,000 is more than three times the fixed cost expense, it is still not enough to turn a profit given a variable rate of 0.741. Finally, (and this may be the most important point) it is easier to generate profits by controlling costs than by increasing sales volume. By dropping the variable rate from 0.741 to 0.641 (line B), the manager saves $15,000 ($111,150 − $96,150), which goes directly toward fixed costs and profit. However, increasing sales by $25,000 (line E) only reduces the loss (negative profit) by $6,475 [− $1,675 − (− $8,150)] because each extra dollar in sales comes with additional variable costs, such as additional food and labor expenses.

Controlling costs and increasing revenue are equally important. Cutting expenses translates to a dollar-for-dollar savings that goes toward fixed expenses and profit, but a manager can only cut costs so far before quality loss and reputation erosion drive business away. Increasing sales volume helps generate additional profit dollars, but they are only a small percentage of the extra revenue. The one scenario to avoid, of course, is one in which sales are dropping from month to month. When a manager is helpless to increase revenue, he has only one choice left—to cut costs—that could drive business down even further. Learning how to drive revenue so that it continually increases while costs are controlled is imperative for a manager to be successful.

The comparison of how a company's profit shifts as business volume and variable costs change is called a *cost/volume/profit analysis.*

13.1.1 Break-Even Point

Of the infinite sales points that can be analyzed using a cost/volume/profit analysis, perhaps the most important one is the break-even point. The *break-even point* is the point at which a business neither loses money nor earns a profit. Mathematically, profit equals zero. The break-even point is typically expressed in sales dollars (the amount of revenue needed to break even), but it can be expressed in number of customers if the average guest check is known. Knowing the break-even point is important as it tells the manager the minimum amount of sales that he must generate to break even given the establishment's variable rate.

To calculate the amount of sales dollars that an establishment must bring in to cover fixed cost and a desired profit, a manager needs the formula:

$$\text{Sales} = \frac{\text{Fixed Cost} + \text{Profit}}{\text{Contribution Rate}}$$

Since Contribution Rate $= 1 -$ Variable Rate, the formula can also be written as:

$$\text{Sales} = \frac{\text{Fixed Cost} + \text{Profit}}{1 - \text{Variable Rate}}$$

To calculate break-even point, there is no need for another formula. Simply assign profit a value of zero; the break-even point is the sales quantity when profit equals zero.

Example 13.3: A restaurant has annual fixed costs of $41,500. The average variable rate for the establishment is 0.603. What is the break-even point in sales for this restaurant?

$$\text{Sales} = \frac{\text{Fixed Cost} + \text{Profit}}{1 - \text{Variable Rate}} = \frac{\$41,500 + 0}{1 - 0.603} = \frac{\$41,500}{0.397} = \$104,534$$

The break-even point is $104,534 in sales.

These formulas can also be used to determine how much sales revenue a business needs to generate to hit a profit goal. Such information comes in handy when owners or investors expect a specific return on their investment.

Example 13.4: The owner of the restaurant in Example 13.3 wants to make a profit of $18,000 next year. Using the data in Example 13.3, how much in sales does the restaurant need to reach this profit goal?

$$\text{Sales} = \frac{\text{Fixed Cost} + \text{Profit}}{1 - \text{Variable Rate}} = \frac{\$41,500 + \$18,000}{1 - 0.603} = \frac{\$59,500}{0.397} = \$149,874.06$$

The restaurant will earn $18,000 in profit at the point at which it has approximately $149,874 in sales.

Sometimes, a manager or owner will prefer to know how many customers rather than sales dollars are needed to hit a given profit target or to break even. To find this out, a manager needs one additional piece of information—the guest check average. To translate any sales amount into a number of customers, simply divide the sales by the guest check average, as follows:

$$\text{Number of Customers} = \frac{\text{Sales}}{\text{Guest Check Average}}$$

Example 13.5: The restaurant in Example 13.4 has a guest check average of $8.73 per guest. How many guests will the restaurant need to serve to hit its target profit of $18,000 (from Example 13.4)?

Since Example 13.4 has already calculated the sales amount for that profit goal, this problem only requires a conversion of sales dollars to number of customers.

$$\text{Number of Customers} = \text{Sales} \div \text{Guest Check Average} = \$149,874 \div \$8.73$$
$$= 17,167.7 \text{ or } 17,168 \text{ customers.}$$

Example 13.6: A hotel restaurant manager is not required to make a profit, but he must break even. His monthly fixed costs are $104,000 and his variable rate is 0.514. How many customers must he serve to break even next month if his guest check average is $36.21?

Step 1: $\text{Sales} = \dfrac{\text{Fixed Cost} + \text{Profit}}{1 - \text{Variable Rate}} = \dfrac{\$104,000 + 0}{1 - 0.514} = \dfrac{\$104,000}{0.486}$

$= \$213,991.77$

Step 2: $\text{Customers} = \text{Sales} \div \text{Guest Check Average} = \$213,991.77 \div \$36.21 =$ 5,909.7 or 5,910 customers

---

In break-even point by customer calculations, because an owner or manager wants to know the point at which the restaurant no longer loses money, the number of customers required to break even should always be rounded up. Therefore, if the calculation for break-even point were 1,428.2 customers, the restaurant officially breaks even on its 1,429th customer. At customer number 1,428, the restaurant still loses a small amount of money.

13.1.2 The Break-Even Point Graph

Managers may prefer to convert their cost/volume/profit analysis into a line graph, sometimes called a break-even point graph. The graph helps a manager locate the break-even point and quickly see profit or loss amounts at various sales levels. (It also serves as a tool to help students understand the concepts behind fixed cost, variable cost, and break-even point.) Figure 13.1 shows a typical break-even point graph.

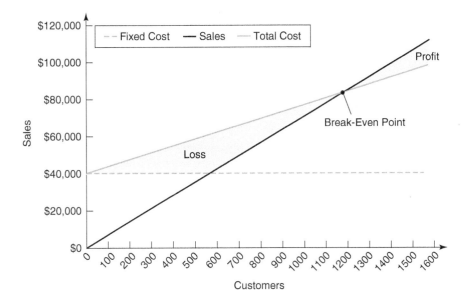

Figure 13.1
Break-Even Point Graph

To create Figure 13.1 (or any break-even point graph), begin by inserting the fixed cost line. Because fixed costs do not change with sales volume or numbers of customers, the line is horizontal. For this particular scenario, the fixed costs are $40,000 whether the restaurant has 1 customer or 1,000 customers. Next, insert the sales line. The sales line is easy to plot from sales data, but one could also be created simply by knowing the average guest check. Each additional customer adds sales dollars in the amount of one more average guest check. Finally, add the total cost line. The total cost line is the sum of fixed and variable costs. At zero sales, the total cost is the same as the fixed cost. Since a manager can calculate the variable costs incurred at various business levels (by multiplying sales by the variable rate), it is simple enough to add the fixed cost total to each of these data points to generate the total cost line.

With a break-even point graph plotted, it is relatively easy to determine the profit or loss at a given business level. The break-even point is the point at which the sales line and the total cost line intersect. In Figure 13.1, that occurs at $83,507 in sales or at 1,177 customers. The triangular wedge to the right of the break-even point represents profit, while the triangular wedge to the left represents loss. The greater the number of customers past the break-even point, the larger the profit. In fact, the profit (or loss) can be measured at a given number of customers by calculating the sales dollars at a given number of customers minus the total cost for that same number of customers.

It should be noted that the break-even point graph is a bit of a simplification of reality. In the real world, the variable costs, and thus total costs, do not necessarily flow in a perfectly straight line. The real total cost line fluctuates like a wave around the average total cost trend. Variable costs include hourly workers, but hourly labor does not correlate exactly to business volume. In layman's terms, an hourly cook might handle forty customers per hour on average. However, the cook might be able to handle up to sixty customers during that same shift before requiring additional labor support. Thus, the variable labor cost (though not the food cost) would remain flat between forty and sixty customers and then jump up at sixty customers—because of the addition of another employee—before leveling out again for another sixty customers. It is easier and more practical to use the *average* total cost, such as the straight line depicted in Figure 13.1.

13.1.3 Break-Even Point and Management Decisions

Managers have the ability to shift a business's break-even point by enacting certain business decisions. Consider the break-even point graph. If a manager raises prices, he will shift the sales line slightly more toward vertical; in other words, each customer generates more dollars in sales (a higher average guest check). Alternatively, a manager could cut variable costs (food cost, beverage cost, and/or labor cost) to flatten slightly the total cost line. Either change would cause the total cost and sales lines to intersect farther to the left; break-even point would occur at a lower number of customers. However, a manager must recognize that raising prices or cutting costs can turn off customers and reduce sales. Thus, a manager must forecast how each of these decisions might impact business volume. As an example, a restaurant might raise its prices 10% but lose 8% of its customers. Determining whether such a move would result in more or less profit becomes obvious with the creation of alternate break-even point graphs using theoretical data.

Similarly, a business might decide to lower prices to generate more profit. How? If lowering prices results in greater numbers of customers, it is possible that the larger business volume will result in higher profit totals. As with raising prices or cutting costs, the only way to know if the change is likely to be good or bad is to forecast some assumptions about changes in business volume and then to chart those assumptions on a graph or in a spreadsheet. In other words, one uses the earlier formulas to calculate the profit predicted under two realities—the current one and one in which prices, costs, and customer volume have changed. Then, the two sets of computations are compared to see which reality is more profitable. Example 13.7 shows how this comparison is made without a graph.

Example 13.7: A restaurant averages 5,000 customers per month with an average guest check of $48.00. The monthly variable cost for this level of business is $149,000, and monthly fixed costs are $81,000. Management forecasts that by raising prices 5%, it will lose 3% of its customers. Would raising prices by 5% generate more or less profit?

Step 1: Calculate the current profit.
$$\text{Profit} = \text{Sales} - \text{Variable Costs} - \text{Fixed Costs}$$
We know variable costs and fixed costs already, but we must calculate sales. Since each customer, on average, generates $48 of sales,

$$\text{Sales} = \text{Customers} \times \text{Average Guest Check} = 5{,}000 \times \$48 = \$240{,}000$$

$$\text{Profit} = \text{Sales} (\$240{,}000) - \text{VC} (\$149{,}000) - \text{FC} (\$81{,}000) = \$10{,}000$$

Step 2: Next, calculate the new sales figure if prices are 5% higher but customer counts are 3% lower.

Any number can be increased by a percentage by multiplying by (1 + the percentage in decimal form). Similarly, a number can be decreased by a percentage by multiplying by (1 − the percentage in decimal form).

$$\text{New Customer count} = 5{,}000 \times (1 - 0.03) = 5{,}000 \times 0.97 = 4{,}850$$

Since prices are 5% higher, the new average guest check is
$$\$48 \times (1.05) = \$50.40$$

$$\text{Sales} = \text{Customers} \times \text{Average Guest Check} = 4{,}850 \times \$50.40 = \$244{,}440$$

Step 3: Note from the problem that prices were increased but costs were left unchanged. Thus, the new variable cost per customer is roughly the same as the old variable cost per customer. To calculate the new variable cost, first determine the old average variable cost per customer and then multiply that amount times the new customer count.

$$\text{Old Variable Cost per customer} = \text{Old VC} \div \text{Old Customer Count}$$
$$= \$149,000 \div 5,000 = \$29.80.$$

$$\text{New Variable Cost} = \text{VC per customer} \times \text{New Customer Count}$$
$$= \$29.80 \times 4,850 = \$144,530$$

In summary, under the new scenario, customers = 4,850; Sales = $244,440; Variable Cost = $144,530

Step 4: Finally, calculate the forecast profit under the new scenario.

$$\text{Profit} = \text{Sales} - \text{Variable Cost} - \text{Fixed Cost}$$
$$= \$244,440 - \$144,530 - \$81,000 = \$18,910$$

Raising prices 5% generates more profit in this scenario.

Under the given assumptions in Example 13.7, the restaurant would nearly double profits by raising prices. However, one must recognize that the 3% customer loss is only a forecast. If the prediction is inaccurate and the loss is closer to 20%, the restaurant's profits will plummet. Admittedly, the math can become quite complex. Adjusting a graph is sometimes easier, especially when done by entering data points into a computer.

Another common management decision is whether to expand business hours. For example, should a restaurant stay open until 11:00 p.m. instead of until 10:00 p.m., or should it offer breakfast in addition to lunch and dinner? To make this determination, a manager simply needs to treat the additional hours as a mini break-even-point case study to determine if the business will break even during the additional hours.

Example 13.8: A restaurant currently ends dinner service at 9:00 p.m. The manager estimates that to extend service until 11:00 p.m., he will need to keep a minimum of three workers on the clock for the extra two hours at an additional daily labor cost of $127. The additional cost for utilities and other fixed expenses is $39 for those two hours. If the restaurant operates with a variable rate (covering food and beverage cost only) of 32.8%, how much in additional late-night sales does the restaurant need to justify staying open?

In this example, the additional labor cost is treated as a fixed cost. Why? Because the manager recognizes that it is a minimum to keep the place open, even if there is only one customer. So, total fixed cost is $127 (labor) + $39 (utilities and other fixed costs) = $166 for the additional two hours. Variable rate is 32.8% or 0.328.

$$\text{Break-Even Point} = \frac{\text{Fixed Cost}}{(1 - \text{Variable Rate})} = \frac{\$166}{(1 - 0.328)} = \$247.02$$

Thus, if the manager believes he can bring in at least $248 in daily sales revenue (without requiring more than the three budgeted workers) between 9:00 and 11:00 p.m., it is worth staying open the extra two hours.

As all of these decisions—increasing or decreasing prices, shifting business hours—are based in part on a cost/volume/profit analysis, it should be stressed that the math behind calculating break-even point is an estimate at best. As stated earlier, the total cost line in a break-even point graph is only an average and doesn't truly move in a perfectly straight line. The forecasts for how price adjustments will impact business levels are based on educated, well-researched guesses, but they are guesses nonetheless.

Break-even point analyses always assume a consistent menu mix. Managers can improve the break-even point simply by shifting the menu mix to get more people to buy higher profit items, which increases the average contribution rate. If the menu mix changes with price shifts or during late-night business hours, the break-even point data will be flawed. Finally, while fixed costs do not typically change across small sales ranges, they can change with large swings in sales volume. For example, the manager might predict that his sales will double if he drops the menu prices by just 5% and stays open three hours later. Such a change might make sense for a given fixed cost line, but in reality, twice as many customers and additional hours likely require the hiring of additional management staff. If the additional hires are salaried, the fixed cost has changed for the business, which would impact the forecast profitability in such a scenario. Similarly, when business is declining, a manager can sometimes conserve profits by cutting fixed costs (e.g., a salaried employee) rather than by raising prices or reducing variable costs. A break-even point analysis does not provide the sure-fire answer to maximizing profits, but it is an excellent starting point for making certain management decisions.

13.2   MARKETING

One of the most important lessons to take away from any cost/volume/profit analysis is that it is easier to make money when sales are increasing than when they are decreasing. So how does a manager increase revenue in a foodservice establishment? In a word—marketing. Marketing technically encompasses a wide range of approaches designed to increase business volume, but these can be classified into four major categories:

- *Market Development*   A company sells its current product line to new customers.
- *Product Development*   A company sells new products to its old customer base.
- *Market Penetration*   A company sells its current product line to its current customer base more frequently.
- *Diversification*   A company sells new products to a new market of customers.

As a simple case study, imagine an upscale burger joint that offers sit-down service to a certain set of customers. Most of its current clientele consists of highly paid business people who take an hour for lunch and who enjoy attentive service. To increase business, the restaurant could develop a loyalty program, in which customers get every tenth burger free, to encourage customers to spend their money there more frequently (market penetration). The restaurant could advertise in local hotel magazines to encourage tourists to dine at the restaurant as well (market development). Management might choose to add desserts and alcoholic drinks to its menu to encourage the sale of new products to its current client base (product development). Finally, a manager might decide to provide a cheaper line of burgers available through a take-out window to attract lower-paid hourly workers, who get only thirty-minute lunch breaks (diversification). Each of these marketing approaches increases revenue, but each does it in a different way.

13.2.1 External Marketing

To attract new customers, managers typically need to market to people outside of the four walls of their establishment. While word of mouth (current customers telling other people about a business) is a powerful tool, managers have a great many other approaches available to them to attract new business proactively.

Advertising.   Advertising is essentially a media spot for which the business has paid to control the message. It comes in many forms, including billboards, magazine and newspaper ads, radio and television commercials, and paid Web site links/banners/ pop-up ads. Though costly, the management gets to control completely the image or message portrayed in the advertisement.

Public Relations or PR. PR is often described as free advertising, but technically it is a means by which a business gets its name in front of the public without paying for that exposure. Sometimes, there are costs involved, but they are usually for labor and food. A few examples of PR include performing a cooking demonstration on a morning news program or at a live cooking show, having a news story about the business in the media, and having an organization promote a business in exchange for providing free samples at the organization's event. The opportunities to have a foodservice operation's name out in public are plentiful, but when the promotion is free, someone other than the business typically controls the message. Getting a TV reporter to say on camera, "Wow! That's the best crab cake I've ever tasted" can be a boon for a restaurant. But a reporter on live TV might just as easily choke on a shell in the crab cake—not the kind of exposure that a business craves. Typically, the more involved in the community a foodservice establishment is, the more likely it is to get ongoing PR.

Signage. One of the simplest ways to market a business is through signage. A prominent sign (see Photo 13.1) or a menu posted in a window can attract foot traffic or cause drivers to stop in for a meal. Ineffective signage can make it difficult for a potential customer to locate a business, even if the management has been effective in building consumer interest in other ways.

Photo 13.1
An Exterior Sign Visible from the Road

Source: © Jonathan Lenz/Shutterstock.

Internet Exposure. In recent years, it has become a near requirement for a foodservice business to have a Web site. More and more customers search the Internet rather than the phone book to find a restaurant, caterer, or other hospitality company. Management can adjust their Web site or pay a fee to search engine companies to ensure that their site comes up near the top of certain Internet search results. Managers can further promote their own Web site on other Web sites through paid advertising or PR. For example, a restaurant could pay to have a Web link on a certain Web site, or its chef could post periodically to food blogs to mention his place of work. Social networking sites often become vehicles for business promotion, too, as restaurants and chefs develop followings and online "friends." Updating one's social networking site regularly helps to keep that chef or business top-of-mind for fans.

13.2.2 Internal Marketing

While attracting new customers is one way to drive revenue, managers can increase sales in small ways simply by marketing to their current customer base. Menus, electronic communication, servers, even the food and service itself are all extremely valuable for encouraging customers to spend more money and to patronize the business more often.

Menus. How a menu looks, kinds of items offered, and the description of menu items all influence what and how much a customer will purchase. To improve menu mix, a manager can arrange high-contribution margin items near the upper part of a menu or highlight them with boxes, colors, or bigger fonts to encourage more sales of those items. Dishes with fabulous-sounding descriptions often sell better than poorly described ones.

Electronic Communication. Ever wondered why so many restaurants offer a drawing for something free to guests who drop a business card into a bowl by the door? The restaurant wants to capture contact information for its customers. Some places outright ask for customer contact information on comment cards or during the reservation-making process. Having a guest's e-mail address (and other information) allows a company to send him special event promotions, coupons, birthday wishes, and other communications that encourage customers to return to that establishment. Some companies encourage customers to become loyal groupies through social networking sites. Guests may learn that they can get discounts via a company's Facebook page, or a manager may use Twitter to advertise free appetizers to the first ten guests to mention the tweet. In the case of mobile food trucks or vendors at farmers' markets, technology can inform customers in real time of the business's current location. Online social networking also helps to keep customers abreast of positive changes in the business and allows a restaurant to highlight its ingredient sources or other characteristics that the customer base values and wishes to support. Such promotions give people a reason to consider a specific foodservice operation their favorite, to patronize it frequently, and to encourage others to do the same.

Loyalty Programs. Some foodservice businesses operate loyalty programs. Through these programs, customers get free food or drink by spending money at the same business over and over. Loyalty programs can be low-tech using stamped cards (think: fill the card with stamps and your next sandwich is free) or high-tech with electronic cards (see Photo 13.2) that record each person's accumulated spending total (think: earn 1,000 points, where $1 = 10$ points, and get a free appetizer). These programs encourage repeat business because a person who is already partway toward something free tends to continue spending in order to earn the reward.

Photo 13.2
An Electronic Loyalty Card
Source: © Dinga/Shutterstock.

Servers.   Servers are extremely influential in persuading guests to spend more money or to select certain items. Servers can recommend high contribution margin foods as their favorites. How well a special sells depends heavily on a server's description at the table. The technique through which servers encourage sales is called *suggestive selling*. Moderately effective suggestive selling encourages guests to think about a certain category of food or drink they might not otherwise consider. A server might do this by asking, "Would you like something to drink besides water?" or "Would you like to start with an appetizer this evening?" These questions are only moderately effective because they offer the guest the opportunity to say "no." Highly effective suggestive selling gives guests a choice, but neither option is to purchase nothing. For example, a server might state, "Our restaurant is famous for its Shrimp Margarita appetizer. May I bring you one of those or would you prefer a different starter among our fabulous menu selections?" Of course, the guest may still decline any appetizer, but framed this way, the question is more effective at encouraging sales. Alcohol is the one area in which servers must be careful not to push sales too heavily. A guest might order ten courses of food, but by the tenth drink, a server has already crossed the limits of propriety and legality for safe alcohol service. Serving a guest to the point of inebriation puts the restaurant and the server at risk of legal liability. The proper technique for driving alcohol sales is *upselling*. In upselling, a server encourages a customer to spend more money on a higher quality product rather than on additional quantity. For example, when a guest asks for a gin and tonic, the server might reply, "Would you like that made with Tanqueray?" If the drink made with Tanqueray costs more than the one made with the well brand, the server has increased the restaurant's sales revenue, his guest check average, and likely, his tip. Suggestive selling and upselling are two of the most effective ways for a server to market to customers to increase sales volume.

Food and Drink Presentation.   Two extremely influential factors for what guests order in a restaurant are what they see and what they smell. (How many times have you heard someone in a restaurant, on seeing a server carry a dish across the dining room, say, "Oooh, what's that?") Spectacular plate presentations may spur a customer to order on the basis of what he sees rather than what is written on the menu. If a bakery smells of brownies coming out of the oven, customers are more likely to buy a brownie in addition to the bread they came to buy originally. Tableside presentation panders to both of these urges. If a customer sees a flaming drink being prepared at another table or smells a neighbor's tableside sautéed shrimp scampi, he is more likely to order one himself. While most restaurants cannot provide tableside service, many can display their dessert choices either on a dessert tray or in a display window at the restaurant's entrance. Beautiful desserts sell better when seen by customers than when merely described to customers.

A cost control manager may market internally or externally, but the most effective managers employ a combination of the two to best increase sales. Whichever marketing approach management takes, a cost control manager has a much easier time generating profits when he focuses on driving revenue as much as he does on controlling costs.

13.3   POS SYSTEMS AND TECHNOLOGY

Technology, including and beyond point-of-sales systems, has come a long way in a generation to help foodservice managers increase revenue and control costs. POS companies typically offer a wide range of computer software and hardware to foodservice and hospitality managers to help them run their businesses. Each component costs additional money, so managers and owners must ultimately decide which technology they will purchase, which software they will develop internally, and which functions they will perform by hand. Usually a smaller operation purchases fewer software suites, while a foodservice business with multiple storefronts requires greater computer support for management and oversight. However, the owner's or management team's preference is usually the biggest deciding factor in whether or not to utilize POS technology.

13.3.1 How Technology Drives Revenue

Current technology on the market has the ability to drive revenue and profit in a variety of ways from increasing service speed to informing menu mix decisions to supporting suggestive selling and marketing approaches. By increasing service speed, a restaurant is able to handle more customers per hour, and when customers are not pressed for time because of service delays, they can order and enjoy multiple courses. POS systems use historical data to know how long the average customer takes during each meal period (see Figure 13.2). Using this information, the system notifies reservationists of exactly how many guests a restaurant can accommodate via reservations for every 15-minute period. Furthermore, POS systems track where each customer is in the meal process. The computer knows which guests have just been seated, which are eating their entrées, and which are due to pay their checks in the next couple of minutes, so it can reliably predict how long a wait will be for customers arriving without reservations. Efficient spacing of reservations and providing guests with accurate wait times helps to maximize the use of each dining room table without irritating customers who do not wish to wait longer than promised for a table.

Today's Service Performance

Day Part	Net Sales	% Sales	Guests	Sales per Guest	Checks	Avg Check	Table Turns	Avg Minutes
Service Totals:	51,578.45	100%	5,119	10.08	3,211	16.06	5,138	45
Breakfast	23,282.31	45.1%	2,539	9.17	1,646	14.14	2,330	43
Lunch	28,296.14	54.9%	2,580	10.97	1,565	18.08	2,808	46

Hour	Net Sales	% Sales	Guests	Sales per Guest	Checks	Avg Check	Table Turns	Avg Minutes
6:00 AM	609.53	1.2%	68	8.96	62	9.83	54	34
7:00 AM	3,364.03	6.5%	369	9.12	251	13.40	233	40
8:00 AM	5,728.02	11.1%	619	9.25	393	14.58	493	44
9:00 AM	6,538.55	12.7%	737	8.87	473	13.82	748	44
10:00 AM	7,042.18	13.7%	746	9.44	467	15.08	802	44
11:00 AM	7,583.39	14.7%	703	10.79	420	18.06	684	45
12:00 PM	11,615.46	22.5%	1,114	10.43	606	19.17	911	45
1:00 PM	6,480.95	12.6%	578	11.21	370	17.52	844	47
2:00 PM	2,446.39	4.7%	183	13.37	160	15.29	361	49
3:00 PM	169.95	0.3%	2	84.98	9	18.88	8	68

All Fixed Periods

Figure 13.2

Sample POS Service Report including Average Minutes for Customer Meal

Source: Printed with the permission of MICROS Systems, Inc.

Keeping customers on schedule during service also helps to turn tables quickly without rushing guests through a meal. Management knows how long each step in the service process should take. Once a guest is entered in the POS system as seated at a table, the computer can notify management if there is a delay in the guest's service at any point along the way. If a server is late taking an order, if the kitchen is slow preparing the food, if the guest is waiting too long to receive a check, a manager is alerted by the computer system, so he can act to relieve the bottleneck (or make contact with the guest before a delayed customer becomes an irate customer). As historical patterns emerge, management can make changes to speed service as well. For example, if the grill station always runs behind schedule, management can decide if the grill cook needs additional help or if the menu mix needs adjustment to drive business to the other cooks.

Technology also has other means for speeding service efficiently. Kitchens can use vibrating pagers to notify servers when their food is ready for pickup. Such a system keeps servers on the floor assisting customers rather than checking on their orders until the moment that the food is ready. Pagers of a different sort are sometimes used to notify waiting guests when their table is ready, which frees those guests from having to cram into a small waiting area for long periods. Similar technology calls a guest's cell phone when a table is available. Servers can use handheld devices to enter a party's food order or to process a customer's credit card right at the table, even allowing the customer to enter the tip electronically on the spot. When a guest wants to pay and leave a restaurant, it is a welcome relief not to wonder how long it will take a server to return with his credit card. Years ago, POS systems sent orders to the kitchen only by printer. Today, the kitchen staff may receive orders on a touch screen display. Without paper to shuffle, cooks operate a little faster. Additionally, the screen notifies the cook if an order is overdue, and the real-time information is shared with both server and manager. The faster customers are served, the faster the restaurant can turn its tables to accommodate more guests each day.

When customers are pressed for time, they are more likely to patronize an establishment with faster service options. Some mobile phone applications, with restaurants that support this technology, now allow customers to set up a tab in a restaurant's POS system, so that a customer can settle the check without waiting for a server. Similarly, a customer can place an order, such as for take-out pizza, without having to go through a human being. The customer can electronically order a pizza in his name to be picked-up at 6:00 p.m. At 5:45 p.m. the order pops-up on the cook's screen automatically, and the computer system processes the credit card without having to go through a person. When the customer arrives at 6:00 p.m., the pizza is ready to go.

POS systems collect data and provide managers with compiled reports to inform their decisions. For example, a POS system can quickly calculate the stars, plowhorses, puzzles, and dogs for a menu mix analysis. It also tracks which time periods are the slowest, so a manager can provide targeted marketing promotions, such as deep discounts between 3:00 and 5:00 p.m. Because data is updated every 15 minutes, a manager could decide to discount a given item's price in the middle of service to sell more of a dish that isn't moving fast enough.

In addition to the other data that a POS system collects, it can store customers' personal information and buying patterns. This gives managers the chance to reward frequent customers with on-the-spot comps or discounts. It also tells managers which customers should receive birthday or anniversary discounts each week. If a regular customer suddenly stops coming, management can reach out to bring that customer back to the restaurant. Since management can add notes to any customer's profile, a server may be able to view all kinds of information about a guest to provide him better service. Such information might include allergies, favorite drinks, preferred seating area, or desired speed of service. Imagine how much more effective suggestive selling is for a server who knows that a guest's favorite drink is Dewar's on the rocks or that he loves seafood. Consider the difference between "Welcome. Have you dined with us before?" and "Welcome back Mr. Jones. Would you care for your usual Dewar's on the rocks?" When a customer feels that the service staff knows him and treats him like a VIP, he is far more likely to return to that establishment often.

With all of the possibilities that technology offers, it should be stressed that not every application is appropriate for every business. An upscale restaurant that prides itself on personal interaction would not want customers to place orders electronically through their phones. Fast food places have no need to employ reservation or waiting area pager systems. More important than any increase in efficiency is the impact on an operation's brand. In most cases, technology supports a business's brand or at least has no effect on it, but when it does, the company's image should almost always come before technology.

13.3.2 How Technology Controls Costs

POS systems do more than just drive revenue. They can aid a manager in the performance of nearly every managerial function (though they are never a replacement for a competent manager). For example, under the umbrella of labor management, a POS system can advise a manager in the process of making employee schedules. Using historical data, a POS system can forecast business in 15-minute increments and suggest time slots for each employee on the schedule. The system can serve as the company's time clock, too. All employees can sign in and out through the POS system. This way, the system tracks which employees are clocking in late or early, which are approaching overtime, and which have attendance problems. The system benefits the workers, too. Employees can request days off and enter preferred work schedules into a POS terminal; the system considers this information when recommending employee work schedules.

As described in earlier chapters, POS systems are exceptional devices for controlling what food is ordered through the kitchen. Using a POS terminal, a server can only order food from the kitchen if it is assigned to a guest check, comp account, employee meal, or transfer account. Thus, servers would have great difficulty obtaining free food to giveaway without someone knowing it. More complex systems allow a manager to control food production even further. Managers can enter recipes into a POS system for each menu item. The system can use historical menu mix data and forecasts to adjust the recipe yields daily, which in turn provides the chef with his daily kitchen production schedule and complementary recipes. If an employee has a recipe question, the recipe can be pulled up on an electronic screen in the kitchen, complete with a picture for plating guidance.

If a purchasing manager has entered each ingredient's cost into the system, the POS system will track standard food cost in real time. It can keep a running tally of the current theoretical inventory on the basis of recipes and guest checks, and it can suggest food purchase orders, including when to place the order and which purveyors to use. (*Note:* The system can only maintain theoretical inventory levels. A manager still needs to take a physical inventory to compare with the system's inventory. If the inventories are the same, then waste and theft are controlled. If there are significant differences, the manager knows exactly which products are not being controlled properly.) Once a real inventory is entered into the system, it can calculate actual food cost and food cost percentage and compare them with standard food cost and its percentage of sales.

POS systems have the ability to notify managers of irregularities in an employee's performance that might necessitate disciplinary action. If an employee has a large number of "voids," "no sales," or guest checks with no orders, the manager knows to investigate for possible employee theft. If an employee has a lot of errors that require correcting in the system, the manager knows that the employee may need additional training. A manager can use the system to research a server's individual checks to see when a guest is seated, when orders are placed, and when payment is made, too. For example, a table with four customers that is seated at 5:00 p.m., orders only two drinks, and does not pay until 10:00 p.m., might raise questions as to whether or not an employee is giving away unauthorized freebies to a table. Tracking that kind of data can be nearly impossible without the aid of a computer system.

Because POS systems also function like cash registers and credit card–processing units, they track exactly how much cash is in a till at a given time and how many sales are processed every 15 minutes. The computer can alert a manager when a till has too much cash in it, so that a manager can transfer some to a locked safe. It can also notify a manager when additional change is required and can recommend what levels of change to pick up at a bank for the next day. It records server credit card tips (and declared cash tips), so the manager can tip out employees properly as well as track employee tip income for tax purposes.

Creating data reports is one of the most valuable functions that a POS system can perform. The system can quickly generate reports—in spreadsheet or graph form—for labor costs, food costs, expense percentages against sales, productivity per person-hour, average guest check per server or per period. In short, a POS system can conduct nearly every mathematical calculation covered in this text and more. It can do so in real time on the basis of the real data that servers, cooks, and purchasing managers enter. Furthermore, in multiunit properties it can compare data across properties or compile everything into a single report for the entire business.

Today's Operations

Total Revenue	13,400.58			Operating Metrics			
Net Sales	13,400.58			Service		Total	Average
Gross Sales	13,932.64			Guests / Avg Spend		266	50.38
Discounts	(532.06)	-3.8%		Checks / Avg Spend		188	71.28
				Table Turns / Avg Spend		0	0.00
Service Charges	0.00			Avg Table Turns / Minutes		0.00	0
Operating Costs	5,155.22	38.5%		Adjustments		Total	Count
				Voids		(22.73)	1
Cost of Goods Sold	5,155.22	38.5%		Returns		0.00	0
Labor Cost	0.00	0.0%		Labor Stats		Total	Hours
				Regular Time		0.00	12.48
Operating Margin	8,245.36	61.5%		Overtime		0.00	0.00
				Sales Per Labor Hour		1,073.76	
Receipts	14,715.45			Avg Hourly Pay		0.00	

The most recent POS transaction included in this report (shown in the local time of the location):   11/2/2007 11:05 AM

Figure 13.3
Sample POS Daily Summary Report

Note: The Labor Cost is listed as "0". Some companies only use their POS systems for certain functions. If a manager does not use the POS system for employee time check-in and check-out, labor is not tracked by the computer and renders the software unable to calculate labor cost. As with all technology, a POS system is only useful if the manager uses it.

Source: Printed with the permission of MICROS Systems, Inc.

13.3.3 Why Learn the Nonelectronic Systems at All?

The incredible capabilities of POS systems beg the question—Why does a current or future foodservice manager need to learn how to calculate anything by hand? Here are some answers.

A POS system is not an all-or-nothing purchase. Each function that it performs requires an additional purchase by the company, and in some cases, an ongoing expense. For example, an electronic inventory management program requires a full-time purchasing or storeroom manager to make it useful. A real inventory must still be conducted and entered into the system. Purveyors' current prices must be entered regularly if the food cost calculation is to be accurate. Sometimes, a manager or owner will decide that it is more cost effective to do something by hand (or using another computer program, such as an Excel worksheet), than it is to purchase that POS system component. Some owners will choose to purchase nothing electronic and to do everything by hand. A close analysis of Figure 13.3 provides the perfect example. In Figure 13.3, labor cost is listed as zero—a scenario that occurs if the company does not purchase and use the employee scheduling and time clock functions available for a POS system. The restaurant depicted in Figure 13.3 may prefer to control labor using other means. A manager should be able to function equally effectively in any of these situations.

Managers must be able to run their operation even when the power is out. If a power failure in the middle of dinner service means that everyone gets a free meal, that no more customers are seated, and that the food and labor cost for that period is simply ignored, a manager will have a difficult time staying profitable—especially in an area prone to power failures. Being able to compute data by hand when a POS system lacks all the information is essential for a manager who wishes to make decisions on the basis of accurate information.

POS systems provide data to inform decisions, but they do not make decisions for managers. So what if a POS system can conduct a menu mix analysis? If a manager does not know what stars, plowhorses, puzzles, and dogs are, the information does not help that manager to improve an operation's profitability. A computer can use historical data to forecast, but a manager must still be able to adjust a forecast on the basis of qualitative data the computer may not know. Abdicating all responsibility for forecasting to a computer is a high-risk gamble that can leave a restaurant shorthanded or overstaffed. Alerts to labor cost or food cost variances are meaningless if a manager does not know what a food cost is, why it is different from a food cost percentage, and when cost overruns are acceptable versus unacceptable. Imagine the problems that could arise for a manager who makes decisions based solely on computer data. The POS system could notify a manager that one particular server has an inordinately large number of comps or unsettled bills. A manager who rushes to fire the employee without an investigation might learn the hard way that the comps were all for the business owner, who always requests his favorite server. Managers need to know what each data report and calculation means and what should be done with that data. The best way to understand this is to know what data the computer uses for its calculations, what the input information and output results signify, and why a manager would want to perform such a calculation in the first place. In short, the best way to understand the computer's information is to know how to do the same spreadsheets without the computer (recognizing that the computer does them much faster).

Finally, a computer is only as good as the data entered into it. When a manager understands how to cost a recipe by hand, he is less likely to enter the wrong information into the system. A POS system can alert a manager when a labor cost variance is too high, but it relies on the manager to enter that variance threshold electronically. A manager who knows how to conduct a wide range of managerial computations by hand is more likely to give the computer the right information to get the results the manager needs for decision making.

While computers and POS systems allow managers to control costs and drive revenue better, they are no substitute for a competent manager. A skilled manager can work faster and make better decisions with the help of a POS system. A manager who does not understand the various costs and cost percentages, yields and the recipe costing process, menu-pricing techniques, purchasing and receiving controls, forecasting, and revenue management is likely to find a POS system fairly unhelpful in assisting him with his responsibilities.

SUMMARY

A cost/volume/profit analysis allows a manager to estimate a business's profit or loss at various levels of business volume given certain variable rates and fixed costs. The variable rate is the average variable cost as a percentage of sales (expressed as a decimal); the percentage remaining that does not go toward variable costs is called the contribution rate (also expressed as a decimal). Total sales are dispersed to cover three areas: variable costs, fixed costs, and profit. The percentage of sales dollars represented by the contribution rate go first to pay fixed costs and then to profit. When fixed costs are not fully covered, the business experiences a loss. Break-even point is the point in sales at which a business earns zero profit but does not have any loss. The break-even point can be expressed in sales dollars, or if an average guest check is known, in number of customers. Managers make decisions on raising or lowering menu prices or on cutting variable costs in part based on how it may impact business and move the break-even point. Decisions to expand business hours are often also made on the basis of whether the additional period is likely to break even on its own. As it is easier to earn a profit when sales are increasing than when they are decreasing, a manager should attempt to drive revenue. Managers have a variety of marketing approaches to increase their business, including market development, product development, market penetration, and diversification. External marketing attracts new customers while internal marketing increases the business from current customers. Suggestive selling and upselling are examples of internal marketing. POS systems have the ability to aid a manager in achieving his revenue and cost control goals. Technology collects data and compiles reports faster than a manager can without a computer, but the manager is still ultimately responsible for understanding and interpreting the computer reports and for making decisions on the basis of all of the information available.

COMPREHENSION QUESTIONS

1. A restaurant has sales of $300,000 during the same period in which its variable costs are $185,300 and its fixed costs are $103,000. What are the restaurant's profits for this period?

2. Using the information from question 1, calculate the restaurant's variable rate.

3. A restaurant has a variable rate of 0.584. In one month, its variable costs are $72,487. What should sales be for that month?

4. What is the contribution rate for a company with a variable rate of 0.664?

5. Variable rate covers all variable costs. What does the contribution rate cover?

6. A restaurant has variable costs of $76,244 and fixed costs of $49,902 for a month. The profit for that month is $3,870. Calculate the total sales dollars, variable rate, and contribution rate for this restaurant.

7. If a restaurant has a variable rate of 0.574 and annual fixed costs of $288,750, what will the profit or loss be on $650,000 in annual sales?

8. Using the information in question 7, what will the profit or loss be if annual sales are $750,000?

9. What is the annual break-even point in sales for a restaurant with a variable rate of 0.673 and annual fixed costs of $187,500? What is the break-even point in number of customers if the guest check average is $67.87?

10. If the owner of the restaurant in question 9 wants to make $20,000 in profit, how many dollars in sales must the restaurant generate? How many customers does that represent?

11. A restaurant manager is considering keeping the business open two hours later. He estimates his labor cost for the additional two hours to be $287 and the cost for additional utilities and other expenses to be $71. If the variable rate (covering all other variable expenses) for the restaurant is 0.614, how much additional business in sales does the manager need to bring in during those two extra hours to break even?

12. What are the four classifications of marketing approaches?

13. List four examples of external marketing and four examples of internal marketing. Describe the difference between internal and external marketing.

14. List three ways in which a POS system helps a manager to drive revenue and three ways in which it helps a manager to control costs.

DISCUSSION QUESTIONS

1. What is the reason for a manager to calculate a break-even point? What would you expect him to do with this information, or is it just nice to know?

2. You conduct a cost/volume/profit analysis for your business in three situations: at current menu prices, with higher menu prices, and with lower menu prices. It just so happens that because of forecast business volume shifts, the break-even point is the same for all three scenarios. Knowing this, would you recommend raising prices, lowering them, or leaving them alone? Why?

3. A restaurant currently operates at a loss. If it could increase its customer base by 5%, it would break even. A marketing study shows that by paying for some local advertising, the restaurant would increase its business by exactly 5%. Should management buy that advertising or look at other marketing campaigns instead? (Assume it cannot afford to do both.) If it just buys the advertising, will it start to break even?

4. A restaurant is operating at maximum capacity. Does it still need to engage in marketing activities?

Why or why not? If yes, what kind of marketing activities would you recommend?

5. Upselling is commonly discussed in relation to alcohol sales because it is safer (legally) to increase alcohol sales dollars by selling higher quality than by selling additional drinks to the same customer. How might a server apply upselling to food sales to get customers to spend more without actually buying additional courses?

6. The text argues that managers must learn how to perform by hand a wide range of computations that a POS system can do for them. Do you agree? Why or why not?

7. POS systems can perform many of the cost control functions that managers do, but they cannot do all of them. What things does a manager do to control costs and drive revenue that a computer cannot do? (List at least three things.)

8. Are there any downsides to using a POS system in a restaurant? When might a manager decide not to use one? When would a manager or owner absolutely want to have a complete POS system with all the bells and whistles?

14

Income Statements and Budgets

Cost control encompasses many separate cost and revenue centers in need of control—sales, food cost, beverage cost, and labor cost, just to name a few. This text has already expounded upon most of those areas. However, none of these cost control subsections works in isolation from the others. They all interconnect and interact to generate a profit. Lower-level managers may focus on just one or two of these areas, but upper management and owners need a bird's eye view of the entire operation and its components to ensure that all the pieces work together to create one thriving business.

The best way to gain a snapshot of how a business's expense and revenue sources interact is through an income statement (sometimes called a profit and loss or P&L statement). Sales that run too low to overcome fixed costs (i.e., to reach the break-even point) are obvious in an income statement. Want to know if cost overruns are coming from overly high food costs, beverage costs, or labor costs? The income statement has the answer. An income statement pinpoints the operational costs that are too high to support a profit; it does the same for sales that are too low. It also notifies a manager if certain cost centers are underspending, which signals a potential threat to long-term customer satisfaction. Income statements help a manager know which parts of the business to adjust and which to leave alone. Budgets, which look similar to income statements, reflect management's response to the prior income statement and its goals for the future. A budget is the roadmap for all lower-level managers to follow, and as such, it is a powerful management control tool. Knowing how to read and how to create an income statement and a budget is a required skill for any future manager.

Objectives

By the end of this chapter, you will be able to:

- Read and interpret an income statement and a budget
- Complete the information on an income statement given only dollars or percentages
- Analyze budget/income statement variances using a common size analysis and a comparative analysis to highlight potential problem areas in an operation
- Create a budget based on historical data, forecasts, and management goals

14.1   HOW TO READ AN INCOME STATEMENT

Students of income statements should know that there are multiple ways to format an income statement. Each expense or sale is classified under an appropriate heading, but what to call those headings and how to arrange the categories on the income statement is management's choice. That said, many restaurants use similar terminology to classify and to order their revenue and expense information. There is a text, *The Uniform System of Accounts for Restaurants*, which is utilized by the National Restaurant Association for its annual reports. By adopting this system, restaurants may make useful comparisons between their own expense and sales data and that of similar restaurants around the country.

Despite the value of employing a common system across the industry, the discussion that follows is *not* the Uniform System of Accounts style. Instead, the forthcoming description of income statements is educationally more straightforward and easier to understand for students new to cost control. Any student who masters this approach first should have little difficulty adjusting to the Uniform System of Accounts format in the future. A sample income statement using *The Uniform System of Accounts for Restaurants* style is located in the Appendix.

14.1.1   Three Types of Statements

While chefs are likely to find the income statement the most valuable financial statement to reference, senior managers use three financial statements. A *balance sheet* reports a company's assets, liabilities and equity since Assets = Liabilities + Equity. It shows property (land, cash, inventory, etc.) that a company owns, known as assets, and it lists the amount that a business owes on debt and expenses to be paid, called liabilities. The equity is the remaining value for owners or shareholders after liabilities are deducted from assets. A *statement of cash flows* depicts the movement of cash through a business to see from a broader perspective where money is going and how much is available on hand. It reports cash flow not only from customer sales and purveyor payments but also from investment activities, such as selling or buying new equipment, from paying debt, and from compensating investors. Both of these reports are important for making major periodic decisions about a business, decisions typically made by an owner or by investors. The third report, the income statement, is the one most often used by managers to control their daily operations.

14.1.2   Income Statements

An income statement may be written to cover any period of time—a day, a week, a month, a quarter, or a half-year—but an annual income statement is the near universal document that most foodservice operations employ, even if they do not use any other type of income statement. A *common size income statement*, a very popular format, lists both dollars and percentages for each line item and category. (When not common-sized, the income statement may include only dollar figures.) For the most part, the percentages express each line item as a percentage of total sales; the exceptions to this rule are the subheadings under the "cost of sales" category. Figure 14.1 depicts a common size income statement.

The sample income statement in Figure 14.1 begins, as all income statements do, with the "sales" category. In most foodservice operations, "sales" is subdivided into "food" and "beverage" sales. The percentages for these two subheadings, calculated as a percentage of total sales, show the sales mix between food and drink. In this sample income statement, food represents 74% of total revenue, while beverages account for the remaining 26%. "Total sales", the sum of food and beverage sales, is always 100%.

USA Restaurant Income Statement 1/1/11–12/31/11		
Sales		
Food	$727,194	74.0%
Beverage	$255,561	26.0%
Total Sales	**$982,755**	**100.0%**
Cost of Sales		
Food Cost	$225,180	31.0% (% of Food Sales)
Beverage Cost	$58,804	23.0% (% of Bev Sales)
Total Cost of Goods Sold	**$283,984**	**28.9%**
Gross Profit	**$698,771**	**71.1%**
Labor		
Salaries and Wages	$275,442	28.0%
Employee Benefits	$52,155	5.3%
Total Labor Cost	**$327,597**	**33.3%**
Prime Cost	**$611,581**	**62.2%**
Controllable Expenses		
Direct Operating Expenses	$48,506	4.9%
Music and Entertainment	$14,300	1.5%
Marketing	$19,325	2.0%
Utilities	$38,992	4.0%
General and Administrative	$24,774	2.5%
Repairs and Maintenance	$14,500	1.5%
Total Controllable Expenses	**$160,397**	**16.3%**
Income before Fixed Costs	**$210,777**	**21.4%**
Fixed Costs		
Occupancy Costs	$98,800	10.1%
Interest	$28,746	2.9%
Depreciation	$31,678	3.2%
Total Fixed Costs (Occupancy, Interest, Depreciation)	**$159,224**	**16.2%**
Profit before Taxes	**$51,553**	**5.2%**
Income Taxes	$12,213	1.2%
Net Income	**$39,340**	**4.0%**

Figure 14.1
Sample Common Size Income Statement

The subcategories under "cost of sales" are the food cost and the beverage cost. The percentages for these two line items are not calculated against total sales. Instead, they are calculated as follows:

Food Cost Percentage = Food Cost ÷ Food Sales

Beverage Cost Percentage = Beverage Cost ÷ Beverage Sales

By calculating these two percentages in this manner, a manager can see whether actual food or beverage costs are out of line with standard food and beverage costs. If these costs were instead compared with total sales, the numbers would shift with the food—beverage menu mix even as food cost and beverage cost percentages remained the same. "Total cost of goods sold" is the sum of the food and beverage costs; its percentage is calculated against total sales to see what percentage of sales is consumed by the direct cost of the items being served. Total cost of goods sold varies somewhat as the sales mix changes. "Gross profit" is the money left from sales after the total cost of goods sold figure has been deducted.

"Labor" is the cost for employees—both their earnings and their benefits. Because labor includes wages, which are variable costs, and salaries, which are fixed costs, this line item is a semivariable cost. "Salaries and wages" is the combined income of the labor force. "Employee benefits" is the cost of all employee benefits. Notice in Figure 14.1 that while employee benefits as a percentage of sales seems low (5.3%), benefits are actually 18.9% of salaries and wages ($52,155 ÷ $275,442). The combined salaries and wages and employee benefits lines are the total labor cost. In Figure 14.1, this labor cost is 33.3% or one-third of all expenses. "Prime cost" is the sum of total cost of goods sold plus total labor cost.

"Controllable expenses" are categorized as such because they are semivariable costs. Like labor cost, all of the expenses listed under controllable expenses fluctuate somewhat with sales but not as a consistent percentage of sales. Controllable expenses, like food, beverage, and labor cost, are prime areas for managers to exercise control over costs.

"Direct operating expenses" is a broad category that includes the costs for items other than food and drink that go toward serving customers. Examples of direct operating expenses are flowers and decorations, china, flatware, glassware, menus, employee uniforms, laundry services, cleaning services, parking services, cleaning and paper supplies, small equipment for the kitchen or bar, licenses, in short, the variable expenses not covered in the other controllable expense categories.

"Music and entertainment" covers the cost of performers as well as licensing fees and royalties for recorded music. If equipment is rented, if performers are fed, or if licenses are required to support a restaurant's music program, those expenses go into this category.

"Marketing" encompasses all costs associated with advertising and public relations. Advertisement creation as well as mailing and postage are included here. When customers are given comp meals or drinks, those costs go here, rather than in food cost or in beverage cost, as their cost is designed for marketing purposes rather than for immediate sales generation.

The "utilities" category includes not only gas, water, and electric, but also the cost for any trash or other waste removal. It also includes the cost of certain types of equipment, such as light bulbs, that are directly related to utility usage.

"General and administrative" costs cover the expenses associated with the infrastructure necessary to operate any business. Telephone, Internet, insurance, office supplies, bank and credit card fees, and recruiting and relocating fees are just some examples. Charitable donations as well as cash register shorts go in this category as well.

"Repair and maintenance" encompasses the cost for all equipment and facility repairs and maintenance, including maintenance contracts and building improvements.

All of the controllable expenses are added together to calculate the "total controllable expenses" line. "Income before fixed costs" is calculated as Total Sales − Prime Cost − Total Controllable Expenses = Income before Fixed Costs. In other words, income before fixed costs is the amount of revenue left after all expenses listed above that line item (but not below it) in the income statement are deducted from total sales.

The "fixed costs" category on the income statement includes three primary cost centers that are fixed costs. "Occupancy costs" includes rent, property taxes, and property insurance. "Interest" is the cost of using someone else's money. Interest may be the interest a company pays on investors' loans or on a mortgage payment.

"Depreciation" is the means by which a company spreads a significant cost across multiple years based on the life expectancy of a purchased item. (These "purchased items" may be large, expensive pieces of equipment or major renovations, but depreciation is not typically used for inexpensive purchases. A restaurant might depreciate a range/oven, for example, but it would not depreciate a single rubber spatula.) For instance, if a restaurant purchases a $4,500 set of computers with a three-year life expectancy, it can (on paper) stretch the cost of that purchase over three years. While there are accounting and tax reasons for doing this, the most logical reason is that the amount paid is returning value over multiple years, so the expense should be divided over those years. Consider the example of the computers. A company pays $4,500 in the first year, but really only uses $1,500 worth of the computers' total value in the first year. The company's profits in the first year look much worse than they should, but in the remaining two years, the profits seem inflated. Without depreciation, the computers are effectively "overcharging the business" for their use in the first year and working for free in the remaining two; it makes more sense to spread the cost across the years that those computers operate. If the computers were rented or leased, their cost would automatically be divided over time, and depreciation would not be necessary. There are various methods to calculate depreciation. Some divide the value equally over an item's life span while others adjust the value of the item year by year. Depreciation also factors in the salvage or resale value of the item after it has outlived its expected usefulness. Whichever technique is used, it should be stressed that depreciation is an accounting tool, not a means to delay payment to an equipment vendor or construction company. A business that sells major equipment to a restaurant expects to be paid right away, not over several years.

The "total fixed costs" line is the sum of the fixed costs (occupancy, interest, and depreciation). "Profit before taxes" is figured by calculating "income before fixed costs" minus "total fixed costs." Finally, income taxes are determined, and the net income is the final profit after income taxes are deducted from profit before taxes.

Notice from the description of each of these line items that as a manager looks down the income statement page, the costs become more and more fixed. Cost of sales is completely variable, labor and controllable expenses are semivariable, and occupancy, interest, and depreciation are completely fixed. This format aids in the creation of budgets from prior income statements, the process for which is discussed later in this chapter.

As described earlier, the percentage column in an income statement is calculated using the following graphic formula:

The cost is the dollar figure for that line item (even when the dollar figure is revenue, not a cost). Sales, with the exceptions of food cost and beverage cost, is the total sales dollars. For food cost and beverage cost, "sales" represents the corresponding food sales or beverage sales figure. As with prior graphic equations, simply cover up the variable being sought, and perform the calculation depicted with the remaining variables.

Example 14.1: On an income statement, "occupancy costs" is listed as $18,000, while total sales are $174,000. What percentage should be written in the column next to "occupancy costs"?

$$\text{Percentage} = \text{Cost} \div \text{Sales} = \$18,000 \div \$174,000 = 0.103 \text{ or } 10.3\%$$

Example 14.2: An income statement lists food sales as $84,000 and beverage sales as $16,000. The manager wishes to operate a 33.2% food cost and a 22.2% beverage cost. To hit these goals, what should the food cost and beverage cost (in dollars) be?

From the graphic, Cost = Sales × %. In this case, "sales" is not total sales but rather food sales and beverage sales separately.

$$\text{Food Cost} = \$84,000 \text{ (Food Sales)} \times 0.332 \text{ (Percentage as a decimal)} = \$27,888$$

$$\text{Beverage Cost} = \$16,000 \text{ (Beverage Sales)} \times 0.222 \text{ (Percentage as a decimal)} = \$3,552$$

14.2   COMPARING INCOME STATEMENTS AND BUDGETS

Income statements and budgets often look similar. Both include the same line item categories, and both can be written in a "common size" format. The primary difference between the two is that an income statement includes real data from history, while a budget is a forward-looking plan for future sales and expenditures. In fact, it is common practice to place budgets and income statements side by side on the same page, so they may be more easily compared. Sometimes a manager wishes to base her current budget on the prior year's income statement; sometimes she wants to see if her current income statement is operating according to the budget prepared for the same period. There are two main approaches to compare a budget to an income statement—common size analysis and comparative analysis.

14.2.1 Common Size Analysis

Since budgets and income statements are typically written in a common-size format, the easiest analysis to perform is a common size analysis. In a common size analysis, managers calculate the differences between the two percentage columns on each budget/income statement being compared. Mathematically, the Variance = Actual Percentage − Budget Percentage, when an actual income statement is being compared with a budget. If two income statements are being compared with each other, then the variance is typically the most recent statement's percentages minus the older statement's percentages. Figure 14.2 demonstrates how an income statement and a budget are analyzed using common size analysis. (*Note:* Some companies use parentheses in financial documents to signify negative numbers; that is the case here as well.)

It should be noted that in Figure 14.2 rounding decimals to one-tenth of a percentage makes certain actual percentage line items appear to be exactly the same as the budgeted percentage. In reality, they are different, but only slightly; in other words, managers who round to one-tenth of one percentage would consider such a difference insignificant. The actual tolerance that management has for variances is typically determined in advance by an owner or senior manager, so other managers know whether a variance is significant. For example, if management decides that a variance of +/− 0.5% is acceptable, than anything within that range is not likely to be a concern for management. In Figure 14.2, any line items with variances greater than the +/− 0.5% threshold have been italicized.

USA Restaurant					
	Budget 1/1/11– 12/31/11	Budget	Actual 1/1/11– 12/31/11	Actual	Variance (Actual%– Budget%)
Sales					
Food	$750,000	75.0%	$727,194	74.0%	*(1.0)*
Beverage	$250,000	25.0%	$255,561	26.0%	*1.0*
Total Sales	**$1,000,000**	100.0%	**$982,755**	100.0%	0
Cost of Sales					
Food Cost	$232,500	31.0%	$225,180	31.0%	0
Beverage Cost	$56,250	22.5%	$58,804	23.0%	0.5
Total Cost of Goods Sold	**$288,750**	28.9%	**$283,984**	28.9%	0
Gross Profit	**$711,250**	71.1%	**$698,771**	71.1%	0
Labor					
Salaries and Wages	$262,000	26.2%	$275,442	28.0%	1.8
Employee Benefits	$49,780	5.0%	$52,155	5.3%	0.3
Total Labor Cost	**$311,780**	31.2%	**$327,597**	33.3%	**2.1**
Prime Cost	**$600,530**	60.1%	**$611,581**	62.2%	**2.1**
Controllable Expenses					
Direct Operating Expenses	$50,000	5.0%	$48,506	4.9%	(0.1)
Music and Entertainment	$15,000	1.5%	$14,300	1.5%	0
Marketing	$20,000	2.0%	$19,325	2.0%	0
Utilities	$38,500	3.9%	$38,992	4.0%	0.1
General and Administrative	$24,500	2.5%	$24,774	2.5%	0
Repairs and Maintenance	$12,500	1.3%	$14,500	1.5%	0.2
Total Controllable Expenses	**$160,500**	16.1%	**$160,397**	16.3%	**0.2**
Income before Fixed Costs	**$238,970**	23.9%	**$210,777**	21.4%	**(2.5)**
Fixed Costs					
Occupancy Costs	$98,800	9.9%	$98,800	10.1%	0.2
Interest	$28,746	2.9%	$28,746	2.9%	0
Depreciation	$31,678	3.2%	$31,678	3.2%	0
Total Fixed Costs (Occupancy, Interest, Depreciation)	**$159,224**	15.9%	**$159,224**	16.2%	**0.3**
Profit before Taxes	**$79,746**	8.0%	**$51,553**	5.2%	**(2.8)**
Income Taxes	$18,899	1.9%	$12,213	1.2%	(0.7)
Net Income	**$60,847**	6.1%	**$39,340**	4.0%	**(2.1)**

Figure 14.2
Common Size Analysis

Once the variances have been calculated, the real analysis begins. Managers must determine the impact of each line item's variance from budget and then decide what to do about it. In some cases, a manager will need to better control expenses. (Remember that "controlling" expenses differs from "cutting" expenses. If an actual cost is well below budget, a manager may decide that increased spending should occur to ensure that quality standards are met.) Sometimes a manager will need to boost marketing to increase revenue. Fixed costs typically cannot be cut, so large variances in fixed costs require additional revenue for them to come in line with the budget. Of course, not every variance signals a problem in the business. A lower-than-expected food cost might represent a reduction in quality standards, but it might also herald an improvement in the purchaser's ability to negotiate lower pricing. Only further investigation from a manager can determine whether an underbudget expense line is cause for concern or for celebration. If budget-beating numbers appear achievable again in future years, upcoming budgets should reflect those new standards. Finally, because total sales are always listed as 100%, a manager must compare total sales in dollars rather than in percentages to see whether actual sales surpassed or fell below budget targets. What follows is an analysis of Figure 14.2.

The first thing to note in a common size analysis of Figure 14.2 is that actual revenue fell slightly short of the budgeted total sales. This difference is not evident in the variance column but rather in a comparison of the two total sales' dollar amounts. The variance in menu mix—food sales versus beverage sales—is outside the range of the +/− 0.5 threshold, but this variance may be good news. Since beverage cost percentage is lower than food cost percentage, the shift in menu mix should help with the overall gross profit from sales.

A review of the cost of sales reveals that the menu mix has helped to keep the total cost of goods sold in line. Both actual and budget numbers are 28.9% despite the fact that the beverage cost percentage is just at the +/− 0.5 tolerance. Still, there is a cause for concern here. A manager would want to investigate why beverage cost is 23.0% instead of the budgeted 22.5%. The answer may be purveyor price increases, which would necessitate an adjustment to future budgets or to menu pricing, or it may result from poor cost control procedures that permit theft or excessive spillage.

The "labor" section reveals significant problems. The 1.8 variance in salaries and wages (i.e., labor cost) is enormous. While a 28.0% versus 26.2% cost difference may not seem like much, tenths of a percentage in an expense line can translate to tens of thousands of dollars in lost profit. For this line item, a manager would investigate why labor costs were out of control and then take corrective action to ensure that the variance does not occur again in the future. Because annual income statements/budgets are sometimes broken down into weekly or monthly income statements/budgets, the large labor cost should not come as a complete surprise. (Though in reality, such news is often a surprise for the many restaurants that only use an annual budget and reference it only once a year). The bigger question is why corrective action wasn't taken earlier to get labor costs back in line with the budget. Prime cost is off by 2.2, but most of that difference comes from the 2.1 variance in total labor cost. The variances under controllable expenses fall within the acceptable threshold, but small percentage differences do ultimately add up. The income before fixed costs is too low by 2.5 points (variance); the majority of that is accounted for through labor cost.

Fixed costs have not changed in dollar terms, but because of the slightly lower revenue, fixed costs consume a larger percentage of sales than management had budgeted for. The 0.3 variance is below the threshold, but realistically, any variance here, no matter how high or low, will be corrected once sales increase to budget targets.

Finally, profit before taxes shows the accumulated effects of small expense overruns, unacceptably out-of-line costs, like labor cost, and revenue shortfalls. Profit before taxes is only 5.2% of sales instead of the budgeted 8.0%—a variance of 2.8 and a difference of over $28,000! Since profit is so far outside the +/− 0.5 threshold, managers must take corrective action in the upcoming year to ensure profits come back in line. Future budgets may be revised to reflect more modest profit goals, but better expense and revenue control will help to make those profit goals more achievable. It should be noted that the profit discussion focuses on profit before taxes rather than on net income because net income derives directly from pretax profit. The taxes must be paid, and all of the controls that improve profit before taxes will similarly improve the business's net income.

14.2.2 Comparative Analysis

While a common size analysis is helpful in assessing a company's performance against a budget or across years, a comparative analysis helps management to identify business trends. A comparative analysis first calculates a variance between two periods (or between an actual and a budgeted period) in dollars. Then, it converts the dollar difference into a percentage change by dividing it by the earlier period (or by the budget). Figure 14.3 illustrates a comparative analysis using the same dollar amounts as Figure 14.2.

By analyzing the variance results in Figure 14.3, a manager would notice that while beverage sales are higher than forecast, food sales and total sales are trending

USA Restaurant				
	Budget 1/1/11– 12/31/11	Actual 1/1/11– 12/31/11	Variance Dollars (Actual–Budget)	Variance % (Variance Dollars ÷ Budget Dollars)
Sales				
Food	$750,000	$727,194	($22,806)	(3.0%)
Beverage	$250,000	$255,561	$5,561	2.2%
Total Sales	**$1,000,000**	**$982,755**	**($17,245)**	**(1.7%)**
Cost of Sales				
Food Cost	$232,500	$225,180	($7,320)	(3.1%)
Beverage Cost	$56,250	$58,804	$2,554	4.5%
Total Cost of Goods Sold	**$288,750**	**$283,984**	**($4,766)**	**(1.7%)**
Gross Profit	**$711,250**	**$698,771**	**($12,479)**	**(1.8%)**
Labor				
Salaries and Wages	$262,000	$275,442	$13,442	5.1%
Employee Benefits	$49,780	$52,155	$2,375	4.8%
Total Labor Cost	**$311,780**	**$327,597**	**$15,817**	**5.1%**
Prime Cost	**$600,530**	**$611,581**	**$11,051**	**1.8%**
Controllable Expenses				
Direct Operating Expenses	$50,000	$48,506	($1,494)	(3.0%)
Music and Entertainment	$15,000	$14,300	($700)	(4.7%)
Marketing	$20,000	$19,325	($675)	(3.4%)
Utilities	$38,500	$38,992	$492	1.3%
General and Administrative	$24,500	$24,774	$274	1.1%
Repairs and Maintenance	$12,500	$14,500	$2,000	16%
Total Controllable Expenses	**$160,500**	**$160,397**	**($103)**	**0.0%**
Income before Fixed Costs	**$238,970**	**$210,777**	**($28,193)**	**(11.8%)**
Fixed Costs				
Occupancy Costs	$98,800	$98,800	$0	0%
Interest	$28,746	$28,746	$0	0%
Depreciation	$31,678	$31,678	$0	0%
Total Fixed Costs (Occupancy, Interest, Depreciation)	**$159,224**	**$159,224**	**$0**	**0%**
Profit before Taxes	**$79,746**	**$51,553**	**($28,193)**	**(35.4%)**
Income Taxes	$18,899	$12,213	($6,686)	(35.4%)
Net Income	**$60,847**	**$39,340**	**($21,507)**	**(35.3%)**

Figure 14.3
Comparative Analysis

lower than the budget goal. Food cost has dropped even more so than food sales (3.1% vs. 3.0%), so food cost is in line. But beverage cost is much higher than it should be for a mere 2.2% increase in beverage sales. All of this translates to gross profits that are 1.8% below budget—not a good thing when discussing profits.

Under labor expense, one sees that labor cost is trending higher (read: costlier). Further research by a manager would reveal whether this is the result of poor scheduling or simply employee pay increases that were not properly accounted for in the budgeting process. Assuming that budgeting was done accurately, management could safely presume that the higher labor costs are partly the result of poor labor control (the variable, wage component of labor cost) and partly the consequence of low sales, which cause fixed salaries to eat up a larger percentage of sales revenue.

Under controllable expenses, direct operating expenses, music and entertainment, and marketing are all below budget while utilities, general and administrative costs, and repairs and maintenance are all over budget. While exceeding budget predictions is good in the revenue half of an income statement, it is not always a good thing in the expense portion of the statement. The total controllable expenses are almost exactly on budget, but this is the result of some underbudget expense lines compensating for overbudget lines. A manager may wish to determine why certain line items, such as repairs and maintenance, are so high. Income before fixed costs is 11.8% underbudget—again, not a good thing; it arises from the combined shortfall in sales and high expense in labor.

Fixed costs, because they have not varied from budget, are unchanged; that is, they have a 0% variance. Unlike a common size analysis, the comparative analysis focuses on trends and on how well actual dollar figures align with the budget. For fixed costs, the expenses are exactly as predicted—a good thing. They will remain at 0% variance whether sales are strong or weak. Consequently, a comparative analysis does not highlight problems that result when managers do not adjust their expense budgets to shifts in revenue, which they cannot do for fixed costs. Where do the problems become evident? In the profit before taxes line. Because the fixed cost dollars do not decline when sales are down, the only place to compensate for lost revenue dollars is through profit. In this case, profit before taxes is down 35.4% from the forecast. Since profits in the foodservice industry represent a very small percentage of total sales, (usually below 5% of sales), small variances in revenue and expenses can impact profit significantly.

Why would a manager perform a comparative analysis instead of a common size analysis? First, a comparative analysis provides dollar differences as well as percentage variances. For example, a manager can quickly see that profit before taxes is $28,193 less than the budget forecast. A comparative analysis also highlights differences in small value line items better than a common size analysis, which emphasizes the line items with the highest dollar amounts the most. For example, because marketing is such a small percentage of total sales, the variance does not even register on a common size analysis; however, a comparative analysis shows that marketing was 3.4% below budget. (Perhaps additional marketing would have helped increase sales to the $1,000,000 target.) Finally, a comparative analysis shows trends that may help with future budgeting, especially when the two columns compared are two years of actual income statement figures. In such a comparison, a 1.3% increase in utility costs might be a sign of a trend. Management might decide to budget utilities 1.3% higher for the upcoming year as well, in anticipation of this continuing trend.

In short, neither common size analysis nor comparative analysis addresses all of management's needs on its own, but together, the two forms of analysis help a management team to better control costs, to plan for future budgets, and ideally, to hit future profit goals.

14.3   CREATING A BUDGET

While it is important for a manager to be able to compare actual income statement data to a budget, it is equally important for a manager to be able to create a realistic budget. Otherwise, large variances will be meaningless. For example, if a manager budgets for a 12% food cost when food cost has never been below 28%, a variance is inevitable. Such a variance may, in fact, reflect good management (the chef's adherence to quality standards) rather than poor cost control.

A budget ultimately has two goals: to predict revenues and expenses accurately and to set aggressive targets for managers to hit. Accurate revenue and expense forecasts are important, so managers can have a road map to use for controlling costs. If the predictions are not even close to accurate, managers will ignore the budget or get frustrated by it. Aggressive targets are also important as they force employees and managers to become a little more efficient in their work and to squeeze as much profit out of sales revenue as possible.

Frontline workers might not normally have an interest in maximizing profits, but they should. Greater profits mean a more stable company and better job security. (There is no job security in a company that is likely to go under.) A company with large profits is better able to expand, which may give senior employees opportunities for raises and promotions. Without enough profit, an owner may decide to cut employees or to freeze pay rates. With large amounts of profit, an owner may invest in equipment or facility upgrades to improve employee working conditions. In short, employees usually benefit when they help a company to achieve its profit goals.

To create a budget a manager (or management team) must first do three things: research historical data and trends for the business, investigate upcoming internal and external variables that may impact the future budget, and set budget goals on the basis of both the information collected through research and the owner's or management team's desires. Only then can a manager effectively write a useful budget.

Historical Data.   The first step in preparing a budget is to analyze historical data. Such historical data includes items such as average guest check, customer counts, expense patterns, and other trends. The data should be tracked over multiple years in long-standing restaurants to see if a trend is evident. Are average guest checks going up or down? Is the customer count growing or shrinking? By what percentage are expenses rising each year? The answers to these questions are easily found in POS system data, but as previous chapters have shown, they can also be calculated by hand. Perhaps the most important research to conduct is a common size analysis and a comparative analysis of prior income statement years. The results will inform a manager of the traditional ranges of certain expense categories. For example, she will see the realistic range for food cost percentages, labor cost percentages, and other expense percentages. She may also find trends, such as a percentage increase that business grows each year or an unexpected annual percentage decrease for direct operating expenses. All of this information, including the most recent year's income statement, provides a manager a starting point on which to found a budget.

Internal and External Variables.   While historical data gives a manager some idea of what to expect in the upcoming year, internal and external variables alert a manager to line items that will likely not follow past trends. An internal variable is a change that has emerged from within the business itself. For example, the restaurant may have just changed the menu mix or replaced the gas ranges with induction burners. Internal variables may help increase profit, such as the recent purchase of an automated beverage dispenser designed to control costs, or they may threaten profit, such as the need to repair equipment that has exceeded its life expectancy. Either way, these variables let a manager know to adjust the upcoming budget accordingly. External variables are those that occur in the outside world. Examples include a new competitor opening next door, changes in government regulations, the closure of a nearby factory, or publicized spikes in the cost of local produce. Each of these examples would impact the business's sales or expenses. Some, like increases in ingredient costs, might necessitate an internal change, such as menu price hikes, to maintain profit. Managers may choose to adjust for other external factors, such as a new competitor, by budgeting for lower revenue. Many external variables are easily discovered through trade publications, professional associations (like the local chamber of commerce), and news reports in general; however, managers can get additional information on future trends from conversations with purveyors and customers. As with internal variables, external variables provide a manager insight into how future line items in the budget should differ from historical trends.

Setting Budget Goals.   Just because a restaurant owner has seen profits drop each year by 1% does not mean that she must resign herself to lower profits in the upcoming year. One of the biggest reasons to budget at all is to plan for profit. Managers may choose to set revenue or expense goals that differ from the researched projections as long as they do something to influence the trend. For example, if a restaurant's sales are expected to remain flat, a manager could choose to set a revenue target of 1.5% growth and invest in marketing to bring that goal to fruition. If local news reports estimate that medical insurance costs will jump 20% next year, a manager could make employees pay a larger percentage of their insurance costs so that the company only sees a 10% increase in its employee benefits expense. The goals that management ultimately sets become the primary guidelines for writing a budget. They must be realistic, achievable, and based somewhat on historical data and on internal and external variables, but they do not have to match data forecasts exactly. For instance, a manager might choose to increase profit forecasts from 2% to 3%, but a jump to 20% is probably unrealistic and would render the budget valueless.

A BUDGETING CASE STUDY: PART I

Assume that Figure 14.4 represents historical data for Restaurant X. (*Note:* Income tax and net income have been dropped; management will only worry about budgeting for profit before taxes.) The chart shows three years of income statements, but it does not provide the analysis. How to analyze and interpret this data is the first step in creating the upcoming year's budget.

There are a few trends to note from Figure 14.4. First, a comparative analysis of food sales (not depicted but easy to calculate from the chart) shows that food sales increased 3.1% from year 1 to year 2 and then 2.5% from year 2 to year 3. Beverage sales, on the other hand, declined in year 3. Food cost has been trending upward, but it has historically remained between 36.5% and 37.4%. Beverage cost has fluctuated in the range of 22.6% to 23.8%.

Under labor, salaries and wages increased 3.3% from year 2 to year 3 (comparative analysis of ($320,766 − $310,592) ÷ $310,592 = 3.3% increase). Employee benefits have been 19%–20% of salaries and wages, but the percentage is slowly increasing each year. (Calculate employee benefits percentage of salaries and wages by computing benefits for one year divided by the salaries and wages for the same year.)

For controllable expenses, direct operating expenses have stayed steady at 4.8%–4.9% of sales. Spending on utilities and on general and administrative has increased slightly each year, both in dollar and in percentage terms, but the dollar spending on marketing and on repairs and maintenance has remained flat for the past two years. The cost for music and entertainment doubled in year 3.

Restaurant X Income Statements						
	Year 1		Year 2		Year 3/Current Year	
Sales						
Food	$727,194	74.0%	$749,377	73.2%	$768,155	73.7%
Beverage	$255,561	26.0%	$274,103	26.8%	$273,894	26.3%
Total Sales	**$982,755**	**100%**	**$1,023,480**	**100.0%**	**$1,042,049**	**100.0%**
Cost of Sales						
Food Cost	$265,180	36.5%	$278,455	37.2%	$286,924	37.4%
Beverage Cost	$60,804	23.8%	$62,075	22.6%	$63,952	23.3%
Total Cost of Goods Sold	**$325,984**	**33.2%**	**$340,530**	**33.3%**	**$350,876**	**33.7%**
Gross Profit	**$656,711**	**66.8%**	**$682,950**	**66.7%**	**$691,173**	**66.3%**
Labor						
Salaries and Wages	$308,442	31.4%	$310,592	30.3%	$320,766	30.8%
Employee Benefits	$59,155	6.0%	$61,388	6.0%	$64,153	6.2%
Total Labor Cost	**$367,597**	**37.4%**	**$371,980**	**36.3%**	**$384,919**	**36.9%**
Prime Cost	**$693,581**	**70.6%**	**$712,510**	**69.6%**	**$735,795**	**70.6%**
Controllable Expenses						
Direct Operating Expenses	$48,506	4.9%	$49,387	4.8%	$50,946	4.9%
Music and Entertainment	$1,000	0.1%	$1,000	0.1%	$2,000	0.2%
Marketing	$19,325	2.0%	$20,000	2.0%	$20,000	1.9%
Utilities	$31,992	3.3%	$33,894	3.3%	$34,910	3.4%
General and Administrative	$21,774	2.2%	$23,476	2.3%	$24,714	2.4%
Repairs and Maintenance	$1,000	0.1%	$2,500	0.2%	$2,500	0.2%
Total Controllable Expenses	**$123,597**	**12.6%**	**$130,257**	**12.7%**	**$135,070**	**13.0%**
Income before Fixed Costs	**$165,577**	**16.8%**	**$180,713**	**17.7%**	**$171,184**	**16.4%**
Fixed Costs						
Occupancy Costs	$90,000	9.2%	$90,000	8.8%	$93,000	8.9%
Interest	$28,746	2.9%	$28,746	2.8%	$28,746	2.8%
Depreciation	$29,678	3.0%	$29,678	2.9%	$29,678	2.8%
Total Fixed Costs (Occupancy, Interest, Depreciation)	**$148,424**	**15.1%**	**$148,424**	**14.5%**	**$151,424**	**14.5%**
Profit before Taxes	**$17,153**	**1.7%**	**$32,289**	**3.2%**	**$19,760**	**1.9%**

Figure 14.4
Income Statements for Case Study

Under fixed costs, interest and depreciation have remained constant. Occupancy costs increased by $3,000 in year 3. Consequently, profit has remained low for the past three years. While there has never been a loss, profit before taxes has never exceeded 3.2% of sales, and last year's profit was only 1.9% of sales.

All of this information is incomplete without the further benefit of management notes from prior years. In this particular case study, the following bits of information were gleaned from notes in the manager's log:

- Menu prices have not been increased in three years even though ingredient costs have gone up.
- Beverage costs declined to 22.6% in year 2 because of new control systems that were implemented; those control systems were not as well maintained in the past year when the bar was shorthanded for a two-month period.
- The cost of health insurance has been rising steadily and has accounted for most of the employee benefit increases.
- The music and entertainment costs doubled when management hired a keyboard player to perform the weekend before Christmas. Sales increased roughly $1,000 that weekend.
- Utility usage has not changed in three years; the increase in that expense line has come entirely from increases in the cost of utilities.
- The equipment maintenance contract costs $2,500. No repairs were needed over the past two years, but the large standing mixer may need a $300 replacement part soon. No other repairs are anticipated.
- Occupancy costs jumped when the lease was renegotiated. The current lease is good for two more years, so occupancy costs will remain the same next year as will interest and depreciation.

With this information in hand, management is ready to study additional internal and external variables that may impact future budget figures. Here is what has been learned from a little bit of research:

- A new housing development less than a mile away is only three months from completion. It is expected to bring 50 new families into the area.
- A restaurant 2 miles away, which used to offer a similar product, just closed. The restaurant that is replacing it sells a very different product and should not provide competition for Restaurant X's customers.
- Market costs for food are expected to rise another 0.2% next year, but beverage costs are forecast to remain flat.
- The cost for employee benefits is expected to increase to 20.5% of salaries and wages.
- The cost of utilities is forecast to rise 2.8% next year.
- Management is considering raising menu prices. Internal analysis shows that a 4% increase in menu prices will result in a 7% drop in customers.

Finally, management is ready to analyze all of this data and to set its own goals. The management team has settled on the following goals for the upcoming year:

- The owner insists that the operation must hit profits of at least 4.0% of sales.
- Management has decided to raise prices for food items on the menu 4%; beverage pricing will remain the same.
- Management believes that by doubling the marketing budget to $40,000, it can capture customers from the new housing development and from the now-closed competitor's clientele. Consequently, it has set the goal of increasing food sales revenue by 5% despite any predicted loss of current customers as a result of the menu price increases. (This information would be determined through a cost/volume/profit analysis, not shown here.)
- Management expects a 4% increase in beverage sales. It plans to achieve this by adding upselling training to the weekly meetings that front-of-the-house employees already attend.

- With the increase in menu prices and a need to control costs better, management is setting the food cost target at 36.5% and the beverage cost at 22.7%—both historically achievable in the past three years.
- Managers will freeze all salaries and only increase wage rates slightly, so total salaries and wages will increase by 1.6%. The benefits package will remain the same, so its cost will be allowed to rise to 20.5% of salaries and wages as forecast.
- The live music before Christmas will be cancelled for next year, so music and entertainment will be cut back to $1,000.
- Management will plan for the purchase of a new part for the standing mixer.

The case study demonstrates how a management team uses researched information to determine budget goals. However, converting those goals into an actual budget often takes a little experimentation. Management begins by adjusting the prior year's income statement's revenue lines per the budget goals. For example, if management predicts a 3.2% increase in food sales, then the upcoming food sales figure is last year's food sales multiplied by (1 + percentage increase in decimal form, in this case, 1.032). With revenue dollars entered, management can calculate the expense dollars in one of three ways: by converting the line item's percentage of sales into dollars, by adjusting last year's line item dollars using a percentage increase or decrease, or by entering a forecast dollar figure directly. Which approach to use is determined by how management expresses its goals. Consider the following examples.

Example 14.3 (calculating budget revenue): Total sales on this year's income statement were $812,500. Management forecasts a 2.7% increase in sales next year. What is the total sales budget for next year?

New Amount = Old Amount × (1 + percentage change expressed as a decimal)

$$= \$812,500 \times (1 + 0.027) = \$821,500 \times 1.027 = \$843,681$$

The new sales budget is $843,681.

Example 14.4 (calculating a line item expense from a percentage of total sales): Management has determined that direct operating expenses should remain at 6.4% of sales. If next year's sales forecast is $843,681, what is the budget for direct operating expenses?

To calculate the cost for a line item when the total sales and percentage of sales figures are known, use the cost-sales-percentage graphic formula to get Cost = Sales × %.

$$\text{Cost} = \text{Sales} \times \% = \$843,681 \times 0.064 = \$53,996$$

Direct operating expenses should be listed as $53,996 in the upcoming budget.

Example 14.5 (calculating a line item expense as a percentage change from last year): Management has determined that utilities will cost 5.5% more next year and that the general and administrative budget will be cut by 2.0%. Calculate the budgets for these two line items if last year's utilities expense was $12,400 and last year's general and administrative expense was $37,200.

This is the same method as calculating a percentage increase or decrease in revenue.

$$\text{New Cost} = \text{Old Cost} \times (1 + \text{percentage change})$$

For utilities, New Cost = $12,400 × (1 + 0.055) = $12,400 × 1.055 = $13,082

For general and administrative, New Cost = $37,200 × [1 + (− 0.02)] = $37,200 × 0.98 = $36,456

Example 14.6 (entering an expense directly): Next year's revenue is forecast to be $843,681. Management has noticed that in addition to the $1,000 annual cost for an equipment maintenance contract, it will have to spend $800 to repair some broken equipment. If there are no other expenses under repairs and maintenance, what is the repairs and maintenance budget for next year?

This answer is simple addition:

$$\$1,000 + \$800 = \$1,800$$

Because the dollar amount is known and its relation to sales is irrelevant to its determination, this expense can be entered directly as a dollar figure into the budget.

Unfortunately, using management's initial budget goals to calculate revenue and expenses does not always result in a final budget. Sometimes, the sales and expense numbers do not generate the desired profit. When this happens, expense guidelines must be readjusted and management goals reconsidered until the profit goal is met. It is generally best to make this adjustment to expenses only, for management has presumably already planned for a best-case scenario on revenue growth. Planning to make up profit shortfalls by increasing revenues even further is a risky gamble unlikely to pay off. If profit expectations are realistic, then cutting expenses usually gets the right result anyway. Part II of the case study demonstrates this process in action.

A BUDGETING CASE STUDY: PART II

Figure 14.5a takes the current year data from Figure 14.4 and adds two columns: The summary of the management goals and other data analyzed from Part I of the case study and the budget that would result directly from that information. The line item dollar amounts are calculated first; they are determined by following the instructions in the management goals/forecasts column. Only once the dollars are entered can the profit be calculated (through addition and subtraction) and can each item's percentage of sales be determined (by dividing each line item amount by the total sales figure).

Once all of the line item figures are computed, the profit line quickly reveals that it will fall short of the 4.0% profit goal. Such a conundrum is not uncommon in the budgeting process. The manager's task now is to adjust some of the expense lines in order to realize the desired profit. Changes to expenses cannot be done willy-nilly as they must be implemented by the managers. Any change that the managers cannot achieve will cause profits to ultimately fall short in the coming year. For example, while it might be desirable to cut utility costs, unless managers can reduce usage, they won't be able to cut those costs—the prices are completely out of their control. One scenario (and there are many alternatives) for cutting costs to realize profits is described through Figure 14.5b. (*Note:* The line items that have been deliberately changed are italicized.)

No change to a budget should come without a plan of action to achieve the new numbers. Otherwise, there is a strong chance that the budget goals will not be met. Even small expense reductions can be extremely difficult. Here is one set of possible approaches to the changes in Figure 14.5b:

- *Food Cost drops from 36.5% to 35.5%*   The chef will manage by seeking less expensive purveyors, by providing specials that utilize trim and produce at risk of spoilage, and if necessary, by cutting protein portion sizes by $\frac{1}{4}$ oz.

Restaurant X Income Statement and Budget					
	Current Year		Management Goals/ Forecasts	Next Year's Budget	
Sales					
Food	$768,155	73.7%	5.0% increase	$806,563	73.9%
Beverage	$273,894	26.3%	4.0% increase	$284,850	26.1%
Total Sales	**$1,042,049**	**100.0%**		**$1,091,413**	**100.0%**
Cost of Sales					
Food Cost	$286,924	37.4%	36.5% of food sales	$294,395	36.5%
Beverage Cost	$63,952	23.3%	22.7% of bev. sales	$64,661	22.7%
Total Cost of Goods Sold	**$350,876**	**33.7%**		**$359,056**	**32.9%**
Gross Profit	**$691,173**	**66.3%**		**$732,357**	**67.1%**
Labor					
Salaries and Wages	$320,766	30.8%	1.6% increase	$325,898	29.9%
Employee Benefits	$64,153	6.2%	20.5% of salaries and wages	$66,809	6.1%
Total Labor Cost	**$384,919**	**36.9%**		**$392,707**	**36.0%**
Prime Cost	**$735,795**	**70.6%**		**$751,763**	**68.9%**
Controllable Expenses					
Direct Operating Expenses	$50,946	4.9%	Trend 4.8%–4.9% of sales (assume 4.9%)	$53,479	4.9%
Music and Entertainment	$2,000	0.2%	Reduce to $1,000	$1,000	0.1%
Marketing	$20,000	1.9%	Double to $40,000	$40,000	3.7%
Utilities	$34,910	3.4%	2.8% increase	$35,887	3.3%
General and Administrative	$24,714	2.4%	Trend slight increase (assume 2.5% of sales)	$27,285	2.5%
Repairs and Maintenance	$2,500	0.2%	$2,800 (for contract and $300 repair)	$2,800	0.3%
Total Controllable Expenses	**$135,070**	**13.0%**		**$160,451**	**14.7%**
Income before Fixed Costs	**$171,184**	**16.4%**		**$179,199**	**16.4%**
Fixed Costs					
Occupancy Costs	$93,000	8.9%	Same dollar amount	$93,000	8.5%
Interest	$28,746	2.8%	Same dollar amount	$28,746	2.6%
Depreciation	$29,678	2.8%	Same dollar amount	$29,678	2.7%
Total Fixed Costs (Occupancy, Interest, Depreciation)	**$151,424**	**14.5%**		**$151,424**	**13.9%**
Profit before Taxes	**$19,760**	**1.9%**	4.0% of sales	**$27,775**	**2.5%**

Figure 14.5a
Income Statement and Budget with Management Goals for Case Study

- *Salaries and Wages Adjusts to No Increase from Past Year* Management will speak with all staff about the need to control labor costs. Managers will make up half of the savings by scheduling more efficiently. The other half of the savings will come from a six-month delay in scheduled pay increases for hourly workers. Salaried workers will receive no pay increase, but their benefits package will remain in place. Workers will be notified of the delay in advance and informed that pay increase amounts will depend on the savings realized from efficiencies in scheduling and greater output per employee in the first six months of the year.
- *Employee Benefits* This savings comes directly from the reduction of the salaries and wages line item.

Restaurant X Income Statement and Budget					
	Current Year		Management Goals/ Forecasts	Next Year's Budget	
Sales					
Food	$768,155	73.7%	5.0% increase	$806,563	73.9%
Beverage	$273,894	26.3%	4.0% increase	$284,850	26.1%
Total Sales	**$1,042,049**	**100.0%**		**$1,091,413**	**100.0%**
Cost of Sales					
Food Cost	$286,924	37.4%	35.5% of food sales	$286,330	35.5%
Beverage Cost	$63,952	23.4%	22.7% of bev. sales	$64,661	22.7%
Total Cost of Goods Sold	**$350,876**	**33.7%**		**$350,991**	**32.2%**
Gross Profit	**$691,173**	**66.3%**		**$740,422**	**67.8%**
Labor					
Salaries and Wages	$320,766	30.8%	*Same dollar amount*	$320,766	29.4%
Employee Benefits	$64,153	6.2%	20.5% of salaries and wages	$65,757	6.0%
Total Labor Cost	**$384,919**	**36.9%**		**$386,523**	**35.4%**
Prime Cost	**$735,795**	**70.6%**		**$737,514**	**67.6%**
Controllable Expenses					
Direct Operating Expenses	$50,946	4.9%	Trend 4.8%–4.9% of sales *(assume 4.8%)*	$52,388	4.8%
Music and Entertainment	$2,000	0.2%	Reduce to $1,000	$1,000	0.1%
Marketing	$20,000	1.9%	Double to $40,000	$40,000	3.7%
Utilities	$34,910	3.4%	2.8% increase	$35,887	3.3%
General and Administrative	$24,714	2.4%	*Trend slight increase (assume 2.4% of sales)*	$26,194	2.4%
Repairs and Maintenance	$2,500	0.2%	$2,800 (for contract and $300 repair)	$2,800	0.3%
Total Controllable Expenses	**$135,070**	**13.0%**		**$158,269**	**14.5%**
Income before Fixed Costs	**$171,184**	**16.4%**		**$195,630**	**17.9%**
Fixed Costs					
Occupancy Costs	$93,000	8.9%	Same dollar amount	$93,000	8.5%
Interest	$28,746	2.8%	Same dollar amount	$28,746	2.6%
Depreciation	$29,678	2.9%	Same dollar amount	$29,678	2.7%
Total Fixed Costs (Occupancy, Interest, Depreciation)	**$151,424**	**14.5%**		**$151,424**	**13.9%**
Profit before Taxes	**$19,760**	**1.9%**	4.0% of sales	**$44,206**	**4.1%**

Figure 14.5b
Modified Income Statement and Budget

- *Direct Operating Expenses Drops from 4.9% to 4.8%.* This lower figure is historically achievable. Lower level managers will brainstorm to suggest cost saving approaches.
- *General and Administrative Drops from 2.5% to 2.4% of Sales* This lower figure is also historically achievable. Management believes that the lower figure can be achieved by purchasing cheaper office supplies and switching Internet service providers.

If management is able to keep to these changes and to the other budget targets, including revenue goals, then the 4.0% of sales profit goal will be attained. (Technically, the profit percentage will be 4.05% or 4.1%, which gives management a small buffer in case any expense lines come in slightly over budget.) It should be noted that a profit of 4% is quite aggressive; it is more than double the previous year's profits. If budget numbers are off and profit drops to 3.0% of sales, the company will still realize higher profits than last year. With expenses cut quite severely as compared with predicted trends and historical patterns, a profit margin of 5% would be unrealistic in this upcoming year.

The method described in the case study is exactly the sort of process that a management team goes through to create an annual budget. The research and forecasting step is quite lengthy, but once done, the budgeting process progresses fairly quickly. Second-round budget adjustments can result in heated debates and a need for further research, but the calculations themselves are not particularly time-consuming.

14.3.1 Dividing a Budget into Smaller Time Frames

While creating an annual budget is an important exercise, it is often an unwieldy tool for managers to use on a day-to-day basis. After all, a manager may not notice until ten months into the year that she is going to be over budget in her department. It is far more practical for managers to have monthly or weekly budgets to reference, so they can modify their control systems (or notify their superiors) early in the year if they are not operating on budget.

Converting an annual budget into a monthly or weekly budget is not as straightforward as dividing by 12 months or by 52 weeks. A restaurant at the beach might bring in half of its annual revenue during July and August while serving only a trickle of customers in the winter. Many restaurants get a bump in sales in December from holiday party business. Figuring out how to divide annual revenue and expenses is complicated, but it becomes markedly easier with historical data.

A foodservice operation with sales history can determine what percentage of annual revenue is brought in each week or month. These computations can be broken down even further by day or by meal, if desired. A manager can take historical percentages and apply them to the upcoming annual budget to generate budgets for shorter periods. For example, if a business typically earns 6.9% of its revenue in January, then next year's January sales budget will be the budgeted annual revenue times 6.9%.

Example 14.7: Using the historical data below, calculate expected revenue by month for next year's budget, if next year's annual revenue is forecast to be $1,300,000.

Month–Last Year	Revenue (Total $1,206,000)
January	$74,000
February	$82,000
March	$85,000
April	$91,000
May	$99,000
June	$107,000
July	$88,000
August	$84,000
September	$103,000
October	$111,000
November	$129,000
December	$153,000

The first step in this problem is to calculate the percentage of total sales that each month represents. To do so, divide each month's revenue by total revenue, which is just the sum of all the monthly revenues. The resulting decimal is the historical percentage of sales earned for that month. Multiply the same decimal (percentage) times the forecast annual revenue for next year to get a monthly revenue budget. The chart that follows illustrates how these steps are performed. (*Note:* The monthly sales forecasts may not add up to the annual forecast due to rounding.)

Month–Last Year	Revenue (total $1,206,000)	Historical Percentage (Month's Revenue ÷ Total Revenue)	Budget with Annual Forecast of $1,300,000 (Multiply Month's % as decimal × $1,300,000)
January	$74,000	6.14%	$79,820
February	$82,000	6.80%	$88,400
March	$85,000	7.05%	$91,650
April	$91,000	7.55%	$98,150
May	$99,000	8.21%	$106,730
June	$107,000	8.87%	$115,310
July	$88,000	7.30%	$94,900
August	$84,000	6.97%	$90,610
September	$103,000	8.54%	$111,020
October	$111,000	9.20%	$119,600
November	$129,000	10.70%	$139,100
December	$153,000	12.69%	$164,970

Of course, historical monthly sales percentages are only constant if the prior year's environment continues in the upcoming year. Managers can and should make slight adjustments to the percentages if they anticipate major changes to the business environment. A major change could be anything from a big convention coming to town to the timing of a nearby construction project to the loss of a big holiday account.

With revenue determined for each month, week, or day, a manager must next calculate the expense lines. This step requires logic, math, and an understanding of the business itself. Variable expenses should remain the same percentage of sales for the shorter time period that they are for the year. Fixed expenses are written on the basis of their payment schedule. For example, if rent is normally paid as equal monthly payments, then the rent portion of occupancy cost is divided evenly across each month, regardless of business levels. Controllable expenses and labor are perhaps the most complicated as they are semivariable. A manager will likely need to separate salaries from wages. Salaries would be divided equally over time while wages would fluctuate as a constant percentage of sales. If pay increases are planned sometime during the year, they should also be factored into the salaries and wages calculation. Certain controllable costs may be scheduled by management only for specific months. For example, if management plans on spending $500 to repair a piece of equipment in March, then the repairs and maintenance line item will have a $500 bump in March. Each individual expense must be considered thoughtfully to determine whether it remains a constant percentage of sales each month, a constant dollar amount each month, or an expense divvied up based on knowledge of the year's management plan.

The logic used to break an annual budget down into monthly or weekly budgets can be used to subdivide budgets by day or by meal. Historical data can tell managers what percentage of business is typically done on the second Tuesday of April, on the Saturday before Valentine's Day, or on the last day of the year. Similarly, historical data reveals prior ratios of lunch to dinner sales and the menu mix of food to beverage sales. These historical trends generate percentages that can be applied to future budgets to determine approximate food and beverage sales dollars for each month of the year. However, wise managers know not to adopt the prior year's percentages without first making adjustments based on planned changes for the year. If management plans a new promotion to increase business on Monday nights next year, then managers may need to adjust the historical percentages accordingly before applying them to next year's budget. Similar tweaks will be required for all sorts of changes, from internal marketing pushes to menu changes to new conventions and festivals coming to town. No manager can accurately predict every change that will come in the following year, but the more that she accounts for, the more accurate her daily, weekly, and monthly budgets are likely to be.

The format of a budget may differ when broken down into very small time frames. For example, managers may decide that there is little value in determining the occupancy cost for the day since it is a monthly expense. When written by month, a budget usually includes all of the line item expenses. When divided into weekly or daily budgets, usually only the variable and semivariable line items are included with the projected sales figures. Managers rely more on the revenue and variable/semivariable cost guidelines to control costs than they do on the fixed cost numbers. If all of the daily and weekly budget line items are met exactly, the monthly and annual profit will materialize as forecast.

Part III of the case study illustrates how specific data is used to generate a monthly, weekly, and daily budget.

A Budgeting Case Study: Part III

This case study will focus on February (for a monthly budget), the second week in February (for a weekly budget), and Friday of the second week in February (for a daily budget), using the budget from Part II of the case study. Historical data for Restaurant X shows that February typically represents 6.8% of annual sales and that the second week in February represents 2.6% of annual sales—a large number because this week includes Valentine's Day. Because of Valentine's Day, the sales mix for February shifts slightly to 73.8% in food sales and 26.2% in beverage sales as guests splurge on more expensive wines. The shift is even greater for the second week of the month when food sales are 71.4% and beverage sales are 28.6%.

This year, Valentine's Day fell on a Tuesday. Next year, it falls on a Wednesday. While each day of the week typically represents a consistent percentage of weekly sales, Valentine's week sales vary depending on when Valentine's Day falls. Historically, when Valentine's Day falls mid-week, the Friday following Valentine's Day represents 21.3% of the week's sales. Management expects this year to follow that pattern.

To create Figure 14.6, the February budget, begin by calculating total sales first. Then, enter all of the remaining line items based on management's notes. The calculations are straightforward. They require either dividing the annual expense by 12 or multiplying the February total sales figure by the percentage of sales that the line item represents. (Note that labor cost is oversimplified for ease of instruction. Normally, salaries and wages would be calculated separately as wages remain a steady percentage of sales but salaries are divided evenly over the year.) Total sales itself is determined by multiplying the annual sales budget ($1,091,413) by the percentage of annual sales that February represents (6.8%).

Restaurant X Budget					
	Annual Budget		Management Notes to Calculate February Budget	February Budget	
Sales					
Food	$806,563	73.9%	73.8% of sales	$54,771	73.8%
Beverage	$284,850	26.1%	26.2% of sales	$19,445	26.2%
Total Sales	**$1,091,413**	**100.0%**	**6.8% of annual sales**	**$74,216**	**100%**
Cost of Sales					
Food Cost	$286,330	35.5%	35.5% of food sales	$19,444	35.5%
Beverage Cost	$64,661	22.7%	22.7% of bev. sales	$4,414	22.7%
Total Cost of Goods Sold	**$350,991**	**32.2%**		**$23,858**	**32.1%**
Gross Profit	**$740,422**	**67.8%**		**$50,358**	**67.9%**
Labor					
Salaries and Wages	$320,766	29.4%	Maintain 29.4%	$21,820	29.4%
Employee Benefits	$65,757	6.0%	Maintain 6.0%	$4,453	6.0%
Total Labor Cost	**$386,523**	**35.4%**		**$26,273**	**35.4%**
Prime Cost	**$737,514**	**67.6%**		**$50,131**	**67.5%**
Controllable Expenses					
Direct Operating Expenses	$52,388	4.8%	Maintain 4.8%	$3,562	4.8%
Music and Entertainment	$1,000	0.1%	$\frac{1}{12}$ of annual cost	$83	0.1%
Marketing	$40,000	3.7%	$2,500 advertising campaign	$2,500	3.4%
Utilities	$35,887	3.3%	Maintain 3.3%	$2,449	3.3%
General and Administrative	$26,194	2.4%	Maintain 2.4%	$1,781	2.4%
Repairs and Maintenance	$2,800	0.3%	$208 payment for maintenance contract	$208	0.3%
Total Controllable Expenses	**$158,269**	**14.5%**		**$10,583**	**14.3%**
Income before Fixed Costs	**$195,630**	**17.9%**		**$13,502**	**18.2%**
Fixed Costs					
Occupancy Costs	$93,000	8.5%	$\frac{1}{12}$ annual cost	$7,750	10.4%
Interest	$28,746	2.6%	$\frac{1}{12}$ annual cost	$2,396	3.2%
Depreciation	$29,678	2.7%	$\frac{1}{12}$ annual cost	$2,473	3.3%
Total Fixed Costs (Occupancy, Interest, Depreciation)	**$151,424**	**13.9%**		**$12,619**	**17.0%**
Profit before Taxes	**$44,206**	**4.1%**		**$883**	**1.2%**

Figure 14.6
Case Study Budget for February

Note that profit is not at the 4% of sales goal. This is the natural result of a month that sees below average sales revenue. Remember that the fixed costs do not change each month, even if sales are low. Months with above-average sales will generate profits greater than 4% of sales. At year's end, the totals will average out to 4% as long as all other budget lines are met.

Figure 14.7 goes through the same process for a weekly budget. Some expense lines have been dropped as they are not weekly expenses that operate as a percentage of sales. In the average restaurant, the most important expenses to control on a weekly or daily basis are the prime costs—food, beverage, and labor. Because the weekly revenue is different from the monthly revenue, all of the dollar amounts computed as a percentage of total sales must be recalculated. In this case, historical data has shown that the second week of February represents 2.6% of annual sales, so the computations begin there and then continue as they did in the monthly budget.

Restaurant X Budget						
	Annual Budget		Management Notes to Calculate February, Week 2 Budget	February, Week 2, Budget		
Sales						
Food	$806,563	73.9%	71.4% of sales	$20,261	71.4%	
Beverage	$284,850	26.1%	28.6% of sales	$8,116	28.6%	
Total Sales	**$1,091,413**	**100.0%**	**2.6% of annual sales**	**$28,377**	**100%**	
Cost of Sales						
Food Cost	$286,330	35.5%	35.5% of food sales	$7,193	35.5%	
Beverage Cost	$64,661	22.7%	22.7% of bev. sales	$1,842	22.7%	
Total Cost of Goods Sold	**$350,991**	**32.2%**		**$9,035**	**31.8%**	
Gross Profit	**$740,422**	**67.8%**		**$19,342**	**68.2%**	
Labor Cost						
Salaries and Wages	$320,766	29.4%	Maintain 29.4%	$8,343	29.4%	
Employee Benefits	$65,757	6.0%	Maintain 6.0%	$1,703	6.0%	
Total Labor Cost	**$386,523**	**35.4%**		**$10,046**	**35.4%**	
Prime Cost	**$737,514**	**67.6%**		**$19,081**	**67.2%**	
Controllable Expenses						
Direct Operating Expenses	$52,388	4.8%	Maintain 4.8%	$1,362	4.8%	

Figure 14.7
Case Study Budget for Second Week of February

Figure 14.8 divides the budget even further into a daily report. However, unlike the previous calculations, the data states that this particular Friday represents 21.3% of *weekly* sales. Thus, the daily total sales figure is derived by multiplying the week's total sales ($28,377) times 21.3%. All other calculations follow as before.

Managers can divide budgets into even greater detail and smaller time frames using historical percentages, so chefs can know their daily budget for every type of ingredient—produce, meat, seafood, dry goods, and such. If desired, all budget line items can be spread across the days of the week to determine a daily profit goal. However, the most important reason to create a daily or weekly budget is to use it as a cost control tool. Creating daily budgets for the sake of making them is a costly waste of time unless they are incorporated into a manager's control processes.

Restaurant X Budget						
	February, Week 2, Budget		Management Notes to Calculate February, 2nd Friday Budget		February, 2nd Friday, Budget	
Sales						
Food	$20,261	71.4%	71.4% of sales		$4,315	71.4%
Beverage	$8,116	28.6%	28.6% of sales		$1,729	28.6%
Total Sales	**$28,377**	**100%**	**21.3% of weekly sales**		**$6,044**	**100%**
Cost of Sales						
Food Cost	$7,193	35.5%	35.5% of food sales		$1,532	35.5%
Beverage Cost	$1,842	22.7%	22.7% of bev. sales		$392	22.7%
Total Cost of Goods Sold	**$9,035**	**31.8%**			**$1,924**	**31.8%**
Gross Profit	**$19,342**	**68.2%**			**$4,120**	**68.2%**
Labor						
Salaries and Wages	$8,343	29.4%	Maintain 29.4%		$1,777	29.4%
Employee Benefits	$1,703	6.0%	Maintain 6.0%		$363	6.0%
Total Labor Cost	**$10,046**	**35.4%**			**$2,140**	**35.4%**
Prime Cost	**$19,081**	**67.2%**			**$4,064**	**67.2%**
Controllable Expenses						
Direct Operating Expenses	$1,362	4.8%	Maintain 4.8%		$290	4.8%

Figure 14.8
Case Study Budget for Second Friday in February

A manager can compare labor budgets to scheduling worksheets to ensure that her employee work schedule falls within budget. If not, she may need to adjust the schedule. Similarly, chefs may need to tighten controls or to look into cheaper ingredient options if weekly food costs exceed budget guidelines. Senior managers may need to shift marketing dollars or to create server incentives for suggestive selling if revenue targets are not achieved. In short, daily, weekly, and monthly budgets allow managers to adjust their controls and their revenue-driving strategies while there is still plenty of time to change and to salvage profit. A manager who relies exclusively on an annual budget will not know whether profits are on target for the year until after the year is over.

Some businesses begin with weekly or monthly budgets and then compile the data to generate an annual budget afterward. Such an approach starts by forecasting business levels week by week or month by month. The revenue numbers are calculated using such information as average guest check, seat turnover rates, number of seats, and number of days open. Once revenue is calculated, costs can be determined. However, the process still requires an adjustment to the annual budget if annual profit goals are not met. Once such an adjustment is made, management must return to the weekly and monthly budgets to modify their expenses as well. This technique works particularly well for a new business without a full year of history. Neither approach is better; they are just different.

14.3.2 The Evaluation Cycle

The final step in the budget process is to evaluate management's budgeting accuracy and the company's adherence to the budget guidelines. The chapter began by explaining how to compare actual income statement data to budget data using a common size or a comparative analysis. That first step in the process is actually just one of many steps in an ongoing cycle. With a budget in hand, managers must continue to assess how well they have performed against the daily, weekly, monthly, and annual budgets. Variances may be the result of poor cost controls, but they could just as easily stem from poor forecasting and budgeting. In time, as a business builds up a long history of sales and expense data and as the managers become more skilled in budgeting for the business, variances between actual numbers and budget numbers will shrink.

SUMMARY

Investors and owners may reference a company's balance sheet and statement of cash flows, but the most valuable financial tool for day-to-day management is the statement of income. Income statements are typically written in "common size" format, meaning that they have dollar and percentage columns. Income statements include lines for revenue, broken into food and beverage sales, and lines for expenses. Expenses are often categorized on the basis of their degree of variability in relation to sales. The percentages on an income statement show the percentage of total sales that each expense represents, except for food and beverage cost percentages, which are a percentage of food sales and of beverage sales, respectively. Two income statements or an income statement and a budget can be compared either using a common size analysis or using a comparative analysis. Both list the variance between the two data sets being compared; managers are left to decide what level of variance is acceptable and which line items require attention. Income statements highlight areas that are out of proportion to the rest of the budget, but a manager must conduct further research to determine why a particular area is not within budget and what to do about it. To create a budget, a manager starts with historical data to determine trends and patterns. Next, she investigates internal and external variables to see how they might influence future revenue and spending patterns. Finally, the manager compiles all of this information to determine a set of goals for the budget. With the goals determined, the manager adjusts the most recent income statement according to those goals and other forecast data. If the profit goal is not met using the manager's new revenue and expense targets, she must adjust certain expense line items to yield the proper profit. These adjustments are not done haphazardly but rather through an honest belief that such cuts can be achieved without sacrificing company standards. Budgets that are not achievable are not effective cost control tools. Annual budgets can be subdivided into monthly, weekly, or daily budgets. Smaller time frame budgets allow managers to check their performance regularly and to correct patterns that exceed budget guidelines well before the budget year is complete.

COMPREHENSION QUESTIONS

1. Most of the percentages in a common-size budget are determined by dividing the line item dollars by total sales dollars. Which expenses are the exceptions to this rule, and how are their percentages calculated?

2. What kinds of expenses might be categorized under "direct operating expenses?" Give at least five examples.

3. List three expenses that might be categorized as "general and administrative."

4. On an income statement, depreciation is listed as $14,795. Total sales are $987,450. What percentage should be written on the depreciation expense line?

5. Using the revenue portion of the income statement and budget below, conduct a common size analysis and a comparative analysis. Fill in all missing sales and percentage data, too.

	Budget (Year 20XX)		Actual (Year 20XX)		Common-Size Analysis (Variance)	Comparative Analysis (Variance)	
	$	%	$	%		$	%
Sales							
Food	$655,000		$648,500				
Beverage	$198,000		$199,200				
Total Sales	$						
Cost of Sales							
Food Cost	$193,225		$191,850				
Beverage Cost	$40,180		$42,400				
Total Cost of Goods Sold	$						
Gross Profit	$						

6. Using the income statement and the following management goals provided, generate a first-draft budget for the upcoming year. (*Note:* Profit is not specified as a goal in this question.) Management Goals:

a) Total sales growth of 1.7%

b) Sales mix of 71% food and 29% beverage

c) Food cost of 32.0% and beverage cost of 20.0%

d) Maintain all controllable expenses at their current percentage of sales

e) Maintain all fixed costs at their current dollar amount

Income Statement and Budget					
	Current Year		Management Goals for Budget	Next Year's Budget	
				$	%
Sales					
Food	$1,013,600	72.4%			
Beverage	$386,400	27.6%			
Total Sales	$1,400,000	100.0%			
Cost of Sales					
Food Cost	$331,447	32.7%			
Beverage Cost	$85,394	22.1%			
Total Cost of Goods Sold	$416,841	29.8%			
Gross Profit	$983,159	70.2%			
Labor					
Salaries and Wages	$403,200	28.8%			
Employee Benefits	$96,600	6.9%			
Total Labor Cost	$499,800	35.7%			
Prime Cost	$916,641	65.5%			
Controllable Expenses					
Direct Operating Expenses	$70,000	5.0%			
Music and Entertainment	$11,200	0.8%			
Marketing	$32,200	2.3%			
Utilities	$63,000	4.5%			

(Continued)

Income Statement and Budget				
	Current Year		Management Goals for Budget	Next Year's Budget
General and Administrative	$37,800	2.7%		
Repairs and Maintenance	$7,000	0.5%		
Total Controllable Expenses	$221,200	15.8%		
Income before Fixed Costs	$262,159	18.7%		
Fixed Costs				
Occupancy Costs	$140,000	10.0%		
Interest	$65,000	4.6%		
Depreciation	$21,000	1.5%		
Total Fixed Costs (Occupancy, Interest, Depreciation)	$226,000	16.1%		
Profit before Taxes	$36,159	2.6%		

7. Referring to question 6, management would like to hit a profit before taxes of 4.5% of sales. Has it hit that profit target with the budget guidelines listed in question 6? If not, what changes would you recommend to the budget to realize a 4.5% profit? (There are many possibilities.)

8. Below is a portion of an annual budget. December's revenues represent 18.2% of annual sales. If management wishes for all sales mix and expense percentages in the spreadsheet to remain the same in December as they are for the annual budget, complete the December budget columns in the spreadsheet.

Budget				
	Annual Budget		December Budget	
			$	%
Sales				
Food	$1,013,600	72.4%		
Beverage	$386,400	27.6%		
Total Sales	$1,400,000	100.0%		
Cost of Sales				
Food Cost	$331,447	32.7%		
Beverage Cost	$85,394	22.1%		
Total Cost of Goods Sold	$416,841	29.8%		
Gross Profit	$983,159	70.2%		
Labor				
Salaries and Wages	$403,200	28.8%		
Employee Benefits	$96,600	6.9%		
Total Labor Cost	$499,800	35.7%		
Prime Cost	$916,641	65.5%		
Controllable Expenses				
Direct Operating Expenses	$70,000	5.0%		
Music and Entertainment	$11,200	0.8%		
Marketing	$32,200	2.3%		
Utilities	$63,000	4.5%		
General and Administrative	$37,800	2.7%		
Repairs and Maintenance	$7,000	0.5%		
Total Controllable Expenses	$221,200	15.8%		
Income before Fixed Costs	$262,159	18.7%		

DISCUSSION QUESTIONS

1. Some foodservice businesses operate without a budget. Are there any benefits to working without a budget? What are the risks of not using a budget?

2. Each expense category plays a role in the overall operation of the business. Pick one controllable expense category. What would be the impact on revenue and/or on other expenses if that category were insufficiently funded?

3. Of the two types of income statement analysis—common size and comparative—which do you prefer? Why?

4. A certain company conducts a common size analysis of its income statement performance against its budget. The variance threshold is +/− 0.2. Revenue is exactly on budget. Every individual expense category has a variance of exactly + 0.1, well below the variance threshold, so no red flags are triggered. Did the management team do a good job in executing this budget or not? What potential problems might come as a result of this job performance?

5. Budgets can be divided to cover daily, weekly, monthly, or annual periods. Which time period would you imagine to be the most useful for managing and controlling revenue and costs? Why? What are the risks/challenges to using that particular time frame?

6. Assume that management has properly prepared an annual budget for a target profit margin. Early in the year, it appears that budget guidelines are not being met. Under what circumstances should management adjust course to maintain the profit goal, and under what circumstances should it decide to accept less profit for the year?

15

A Discussion of Other Expenses

An income statement for a foodservice establishment lists numerous categories into which all sales and expenses can be placed. This text has covered sales quite thoroughly, but in terms of expenses, it has focused mainly on the prime costs—food cost, beverage cost, and labor cost. A manager must control these three costs if he is to have any chance of generating a profit. However, the income statement includes other expenses that also impact profit, and it would be a significant oversight not to include a discussion of those expenses.

As food, beverage, labor, and marketing costs have been covered elsewhere in the text, this chapter deals with direct operating expenses, music and entertainment, energy and utilities, administrative and general expenses, and repairs and maintenance—the remaining controllable expenses. It also includes some thoughts on occupancy costs and capital budgeting, which impacts interest and depreciation. As with the prime costs, there are no one-size-fits-all solutions for controlling these expenses effectively. The best approach is first to consider the possible options for each of these line item expenses and then to balance the company's quality and quantity standards against each expense's cost.

Cost of goods sold requires a manager to understand recipe costing, which involves yields and costs per portion. Scheduling employees efficiently and managing overtime are essential elements to controlling labor cost. The other controllable expenses do not involve such complexity. While each customer pays a different amount on the basis of the value of the food and drink he orders, every customer receives the same linens, china, parking access, music, light, and atmosphere. Consequently, these costs are best reviewed and controlled collectively rather than per customer. As long as the expense categories fall within certain percentage ranges on the statement of income, the business should be able to maintain a profit.

The purpose of this chapter is neither to describe mathematical procedures for computing costs per customer nor to rehash the discussion on calculating expenses as a percentage of sales on an income statement. Instead, this chapter introduces the many considerations that go into controlling these other expense categories. How a manager or owner progresses after considering the various expense options depends entirely on the business's concept and its quality and quantity standards.

Objectives

By the end of this chapter, you will be able to:

- List examples of costs that comprise most of the controllable expense categories
- Describe some of the considerations that go into controlling the various controllable expense categories
- Describe the pros and cons of owning versus renting a property
- Describe some of the factors considered in the capital budgeting process

15.1   CONTROLLABLE EXPENSE CONSIDERATIONS

Many of the controllable expense decisions are made by senior managers or owners before a foodservice business opens its doors or as part of a budgeting process. While the consideration controllable expenses receive is less frequent than the attention paid to the prime costs, it is a result of the nature of the expenditures and not a sign that these expenses are less important to control. As an example, food is purchased daily, so there is an ongoing opportunity to source new products through new purveyors. Flatware and china may be purchased only once a year, so it is not a subject of daily discussion among cost control managers. What follows is a description of some of the alternatives management considers when making cost control decisions for controllable expenses.

15.1.1 Direct Operating Expenses

Utensils.   Forks, spoons, knives, and other flatware (see Photos 15.1 and 15.2) are required expenses for nearly every type of foodservice establishment. For higher-end establishments, utensils may be silver or stainless steel; in more casual restaurants, they may be single-use disposable plastic. Which to purchase depends on the business's quality standards. However, within each category of disposable or reusable wares, there are several options at varying prices. Metal silverware can be plain or ornate, heavy or lightweight, silver or steel. Ornate, heavy, and silver are the pricier options, but establishments that cater to the very rich may need to provide the most luxurious choices (for which guests pay via hefty menu prices). Disposable flatware also comes in a range of options from flimsy to heavy duty. Some types are even compostable—a nod to responsible environmental stewardship. If a restaurant concept could justify either disposable or reusable flatware, management typically weighs all of the costs involved before choosing between the two. Metal silverware is more expensive upfront, but it is not repurchased with each use, as are plastic utensils. That said, metal flatware is not cost free after the initial purchase. Some pieces will be damaged, some stolen, and all must be washed, which requires labor, utilities, and detergent. Over time, metal flatware must be supplemented, even if only to replace lost or damaged pieces. For this reason, managers should always check to ensure that the style chosen is not a pattern going out of production. It is much cheaper to buy an additional 100 spoons for a restaurant than to replace the entire 2,000-unit inventory because the pattern is out of stock. How much inventory to have on hand depends on four variables: number of

Photo 15.1
Basic Flatware

Source: © Shutterstock.

Photo 15.2
High-end Flatware

Source: © Dr. Margorius/Shutterstock.

seats, the time it takes to turn a table, the utensils needed to serve the average customer, and the rate at which dishwashers turn around soiled flatware. Having a few additional pieces to cover future loss allows a restaurant to purchase replacement flatware less frequently without creating a shortage for customers.

China and Glassware. Choosing dishes and glassware involves many of the same considerations as selecting utensils. How fancy and upscale should the plates and glasses be? Are reusable or disposable pieces more appropriate to the business's style of service? When considering china and glassware, durability is also an extremely important factor. Thin and delicate options convey a message of elegance and luxury, but if the pieces break in the process of normal dishwashing, they become an overly costly expense. Whatever china and glassware is chosen, they ought to be able to endure normal restaurant wear and tear. Nowadays, china comes in many shapes and colors, in addition to a range of styles. Managers can decide to purchase triangular, rectangular, and wavy plates in addition to traditional round ones. The types of china (bowls, plates, cups, etc.) to purchase depend heavily on the menu. Family-style restaurants will need lots of serving platters as will catering halls. Hotels offering high tea will need a bounty of teapots. Even types of salt and pepper shakers and flower vases must be considered for those establishments that use them on the table. Glassware choices, too, depend on menu offerings and on a restaurant's concept. Full-service bars require various styles of glassware. Specialty beer establishments may have a different kind of glass for each beer or just a single, universal mug. Managers can decide to stock wine glasses for red versus white, or they may offer guests different glasses for white burgundy, American chardonnay, and Riesling. Finally, managers who utilize real china and glass are not necessarily absolved from maintaining a supply of disposables. Breakfast guests may ask for coffee to-go; leftovers may be placed in a plastic container rather than wrapped in foil. The inventory that a foodservice business maintains impacts the level of service the employees are empowered to provide.

Linen and Uniforms. While china, utensils, and glassware are almost always washed in-house (unless they are disposable), linens require some consideration of how to launder them. While a restaurant can purchase its own linens and launder them on site, many operations rent linens from a linen company. Rentals cost more per use than simply sending one's own linen out for laundering, but a linen company assumes the cost of replacing damaged rented cloths and napkins. There is no upfront purchase cost for using a linen rental company either. Still, if a specific type of linen is desired but unavailable, purchasing linens may be the only option. Uniforms operate similarly. A company can purchase uniforms for its employees and send them out to be laundered or wash them in-house. However, many uniform companies offer the ability to both design and launder uniforms for foodservice businesses; these companies also assume the cost of replacement. Unlike linen rentals, uniform companies typically charge an upfront fee for uniform design as many restaurants now embroider their logo or an employee's name on the uniform. Consequently, renting uniforms is not as straightforward as borrowing from the company's current inventory. For both uniforms and linens, there are lower-cost alternatives. A company may decide to use easy-to-clean polished tables without cloths, or it might use butcher paper or other disposable cloths that better fit the restaurant's concept. Uniforms may be as simple as a dress code for employees. Asking employees to launder their own uniforms is a low-cost approach, but managers run the risk that an employee's ironing or washing job represents the company poorly.

Cleaning.   Cleaning supplies come either concentrated or pre-diluted, which gives managers options. Concentrates are often cheaper, but if improperly diluted, they become very expensive or ineffective. Dispensers help control the overuse of cleaning supplies. For example, a soap dispenser that provides foam rather than liquid hand soap uses less soap per customer. Management can choose between washable wiping cloths or disposable ones for kitchen cleaning; the cost of laundering often impacts management's choice. As a major labor saver, a manager may contract certain cleaning responsibilities to an outside company. Outsourcing allows cooks and servers to leave the kitchen and dining room cleaning to outsiders, who work when the establishment is closed. The decision to outsource is a financial one because it may be more economical to hire outside laborers than to pay employees.

Kitchen and Bar Utensils.   This category represents the smallwares used in food and drink production. There is not always a lot of flexibility in these purchases because commercial grade equipment is required by law for most foodservice businesses. However, management may decide to pay more for a laborsaving device than to go with a cheaper option. For example, a food processor will pay for itself many times over in labor savings over knives. Similarly, a buffalo chopper will plow through more produce faster than a small food processor will. How expensive and complete an inventory to purchase depends on the menu, storage space, and business volume. A buffalo chopper is a wasted expense if a cheaper food processor can handle the business volume.

Decorations.   Foodservice managers and owners have a wide range of price points from which to choose when deciding how to decorate a dining room. Flowers on tables and in waiting areas can be fresh (and expensive because of ongoing replacement) or artificial. Art on the wall can be extremely valuable or quite cheap. Some restaurants have sidestepped the cost of wall art by using their dining room as an art gallery (see Photo 15.3). Local artists display their work for free as long as the restaurant posts the artist's name and the cost of each painting, which alerts guests that the art is for sale. The decorations used should always reinforce the restaurant's concept. A French bistro may display old advertisements of French products. Private clubs with a hunting tradition may display works of taxidermy. Seafood places may maintain a large aquarium. How the manager chooses to decorate the dining room depends on available budget and marketing strategy. Some guests place more importance on a restaurant's décor than they do on its food and service. Having decorations that meet customers' expectations helps build up a regular clientele.

Menus.   As with other direct operating expenses, the cost for printing menus correlates somewhat to the business's concept. High-end restaurants may print daily menus on heavyweight paper, or they may print permanent menus in leather-bound books. More casual operations may laminate menus in plastic to protect them from spills. Certain concept restaurants print menus on brown paper bags or design menus to look like newspapers. Some have even given their menus alternate purposes—embedded

Photo 15.3
Restaurant with Significant
Art on the Walls

Source: © Enrique Uranga/DK/
Pearson.

with flower seeds that can be planted in a garden or printed with edible ink on a cracker-like material that can be eaten as part of the dining experience. A small coffee house or bistro may not print menus at all but instead list food and drink options on a highly visible chalkboard. Any restaurant that provides take-out or delivery should have inexpensive paper menus available for guests to take from the restaurant; these menus are inexpensive marketing tools that help to drive off-premise business.

Licenses and Permits.   While listed as a direct operating expense, licenses are not typically "controllable." They must be purchased for a business to comply with the law. Managers may choose not to purchase a license if it does not make financial sense—purchasing a multimillion dollar liquor license, for example—but no restaurant should operate without the licenses and permits that its business requires.

Other Direct Operating Expenses.   Managers may choose to fund any number of additional operating expenses. Every extra cost should go toward supporting the business concept or toward marketing. Giving away matchbooks or magnets with the company's logo and phone number is not only a customer service but also a marketing strategy. Postcards or logo-emblazoned paper cups serve the same purpose. Happy Meal toys can be the primary draw that brings entire families to McDonald's. Other guest supplies may be provided simply as a goodwill gesture to leave the customer with something extra on the way out the door. Peppermint candies or toothpicks are inexpensive examples. Other direct operating expenses include fuels not classified under utilities, such as charcoal or wood chips, which may be a draw for customers who want an authentic "grilled" taste. For restaurants that make deliveries, certain car and truck expenses, such as gas and tolls, fall into this category. Whether or not a business takes on any of these additional expenses is typically a financial decision. When an expenditure brings in additional business or allows management to charge a premium for a product, the profit realized may justify the expense.

15.1.2 Music and Entertainment

Managers and owners have a lot of flexibility in their music and entertainment expenses. Some establishments utilize only recorded music and pay small royalty fees. Others use live

Photo 15.4

Live Music in a Restaurant

Source: © Chris Stowers/DK/Pearson.

performers, regularly or intermittently, as a draw for business. Live music might be as basic as a single guitarist or pianist or as complex as a string quartet or mariachi band. Live music is not the sole purview of fine restaurants (see Photo 15.4). Irish pubs sometimes host musicians, and concert venues make music the focus over food. However, music is not the only form of entertainment at a manager's disposal. Sports bars (and many other casual establishments) offer television broadcasts on multiple screens. Recorded films are also an entertainment draw, especially animated movies or cartoons in a kid-friendly restaurant. Live performers may include magicians, comics, ventriloquists, or clowns. Coffee houses, for the cost of stage space and a microphone, may host authors, political speakers, or even amateur poets (think poetry slam) as a business draw. In the case of live performers, both the performers and their agents may require a fee. Any entertainment cost should always be compared with the corresponding increase (or decrease) in sales revenue to determine whether the expense adds to or undermines profits. Finally, as with all other expenses, the entertainment should always support the business's concept, not clash with it.

15.1.3 Energy and Utilities

While a manager may not have control over the prices charged for utilities, he can greatly impact the quantity of energy and water used in a foodservice business. Currently, much of the control of utility expenses at foodservice operations occurs through lower usage or conservation. Managers can select energy-saving equipment or train their employees to incorporate energy-saving techniques into their everyday tasks. However, technologies that allow companies to generate their own energy through sun, wind and geothermal sources are available and may soon become commonplace in large-scale operations. The decision to invest in infrastructure to generate one's own solar, wind, or geothermal energy rests at the highest level with a company's owner or managers because of the substantial upfront costs. Because any manager can reduce utility usage in small ways, this section focuses primarily on opportunities for cost savings through conservation. As waste removal is typically categorized under "utilities," it will also be discussed in this section.

Energy Conservation.   By reducing the amount of energy used in a company, a manager not only helps the environment but also reduces utility costs. Conservation can be done in small, low-cost ways that require little more than employee training or in larger ways through equipment replacement and facility upgrades. Both can make a difference in a business's utility expense.

Refrigeration.   Refrigerators and freezers are notorious sources of wasted energy. Employees may leave the cooler door open, place products in ways that restrict airflow, or throw extremely hot foods directly into a refrigerator or freezer. To maximize a cooler's efficiency, managers should keep the compressor well maintained. Clean coils and compressor units operate more efficiently than do dirty ones. Employees should arrange foods on shelves in ways that maximize airflow and should not place anything directly in front of the cooler's fan. Managers should make sure that gaskets are in good condition so that they do not allow cold air to leak from a refrigeration unit. Plastic pass-through curtains help keep cool air in a walk-in while people are entering and exiting the unit. Employees can further reduce a walk-in's energy consumption by turning off the light when the cooler is unoccupied, by thawing frozen food in the refrigerator to help maintain the unit's cool temperatures, and by cooling hot foods down to room temperature before placing them in a refrigerator or freezer. Gathering one's entire daily mise en place in a single trip prevents repeated opening and closing of the walk-in's doors, which further reduces energy waste. Though it requires a major renovation (or proper planning in the initial construction), locating the walk-in freezer inside the walk-in refrigerator prevents room temperature air from filling the freezer.

Lighting.   Switching to low-energy light bulbs is a quick and simple approach to saving energy; turning off lights until they are needed is another. Managers can check bulbs to see if a lower wattage would provide similar lumens or sufficient brightness. Light-colored décor and windows help brighten a room without using lots of energy (though multipane windows should be utilized to minimize heat transfer through the windows).

HVAC and hoods.   As with refrigeration, a clean and well-maintained system operates more efficiently than does a dirty or blocked one. Maintenance or contract workers should clean HVAC units and kitchen hoods regularly. Keeping thermostats at the proper temperature helps reduce energy usage. While 68°F is a comfortable room temperature in cold weather, thermostats should be set higher in the summer. During renovations, managers should ensure that walls are properly insulated, and they may consider energy-efficient windows. Kitchen hoods come in various types. Hoods that vent a portion of unconditioned make-up air reduce the amount of cooled or heated air taken from the kitchen. These hoods still evacuate smoke and grease from the kitchen, but in the process, they use some air from outside rather than that conditioned by the HVAC unit.

Cooking equipment and technique.   Some equipment is naturally less energy intensive than are others. Steamers and microwaves cook food quickly in well-insulated environments, so they are quite efficient. Ranges, especially flattops, disperse a lot of heat into their surroundings as part of the cooking process, which not only wastes the burner's energy but also works at cross-purposes with air-conditioning units. Induction burners help to minimize energy dispersal for stovetop cooking. Ovens lose considerable heat when opened, so cooks should be trained to leave food alone in the oven if it does not need immediate attention. Cooking multiple items at once in an oven also helps to use the oven's heat efficiently. In some operations, cooks turn on the ovens as soon as they walk in the door, even if those ovens won't be used for hours. Creating a schedule so that ovens are turned on only when they are needed reduces energy consumption. Covering pots on the range helps them to heat up faster, too, so they will not need to be left on a burner all day long. Finally, keeping cooking equipment clean and unclogged helps it to operate more efficiently.

Energy Creation.   Some "green" buildings have energy creation devices incorporated into their construction, and there is no reason foodservice operations cannot do the same. Photovoltaic cells (solar panels) can be placed on rooftops to produce electricity for a restaurant. In locations that experience a lot of wind, windmills may generate enough electricity to power a foodservice business. Geothermal energy can be tapped to heat or to cool a facility without relying entirely on an HVAC unit. While these types of infrastructure investments are not cheap, they do eventually pay for themselves. As the cost of utilities rises, energy-generation devices may cover their costs in just a few years' time.

Water. Water is one of the most highly used resources in any foodservice operation, but it isn't always conserved properly. A broken pipe, a leaky faucet, or a perpetually running toilet all waste gallons of water daily until fixed. Repairs are relatively inexpensive compared with the cost of weeks' worth of wasted water. Hard water, which leaves mineral deposits on surfaces, reduces the effectiveness of detergents. Using a water softener or periodically de-liming dishwashers helps keep this equipment working properly without the overuse of detergents.

Managers can and should train cooks not to waste water as part of the cooking process. While the health department permits the thawing of food by running it under cold water, thawing under refrigeration is far less water intensive. A large pot of boiling water can be used to blanch multiple sets of vegetables rather than being thrown out after just one use. Three-compartment sinks should be filled and used as "dunking" tanks instead of as locations for rinsing dishes with a constant stream of water. Some large-scale food manufacturers have even installed water reclamation systems, so water that is used in one place in the business can be salvaged and used for another purpose. (New Belgium Brewing Company in Fort Collins, Colorado, provides an excellent example of water conservation and reclamation for a beverage business.)

Waste Management. Trash removal has always been a necessary expense for any foodservice business, but new approaches to waste management allow a company to not only protect the environment but also save money in the process. Some companies purchase excess fat from restaurants for use in soaps or other products. Farmers can utilize food waste for compost or as slop for pigs. In some jurisdictions, recycling of glass, metal, plastics, cardboard, and other materials is a legal requirement. In all of these examples, materials that would have otherwise gone into the trash dumpster are sent elsewhere, which allows a restaurant to pay for fewer trash pickups. Not all of the alternatives to trash removal are free; for example, a company may have to pay as much for recycling pickup as it does for trash removal. However, some are either low-cost or moneymaking options. A farmer may pick up food waste for free as long as the restaurant bags and saves it; soap companies may pay for fat. Highly inventive businesses have even found ways to convert the decomposition of waste into energy creation by trapping methane for fuel, but small operations with limited space may need to rely on simpler waste management approaches.

15.1.4 Administrative and General

Administrative and general encompasses a wide range of overhead costs, including postage, telephone and Internet, membership dues and subscriptions, travel expenses, cash shortages, doubtful accounts, security, and credit card commissions. How a manager chooses to approach these expenses will differ greatly from one business to the next. For example, a high-end restaurant with an international menu may pay to send its chef overseas each year and may invest in membership in several international associations. A small carryout shop may budget nothing for travel or membership expenses. This section focuses on just a few of the many possible expenses listed under "administrative and general."

Insurance. While different foodservice operations require different types of insurance, most culinary businesses have some form of insurance. Insurance protects a business against theft, against loss from equipment malfunction, and against lawsuits for public liability, for Dram Shop Act violations, or for food poisoning. (Property insurance, such as fire or flood insurance, is also essential, but it is classified under Occupancy Costs.) Some companies specialize in only one type of insurance while others provide most of the coverage that a foodservice business needs. Insurance costs money that might otherwise go toward profits, but it protects the company from going belly up after a single lawsuit. Still, managers and owners should not rely solely on insurance to protect themselves. Risk management helps to keep a company's insurance costs from skyrocketing, and it reduces the frequency of lawsuits that can distract and overwhelm a manager or owner. Examples of risk management include enforcing food safety and sanitation procedures and safe alcohol service standards, maintaining all equipment so that it operates safely and properly, securing surplus cash in a safe or in the bank, and training employees in safe work habits. While some of these investments may seem costly, they are all less disruptive to a business than a fire or a major lawsuit is.

Security. Security spans a wide range of possibilities from simple door locks to security guards and cameras. The level of security a restaurant or other foodservice operation needs depends heavily on its location, hours, and type of business. Many of the control techniques in earlier chapters have focused on theft by employees and customers, but security against violent robberies or break-ins by outsiders is equally important. Frequent burglaries not only result in lost cash, but they also cause property damage that must be repaired before customers return. Some businesses employ metal gates or other enclosures to seal off their facility completely from the outside world when no one is on the property. Others employ cameras and alarm systems to alert security teams and the police to potential burglaries. The investment in security may be thought of like insurance: The payments for protection are there to minimize or to deter substantial business disruptions. In today's world, security and safety training for employees is also a must. Workers must know how to handle robbers so that all customers and staff remain safe and unharmed. Disaster scenarios should be created and periodically reviewed with employees so that they know how to deal with natural disasters, terrorist attacks, or just simple power failures. Different scenarios may call for immediate evacuation or for sheltering in place. Often, the natural reaction to an unexpected threat is not the best approach to keeping guests and employees out of harm's way.

Back Office. In a single small business, managers or owners may include accounting and other overhead-related paperwork as one of their many duties. However, in multi-unit businesses, it often makes financial sense to hire a back office manager to handle this type of paperwork for all of the retail outlets. Such an employee provides the expertise, time, and focus to handle insurance, license, and accounting issues that would else distract other managers from their normal responsibilities. Some foodservice operations outsource this job to another company while others prefer to keep it in-house. If a back-office manager is hired on staff, that person not only requires a salary but also needs office space and furniture. Still, if these costs are divided over five restaurants, it may be much cheaper than outsourcing the job.

15.1.5 Repairs and Maintenance

The repair and maintenance of equipment is critical to avoid serious financial loss. A broken dishwasher or oven may hamper a kitchen's ability to serve customers at an acceptable pace. Nonfunctioning HVAC units can make a room uncomfortably hot or cold. While some damaged floors may simply be an eyesore, others can cause customers to fall and to injure themselves—a lawsuit in the making. Every foodservice operation periodically needs repairs. While some repairs do occur as unforeseen emergencies, many are predictable and controllable through regular maintenance.

Maintenance may be performed by the organization's own staff, but many small foodservice companies obtain preventive maintenance contracts with businesses that specialize in equipment maintenance and repair. A preventive maintenance contract stipulates that a repairperson will periodically check certain equipment for possible damage and perform maintenance work on it to keep it in proper working order. Maintenance might include cleaning, greasing, calibrating, or otherwise adjusting equipment to help it run better. A preventive maintenance worker can notify management of equipment that needs repair before it becomes an emergency. For example, it is better to learn that a dishwasher pipe is likely to burst in the coming months if not repaired than to discover the issue after the pipe has burst in the middle of service. Maintaining a refrigerator compressor not only helps it run more efficiently and last longer but also reduces the odds that a business will lose its refrigerated inventory because the walk-in cooler fails unexpectedly. Repairs and maintenance are an expense, but with proper planning, the expense can be budgeted for and controlled. Maintenance that extends the usable life of equipment and helps that equipment to run on less energy may pay for itself in the long run. The cost of unexpected equipment failure that requires emergency repair or causes temporary business loss is far higher than is the cost of preventive maintenance.

One of the challenges to budgeting for equipment repair is the condition of a piece of equipment at purchase time. While new equipment should not break immediately and may be under warranty, a used piece of equipment is of unknown quality. Some foodservice businesses, in order to save upfront money, purchase used equipment at auction. The equipment sold at auction typically comes from another foodservice operation that has recently gone out of business. The used equipment may work at the time of sale, but the buyer has no idea of how well that unit was maintained by the previous owner. It may last for ten years without needing repair, or it might fail within ten days. Saving money upfront on used equipment often requires a higher repair and maintenance expense over time. However, a manager or owner will know if current cash flow limitations make purchasing new equipment cost prohibitive.

One way to obtain equipment cheaply without worrying about additional maintenance costs is to receive that equipment for free through a certain supplier. Some businesses, particularly beverage companies, supply display refrigerators, coffee machines, or soda fountains in exchange for exclusivity rights in a restaurant. For example, a coffee company may provide the coffee brewing apparatus and thermoses to a restaurant that promises to buy coffee only from that company. The coffee company owns the equipment and is responsible for repairing or replacing it if it breaks. However, the restaurant loses the equipment if it switches to a different coffee supplier to get a better product or a cheaper purchase price.

There are many ways to source new or used equipment for a foodservice business. Each approach comes with pros and cons. An analysis of current cash flow and future budget plans helps a manager to determine the best approach for his operation. Initial investment costs must always be balanced against long-term repair and maintenance expectations.

While repairs and maintenance are often thought of in terms of equipment, landscaping and exterior maintenance is also a consideration for this expense category (see Photo 15.5). How a property is landscaped has a direct impact on the cost of landscape

Photo 15.5
An Outdoor and Landscaped Restaurant Requires Maintenance

Source: © qingqing/Shutterstock.

maintenance. For example, a rock garden with cacti may require little water and upkeep while a green lawn with embedded lighting and a running fountain may have a high maintenance cost. One of the benefits of an urban restaurant in an office building is the minimal landscaping cost, but large rural operations have the ability to convert their outdoor property into a functional space. Large properties may be used for outdoor events, such as catered weddings or parties, or they may be converted into miniature farms, producing vegetables and herbs for the restaurant. The decisions an owner makes on landscaping affect whether the business's outdoor space provides functionality (and financial benefit) or strictly ambience that attracts guests and enhances their dining experience.

Parking lot maintenance is another "repair and maintenance" cost (for those businesses responsible for their parking facilities). While repaving and drawing parking space lines may not be required even once per year, snow removal from parking lots (and walkways) is a major business cost in some parts of the country. A parking lot that customers cannot use is a deterrent to business. Proper lighting is also required, so customers feel safe walking to their cars. In large hotels, parking may be a revenue source as guests may be charged a fee to park their cars. In urban restaurants, there may be no parking available at all. In such cases, the business may choose to hire or to contract out valets to park cars for guests. The decision to charge guests directly for valet service depends on whether or not the valets can park the cars for free. If local street parking is available or if the restaurant has a relationship with a nearby garage that allows them access to the garage for minimal expense, the business may choose to absorb the cost of valet parking as a service to restaurant patrons (and to account for the cost in menu pricing).

Finally, facility upgrades and maintenance are expenses for which a business should always budget. Small bits of damage to a wall or floor may not seem like a big deal, but as a space begins to look old and worn, customers may be less inclined to patronize that business. Rusted bathroom fixtures, peeling wallpaper, and stained carpets all communicate a message of low quality that can make a menu's prices seem inflated. Small repairs can often be carried out by a restaurant's staff, but major repairs should be planned and budgeted in advance. It is not uncommon for a foodservice business to undergo a major renovation every ten years or so. If the business must close down during renovations, that loss of revenue must be factored into the budget as well.

15.2   FIXED EXPENSE CONSIDERATIONS

As with controllable expenses, fixed expenses on an income statement do not typically receive daily attention from management. Still, the decisions that a manager or owner makes on a fixed cost expense can lock a company into a set financial commitment for years to come. For that reason alone, the decision-making process regarding fixed expenses is critical. What follows is a discussion of some of the variables that a manager or owner should consider when deciding the type of fixed expense to adopt.

15.2.1   Occupancy Costs

The biggest decision to impact a company's occupancy cost is the choice between buying and renting. Buying a property has long-term advantages. An owner has greater control over how the property is modified, and once the business pays off the mortgage, the occupancy cost drops significantly. Furthermore, as the business owns the building and the property, it has the ability to take out credit against the equity should the company need significant credit at some point. Should the business go under, the owner has the ability to sell off the land and property to recoup some of his investment.

Purchasing a building and/or property is not always feasible for an owner or for a business, however. The initial purchase price and subsequent down payment may be too large for a company to afford. Depending on the real estate and financial markets, the mortgage payment may be higher than a monthly rental payment elsewhere would be. Additionally, when a company owns a property, it is responsible for all of the taxes and costs associated with maintaining that property. Even if purchasing were the better long-term investment, a business saddled with the burden of a large mortgage might not survive long enough to benefit from the investment.

Some of the expenses associated with the ownership of a property may be the responsibility of the landlord in a rental space. Landscaping, property taxes, parking lot maintenance, and periodic facility upgrades are sometimes negotiable in a lease agreement such that they become the responsibility of the landlord rather than of the tenant. Landlords may also be responsible for certain HVAC, plumbing, and electric maintenance and repairs. A high rent that includes a large number of these controllable expenses may be cheaper than a market-rate rent that requires management to contract out these services. In some cases, leases will charge separate maintenance fees for certain services, but a tenant may be justified in withholding payment if the work is not done properly. By thoroughly comparing all of the costs associated with owning versus renting a property, an owner can more effectively decide which option is best for a business.

15.2.2   Capital Budgeting

Deciding whether to invest in significant improvements to a facility is a difficult decision. Major facility upgrades cost tens or hundreds of thousands of dollars. Putting that money into a facility may create a multiyear depreciation expense and/or an interest expense—fixed costs that at certain business levels can mean the difference between generating a profit and breaking even (or worse). Capital budgeting is the process for deciding between major investments whose expenses and returns span multiple budget cycles. Managed properly, capital budgeting helps a manager to determine which large-scale projects make the most financial sense.

The first factor in capital budgeting is to consider the impact an investment will have on sales. For example, will a renovation expand the dining room and seating capacity, thus increasing sales by a forecast 20%? Will a facility upgrade stem the current trend of steadily declining revenue? Some investments have significant impact on sales, while others do not. A kitchen expansion that allows for take-out and catering services will likely help sales, while the purchase of a new dishwasher and range probably will not.

Next, a manager should consider any adjustments to other expense lines. Will a new dishwasher reduce water and electricity usage? Will its larger capacity reduce labor costs? Sometimes, an investment can pay for itself through long-term savings in other expense areas. But then, if a business must borrow the money to invest in a renovation, it will increase its interest expense line.

Management should next compare various alternatives to see which is the best investment option. For example, should the restaurant purchase a complete POS system or simply purchase one POS module? Which makes more sense, the purchase of a grill and a range or the purchase of a combined grill/range unit? Cost is one factor to consider at this point. However, any cost discussion should include a comparison of potential depreciation expenses, for each alternative may have a different salvage value and life span. A $10,000 piece of equipment with an expected life span of five years may be more expensive in depreciation terms than a $20,000 piece of equipment with a twenty-year life span.

Finally, a manager should consider alternate uses for the financial capital to see if making an investment in a given area is a good use of money. After all, while an expense may be depreciated over several years, the company will surely have to outlay the money (or to secure credit) as soon as the upgrade or renovation is complete. Will a $50,000 investment generate or save more money than simply putting $50,000 into a bank account to earn interest will? With the company's cash flow, is there even $50,000 available to invest now that won't be needed later? Thoroughly analyzing the impact that a major expense will likely have on a business helps a manager to decide how best to budget a company's capital.

SUMMARY

There are a great number of questions to answer when considering how to manage controllable expenses and, when possible, fixed expenses. Direct operating expenses are the costs associated with utensils, china, glassware, linens, uniforms, cleaning supplies, kitchen and bar utensils, decorations, menus, licenses, permits, and other expenses. While not often reviewed on a daily basis, many of these expenses can be controlled through a periodic analysis of alternatives. Managers must recognize, however, that any change must not only maintain company standards but also support the theme and mission of the operation. Music and entertainment play a role in most foodservice businesses, so these expenses should be considered in the budgeting process. Energy and utilities expenses can be controlled not only through conservation but also through energy creation—a relatively new concept for hospitality businesses. Water can be conserved and reclaimed, and waste management offers opportunities for cost savings through recycling, composting, and the sale of certain types of waste. Administrative and general expenses encompass insurance, security, and back office expenditures in addition to general overhead costs; each of these expense areas can be controlled in a range of ways that best suit the needs of the company. Repairs and maintenance expenses are necessary and somewhat predictable costs that can keep a foodservice operation from falling victim to a business-shuttering emergency. Repair costs depend not only on how long a company has owned a piece of equipment but also on the equipment's condition at the time of purchase. Landscaping, parking maintenance, and facility repair also fall under the heading of repairs and maintenance. While fixed expenses can rarely be changed once set, they do periodically come up for review and possible adjustment. Perhaps the biggest influence on a company's occupancy costs is the decision to rent or to buy the property; each choice comes with pros and cons. Capital budgeting and major investment decisions can affect a company's interest and depreciation expense lines. While all of these expenses combined typically represent less than half of a foodservice business's total expenses, they are essential elements of any income statement. The better they are controlled, the easier it is for a company to make a profit.

COMPREHENSION QUESTIONS

1. List seven types of expenses that fall under the heading "direct operating expenses."
2. Pick one example of a direct operating expense. Provide an example of how that expense could be made high cost or low cost.
3. List three types of expenditures that would be classified as "music and entertainment."
4. Provide three examples of ways to reduce utility costs through energy conservation.
5. List three categories into which "waste" might be separated as part of a waste management system.
6. List three things for which insurance might protect or cover a foodservice business.
7. List three types of expenses that fall under the heading "Repairs and Maintenance."
8. List two advantages of buying a property for a restaurant and two advantages of renting a space for a restaurant.
9. List three bits of information to consider in the capital budgeting process.

DISCUSSION QUESTIONS

1. Choose a restaurant concept (high-end, mid-range, or low-cost). For each of the italicized subheadings under section 15.1.1, describe the type of product you would purchase to support that restaurant. Be prepared to defend your choices.
2. Think of an example of energy creation that you have seen or heard of in a business (not necessarily a food business). Describe how that technology might be applied to a small restaurant in your area. How feasible and practical would it be to implement?
3. Describe one way (not already stated in the chapter) that a restaurant could conserve or reclaim water. Be specific.
4. Select a specific location in your neighborhood to open a restaurant of your creation. Describe the restaurant briefly. Then, describe the type of security program you would create for that restaurant. Defend your approach to security.
5. If you had the choice between owning or renting the space to create your dream restaurant, which would you choose? Why?

Industry Standard Statements of Income

The Uniform System of Accounts for Restaurants by Jim Laube provides the standard format and revenue and expense categories used by the National Restaurant Association. While a business could use any number of categories and formats to suit its needs, there is a benefit to using this standardized approach to income statements.

The National Restaurant Association collects data from many of its members and compiles that data into annual reports. Through these reports, a restaurant owner or manager can compare his income statement performance against similar restaurants' results nationwide. However, in order to compare apples to apples, or expense lines to expense lines, it is important that all restaurants include the same kinds of expenses in categories of the same name. For example, it would be meaningless to compare your repairs and maintenance line item expense to other restaurants' repairs and maintenance costs if your income statement places the wages for an on-staff repairperson under "repairs and maintenance" but other businesses place that salary under a "staff wages" expense line.

Our text has provided a statement of income format that works well as a teaching tool. It separates variable (food and beverage), semivariable (labor and controllable), and fixed expenses to stress those concepts. It also works as a simplified model in that it assumes that all of a business's income stems only from food and drink. Once you have mastered this approach, making the leap to Laube's *The Uniform System of Accounts for Restaurants* style should be easy.

The sample statement of income (see Figure A) follows Laube's format. It should be noted that this is the latest format presented in the 2011 edition of *The Uniform System of Accounts for Restaurants* and supersedes prior editions of that text.

First, compare the similarities between this income statement and the format described in Chapter 14. Sales still includes food and beverage sales, and the food and beverage cost percentages are based on the separate food and beverage sales, respectively. Controllable expenses use the same line item terminology as well.

The differences, however, are significant. Laube includes a sales line for "Merchandise & Other," which accounts for any non-food or -beverage sales that a restaurant may have. Just as with food or beverage, the cost of sales' percentage for "Merchandise & Other" is compared only to this line item's sales total. Many of today's restaurants find ways to generate revenue beyond mere food and beverage sales. This additional category allows a restaurant to account for the sale of embroidered shirts and hats, books by the chef, restaurant-logo mugs, in short, anything that the restaurant sells beyond food and drink. Students who can navigate the calculations for food sales and cost and beverage sales and cost should have little difficulty in comprehending the math behind this additional revenue center.

Laube divides labor into management, staff, and employee benefits. By dividing management and staff into two separate line items, the model allows managers to control the fixed and the variable cost components of labor separately. Tracked separately, management can more readily see if a department's frontline worker expense remains a consistent percentage of sales even though manager's salaries will not vary with sales volume.

Noncontrollable (a.k.a. fixed) expenses, in the Laube model, adds a line item for equipment leases and moves interest to a location separate from noncontrollable expenses. Laube also includes two additional line items—corporate overhead and other

Name of Restaurant Company Statement of Income for the Period Ended (Insert Date)	Amounts	Percentage*
Sales		
Food	$ 700,000	77.8
Beverage	175,000	19.4
Merchandise & Other	25,000	2.8
Total Sales	900,000	100.0
Cost of Sales		
Food	210,000	30.0
Beverage	50,000	28.6
Merchandise & Other	10,000	40.0
Total Cost of Sales	270,000	30.0
Labor		
Management	90,000	10.0
Staff	165,000	18.3
Employee Benefits	56,100	6.2
Total Labor	311,100	34.6
Prime Cost	581,100	64.6
Other Controllable Expenses		
Direct Operating Expenses	55,000	6.1
Music & Entertainment	2,500	0.3
Marketing	25,000	2.8
Utilities	35,000	3.9
General & Administrative Expenses	45,000	5.0
Repairs & Maintenance	15,600	1.7
Total Other Controllable Expenses	178,100	19.8
Controllable Income	140,800	15.6
Non-Controllable Expenses		
Occupancy Costs	70,000	7.8
Equipment Leases	5,000	0.6
Depreciation & Amortization	15,000	1.7
Total Non-Controllable Expenses	90,000	10.0
Restaurant Operating Income	50,800	5.6
Corporate Overhead	2,500	0.3
Interest Expense	955	0.1
Other (Income)/Expense	1,500	0.2
Income before Income Taxes	$ 45,845	5.1

* All percentages are calculated as a percentage of Total Sales except Food, Beverage and Merchandise & Other Costs which are based on their respective sales.

Figure A

The Uniform System of Accounts for Restaurants Style Sample Statement of Income

Source: Printed with the permission of the National Restaurant Association.

income/expense. Corporate overhead becomes particularly important for multiunit properties that must share the cost for their corporate office's expense. The "other income/expense" line allows for flexibility for an operation that has additional income or expenses that do not fit into any of the other line items.

In short, *The Uniform System of Accounts for Restaurants* statement of income model may be more difficult to learn than the format described in this text, particularly for the novice culinary or hospitality student unfamiliar with income statements. However, as future managers gain more comfort with income statements and accept jobs managing real-world restaurants, they should find that Laube's format better accounts for the complexity of all but the simplest restaurants.

Note: Page numbers followed by *f* representing figures and page numbers followed by *t* representing tables.